PENGUIN BOOKS

THE PORTABLE

Each volume in The Viking Portable Library
either presents a representative selection
from the works of a single outstanding writer
or offers a comprehensive anthology on a
special subject. Averaging 700 pages in length
and designed for compactness and readabil-
ity, these books fill a need not met by other
compilations. All are edited by distinguished
authorities, who have written introductory
essays and included much other helpful ma-
terial.

"The Viking Portables have done more for
good reading and good writers than anything
that has come along since I can remember."
—Arthur Mizener

Theodore Morrison has published several
books of poetry and is emeritus Professor of
English at Harvard. He is currently working
on a brief history of the Bread Loaf Writers'
Conference.

The
Portable
CHAUCER

REVISED EDITION

ﮩﻮﻬ ﮩﻮﻬ ﮩﻮﻬ ﮩﻮﻬ ﮩﻮﻬ ﮩﻮﻬ ﮩﻮﻬ ﮩﻮﻬ ﮩﻮﻬ ﮩﻮﻬ

Selected, Translated, and Edited by
THEODORE MORRISON

PENGUIN BOOKS

PENGUIN BOOKS
Published by the Penguin Group
Viking Penguin Inc., 40 West 23rd Street,
New York, New York 10010, U.S.A.
Penguin Books Ltd, 27 Wrights Lane,
London W8 5TZ, England
Penguin Books Australia Ltd, Ringwood,
Victoria, Australia
Penguin Books Canada Ltd, 2801 John Street,
Markham, Ontario, Canada L3R 1B4
Penguin Books (N.Z.) Ltd, 182–190 Wairau Road,
Auckland 10, New Zealand

Penguin Books Ltd, Registered Offices:
Harmondsworth, Middlesex, England

First published in the United States of America
by Viking Penguin Inc. 1949
Paperbound edition published 1956
Reprinted 1958 (twice), 1959, 1960 (twice), 1961 (three times),
1962 (twice), 1963 (twice), 1964 (twice), 1965, 1966 (twice),
1967, 1968, 1969 (twice), 1970 (twice),
1971 (twice), 1972, 1974, 1975
Revised edition published
by Viking Penguin Inc. 1975
Published in Penguin Books 1977

15 14 13 12 11

LIBRARY OF CONGRESS CATALOGING IN PUBLICATION DATA
Chaucer, Geoffrey, d. 1400.
The portable Chaucer.
Reprint of the rev. ed. published in 1975 by The Viking
Press, New York
Bibliography: p. 49.
I. Morrison, Theodore, 1901– II. Title.
[PR1855.M6 1977]   821'.1   77-1097
ISBN 0 14 015.081 1

Printed in the United States of America
Set in Linotype Times Roman

To the Memory of F. N. Robinson who patiently read in typescript the original edition of this book and extended every kindness that a leading Chaucerian scholar could show to a former pupil whose importunities he might as easily have dismissed.

ঝ৬ ঝ৬ ঝ৬ ঝ৬ ঝ৬ ঝ৬ ঝ৬ ঝ৬ ঝ৬ ঝ৬

Contents

vii

viii Contents

Introduction

CHAUCER'S TIMES

Geoffrey Chaucer lived in medieval England, which despite its outlying position was bound into the medieval culture of Europe by religion, war, commerce, poetry, philosophy, and science, and by the common institutions of feudalism. This turbulent world rubbed edges with the near and even the far East. "Tamerlane's life," as J. L. Lowes points out, "just overlapped Chaucer's at each end, and . . . it was in the year in which Chaucer was appointed Justice of the Peace that the Great Turk boasted that he would make his horse eat oats on the high altar of St. Peter's." The peak of the Crusades had long passed, but, to quote Lowes again, "Chaucer's Knight had fought in Europe, Asia, and Africa against the Moors, the Turks, the Tartars and the heathen of the North— in Turkey, Spain, Prussia, Lithuania (then a Tartar outpost) and Russia, and also with 'that valorous champion of impossible conquests,' Pierre de Lusignan, king of Cyprus, at the taking of Alexandria, and at Lyeys and Satalye. And the Knight was a composite portrait of men whom Chaucer personally knew."

England was engaged during Chaucer's lifetime and for some fifty years after his death in the Hundred Years' War with France. Chaucer was probably born somewhat later than 1340; he died in 1400. The first celebrated English victory in the war, Crécy, occurred in 1346, and the last, Agincourt, in 1415. Joan of Arc was martyred in 1431, and the final reversal of English fortunes in the struggle began.

1

The dynastic claims of the English throne to continental territory do not account for the energy that sustained a century of conflict. "The Hundred Years' War," says G. M. Trevelyan, "was the diplomatic and military aspect of the period of transition from the feudal to the national, from the Middle Ages to the Renaissance." The first notable action was the English naval victory at Sluys. Later England lost control of the sea for some fifteen years. Chaucer's Merchant, in the Prologue to *The Canterbury Tales,* wants the sea kept open at all costs between Middleburg, in Holland, and the river Orwell. The contest involved trade, sea power, and middle-class interests. The English land victories were won by abandoning or modifying feudal tactics. The yeoman archers who decided the issue at Crécy and Agincourt against French knights who clung to chivalric arms and tactics came from a population which had not only been allowed but compelled to bear arms. The commoner brought home booty, and the noble brought home his noble French captives, who paid appropriate ransoms to their English hosts, besides dancing, flirting, banqueting, and hawking with them. The war provided outlets for other kinds of ambition also. Chaucer's Squire, doing well for one of his age in forays through Flanders and Picardy, hoped "to stand the better in his lady's grace."

The war was accompanied by landmarks of social change at home. In 1348-49, the Black Death reduced the nation in sixteen months from perhaps four million to perhaps two million five hundred thousand, and "precipitated the class struggle," in Trevelyan's phrase, since "the market value of labor had been doubled at a stroke." Free laborers demanded better wages; peasants bound to compulsory labor on the estates of their feudal overlords began to struggle for freedom. But while farmland was going back to wilderness, the war went on, still regarded as a source of plunder and profit. "Poitiers followed Crécy," says Trevelyan, "as though half the world had not died in the interval." In 1381, the resentments and the improved bargaining power of feudal labor broke out briefly in the Peasants' Revolt. Wat Tyler led contingents of the rebels to London, where they killed the Archbishop of Canterbury—a tribute to the secular power of the church and its position in the social and economic structure. They also attacked the Flemish weavers who had been brought in to help develop English cloth making, evidently looking on them as unwelcome competitors. They dispersed after two meetings with the young king Richard, at which he promised concessions he did not mean to carry out, and at the second of which Wat Tyler was killed, together with his lieutenant Jack Straw (unless the latter was a contemptuous name for Tyler himself).

In the Prologue to *The Canterbury Tales*, the Physician, who was not a free spender, as Chaucer tells us, carefully saved up the fees he collected in time of plague. The good Parson did not desert his parish flock in favor of a sinecure singing masses for the dead, an opportunity other priests discovered after the wholesale mortality of the Black Death. The Peasants' Revolt supplies Chaucer with a comic comparison in one of his gayest and most sophisticated tales: Jack Straw and his retinue did not make such a racket over some Fleming they were going to kill as Partlet and her sister hens made when they saw the fox carrying off Chanticleer. These allusions are characteristic. Chaucer lived in a time of social change, but he was not what we should call a social thinker, nor does his work contain what we should recognize as the note of social protest. He believes in the Church and makes unholy comedy of its abuses. He is not the man to undertake either the intellectual or the practical work of reform, as his contemporary John Wycliffe did. Wycliffe, taking the radical position that only secular influence could reform the Church, giving reasoned support to those who had advantages to gain by opposing the local power of the papacy, and translating the Bible into current English, anticipated the work of the Reformation, though he eventually pushed his teaching to the point of heresy, and his followers, who acquired the name of Lollards, were persecuted for several generations. When Chaucer's Host, in *The Canterbury Tales*, first calls on the good parish Parson for a story, the Parson rebukes him for swearing. "I smell a Lollard in the wind," the Host answers, and warns the company to expect a sermon. The Shipman, no very reputable character, will not listen to preaching from a Lollard. "He will sow some difficulty, or scatter tares through our clean wheat." It is characteristic of Chaucer to see the great event, the important doctrine or movement, in its effect on some person or group of people, and to see it with a sense of humor, a sense of comic byplay and entanglement, that seldom goes to sleep or yields for long to earnestness.

In this energetic and contentious period, Chaucer sought bread and butter and comforts through preferment in the public service of three kings and another almost royal patron, John of Gaunt. Of the kings Chaucer served, the second and third, Richard II and Henry IV, received dramatic treatment at Shakespeare's hands. To John of Gaunt, in *The Tragedy of King Richard II*, Shakespeare gave his most famous speech of impassioned nationalism:

> This royal throne of kings, this sceptered isle . . .
> This precious stone set in the silver sea . . .
> This blessed plot, this earth, this realm, this England.

Chaucer was sent in 1377 on a secret continental mission with the subsequent Earl of Worcester, who later rebelled and was vanquished by Henry IV at Shrewsbury. If Chaucer had lived three years longer, as G. G. Coulton points out, he "would have seen his old fellow envoy's head grinning down from the spikes of London Bridge side by side with 'a quarter of Sir Harry Percy' " —the Harry Percy who was Shakespeare's Hotspur. Had there been a Falstaff outside Shakespeare's pages, Chaucer would have known him in London, an unsanitary medieval town of some forty thousand people, where together with Westminster and St. Paul's and the Tower and the quays along the Thames were houses in which people wore their heaviest clothes in winter as they nursed their chilblains by the hearth, houses with walls so flimsy that in case of fire they could be pulled down by ropes and grapples.

In this "flower of cities all," as Chaucer's Scots follower Dunbar called it, books were rare and costly, and the King's English was in the process of creation. Books in Chaucer's day were manuscripts copied by hand and bound. A book might include copies of several or even a considerable number of separate works or compilations; thus the sixty books that Chaucer refers to as his own constituted in his day an unusual private library. Printed books only began to appear in Europe half a century after Chaucer's death, and not till 1475 did *The Canterbury Tales* appear in an edition printed from type by Caxton, the first English printer. Reading aloud was a common form of polite entertainment, as we see when Pandarus visits Cressida in the *Troilus* and finds his niece and her circle listening to a girl reading the story of Thebes. Chaucer himself read aloud from his works at court, where by no means all his auditors would have been able to read for themselves. French of Norman origin gave way during Chaucer's lifetime as the spoken language of the court and of law pleadings to the English dialect of the London region, which became the progenitor of modern English. Edward III, who reigned as

Chaucer entered life, may not have known how to address the Commons in the native tongue, but Henry IV in 1399 accepted the throne in English. "God save the King," writes Chaucer in 1391, "who is the lord of this language."

Chaucer's contemporary and acquaintance John Gower, also prominent at court, wrote poems in Latin, French, and English. While Chaucer did not use the pre-Norman, Old English metric inherited from *Beowulf* and Cædmon, the alliterative *rum-ram-ruf* of which the Parson makes fun in the prologue to his tale and which showed its expiring vigor in the contemporary poem or group of poems known as *Piers Plowman*, he did throw his whole strength, both as translator and poet, into the use of English as it was spoken in his day. He was the first great poet to use English and to show its capacity for expression equal to the best in other languages, but only at the cost of long being seen through a glass darkly. For it was English in process of breakdown and fresh formation, and had to undergo considerable and rapid changes before it became the English of the Renaissance and later times. "Go, little book, and since there is so great diversity in English and the writing of our tongue, I pray God that no one miswrite or mismeter you through ignorance of language, and wherever you may be read, I pray God that you may be understood." This is Chaucer's petition at the end of the *Troilus*, and it is due to the labors of a large number of scholars, especially from the latter part of the nineteenth century on, that accurate understanding of what Chaucer wrote is now possible as it would not have been for centuries after his death.

CHAUCER'S LIFE

We do not have the literary gossip about Chaucer that Johnson could record of Dryden, Addison, or Pope; we do not have the memorabilia, letters, diaries, personal reminiscences, that cluster thickly around such later figures as Byron, Shelley, or Yeats. The traces of Chaucer's life are numerous but impersonal and official. They are stored up for the most part in public documents, in legal proceedings, in notices of appointments and payments. How Chaucer's life felt to the man who lived it has to be gathered from his work, from the expression his temperament finds in the Canterbury pilgrimage and the *Troilus*, together with a few references to himself, mostly humorous.

Chaucer's name, derived from the French *"chaussier,"* implies that his family were at one time shoemakers, but his father and grandfather were both wine merchants, apparently successful and rising men. His father, John Chaucer, with other citizens interested in stimulating commerce, was among the company attending King Edward III in 1338 when he set out for the Rhine to form an alliance with the emperor Louis IV. Geoffrey Chaucer himself makes his first appearance in the household accounts of Elizabeth, countess of Ulster and wife of Prince Lionel. These accounts note that Chaucer received clothing from Elizabeth's wardrobe and in 1357 an allowance "for necessaries at Christmas." From his early years until 1399, when King Henry IV confirmed and increased the pension which together with an annual hogshead of wine Chaucer had received from Richard, his life appears externally to be a crowded series of appointments and missions at the hands of his various patrons, royal and noble, not without setbacks along the way.

To summarize first the more important posts that Chaucer held in the English court and public service, he is enrolled, perhaps as early as 1368, among the Esquires of the Royal Household of Edward III. It seems as though Chaucer must have exceeded the usual employments and privileges of squires, such as running errands, attending at meals, and sleeping two by two in appointed rooms. He may have been married as early as 1366, he received a life pension from Edward in 1367, and during the ensuing years he was frequently on state business abroad. In 1374 he was appointed Controller of Customs and Subsidy of Wools, Skins, and Hides in the port of London, a lucrative post, the duties of which he was allowed from time to time to perform by deputy when he was absent on the king's or other business. While holding this office, he received a handsome prize, the large fine imposed on John Kent, who was discovered by Chaucer or his subordinates trying to smuggle a cargo of wool from London without paying the duties. In 1386, a year after being granted a permanent deputy, he either resigned the controllership or was removed from it by a Parliamentary commission. Chaucer left the rent-free house over Aldgate in London where he lived as customs officer and took up residence in Kent, which he represented in Parliament in 1386 as Knight of the Shire. He was not re-elected, and writs protecting him against attachment for debt in the spring of 1388 suggest a bad turn in his affairs. In 1389, when the young king Richard came of age, Chaucer was appointed Clerk of the King's Works. In this and related appointments, Chaucer became responsible for construction and repairs affecting royal residences and parks, and also the walls, bridges, and sewers along a stretch of the Thames. He had to handle payrolls, manage labor, and travel industriously. He was robbed at least twice, and once beaten up. He resigned his clerkship the next year. Chaucer's last considerable appointment came in 1391 as deputy forester of the royal forest of Petherton. He continued to receive annuities, gifts for services, and employments of various kinds, but his pension from Richard seems to have been very irregularly paid. "Twice he dunned his royal patron," says G. G. Coulton, "for the paltry sum of 6s. 8d."

In the earlier part of his active life, Chaucer was frequently abroad on military or diplomatic errands. In 1360, after Chaucer had been captured in France, King Edward contributed to his ransom. A number of times expense allowances or grants of legal protection during his absence show Chaucer being sent to the continent on royal business, often unknown business; when he accompanies the subsequent Earl of Worcester, it is "on the King's secret affairs." For English letters and culture the most important of Chaucer's journeys were those that took him to Italy, where, if he did not meet Petrarch in person, he began or improved acquaintance with the language of Dante, Petrarch, and Boccaccio. Chaucer probably first saw Italy in 1373, when he was one of a commission to negotiate with the Genoese for the use of an English commercial port, and when he also visited Florence. In 1378 he was a member of a military-diplomatic mission to the court of Bernabo Visconti, whom he later celebrated as "the scourge of Lombardy" in the string of tragedies, or catastrophes to men of high position, which the Knight will not let the Monk finish in *The Canterbury Tales.* This was the Bernabo suspected of poisoning Chaucer's early master, Prince Lionel, after Lionel's Italian marriage. It is largely the Italian journeys, which enlarged and liberated his mind and work, that make it possible for Coulton to say: "For a hundred and fifty years, Chaucer was practically the only channel between rough, strong, unformed English thought and the greatest literature of the Middle Ages."

This incomplete recital of some of Chaucer's more conspicuous political appointments and diplomatic missions establishes him as a man whose career was active and who lived his life in the world's eye. It leaves us wondering when Chaucer wrote his works; he, if any of the great writers, might plausibly be the victim of a Baconian theory, on the ground that his life does not seem to leave a loophole for the amount of learning he absorbed and the bulk of writing he accomplished. But what kind of man lies behind the external record? Chaucer has been pictured as an incompetent man of business, removed from his controllership by an investigating committee, dismissed from his clerkship for irresponsibility or incapacity. He has been pictured also as an able public servant, a man who held important administrative posts and was entrusted with a share in delicate royal negotiations which could not have been left to slack hands. Such a man could not have escaped some of the ordinary reverses of a career dependent on the favor of patrons in a bustling court full of "pacts and sects of great ones that ebb and flow by the moon." It is unnecessary to magnify Chaucer's purely practical ability, and it seems unreasonable to deny that he had any at all.

Chaucer as a man of affairs was probably neither much above nor below the enlightened wordly conscience of his age. In 1381, a certain Cecily Chaumpaigne relieved Chaucer of any kind of legal liability for "raptus." What specifically lies behind the incident is unknown. Cecily was doubtless an heiress and a ward, and "raptus" in her case, as in other known cases, meant not rape but abduction. In the Middle Ages, when marriage contracts were frequently arranged between children, heirs and heiresses were not uncommonly abducted with the design of marrying them off in a profitable quarter. An attempt of the sort had been made on Chaucer's father in his boyhood. Chaucer's implication in the affair of Cecily may well have amounted to nothing at all, but there can hardly be any doubt that he was quite capable of taking action for his personal advancement and profit. He must have known how to say what was pleasing to kings and patrons. He must have known how to satisfy them at least reasonably well as an agent in their business, though his poetry also served the entertainment and prestige of the court and no doubt helped bring him his rewards. He kept himself afloat through three reigns in a turbulent time. He liked and sought the comforts if not the fleshpots of this world. Whatever the sins for which he asked forgiveness at the end of *The Canterbury Tales,* beyond the writing of some rowdy stories that have survived and some "lecherous lays" that have not, we may be confident that in itself the search for preferment and ease was not one of them.

Chaucer is no doubt to be taken literally when, in *The House of Fame,* he describes himself coming home from the customs after balancing his accounts and burying himself in a book until his eyes were glazed, living a hermit's life, though not, as he says, with a hermit's abstinence. I take him literally also when, in the course of determining the time of day by practical astronomy and geometry, he alludes to his "six feet of height" and the length of shadow it casts. He makes fun of himself to Scogan as "round in figure," again no doubt accurately. "Here's a trim little puppet for a woman to embrace," the Host says to him jocosely, "as well shaped around the middle as I am myself!" From such indications it seems that Chaucer belonged to the tall and portly variety of Englishman, portly at any rate in later life.

Chaucer married Philippa, the daughter of Sir Payne Roet and sister of Katherine Swynford, John of Gaunt's mistress and later his third wife. Philippa died or vanishes from the record in 1387. Some commentators have been at pains to suggest that Chaucer's marriage did not lead to domestic felicity, but while virtually nothing is known of his personal relations with Philippa, the suggestion rests on literal-minded interpretation of passages in his work. In *The House of Fame,* the Eagle, when Chaucer is borne aloft in a terrified swoon, speaks to him in the "voice of one I could name," a voice that used to rouse him brusquely from his sleep. Was Philippa the one he could have named, or was Chaucer indulging in a standard joke about marriage? Chaucer's Wife of Bath and his Merchant and his "Envoy to Bukton" hardly present a romantic view of marriage, but the "Envoy to Bukton" speaks out of a perennial tradition of banter at the expense of any man about to be married, and in any case marriages in the court circle were customarily alliances of property or family advantage. By courtly convention, love was not to be expected between man and wife. The exception in Chaucer's work is worth noting: the Franklin, in his tale, declares that the "law of love" accords with love in marriage, but love of any sort depends on patience and forbearance. Similarly, Chaucer's habitual pretense that he was unsuccessful in love and acquainted with it only through books hardly establishes that he spent a substantial part of his life pining away for an unrequited passion. This too is joking and play with the conventions.

However their marriage fared, Chaucer and Philippa are generally credited with producing two sons and perhaps a daughter, Elizabeth Chaucy. Efforts have been made to deprive Chaucer of his sons, but the evidence in favor of Thomas Chaucer, an eminent man who became a member of the King's Council and served several times as Speaker of the House of Commons, is strong enough to withstand the contention that his father was not Chaucer but Chaucer's patron and brother-in-law, John of Gaunt. Chaucer's prose *Treatise on the Astrolabe*, a description of the medieval predecessor of the sextant, with problems involving its use, "the oldest work written in English on an elaborate scientific instrument,"[1] is addressed to "little Lewis my son," who knew small Latin as yet, but had shown unmistakable signs of his "ability to learn sciences dealing with numbers and proportions." It has been questioned whether "little

---

[1] Quoted by F. N. Robinson from R. T. Gunther.

Lewis" was Chaucer's own child, or whether he was a
godson, a child of Chaucer's friend Sir Lewis Clifford.
But discovery of the name of Lewis Chaucer in a record,
as Robinson notes, strengthens the natural interpretation
of Chaucer's words. The child to whom he gave an
"adequate Astrolabe for our horizon, constructed accord-
ing to the latitude of Oxford," and for whom he wrote
the unfinished elementary treatise on its use, in English
meant for children to understand, may safely be thought
of as his own.

CHAUCER'S FOLLOWERS AND CRITICS

No poet equal to Chaucer appeared in England until
Elizabeth's time. In the century and more after his death
the language whose literary capacity Chaucer had es-
tablished changed rapidly, while the Wars of the Roses
set back English thought and society and interrupted its
progress toward the Renaissance. Though Chaucer was
venerated and hailed as a master and example by poets
both in England and Scotland, poetry, especially in Eng-
land, fell into a decline of talent. Chaucer's work, both
in learning to use English as an instrument of poetry
and in bringing the world and the desires and characters
of men into full expression, had to be done over again,
in altered speech and in a different age.

But Chaucer and his work, however imperfectly un-
derstood, at no time passed unnoticed or unknown, as his
work never has in any century since his death. In the time
of Elizabeth, Spenser adopted Chaucer as his master,
characteristically alluding to him under the name of
Tityrus. "Spenser more than once insinuates," says Dry-
den, "that the soul of Chaucer was transfused into his
body, and that he was begotten by him two hundred
years after his decease." The transfusion is questionable
in many ways. The allegorizing and idealizing tempera-

ment of Spenser is at the opposite pole from Chaucer, the comic realist of *The Canterbury Tales,* and Spenser as a stylist is equally remote from Chaucer at his best. No vessel could be less suited to receive the soul of the man who created the Wife of Bath than Edmund Spenser, who created *The Faërie Queene.* Take three lines from that poem (Book III, Canto I, stanza 25):

> Ne may love be compeld by maisterie;
> For soon as maistrie comes, sweet love anon
> Taketh his nimble wings, and soon away is gone.

Spenser has taken over these lines from Chaucer, with characteristic changes. Here they are as Chaucer wrote them in the Franklin's Tale:

> Love wol nat be constreynéd by maistrye. [authority]
> When maistrie comth, the God of Love anon
> Beteth his wynges, and farewel, he is gon!

Aside from the element of the affected antique in Spenser, "sweet love," "nimble wings," "soon away is gone," and the dropping out of the direct "farewell," with its tone of speech, show what happens when Chaucer becomes Tityrus. In his whole mind and temperament Spenser was another man from Chaucer; but it was necessary for him to create a language and a versification for his own kind of poetry, and he did find both incentive and example in what Chaucer had done with English at an earlier stage. Spenser expressed his essential debt to Chaucer in the famous tribute "well of pure English, undefiled." He saw in Chaucer's work the first great use of the English language as an instrument of poetry, and looked on him therefore as a source and wellspring of the language itself. Poets after Spenser repeatedly echo this praise of Chaucer, which has its real historical foundation. Yet it is necessary to remember that even without the diffraction of his own temperament, Spenser could not have seen Chaucer clearly because he did not have the means of understanding his language accurately.

The same ignorance of Chaucer's language, brought about by the rapid loss of the remaining inflections in Chaucer's English and by changes in idiom and vocabulary, accounts in part for the distortions in Dryden's view of Chaucer. For Dryden, Chaucer was the first poet who "refined" the mother tongue; yet he thought Chaucer had the "rude sweetness of a Scotch tune" and found his verse not "harmonious" to the Restoration ear. Chaucer was in fact anything but a "rude" versifier. When the pronunciation of many of his words and phrases became lost or obscured, both his regularity and his irregularity as a versifier became obscured also. Chaucer in his mature poems was one of the most scrupulous of English versifiers, and one of the most harmonious when he chose to be. But his harmonies can be complex. He shows himself an early master of the art of "counterpointing" the tones of lively natural speech against the structure of the pentameter line. This sophisticated treatment of verse reaches a high point of expertness, as J. L. Lowes has admirably illustrated, in the talk of Pandarus in *Troilus and Cressida*, but it is generally characteristic of Chaucer and is of course richly strung through the talk of the Canterbury pilgrims.

But despite his errors of fact and information, particularly about Chaucer's language, despite the patronizing Restoration eye that saw Chaucer as a "rough diamond," an early and incomplete "refiner" needing in his turn to be refined, Dryden's criticism of Chaucer is remarkable for its large, understanding, independent view. Dryden on Chaucer does not read like a man who has listened to what others have been saying and who moves cautiously within lines already laid down. His response to Chaucer is unstaled and unconditioned. He has the air of a little Aristotle, surveying objects as they come before his in-

telligence, comparing and analyzing them as if for the
first time. He compares Chaucer with Ovid, and takes
occasion to remark that "both of them were well-bred,
well-natured, amorous, and libertine, at least in their
writing, it may be also in their lives." He compares him
with Vergil and Homer, and says that Chaucer

> . . . matched their beauties, where they most excel;
> Of love sung better, and of arms as well.

One only wishes that if Dryden were going to say this
much, he had said it of *Troilus and Cressida* instead of
the Knight's Tale! Dryden finds Chaucer a "perpetual
fountain of good sense; learned in all sciences," and in
the medieval sciences Chaucer in fact acquired a re-
markable layman's learning. "He must have been a man
of a most wonderful comprehensive nature," says Dry-
den, "because, as it has been truly observed of him, he
has taken into the compass of his *Canterbury Tales* the
various manners and humours (as we now call them) of
the whole English nation, in his age. Not a single char-
acter has escaped him. All his pilgrims are severally dis-
tinguished from each other. . . . Even the grave and
serious characters are distinguished by their several sorts
of gravity: their discourses are such as belong to their
age, their calling, and their breeding. . . . Some of his
persons are vicious, and some are virtuous; some are un-
learned or (as Chaucer calls them) lewd, and some are
learned. Even the ribaldry of the low characters is dif-
ferent: The Reeve, the Miller, and the Cook are several
men, and distinguished from each other, as much as
the mincing lady Prioress and the broad-speaking gap-
toothed Wife of Bath. . . . 'Tis sufficient to say, accord-
ing to the proverb, that here is God's plenty. We have
our forefathers and great-grandames all before us, as
they were in Chaucer's days; their general characters are
still remaining in mankind . . . for mankind is ever the

same, and nothing lost out of nature, though everything is altered." No summing up is ever likely to put better than Dryden's the qualities which have kept Chaucer alive and for which he is chiefly valued today. They are the qualities found in the best of *The Canterbury Tales,* in its Prologue and in the byplay of the pilgrimage itself. Dryden does not speak as though he had read *Troilus and Cressida;* if he did know it, his silence about its three principal characters, especially Pandarus, is remarkable. The one great quality in Chaucer to which Dryden fails to make adequate acknowledgment is the one that time cannot wither nor custom stale, the almost but never quite naïve charm of his best lyrical passages. It is to these passages that Dryden's ear was more than half closed, partly by ignorance of Chaucer's metric, partly by Restoration taste; only a "rude sweetness" sifted through.

In the eighteenth century, Pope and no small number of lesser writers produced Augustan versions of Chaucer or free improvisations on his poems, again "refining" the first refiner of the English tongue. This is not the place for a detailed history of Chaucerian imitation and criticism. But it is interesting that Blake, a man quite as different from Chaucer as Edmund Spenser had been, "said more in print about Chaucer than about any other poet," as Mark Schorer points out. Blake's comments were occasioned by his fresco painting, of which he later made the familiar engraving, which shows the pilgrims at the start of their journey. "The time chosen," says Blake, "is early morning, before sunrise, when the jolly company are just quitting the Tabarde Inn." Blake may seem to repeat the praise that Dryden had given Chaucer—"we have our forefathers and great-grandames all before us." But while Chaucer idealized his figures in one way, Blake idealized them in another. Chaucer's scoundrels are scoundrels of consummate type, complete and pure, and his student, parson, and plowman are similarly types of complete virtue and simplicity. One feels that pure zest and delight in his own creations had a good deal to do with Chaucer's idealizing. Is a man to be a scoundrel? Make him a scoundrel up to the limit, no pindling or half-hearted specimen! Yet whether presented as portraits in the Prologue or later set to work reacting on each other in the pilgrimage itself, each character strikes us as an individual, as though he had suffered a life history of his own and could speak with his own voice. Blake by contrast sees Chaucer's types as walking myths or principles. "Chaucer's characters live age after age. Every age is a Canterbury Pilgrimage; we all pass on, each sustaining one of these characters; nor can a child be born, who is not one of these characters of Chaucer." This much might be Dryden's criticism, a little heightened; but this is not enough for Blake. "Chaucer makes every one of his characters perfect in his kind; every one is an Antique Statue; the image of a class, and not of an imperfect individual. . . . Chaucer has divided the ancient character of Hercules between his Miller and his Plowman. . . . The Plowman . . . is Hercules in his supreme eternal state, divested of his spectrous shadow; which is the Miller, a terrible fellow, such as exists in all times and places for the trial of men, to astonish every neighborhood with brutal strength and courage." The temperament of Chaucer and the real lineaments of his Miller and his Plowman begin to disappear in such Platonizing.

In the nineteenth century, at about the time when modern scholarship was beginning its elaborate recovery of Chaucer's language and text, Chaucer's reputation received from Matthew Arnold its most magisterial snub. Arnold contributed the general introduction to Ward's *English Poets*, a historical library of selections from English poetry, taking the middle ages and Chaucer himself as a beginning point. Arnold issued a solemn warning against two sources of error in judging whether a poet's work "belongs to the class of the very best": the historical estimate and the personal estimate. He proceeded to deny Chaucer a place among the very best. It is not that he was ungenerous to Chaucer, nor that he failed to respond to him. Rereading Arnold, I found him actually more hospitable to the spirit of Chaucer than I had expected from memory. "Chaucer's power of fascination," he says, "is enduring; his poetical importance does not need the assistance of the historical estimate; it is real. He is a genuine source of joy and strength, which is flowing still for us and will flow always. He will be read, as time goes on, far more generally than he is now." Arnold quotes from Dryden's praise of Chaucer as "a perpetual fountain of good sense," and shows a responsiveness to Chaucer's diction and to the "fluidity of movement" in his verse which we should expect of a man of Arnold's immense reading and cultivated taste, and toward which Dryden's perceptions were necessarily blunted. Arnold praised the work of Chaucer for its "truth of substance," the result of "his large, free, simple, clear yet kindly view of life." Elsewhere Arnold transforms his series of adjectives into nouns, and finds in Chaucer "largeness, freedom, shrewdness, benignity." All this is surely no ungenerous tribute, nor is it off the mark, though Arnold may seem to be bowing a little stiffly, and the word "benignity" may ring a little oddly in association with the Wife of Bath and the Pardoner. One thinks of Dryden's "well-bred, well-natured, amorous, and libertine," and feels that these words suggest one man of the world ferreting out the disposition of another at least as well. But Arnold denies Chaucer a place among the very best, a place with Homer or Dante, because Chaucer lacked "the high and excellent seriousness, which Aristotle assigns as one of the grand virtues of poetry." Already one's risibilities begin to be touched. I am not concerned, myself, to set Chaucer above Dante or Dante above Chaucer. In English literature we have had one greater than Chaucer, though in my own view Shakespeare is the only one. The world of imagination that Shakespeare peopled seems even more densely populated and representative than Chaucer's world, partly because the inward perspectives of Shakespeare's characters are generally richer, subtler, and deeper; partly because the problem of justice and the sense of evil shook the imagination of Shakespeare more profoundly; and partly because at its best the rhetoric of Shakespeare, while remaining clear and unaffected, reached degrees of complex association quite beyond anything that Chaucer, with his prevailing virtue of simplicity, would or could in his age have thought of attempting. The one element of Chaucer's *Troilus and Cressida* that remains in Shakespeare's dramatization of the same story is the youth of Troilus, his character as a very young man for whom the excitement of sexual experience is just opening.

> I am giddy, expectation whirls me round.
> The imaginary relish is so sweet
> That it enchants my sense. What will it be
> When that the watery palate tastes indeed
> Love's thrice repured nectar? Death, I fear me;
> Sounding destruction; or some joy too fine,
> Too subtile-potent, tun'd too sharp in sweetness
> For the capacity of my ruder powers.
> I fear it much; and I do fear besides
> That I shall lose distinction in my joys,
> As doth a battle when they charge on heaps
> The enemy flying.

Chaucer's Troilus was in the same state of emotion, but Chaucer could not have expressed it for him as Shakespeare did, would not have attempted to, and did not need to. The moments of dialogue in Chaucer when the courses of action among the characters come to a head and are forced into expression take a much simpler form. (I translate in prose at this point; a verse rendering will be found later in the volume.)

This Troilus began to strain her in his arms, and said, "O sweet, as I ever hope to thrive, now you are caught, now there is but we two! Now yield, for there is no other remedy." To that Cressida answered, "Had I not before now, my sweet, my dear heart, yielded, surely I should not now be here!"

The answer to Arnold's criticism of Chaucer is partly that he was himself making the kind of personal estimate he condemned. He was expressing a preference for poetry of a kind and tone he did not find in Chaucer. Arnold tried to do justice to the comic and the robust, but he lacked the stomach for it, and lacking that, he failed to do justice to the nature of seriousness itself. "Arnold," says Lionel Trilling, "does not really mean seriousness at all. He means solemnity; he means the knowledge of how to be 'sick or sorry.' . . . But if Chaucer is not serious, then Mozart is not serious and Molière is not serious and seriousness becomes a matter of pince-nez glasses and a sepia print of the Parthenon over the bookshelf." But like Dryden, Arnold does not speak as though he had a real acquaintance with *Troilus and Cressida*. This work does not give us the "God's plenty" we find in the fragments of the Canterbury pilgrimage. But as a sustained fiction, subtle in characterization, intense in emotion at its points of climax, interweaving irony, comedy, and the tragic sense of disillusionment, it takes rank with *The Canterbury Tales* as one of Chaucer's two great achievements. One might have expected Arnold to find in the *Troilus* more fortunate examples of what he meant by seriousness than the example he actually took from the Prioress's Tale. This story, based on the raw superstition of "ritual murders" of Christians by Jews, is as good an example as any in *The Canterbury Tales* of dramatic propriety. It is unmistakably the Prioress who speaks, in the choice of the story she tells, in every inflection of style, in the exacerbated tenderness of the nun toward the idea of innocent childhood, in the hypertrophic medieval piety she expresses. In content, of course, the tale hardly adds luster to Christian belief or practice. It seems odd that Arnold, in search of lines or snatches of poetry that might serve as "touchstones" to detect "the very best" and distinguish it from the spurious or the inferior, should have chosen from Chaucer the cry of the murdered little Christian pupil miraculously kept alive by the "grain" which the Virgin had placed on his tongue:

My throte is cut unto my nekke bone.

This is effective enough in its place, but a quaint piece of baggage to carry in one's mind as a talisman!

CHAUCER'S LEARNING

Dryden praised Chaucer as "learned in all sciences," and some awareness of the range of his reading and knowledge will give the modern reader a better understanding of Chaucer. Little is known of how or where Chaucer got his extensive education. Robinson, relying on records cited by Professor Crow, thinks it probable that he obtained part of his early training at St. Paul's Cathedral School in London. An old tradition, which has recently gained new favor, holds that he was a member of one of the Inns of Court, where suitable candidates studied law, a helpful preparation for Chaucer's diplomatic missions and administrative posts. This tradition includes the detail that Chaucer was fined two shillings for beating a

Franciscan friar. In any case, he was no doubt brought up to read and speak French; he learned Latin early and later made himself at home in Italian before he was well into his twenties. He used these languages, besides his native English, to acquire not only a stock of literary learning, but a remarkable layman's grasp of the interconnected medieval sciences of astronomy, astrology, medicine, physiognomy, alchemy, and what we should now call psychology, especially the psychology of dreams. His elementary textbook on the astrolabe, taken mostly from an Arabian original which reached him through Latin, has already been mentioned; he also translated *The Consolation of Philosophy* from the Latin of Boëthius, a work that frequently supplies Chaucer or his characters with moral or metaphysical reflections.

In the strictly literary development of Chaucer, as J. L. Lowes has described his progress, "French poetry yielded first place to Italian, and both to an absorption in human life." Chaucer began by adopting the standard convention of later French courtly love poetry, the allegorical dream, which gave him the basis of *The Book of the Duchess, The House of Fame*, and *The Birds' Parliament;* he returned to this convention as late as the Prologue to *The Legend of Good Women*, written after *Troilus and Cressida*. But in the *Troilus* he is taking his story from Boccaccio, re-creating the Italian work with important independent transformations of character and structure, and the direct stimulation from life itself is already working at full power. By the time Chaucer wrote the Prologue to *The Canterbury Tales*, the best of the tales themselves, and even more the byplay of the pilgrimage, both his literary learning and his layman's grasp of what passed for science nosed their way into line after line, but they did so as allies of Chaucer's personal and direct view of life and people. Yet Chaucer never forgot anything he had picked up along the way, from French poetry on. His texture of life and learning together became more complex. His allusions to Machaut, *The Romance of the Rose,* Vergil, Statius, Ovid, Boccaccio, Dante, Petrarch, Boëthius, grew denser and more complicated. Recalling the table manners prescribed for ladies in *The Romance of the Rose,* the long French allegory which he had at least in part translated, he could apply the standard prescription with novel effect to his portrait of the Prioress, who "took pains to imitate court manners." Chaucer was a man of voracious intellectual curiosity, and a man who obviously delighted in the exercise of this curiosity. His delight in applying a proverb is the same as his delight in applying a text from Augustine or St. Paul; it gives him pleasure to recognize any relation between thought, whether homely traditional wisdom or the "authority of learned clerks," and the experiences of men and women in the common world.

As for the sciences, Chaucer's use of astronomy and astrology and his references to medieval medicine, based on the theory of the four "humors" or fluids of the body, will strike anyone who looks at his work. The presence of another medieval science, physiognomy, the art of interpreting psychological and constitutional characteristics by outward physical traits, will be less obvious, and an illustration drawn from it may suggest how Chaucer used his acquaintance with the sciences to apply all the known or supposed modes of understanding human beings to his gallery of pilgrims. W. C. Curry, in *Chaucer and the Mediaeval Sciences,* outlines the beliefs of the Middle Ages about physiognomy. The position of the planets at their birth gives men and women certain constitutional traits and inclinations; these can be detected with empirical certainty by means of corresponding outward physical traits. Perhaps the most striking case is the Pardoner. With his high, thin goat's voice, staring eyes, yellow hair, and other distinguishing marks, he was, to the educated medieval eye, a glutton, a hypocrite, and a eunuch, as Chaucer makes plain enough when he says, "I think he was a gelding or a mare." This fundamental fact, established in the Prologue, explains the altercation between the Pardoner and Harry Bailly, the Host, after the Pardoner has told his tale. The Pardoner reveals himself as a hypocrite and a glutton; he preaches always on the same text, he says, "avarice is the root of evil," because that enables him to preach against the very sin he practices. No doubt, as G. L. Kittredge observed, the Pardoner takes an artist's pride in his exposure of his own skill in playing on the credulity of simple people. And very likely the Pardoner for a moment drops the role of hypocrite when he says, "Christ grant you his pardon, for I will not deceive you, that is best." But he goes on to urge the company to kiss his relics, after cheerfully confessing them fakes, and suggests that Harry Bailly should be first, "since he is most enveloped in sin." The Host, the genial master of the company, ought to have answered, "Well, you old fraud, you've put on a good show. I'll kiss your fake relics for you if you want." Instead he takes the shortest and crudest way, whether knowingly or not, to hit the Pardoner below the belt, by a series of remarks that could not help reminding the Pardoner of the defect that the planets had given him and that his obvious physical traits would have betrayed to any of the pilgrims who knew their contemporary science. To this blow there was no answer; the one possible response was speechless and helpless rage, which only the intervention of the Knight could mollify. A literature and a theory lie also behind the wart on the Miller's nose and the gaps between the Wife of Bath's teeth. All this science did not obscure Chaucer's characters as individuals. Chaucer did not let science, or supposed science, create his characters for him as types or case histories, but used the best available knowledge to understand and interpret in the fullest degree men and women independently observed and imagined.

CHAUCER'S BAWDY TALES

Dryden, late in his life modernizing for his own age the Knight's Tale, the Nun's Priest's Tale, and the Wife of Bath's Tale, and conscious that some of his own plays were open to the moral objections brought against the Restoration stage, remarked self-righteously of his Chaucerian adaptations: "I have written nothing which savours of immorality or profaneness." What once would have been called obscenity in Chaucer is not likely to ruffle many sensibilities in the latter twentieth century. Yet Chaucer himself apologized for his vulgar yarns. In the general Prologue to *The Canterbury Tales* and the Prologue to the Miller's Tale, the apology is at least partly ironic, though the irony itself shows that the tales were open to objection on the part of some readers or listeners. In his "retractation," if, as is reasonable to suppose, he actually wrote it, Chaucer apologized without irony for those of his writings that "tended toward sin," including many that would now seem entirely innocent. The interesting question is what would have made the Miller's Tale or the Reeve's Tale objectionable to some of those who might have listened to them.

In reading his bawdy stories, one does not feel that Chaucer is violating tabus either of language or subject matter. He does not have the air of defying convention or exploiting forbidden ground. Partly this effect comes from his naturalness and health of temperament, but no doubt it was also due in part to the social conditions of his time. Chaucer and his age had little opportunity to make a secret of bodily functions. It was a luxury denied them. In the public rooms of great houses, the silks of the ladies trailed over a compost of rushes and dog's filth. In such a cottage as the poor widow inhabited with her two daughters in the Nun's Priest's Tale, the distinction between public and private rooms, between "hall and bower," was lost. Chanticleer and his paramours roosted on the beams overhead while widow and daughters slept in the one hovel-room below. The Wife of Bath, describing her methods of keeping husbands in subjection, confesses cheerfully that "if my husband had pissed on a wall or done a thing that might have cost his life," in other words a common act or a seriously criminal act, she would let her "gossips" know about it immediately. In such a context, Chaucer's openness about the sexuality and other physical functions of his characters is not surprising.

But linguistic as well as sanitary conditions help throw light on Chaucer's rowdy tales. Chaucer's vocabulary does not contain the four-letter word for copulation which until recently was tabu in decent social intercourse, but is now so universally common that it threatens to lose its meaning and become a mere verbal tic. Chaucer's verb "swyven" is used freely and naturally, without any sense that it ever needed to burst up from an outlawed level of speech. It was in more recent times that a split occurred between a vocabulary regarded as fit for writing and respectable conversation and another vocabulary, regarded as vulgar or obscene and limited to unrespectable society or exclusively male conversation. Chaucer's vocabulary is more unitary, all "pure English undefiled," even in his rowdy scenes or tales. Chaucer's language, so far as I can see, does not even contain any very distinct class of words that can be called slang. The Canon's Yeoman's Tale, exposing alchemical frauds, of course uses the jargon of alchemy. The students in the Reeve's Tale speak in a northern dialect. But slang, although I have had to resort to it in the effort to sustain Chaucer's liveliness and humor, does not really represent his linguistic manner.

Chaucer's fabliaux would have been open to objecttion in his day not because they aroused the sense of the obscene, but because, as Chaucer himself says, they were tales of sin. They were unedifying in a day when the edifying could also be entertaining. They were "lewd," meaning ignorant, uneducated, characteristic of the manners of those who could not boast of being well born or "gentle." All the pilgrims were delighted with the Knight's tale of love and chivalry, but especially the "gentles." When the drunken Miller had finished his "lewd" story, different pilgrims had different things to say, but "for the most part they laughed" and took it sportingly. The Knight did not interrupt the Miller; he interrupted the tedious but thoroughly dignified string of catastrophes related by the Monk under the heading of tragedy. Chaucer's fabliaux are represented as being told openly in the hearing of the Knight, the lady Prioress, and the Monk. No doubt Chaucer himself read aloud at court from his "lewd" tales.

The sense of the corrupt, it seems to me, is almost nowhere to be found in Chaucer. Perhaps elements in the Merchant's Tale are distasteful enough to be offensive, but its ridiculous and ingenious conclusion has a redeeming charm. The fabliaux are vulgar, but not with the vulgarity that means coarseness of perception in the author, rather the vulgarity that comes from heartiness of palate and the capacity to share in the common life of the world at its lower as well as higher levels. The disturbing note, to the sensitive mind, in the tales of the Miller and the Reeve, is their cruelty. But broad comedy can hardly escape a strain of the cruel. Someone is bound to get hurt, and in Chaucer it is credulity, vanity, jealousy, hypocrisy, and shrewdness overreaching itself that commonly get hurt. The reader may wince, but he is squeamish indeed if he can refuse his laugh. The Miller's Tale, after all, is more than a farcical anecdote which folklorists assign elegantly to the category of the "misdirected kiss," joined with another frequent anecdote about a character who is induced to dread a return of Noah's flood. One of the root themes of the comic, or for that matter the tragic, is human credulity. It has seldom received such drastic treatment as in the Miller's Tale. Consider the deluded carpenter going up with his choreboy to pry open the door behind which he thinks Nicholas is sitting bemused and out of his wits in an astrologer's trance. "Wake up, Nicholas, and think of Christ's passion," the carpenter implores. "Think of God, as we do, we working men!" One is reminded of scenes in Ben Jonson. Rare Ben himself could hardly make comedy hit a more devastating blow.

CHAUCER AND RELIGIOUS BELIEF

Religion possessed an extraordinary vitality in Chaucer's times. The Church exerted its force in social and private life on a scale and with an acceptance of its prerogatives very different from anything to be seen in English-speaking societies today. Chaucer's clerics, with the exception of the good parish Priest, suggest the extent to which ecclesiastical authority was everywhere present and the extent to which it could be abused. Resentment against clerical and institutional abuses was vigorous, but without much effect, to all appearances, on fundamental belief. Everyone was a Christian and a Catholic, up to the point, at any rate, when Wycliffe and his followers fell under condemnation of heresy. And in Chaucer the impression is lively that religion existed for sinners. It owed its vitality to the remarkable human energies that religion exists to control, direct, and sometimes to suppress or sublimate, but which insist on breaking out in peculiarly human manifestations. The imaginative resourcefulness of the Middle Ages in profanity and blasphemy is everywhere evident in Chaucer, and can only be a paradoxical token of the vigor of religious belief itself. God was a very personal God, for purposes of swearing as well as for higher theological purposes. His body could be torn to shreds, as the hypocritical Pardoner observes, in the oaths of revelers and blasphemers. God's body, God's arms, the nails that held Christ's hands to the cross, the relics and holy places of saints were freely levied on for picturesque and profane images.

Amid all this paradoxical vigor, Chaucer was himself a good Catholic, a believer and an acceptable member, no doubt, of the Christian community. More than this, he expressed at times a genuine and deep piety, which rises now and again in his work to the exalted and true accent of notable religious poetry. A very large part of his total production in poetry and prose was pious or edifying, a side of Chaucer not well represented in this volume, I must admit. For after all it is by the worldly part of his work that Chaucer is remembered. The force of his distinct gifts as a poet went more frequently by far into human than divine comedy or tragedy. When the Parson, introducing his tale, which is to wind up the Canterbury pilgrimage with "something edifying," says to his audience, "And Jesus, for his grace, give me the wit to show you, on this journey, the way of that perfect, glorious pilgrimage which is called the heavenly Jerusalem," the lines are simple, touching, and fully genuine. But they are also "in character." It is the Parson speaking. Chaucer was no doubt in full sympathy, but if his personal belief was at work, the artist of *The Canterbury Tales* was just as much at work, and we smile as we think of the Parson addressing his words to the Wife of Bath, the Franklin, the Miller, the Friar, the Summoner, and the

Physician, "who paid little attention to the Bible." They too, for that matter, were all good Catholics and Christians; nothing would have astonished them more than to be classified with Turks, Jews, and infidels, the only alternative they would have known to being Christian and Catholic.

Perhaps the most exalted and most nearly personal note of piety to be found in Chaucer at his best occurs at the end of the *Troilus*. "O young people, he or she, in whom love springs up with the freshness of your age," he says, and invokes the love of Christ instead of fleshly love as the only stable and certain allegiance of human affections. "He will be false to no man, I dare say," and Chaucer ends the poem with a prayer to the Trinity which is in part translated from Dante. "Defend us from visible and invisible foes!" But even here the expression of piety, fully genuine as it no doubt is, can hardly be detached from its context and taken as an independent religious poem. The hymn to the Trinity is also dramatic, in a more oblique fashion than the Prioress's Tale or the Parson's lines on the heavenly Jerusalem. For the end of the *Troilus* is a blended compound of many tones, including the ironical dedication to Gower, which suggests Byron's ironical dedication of *Don Juan* to Southey. The imagination of the artist is completing a very worldly tragicomedy by extending it into the final dimension, into the perspective we take when the story is over, when the play has run its course, and we see the necessary instability of all worldly relations and goods. This perspective is aesthetically necessary to the conception of tragedy pursued to its limits.

There is no question that Chaucer was a believer and had a genuine strain of personal piety. But how far can a man go in satire of clerical abuses without trespassing on the fundamentals of belief? Chaucer went pretty far at a number of points. In his portrait of the Summoner, he

seems to come very close to calling in question the power
of excommunication as represented by the archdeacon's
curse. It is hard to resist the impression of an underlying
savage thrust that just stops short of challenging an ulti-
mate power of the Church.

The answer to all questions about Chaucer's personal
religious belief, it seems to me, lies in his predominantly
worldly temperament. Whatever the reader may think of
him for it, Chaucer had neither an innovating nor a rebel-
lious mind. He was of all poets the one who could accept
the world as he found it, and without craving to reform
society, could be tickled to the root, like the Wife of
Bath, that he had "had his world in his time." Manifest
absurdities, abuses, and corruptions he could ridicule, as
any man of the world with a moral sense can do; but he
did so, as far as I can see, without the impulse either to
construct in his mind a new plan for an ideal society, or
to reform existing society by some political program.
Chaucer was mainly a moral rather than a religious poet,
and moral not as a reformer, but as one who shared,
enjoyed, and understood common life. In Chaucer, with
the fewest possible exceptions, the reader always knows
where right and wrong lie. If he had a strong enough
comic stomach to relish the character of a scoundrel as
much as the character of a just and upright man, he
never blurred the distinction between them. In his own
age, he would never have questioned nor doubted funda-
mental Christian beliefs, the providence and trinity of
God, the redemption from sin and entrance into eternal
bliss offered by Christ, the Son of God, the sanctity and
ideal beauty of the virgin mother of Christ, the authority
of the Church visible as the trustee on earth of the keys
of salvation and the doctrines of the true faith. If we
could imagine Chaucer, with his worldly temperament,
his intellectual curiosity, his eagerness for all sorts of
knowledge, including the sciences, transplanted to a later

and more secular age, we might well expect his beliefs also to become secularized, but without loss of that fundamental piety which the natures of those who accept the world and are glad to have lived in it must feel toward the sources of being.

CHAUCER AND LATER POETRY

Chaucer, who foreshadowed the Renaissance, would have been at home in it as a poet-playwright both comic and tragic. As the Elizabethan age passed into the Jacobean, we can hardly imagine a transplanted Chaucer writing the Holy Sonnets of Donne or following the example of the metaphysicals. In the disciple of "rare Ben," Herrick, who combined worldliness with piety of mind and simplicity of expression, he would have found a more congenial note. Milton, so often taking his own sense of divine mission as his theme, writing with dignified pathos of his personal misfortunes and the defeat of his socio-theological hopes, identifying himself with Samson, the chosen champion of the Lord, "eyeless in Gaza at the mill with slaves," brings into poetry a strain altogether foreign to Chaucer, who always speaks of himself with self-deprecation and humor. Chaucer could have matched wits with Pope and Swift, but only his worldliness would have been satisfied in their select circle, not the humanity by which it was enlarged and kept true. Savage indignation could never have been Chaucer's role. In the eighteenth century, he would have been a friend of Henry Fielding, and would have written another *Tom Jones*, not another *Dunciad*.

Among the Romantic poets, Chaucer would have been hard put to it to find a place. He would have relished *Don Juan*, but could never have taken himself seriously enough to wear the Byronic character. Dickens and Mark Twain are more nearly heirs of Chaucer in the nineteenth century than is any poet. We can see the radical differences between Chaucer and the Romantics, and much poetic doctrine and practice that has followed them, by thinking of the way in which Chaucer spoke of himself and his poetry in contrast with some characteristic utterances of the Romantics. "Scatter my dead leaves over the universe," implored Shelley, apostrophizing the West Wind; "Be thou me, impetuous one!" Chaucer, I feel sure, could never have identified himself with the universe, or given his leaves a role to play in the natural process of death and renewal. He could never have conceived of the poet as legislating for mankind, consciously or unconsciously, through the possession of a special sensibility that could redeem and reconstruct society. It is not so that Chaucer speaks of himself. Rather he reminds his friend Scogan to put in a word for him at court, or protests to his empty purse, alias King Henry, that he is "shaved as close as any friar." Chaucer is without Romantic egotism, without Romantic self-preoccupation. He sees himself cheerfully as a member of the social scene, a man moving among men, and in scale with the sprawling human spectacle. Byron could say:

> But there is that within me which shall tire
> Torture and Time, and breathe when I expire.

Chaucer says:

> All that men write shall pass, in prose or rhyme.
> Take every man his turn in his own time.

And as Chaucer is free from self-preoccupation, he is free from self-pity. He does not fall upon the thorns of life and bleed, at least in public. He complains, humorously, of unlucky turns in his personal fortunes, hoping to repair them. He does not drag the pageant of a bleeding heart before an admiring world; he twits himself on being one whom the god of love does not favor in the dance.

Chaucer was free from world-sickness and rebelliousness. He was acquainted with human pity and believed in divine compassion, but they did not lead him to a sense of guilt, loathing, or anxiety in his relations to the world and its people.

The beguiling simplicity of Chaucer at his best is so great that it becomes puzzling. From time to time Chaucer has been thought naïf, but a little familiarity with his shrewd and worldly intelligence is enough to dismiss the notion that he was a child-minded unsophisticate. The secret is, I think, that for all his worldliness Chaucer never lost the faculty of delight, whether in the opening and closing daisies in May, or in old books, or in what purported to be scientific knowledge in his time, or in the London streets crowded with people in all their species. Delight, not bitterness, is the mainspring even of Chaucer's irony, even of his satire at its sharpest. It is a pleasure to recognize the folly of the fool and the vice of the scoundrel, his lines seem to say. They, too, are human; they, too, are natural, as the birds are, and it would be a pity not to grant them the spontaneous admiration that a healthy eye takes in discerning any of God's creations.

As Chaucer's response to the world and its people was direct and wholehearted, so he was by every inclination a communicator. He began by using the allegorical conventions that fashion provided him, but in his fully mature work he put his plain sense in plain words. He did not entrust his meaning to schemes of symbolism. He uttered himself directly, and his prayer was to be understood. He had that simplicity of character which Emerson defined when he said that a man's simplicity consists in "his desire to communicate the truth without loss."

The same simplicity shows itself in Chaucer's moral sense. He was a moralist in the sphere in which the comic spirit moves with authority, the sphere of observable

common life and recognizable experience. His moral
sense was shrewd, clear, and plain, uncorrupted by inner
confusion. It was active in a world of people; it traced
the moral lineaments of human beings, and pursued acts
and traits to their consequences in human lives. It rel-
ished the wisdom of proverbs and delighted in applica-
tions of homely sense. It was not directed toward ideal
constructions of society; it did not try to shatter the sorry
scheme of things and remold it closer to some revolu-
tionary concept. One does not feel in Chaucer that pro-
found, personal, metaphysical sense of evil that some-
times in Shakespeare's tragedies destroys the fabric of
political and domestic relations and even obscures for a
time the order of the universe itself. But give Chaucer
his men, women, and proverbs, and his sound moral un-
derstanding is seldom at fault.

What put such traits within a poet's possession? Was
it the age in which he lived? Was it the special conditions
of his time alone that gave him a station in society and
spared him the sense of isolation, of being at odds with
his world, which became so prominent a note among
poets and their critics and interpreters during the Roman-
tic movement and the wars and social upheavals of the
twentieth century? One point, at any rate, seems clear.
The exact degree of Chaucer's skill as a man of affairs is
open to controversy or conjecture; but the irresistible
impression of his life and his writings taken together is
that he got his grasp of life by living as the world lives,
by engaging in the often humdrum business of bread-
winning, by seeking position and employment, accepting
responsibility and expecting to be held to account; by
marrying, begetting children, and planning and working
for their education and advancement, as he sought his
own advancement and comfort in the ways open to a
man of the world. Here was Chaucer's link with his
society, here was the price he paid for the great mass

of raw material on which his comic genius went to work, the mass of humanity itself. Of all poets, Chaucer was the poet of this world. For him this world, the center of the Ptolemaic cosmos that now seems so tidy and small, was rendered intelligible and given comfort by the scheme of Christian redemption, however transitory and full of the terrors of disease and misery earthly life itself may have been. But it was this present world of men and women in their rough, energetic, and hazardous society that Chaucer knew, reported, and loved. If he did not seek to reform it, if our own twentieth century seems to stand in more terrible and imminent danger than any preceding society on earth, we may reflect that there is danger also in the attempt to legislate for mankind. It is the danger that the legislator himself will only be able to look on men and women as they are, in their world as it is, with loathing and rejection, and will only be able to love, if he can love at all, some ideal and imagined humanity in some state of things that is not now and never yet has been. Chaucer was able to love the actual world he saw round him, the only world he would ever know. In the simplicity of his nature, he was able to speak directly, and to be what Dryden called him, in words that since the Romantic movement we might well rub our eyes in astonishment at hearing applied to a poet, "a perpetual fountain of good sense."

ON MODERNIZING CHAUCER

The game of modernizing Chaucer is an old one. It has gone on steadily since Dryden produced his versions of Chaucer toward the end of the seventeenth century. Dryden and Pope are the two most expert versifiers in English who undertook to adapt considerable portions of Chaucer to the taste and style of their times. A look at their procedure may be interesting.

Here is the beginning of the Wife of Bath's **Tale in** Chaucer's language (text from Robinson's edition):

> In th'olde dayes of the Kyng Arthour,
> Of which that Britons speken greet honour,
> Al was this land fulfild of fayerye.
> The elf-queene, with hir joly compaignye,
> Daunced ful ofte in many a grene mede.
> This was the olde opinion, as I rede;
> I speke of manye hundred yeres ago.
> But now kan no man se none elves mo,
> For now the grete charitee and prayeres
> Of lymytours and othere hooly freres,
> That serchen every lond and every streem,
> As thikke as motes in the sonne-beem,
> Blessynge halles, chambres, kichenes, boures,
> Citees, burghes, castels, hye toures,
> Thropes, bernes, shipnes, dayeryes—
> This maketh that ther been no fayeryes.
> For ther as wont to walken was an elf,
> Ther walketh now the lymytour hymself
> In undermeles and in morwenynges,
> And seyth his matyns and his hooly thynges
> As he gooth in his lymytacioun.
> Wommen may now go saufly up and doun
> In every bussh or under every tree;
> There is noon oother incubus but he,
> And he ne wol doon hem but dishonour.

Here is a translation of Chaucer's lines, arranged as prose, without suppression of some of his rhymes:

> In the old days of King Arthur, of whom Welshmen speak with great reverence, this whole land was full of fairy enchantment. The elf-queen, with her jolly company, danced often in many a green meadow. This was the old opinion, as I read; I speak of many hundred years ago. But no man now can

see any more elves, for now the great charity and prayers of limiters [friars authorized to beg in assigned districts] and other holy friars, who haunt every stream and every part of the country, thick as motes in a sunbeam, blessing halls, chambers, kitchens, bowers, cities, towns, castles, lofty towers, villages, barns, stables, dairies—this is the reason why there are no fairies, for where there used to walk an elf, there now walks the limiter himself, in the mornings and the afternoons, and says his matins and his holy things as he goes about his district. Women may now go safely up and down in every thicket or under every tree. There is no other incubus but him, and he will do them no more than dishonor. [The Wife of Bath's concluding joke rests on the belief that intercourse with an incubus always caused pregnancy.]

Dryden expands Chaucer's twenty-five lines to forty-five. I quote only in part:

In days of old when Arthur filled the throne,
Whose acts and fame to foreign lands were blown,
The king of elves and little fairy queen
Gambolled on heaths, and danced on every green . . .
Nor darkling did they dance; the silver light
Of Phoebe served to guide their steps aright,
And, with their tripping pleased, prolonged the night . . .
    I speak of ancient times; for now the swain
Returning late may pass the woods in vain,
And never hope to see the nightly train . . .
For priests with prayers, and other goodly gear,
Have made the merry goblins disappear . . .
And friars that through the wealthy regions run,
Thick as the motes that twinkle in the sun,
Resort to farmers rich, and bless their halls,
And exorcise their beds, and cross the walls;
This makes the fairy quires forsake the place,
When once 'tis hallowed with the rites of grace,

and so on.[1] Dryden had remarked in his preface that Chaucer lacked "the modern art of fortifying," an observation for which A. E. Housman properly twits him in *The Name and Nature of Poetry.*

Turning back to the Wife of Bath's Prologue, we find Chaucer beginning thus:

> Experience, though noon auctoritee
> Were in this world, is right ynogh for me
> To speke of wo that is in mariage.

"Experience," says the Wife of Bath, "though there were no learned authority on the subject in this world, is plenty to enable me to speak of the woe that is in marriage." Thus Pope, paraphrasing Chaucer:

> Behold the woes of matrimonial life,
> And hear with rev'rence an experienced wife.

It is obvious enough what Dryden and Pope are doing. Brilliant versifiers in their own right, each a follower and a molder of the special fashions and tastes of his own time, they frankly transform Chaucer into something like a fashionable poet of the period, cast in their own image. They add, alter, or modify at will. They are totally unlike Chaucer except as they take over roughly the substance of what he said or told. Neither has the simplicity of Chaucer's nature or style. They share the gift of satire with him, but they give satire not the worldliness of Chaucer's wholehearted delight in things, but a kind of *beau monde* worldliness of entirely different taste. And their rhetorical instrument, the rhyming couplet so designed as to encourage parallelism, antithesis, and epigrammatic self-sufficiency, is entirely different from Chaucer's natural, simple, narrative, forward-

---

[1] The reader who wants to anticipate at this point and see how I have rendered the first lines of the Wife of Bath's Tale may turn to page 230.

moving couplet, with its loose syntax, plain and idiomatic diction and phrasing, and conversational ease. It is amusing to see Chaucer's "jolly company" become Dryden's "fairy quires"; it is amusing to see Pope turn "experience is enough for me to speak of the woes in marriage" into "Behold the woes of matrimonial life," almost extinguishing the Wife of Bath herself into a general principle. But Pope, in his free version of the Merchant's Tale, produced what I suspect is the most spirited and racy refashioning of a Chaucer story, the story that of all Chaucer's is closest to the embittered tone of cynicism, a quality that Pope seized on with full relish.

Very different is Wordsworth's way of going at Chaucer. Introducing his version of the Prioress's Tale, he says: "In the following Poem no further deviation has been made than was necessary for the fluent reading and instant understanding of the Author [*i.e.:* of Chaucer]. ... The ancient accent has been retained in a few conjunctions, as *alsò* and *alwày*, from a conviction that such sprinklings of antiquity would be admitted, by persons of taste, to have a graceful accordance with the subject." And so we have the Prioress saying, in Wordsworth:

A little school of Christian people stood
Down at the farther end, in which there were
A nest of children come of Christian blood,
That learnèd in that school from year to year
Such sort of doctrine as men usèd there
That is to say, to sing and read alsò,
As little children in their childhood do.

Among these children was a Widow's son,
A little scholar, scarcely seven years old,
Who day by day unto this school hath gone,
And eke, when he the image did behold
Of Jesu's Mother, as he had been told,
This child was wont to kneel adown and say
Ave Marie, as he goeth by the way.

Here is a method of modernizing which is more reverential toward Chaucer than Dryden or Pope and also a great deal stuffier. It might be called the school of modernizing Chaucer by "sprinklings of antiquity," a school that did not cease with Wordsworth. It is superficially more faithful to its original; it does not add, does not alter, does not transform Chaucer into a fashionable poet of a different period. But it is faithful only to Chaucer's content; its effect and tone are even farther from Chaucer than Dryden and Pope are, inasmuch as it falls short of the spiritedness of their versions. "Sprinklings of antiquity," it seems to me, are likely to give the reader unacquainted with Chaucer's language and metric the blasphemously wrong impression that Chaucer wrote, in his own time, a kind of bastard, pedantic, schoolmaster's jargon, full of departures from ordinary usage, pronunciation, and idiom, and remote from speech. How it is possible to capture any of Chaucer's tone except in a reasonably natural and current language, close to good conversation in whatever time the "modernizing" may be undertaken? For it was in precisely such a language that Chaucer wrote in his own day.

The translation of poetry at full value from one language or dialect to another is notoriously impossible. And "modernizing" Chaucer is a problem in the translation of poetry, perhaps in some respects an easy one, but in others as hard as any such problem. It is a question what the aims of the translator should be. As Arnold noted in his lectures "On Translating Homer," everyone will agree that fidelity to the original is the first object. But what is fidelity?

There is of course a belief at present that in a sense no translation can be faithful. Translation goes by periods, this view holds; every age must translate the great writers of the past all over again, for it must, by a law of taste and sensibility, re-create them in its own image.

What it sees is never the original writer as he was in his own time or under some absolute, eternal view, but its own lineaments reflected back from the original. Dryden and Pope exemplify the measure of truth in this view in their versions of Chaucer. They were not actually attempting to translate Chaucer with such close and detailed faithfulness as human possibility would allow them to achieve; they were freely embroidering Chaucerian themes and stories. Even so, they were more faithful to Chaucer than Wordsworth in so far as they rendered him with spirit and in a language natural to their own time and circle. But is no higher degree of fidelity possible?

I have at any rate attempted translation, not embroidery, in this volume, and have taken the translator's duty of faithfulness as my first obligation. But the notion that in order to be faithful a translator must set down a word for every word in the original, for each of Chaucer's nouns an equivalent, current noun, or for each of his lines exactly one parallel line, leads, it seems to me, not to faithfulness but its opposite. The first point in fidelity is to the content; it is truly to represent the meaning of the original, to say as far as possible just what Chaucer said, to tell his stories as he told them. But the next and far more difficult problem is faithfulness to the tone and effect of the original, to catch the notes of gaiety or irony or gravity as they succeed each other in Chaucer's pages. Here is the problem of style and language; here is the point at which the translator is bound to lose the game, to ache with private chagrin as he sees what he has done to his original, how the magic has leaked away, how the charm has flattened out, how the light-wine sparkle of Chaucer has been turned into beer if not outright dishwater. Only a measure of independence will sustain the translator or "modernizer" who aims at catching as much as he can of the tone and effect of

the poet he translates. Where he can follow closely, even
word by word, and feel that he has preserved some of
the effect, he will be most deeply satisfied with his work.
Where this is impossible, he must, in the most appro-
priate language of his time that he can command, try to
convey the meaning, character, and spirit of the original
in other terms.

The translator who wants to be faithful to the style
of his original will look for the main traits of that style,
and seek to preserve them despite the changes of time,
tongue, and fashion. In Chaucer, the difficult trait to
catch now is his extreme simplicity. So many changes
of culture have intervened, with their corresponding
changes in expression, that a modernizer is subject to
powerful gravitational drags away from Chaucer's ac-
tual manner. The epigrammatic couplet of Pope and
Dryden tempts him to render some of Chaucer's cou-
plets in sharper, more self-contained antitheses than the
loose, easy, forward-moving Chaucerain fashion. The
satiric portraits in the Prologue are a temptation to
Byronic rhyming. In some passages a kind of phrasing
left over from Romantic rhetoric seems to offer an easy
way out. I have tried to represent Chaucer's simplicity as
faithfully as I was able, his plain diction, his active,
simple, but often highly idiomatic predicates, his loose-
ness of syntax, even his freedom with pronouns, which
often wander about with happy disregard for the logic
of unambiguous reference. I have, I admit, tightened
and formalized his syntax in places and straightened
out some of his pronouns, and with another Chaucerian
trait I have followed him even less faithfully. Chaucer is
an odd mixture of the prolix and the concise. The mod-
ern reader marvels equally at the rapidity with which
he can wind up a tale or a scene, the happy, summary
brevity with which he can state and leave a point when

he chooses to, and at the same time the astounding length at which he can embroider, dilate, postpone the issue, furnish twenty or forty "old examples," and hammer the obvious with a truly formidable array of "authorities." Chaucer is also full of tag lines and stock filler phrases. I have tried to give the reader enough of his prolix side so that this trait will be abundantly clear, but I have not hesitated to condense. My versions of the Knight's Tale and the *Troilus* are about half as long as Chaucer's, and yet I have achieved the reduction by the outright omission of very little indeed in the originals. Most of it is the result of simple squeezing down of expression. The other poems and passages I have rendered have been condensed far less, many scarcely at all. But I have gone on the principle that expansion was everywhere to be avoided, and condensation, within limits, welcomed.

I have not tried to make Chaucer sound as though he were writing in the mid-twentieth century; rather as though, if he were writing now, he would use a language familiar to us in conversation and reading. Not the language or literary method of "modern poetry" since *The Waste Land*, into which it would be impossible to render Chaucer at all, but a language drawn from the diction and usage of good talk and general literate expression, prose or verse. I well know that my resources have not been equal to this task, and I have found modifications necessary in two directions. I have tried to avoid "sprinklings of antiquity," obsolete or archaic words or forms, except for the names of objects or occupations which no longer exist, and for which it would be foolish to try to find modern substitutes. But I have had to admit some words and phrases that no doubt will seem bookish, drawn from a literary background which is receding, and with reluctance I have had to admit some slang, in contexts where slang seemed the nearest match for the natural, unself-conscious physical words that in Chaucer's time would have been pure current English.

Chaucer was an exact rhymer, so exact that scholars have been able to use rhyme as one criterion in determining whether poems attributed to him were in fact his, and in determining the pronunciation of some of his vocabulary. To attempt to reproduce Chaucer's thousands of exact rhymes in modern English is an effort that few people will envy me. I have of course had to change many hundreds of Chaucer's rhyming pairs. I have used exact rhymes in the main, but have not hesitated to use imperfect rhymes where I could gain what seemed greater naturalness of expression.

Many of Chaucer's words, whether through inflectional endings now lost or contracted (*bokës*, plural of *books*), or through difference of pronunciation as such, had more syllables than the same words have in their present form: *creature* would have had three syllables in Chaucer (*cráyature*). When it occurred at the end of a line as a rhyme word, the final short "e" would have been lightly sounded, not with any stress, not at the length of a full syllable, rather as though one said the "u" of "up" without sounding the "p": *crëätûrë*. This very light sounding of final short "e" in rhyme words gave Chaucer many hundreds of rhymes which did not have the weight of outright feminine (two syllable) rhymes, such as *lightest* and *brightest*, but hovered between feminine and masculine (one syllable) rhymes. Thus our *game* and *shame*, used as rhyme words, would have been pronounced by Chaucer *gámë* and *shámë* (the "a" pronounced "ah"). The sum of these differences gives both the metric quality and the quality of rhyme in Chaucer an effect of indescribable lightness and charm, and distinguishes his verses both in weight and motion from modern English verses in the same meter.

Chaucer's pentameter line has been somewhat despair-
ingly called liquid, flowing, sinuous. The modern Eng-
lish pentameter seems to me acoustically heavier and
thicker by comparison. We can get more words, or a
closer tissue of words, into a line—another reason for
condensing Chaucer, unless the modernizer wants to
pad outrageously. But the lightness and charm of Chau-
cer's easy motion is, I am afraid, almost impossible to
approximate in English today. With the exception of
the *Troilus,* I have reproduced Chaucer's verse forms
and rhyme schemes in my versions, but I cannot pretend
to have caught the quality of his rhyming or of the mo-
tion of his lines. I doubt whether the language today is
capable of doing so.

As a metrist, the aesthetic accomplishment of Chaucer
is so great as to tax the imagination. In *The Book of the
Duchess* and *The House of Fame,* we find him, in the
early stages of his career, rattling along in half-doggerel
four-stress couplets, a form in which he could not have
written his mature work. There are lines in *The Book of
the Duchess* as lovely as he ever wrote, but the short
couplet was an open temptation to his prolixity. Chau-
cer, needing a more resourceful and more exacting verse
form, found it and brought it to perfection. Whatever
partial and irregular precedents he may have profited
by, he virtually created the English pentameter, the
meter of Marlowe's and Shakespeare's dramatic verse,
of Spenser's and Milton's epic verse, the line that by its
flexibility, its capacity to absorb variations and contra-
dictions of every sort without losing its identity as a
rhythmic structure, has been the chief metric property
of the English tongue since he used it. Whether French
or Italian verse suggested the five-foot line to Chaucer
does not much matter. English is neither French nor
Italian. He first heard the pentameter in English, first
heard and caught in English words its full right and

claim as the dominant natural measure implicit in the language. True enough, after the rapid linguistic changes following Chaucer's death, the pentameter had to be rediscovered and retuned, but Chaucer first found and perfected it. He used it not only for the couplets of most of *The Canterbury Tales,* but built more elaborate structures of it as well. His favorite was the seven-line rhyme-royal stanza. To the eight-line stanza of the Monk's Tale, Spenser added an Alexandrine as ninth line and so created the stanza that bears his name. Only two really notable verse forms have come into wide and continued employment in English since Chaucer's day, the sonnet and blank verse, and both use the pentameter as their metric line.

There is no use denying that rhyme and meter present the translator with a long series of exasperations and exigencies. Distortions, alterations, and additions become unavoidable. I think that even in my rhymed versions I can claim a substantial faithfulness to Chaucer's content, but I have had to condense, pad, fob up, and change here and there. The Miller, speaking to the Reeve, remarks:

> Leve brother Osewold,
> Who hath no wyf, he is no cokewold.

This becomes, in my version, for reasons that will be obvious enough:

> Oswald, my brother, *true as babes are suckled,*
> The man who has no wife, he is no cuckold.

I believe I have made few such outright additions to Chaucer as the italicized words in this couplet, but departures of some sort have frequently seemed unavoidable. I have considered that the greatest sin against Chaucer, the worst breach of faithfulness by the translator, would be to make him sound stuffy or pedantic, to make him sound as though he wrote without naturalness and with-

out spirit. All other sins are minor by comparison. I
have tried to avoid both major and minor sins, but I am
conscious of many that I have been compelled to com-
mit. Singer, humorist, tough-minded moralist, and man
of compassion that Chaucer was, I can only hope that
I have not too far debased the English that he made so
"sweet upon his tongue."

SUGGESTED READINGS AND OTHER AIDS

The general reader who wants to make a first-hand ac-
quaintance with Chaucer, and the teacher and student
at any stage up to advanced original research, will find
all their ordinary needs satisfied by a single volume, *The
Works of Geoffrey Chaucer*, edited by F. N. Robinson
(Boston: Houghton Mifflin, second edition, 1957). This
contains the text of all Chaucer's known works, records
the facts of his life, summarizes his grammar, pronun-
ciation, and metrics, provides textual and explanatory
notes, bibliographical references, and a glossary.

Albert C. Baugh, *Chaucer's Major Poetry* (New York:
Appleton-Century-Crofts, 1963), provides a text less
elaborate in its editorial apparatus than Robinson but
amply sufficient for the classroom or for readers of Chau-
cer in the original.

R. K. Root, *Troilus and Criseyde* (Princeton: Princeton
University Press, 1926), will aid readers who wish to
pursue the text, sources, and problems of the *Troilus*.

R. D. French, *A Chaucer Handbook* (New York: F. S.
Crofts and Company, 1927), is a standard, useful guide.

Nevill Coghill, *The Poet Chaucer* (New York: Oxford
University Press, 1964 edition), offers a lively, compact
introduction to Chaucer.

Marchette Chute, *Geoffrey Chaucer of England* (New
York: E. P. Dutton and Company, 1946, paperback
1958), presents the documented facts of Chaucer's life,
traces his literary development, and fills in the social
and historical picture of his times both readably and
thoroughly.

G. G. Coulton, *Chaucer and His England* (London: Methuen and Company, 1908), is permanently valuable.

C. S. Lewis, *The Allegory of Love* (New York: Oxford University Press, 1936, paperback 1958), deals in a wider historical context with the courtly love tradition, which is important in Chaucer.

W. C. Curry, *Chaucer and the Mediaeval Sciences* (New York: Oxford University Press, 1926), throws light on an important side of Chaucer's knowledge and its literary use.

G. L. Kittredge, *Chaucer and His Poetry* (Cambridge, Mass.: Harvard University Press, 1915), is still admirable for interpretation and criticism.

Two works by J. L. Lowes, *Geoffrey Chaucer and the Development of His Genius* (Boston: Houghton Mifflin, 1934), and *The Art of Geoffrey Chaucer* (New York: Oxford University Press, 1931), are notable for lively and discriminating criticism and appreciation.

Sheila Sullivan, editor, *Critics on Chaucer* (London: George Allen and Unwin, Ltd., 1970), is an anthology of critical and interpretive selections ranging from Dryden through Virginia Woolf and C. S. Lewis.

J. A. Burrow, *Geoffrey Chaucer, A Critical Anthology* (Penguin Books, 1969), offers a similar body of mostly short critical selections.

R. S. Loomis, *A Mirror of Chaucer's World* (Princeton: Princeton University Press, 1965), is an attractive picture book, with descriptive and explanatory text, containing a wide variety of illustrations reproduced from sources contemporary or nearly contemporary with Chaucer.

For those who wish to become acquainted with at least an approximation to the sound of Chaucer's Middle English, recordings are available by various readers. Three readings by J. B. Bessinger, Jr., are recommended: "General Prologue," "Prologue to the Parson's Tale," "Retraction" (Caedmon, TC 1151); "Miller's Tale" and "Reeve's Tale" (Caedmon TC 1223); "Parliament of Fowls" and six lyric poems (Caedmon TC 1226).

THE
CANTERBURY
TALES

Prologue

As soon as April pierces to the root
The drought of March, and bathes each bud and shoot
Through every vein of sap with gentle showers
From whose engendering liquor spring the flowers;
When zephyrs have breathed softly all about
Inspiring every wood and field to sprout,
And in the zodiac the youthful sun
His journey halfway through the Ram has run;
When little birds are busy with their song
Who sleep with open eyes the whole night long
Life stirs their hearts and tingles in them so,
Then people long on pilgrimage to go,
And palmers to set out for distant strands
And foreign shrines renowned in sundry lands.
And specially in England people ride
To Canterbury from every countyside
To visit there the blessed martyred saint
Who gave them strength when they were sick and faint.
   In Southwark at the Tabard one spring day
It happened, as I stopped there on my way,
Myself a pilgrim with a heart devout
Ready for Canterbury to set out,
At night came all of twenty-nine assorted
Travelers, and to that same inn resorted,
Who by a turn of fortune chanced to fall
In fellowship together, and they were all
Pilgrims who meant toward Canterbury to ride.
The rooms and stables were well kept and wide

And we were well provided with the best,
And shortly, when the sun had gone to rest,
I had so talked with each that presently
I was a member of their company
And promised to rise early the next day
To start, as I shall show, upon our way.

But none the less, while I have time and space,
Before this tale has gone a further pace,
I should in reason tell you the condition
Of each of them, his rank and his position,
And also what array they all were in;
And so then, with a knight I will begin.

A Knight was with us, and an excellent man,
Who from the earliest moment he began
To follow his career loved chivalry,
Truth, openhandedness, and courtesy.
He was a stout man in the king's campaigns
And in that cause had gripped his horse's reins
In Christian lands and pagan through the earth,
None farther, and always honored for his worth.
He was on hand at Alexandria's fall.
He had often sat in precedence to all
The nations at the banquet board in Prussia.
He had fought in Lithuania and in Russia,
No Christian knight more often; he had been
In Moorish Africa at Benmarin,
At the siege of Algeciras in Granada,
And sailed in many a glorious armada
In the Mediterranean, and fought as well
At Ayas and Attalia when they fell
In Armenia and on Asia Minor's coast.
Of fifteen deadly battles he could boast,
And in Algeria, at Tremessen,
Fought for the faith and killed three separate men
In single combat. He had done good work
Joining against another pagan Turk

With the king of Palathia. And he was wise,
Despite his prowess, honored in men's eyes,
Meek as a girl and gentle in his ways.
He had never spoken ignobly all his days
To any man by even a rude inflection.
He was a knight in all things to perfection.
He rode a good horse, but his gear was plain,
For he had lately served on a campaign.
His tunic was still spattered by the rust
Left by his coat of mail, for he had just
Returned and set out on his pilgrimage.

   His son was with him, a young Squire, in age
Some twenty years as near as I could guess.
His hair curled as if taken from a press.
He was a lover and would become a knight.
In stature he was of a moderate height
But powerful and wonderfully quick.
He had been in Flanders, riding in the thick
Of forays in Artois and Picardy,
And bore up well for one so young as he,
Still hoping by his exploits in such places
To stand the better in his lady's graces.
He wore embroidered flowers, red and white,
And blazed like a spring meadow to the sight.
He sang or played his flute the livelong day.
He was as lusty as the month of May.
His coat was short, its sleeves were long and wide.
He sat his horse well, and knew how to ride,
And how to make a song and use his lance,
And he could write and draw well, too, and dance.
So hot his love that when the moon rose pale
He got no more sleep than a nightingale.
He was modest, and helped whomever he was able,
And carved as his father's squire at the table.

   But one more servant had the Knight beside,
Choosing thus simply for the time to ride:

A Yeoman, in a coat and hood of green.
His peacock-feathered arrows, bright and keen,
He carried under his belt in tidy fashion.
For well-kept gear he had a yeoman's passion.
No draggled feather might his arrows show,
And in his hand he held a mighty bow.
He kept his hair close-cropped, his face was brown.
He knew the lore of woodcraft up and down.
His arm was guarded from the bowstring's whip
By a bracer, gaily trimmed. He had at hip
A sword and buckler, and at his other side
A dagger whose fine mounting was his pride,
Sharp-pointed as a spear. His horn he bore
In a green sling, and on his chest he wore
A silver image of St. Christopher,
His patron, since he was a forester.
  There was also a Nun, a Prioress,
Whose smile was gentle and full of guilelessness.
"By St. Loy!" was the worst oath she would say.
She sang mass well, in a becoming way,
Intoning through her nose the words divine,
And she was known as Madame Eglantine.
She spoke good French, as taught at Stratford-Bow,
For the Parisian French she did not know.
Also at table she was schooled so well
That from her lips no morsel ever fell.
She wet her fingers lightly in the dish
Of sauce, for courtesy was her first wish.
With every bite she did her skillful best
To see that no drop fell upon her breast.
She always wiped her upper lip so clean
That in her cup was never to be seen
A hint of grease when she had drunk her share.
She reached out for her meat with comely air.
She was a great delight and always tried
To imitate court ways, and had her pride,

Both amiable and gracious in her dealings.
As for her charity and tender feelings,
She melted at whatever was piteous.
She wept if she but came upon a mouse
Caught in a trap, if it were dead or bleeding.
Some little dogs that she took pleasure feeding
On roasted meat or milk or good wheat bread
She had, but how she wept to find one dead
Or yelping from a blow that made it smart,
And all was sympathy and loving heart.
Neat was her wimple in its every plait,
Her nose well formed, her eyes as gray as slate.
Her mouth was very small and soft and red.
She had so wide a brow I think her head
Was nearly a span broad, for certainly
She was not undergrown, as all could see.
She wore her cloak with dignity and charm,
And had her rosary about her arm,
The small beads coral and the larger green,
And from them hung a brooch of golden sheen.
An A inscribed beneath a crown it bore,
And under that *Omnia vincit amor.*

   A Priest accompanied her toward Canterbury,
And an attendant Nun, her secretary.

   There was a Monk, and nowhere was his peer,
A hunter and a roving overseer.
He was a manly man, and fully able
To be an abbot. He kept a hunting stable,
And when he rode the neighborhood could hear
His bridle jingling in the wind as clear
And loud as if it were a chapel bell.
Wherever he was master of a cell
The principles of good St. Benedict,
For being a little old and somewhat strict,
Were honored in the breach, as past their prime.
He lived by the fashion of a newer time.

He would have swapped that text for a plucked hen
Which says that hunters are not holy men,
Or a monk outside his discipline and rule
Is too much like a fish outside his pool;
That it to say, a monk outside his cloister.
But such a text he deemed not worth an oyster.
I told him his opinion made me glad.
Why should he study always and go mad,
Mewed in his cell with only a book for neighbor?
Or why, as Augustine commanded, labor
And sweat his hands? How shall the world be served?
To Augustine be all such toil reserved!
And so he hunted, as was only right.
He had greyhounds as swift as birds in flight.
His taste was all for tracking down the hare,
And what his sport might cost he did not care.
His sleeves I noticed, where they met his hand,
Trimmed with gray fur, the finest in the land.
His hood was fastened with a curious pin
Made of wrought gold and clasped beneath his chin,
A love knot at the tip. His head might pass,
Bald as it was, for a lump of shining glass.
His face was glistening as if anointed.
Fat as a lord he was, and well appointed.
His eyes were large, and rolled inside his head
As if they gleamed from a furnace of hot lead.
His boots were supple, his horse superbly kept.
He was a prelate to dream of while you slept.
He was not pale nor peaked like a ghost.
He relished a plump swan as his favorite roast.
He rode a palfrey brown as a ripe berry.

   A Friar was with us, a gay dog and a merry,
Who begged his district with a jolly air.
No friar in all four orders could compare
With him for gallantry; his tongue was wooing.
Many a girl was married by his doing,

And at his own cost it was often done.
He was a pillar, and a noble one,
To his whole order. In his neighborhood
Rich franklins knew him well, who served good food,
And worthy women welcomed him to town.
The license that his order handed down,
He said himself, conferred on him possession
Of more than a curate's power of confession.
Sweetly the list of frailties he heard,
Assigning penance with a pleasant word.
He was an easy man for absolution
Where he looked forward to a contribution,
For if to a poor order a man has given
It signifies that he has been well shriven,
And if a sinner let his purse be dented
The Friar would stake his oath he had repented.
For many men become so hard of heart
They cannot weep, though conscience makes them smart.
Instead of tears and prayers, then, let the sinner
Supply the poor friars with the price of dinner.
For pretty women he had more than shrift.
His cape was stuffed with many a little gift,
As knives and pins and suchlike. He could sing
A merry note, and pluck a tender string,
And had no rival at all in balladry.
His neck was whiter than a fleur-de-lis,
And yet he could have knocked a strong man down.
He knew the taverns well in every town.
The barmaids and innkeepers pleased his mind
Better than beggars and lepers and their kind.
In his position it was unbecoming
Among the wretched lepers to go slumming.
It mocks all decency, it sews no stitch
To deal with such riffraff; but with the rich,
With sellers of victuals, that's another thing.
Wherever he saw some hope of profiting,

None so polite, so humble. He was good,
The champion beggar of his brotherhood.
Should a woman have no shoes against the snow,
So pleasant was his *"In principio"*
He'd have her widow's mite before he went.
His profits were much greater than his rent
For begging rights within appointed bounds.
None of his brethren trespassed on his grounds!
He loved as freely as a half-grown whelp.
On arbitration-days he gave great help,
For his cloak was never shiny nor threadbare
Like a poor cloistered scholar's. He had an air
As if he were a doctor or a pope.
It took stout wool to make his semicope
That plumped out like a bell for portliness.
He lisped a little in his rakishness
To make his English sweeter on his tongue,
And twanging his harp to end some song he'd sung
His eyes would twinkle in his head as bright
As the stars twinkle on a frosty night.
Hubert this gallant Friar was by name.

   Among the rest a Merchant also came.
He wore a forked beard and a beaver hat
From Flanders. High up in the saddle he sat,
In figured cloth, his boots clasped handsomely,
Delivering his opinions pompously,
Always on how his gains might be increased.
At all cost he desired the sea policed
From Middleburg in Holland to Orwell.
He knew the exchange rates, and the time to sell
French currency, and there was never yet
A man who could have told he was in debt
So grave he seemed and hid so well his feelings
With all his shrewd engagements and close dealings.
You'd find no better man at any turn;
But what his name was I could never learn.

There was an Oxford Student too, it chanced,
Already in his logic well advanced.
As skinny as a rake the horse he rode,
And he himself was hardly a plump load,
Rather his look was hollow and sober enough.
He wore an outer coat of threadbare stuff,
No benefice was yet in his enjoyment
And he was too unworldly for employment
In some lay office. At his couch's head
His twenty volumes bound in black and red
Of Aristotle's philosophy pleased him more
Than a rich wardrobe or a gay guitar,
For though he knew philosophy could offer
Promise of gold, there was little in his coffer.
Whatever he got by touching up a friend
On books and learning he would promptly spend
And busily pray for the soul of anybody
Who furnished him the wherewithal for study.
His scholarship was what he truly heeded.
He never spoke a word more than was needed,
And that was said with dignity and force,
And quick and brief. He was of grave discourse,
Lending his weight to virtue by his speech,
And gladly would he learn and gladly teach.

There was a Lawyer, cunning and discreet,
Who'd often been to St. Paul's porch to meet
His clients. He was a Sergeant of the Law,
A man deserving to be held in awe,
Or so he seemed, his manner was so wise.
He'd often served as Justice of Assize
By royal appointment, with a broad commission,
For his knowledge and his eminent position.
He'd many a handsome gift by way of fee.
There was no buyer of land as shrewd as he.
All ownership to him became fee simple.
His titles were never faulty by a pimple.

None was so busy as he with case and cause,
And yet he seemed much busier than he was.
In every case and verdict he was schooled
Through the whole record since King William ruled.
No one could pick a loophole or a flaw
In any lease or contract he might draw.
Each statute on the books he knew by rote.
He traveled in a plain, silk-belted coat.

    A Franklin traveled in his company.
Whiter could never daisy petal be
Than was his beard. His ruddy face gave sign
He liked his morning sop of toast in wine.
He lived in comfort, as he would assure us,
For he was a true son of Epicurus
Who held the opinion that the only measure
Of perfect happiness was simply pleasure.
Such hospitality did he provide,
He was St. Julian to his countryside.
His bread and ale were always up to scratch.
He had a cellar none on earth could match.
There was no lack of pasties in his house,
Both fish and flesh, and that so plenteous
That where he lived it snowed of meat and drink.
With every dish of which a man can think,
After the various seasons of the year,
He changed his diet for his better cheer.
The partridge in his coops were fat as cream,
He had a fishpond stocked with pike and bream.
Woe to his cook for an unready pot
Or sauce that wasn't seasoned and spiced hot!
A table in his hall stood on display
Prepared and covered through the livelong day.
He presided at court sessions for his bounty
And sat in Parliament often for his county.
A well-wrought dagger and a purse of silk
Hung at his belt, as white as morning milk.

He'd been a sheriff and county auditor.
On earth was no such rich proprietor!
   There were five Guildsmen, in the livery
Of one august and great fraternity,
A Weaver, a Dyer, and a Carpenter,
A Tapestry-maker and a Haberdasher.
Their gear was furbished new and clean as glass.
The mountings of their knives were not of brass
But silver. Their pouches were well made and neat,
And each of them, it seemed, deserved a seat
On the platform at the Guildhall, for each one
Was likely timber to make an alderman.
They had goods enough, and money to be spent,
Also their wives would willingly consent
And would have been at fault if they had not.
For to be "Madamed" is a pleasant lot,
To march in first at feasts for being well married
And royally to have their mantles carried.
   These Guildsmen had a Cook with them, their own,
To boil their chickens with the marrow bone
With seasoning powder, capers, and sharp spice.
In judging London ale his taste was nice.
He well knew how to roast and broil and fry,
To mix a stew, and bake a good meat pie,
Or capon creamed with almond, rice, and egg.
Pity he had an ulcer on his leg!
   A Skipper was with us, his home far in the west.
He came from the port of Dartmouth, as I guessed.
He sat his carthorse pretty much at sea,
His coarse smock joggling on his either knee.
A dagger on a string from his neck hung down
Beneath his arm. His face was burnished brown
By summer sun. He was a true good fellow.
Many a time he had tapped a wine cask mellow
Sailing from Bordeaux while the owner slept.
Too nice a point of honor he never kept.

In sea fights, if he got the upper hand,
Drowned prisoners floated home to every land.
In navigation, whether reckoning tides,
Currents, or what might threaten him besides,
Harborage, pilotage, or the moon's demeanor,
None was his like from Hull to Cartagena.
He knew each harbor and the anchorage there
From Gotland to the Cape of Finisterre
And every creek in Brittany and Spain,
And he had called his ship the *Madeleine*.

With us came also an astute Physician.
There was none like him for a disquisition
On the art of medicine or surgery,
For he was grounded in astrology.
He kept his patient long in observation,
Choosing the proper hour for application
Of charms and images by intuition
Of magic, and the planets' best position.
For he was one who understood the laws
That rule the humors, and could tell the cause
That brought on every human malady,
Whether of hot or cold, or moist or dry.
He was a perfect medico, for sure.
The cause once known, he would prescribe the cure,
For he had his druggists ready at a motion
To furnish the sick man with some pill or potion—
A game of mutual aid, with each one winning.
Their partnership was hardly just beginning!
He was well versed in his authorities,
Old Aesculapius, Dioscorides,
Rufus, and old Hippocrates, and Galen,
Haly, and Rhazes, and Serapion,
Averroës, Bernard, Johannes Damascenus,
Avicenna, Gilbert, Gaddesden, Constantinus.
He urged a moderate fare on principle,
But rich in nourishment, digestible;

Of nothing in excess would he admit.
He gave but little heed to Holy Writ.
His clothes were lined with taffeta; their hue
Was all of blood red and of Persian blue,
Yet he was far from careless of expense.
He saved his fees from times of pestilence,
For gold is a cordial, as physicians hold,
And so he had a special love for gold.

A worthy woman there was from near the city
Of Bath, but somewhat deaf, and more's the pity.
For weaving she possessed so great a bent
She outdid the people of Ypres and of Ghent.
No other woman dreamed of such a thing
As to precede her at the offering,
Or if any did, she fell in such a wrath
She dried up all the charity in Bath.
She wore fine kerchiefs of old-fashioned air,
And on a Sunday morning, I could swear,
She had ten pounds of linen on her head.
Her stockings were of finest scarlet-red,
Laced tightly, and her shoes were soft and new.
Bold was her face, and fair, and red in hue.
She had been an excellent woman all her life.
Five men in turn had taken her to wife,
Not counting other youthful company—
But let that pass for now! Over the sea
She'd traveled freely; many a distant stream
She crossed, and visited Jerusalem
Three times. She had been at Rome and at Boulogne,
At Compostella's shrine, and at Cologne.
She'd wandered by the way through many a scene.
Her teeth were set with little gaps between.
Easily on her ambling horse she sat.
She was well wimpled, and she wore a hat
As wide in circuit as a shield or targe.
A skirt swathed up her hips, and they were large.

Upon her feet she wore sharp-roweled spurs.
She was a good fellow; a ready tongue was hers.
All remedies of love she knew by name,
For she had all the tricks of that old game.

  There was a good man of the priest's vocation,
A poor town Parson of true consecration,
But he was rich in holy thought and work.
Learned he was, in the truest sense a clerk
Who meant Christ's gospel faithfully to preach
And truly his parishioners to teach.
He was a kind man, full of industry,
Many times tested by adversity
And always patient. If tithes were in arrears,
He was loth to threaten any man with fears
Of excommunication; past a doubt
He would rather spread his offering about
To his poor flock, or spend his property.
To him a little meant sufficiency.
Wide was his parish, with houses far asunder,
But he would not be kept by rain or thunder,
If any had suffered a sickness or a blow,
From visiting the farthest, high or low,
Plodding his way on foot, his staff in hand.
He was a model his flock could understand,
For first he did and afterward he taught.
That precept from the Gospel he had caught,
And added as a metaphor thereto,
"If the gold rusts, what will the iron do?"
For if a priest is foul, in whom we trust,
No wonder a layman shows a little rust.
A shame it is, that priests in mind should keep,
To let a filthy shepherd tend clean sheep.
By his own purity a priest should give
The example to his sheep, how they should live.
He did not rent his benefice for hire,
Leaving his flock to flounder in the mire,

And run to London, happiest of goals,
To sing paid masses in St. Paul's for souls,
Or as chaplain from some rich guild take his keep,
But dwelt at home and guarded well his sheep
So that no wolf should make his flock miscarry.
He was a shepherd, and not a mercenary.
And though himself a man of strict vocation
He was not harsh to weak souls in temptation,
Not overbearing nor haughty in his speech,
But wise and kind in all he tried to teach.
By good example and just words to turn
Sinners to heaven was his whole concern.
But should a man in truth prove obstinate,
Whoever he was, of rich or mean estate,
The Parson would give him a snub to meet the case.
I doubt there was a priest in any place
His better. He did not stand on dignity
Nor affect in conscience too much nicety,
But Christ's and his disciples' word he sought
To teach, and first he followed what he taught.

   There was a Plowman with him on the road,
His brother, who had forked up many a load
Of good manure. A hearty worker he,
Living in peace and perfect charity.
Whether his fortune made him smart or smile,
He loved God with his whole heart all the while
And his neighbor as himself. He would undertake,
For every luckless poor man, for the sake
Of Christ to thresh and ditch and dig by the hour
And with no wage, if it was in his power.
His tithes on goods and earnings he paid fair.
He wore a coarse, rough coat and rode a mare.

   There also were a Manciple, a Miller,
A Reeve, a Summoner, and a Pardoner,
And I—this makes our company complete.
   As tough a yokel as you'd care to meet

The Miller was. His big-beefed arms and thighs
Took many a ram put up as wrestling prize.
He was a thick, squat-shouldered lump of sins.
No door but he could heave it off its pins
Or break it running at it with his head.
His beard was broader than a shovel, and red
As a fat sow or fox. A wart stood clear
Atop his nose, and red as a pig's ear
A tuft of bristles on it. Black and wide
His nostrils were. He carried at his side
A sword and buckler. His mouth would open out
Like a great furnace, and he would sing and shout
His ballads and jokes of harlotries and crimes.
He could steal corn and charge for it three times,
And yet was honest enough, as millers come,
For a miller, as they say, has a gold thumb.
In white coat and blue hood this lusty clown,
Blowing his bagpipes, brought us out of town.

 The Manciple was of a lawyers' college,
And other buyers might have used his knowledge
How to be shrewd provisioners, for whether
He bought on cash or credit, altogether
He managed that the end should be the same:
He came out more than even with the game.
Now isn't it an instance of God's grace
How one of little knowledge can keep pace
In wit with a whole school of learned men?
His masters, to the number of three times ten,
Knew every twist of equity and tort;
A dozen in that very Inn of Court
Were worthy to be steward of the estate
To any of England's lords, however great,
And keep him to his income well confined
And free from debt, unless he lost his mind,
Or let him scrimp, if he were mean in bounty;
They could have given help to a whole county

In any sort of case that might befall;
And yet this Manciple could cheat them all!
   The Reeve was a slender, fiery-tempered man.
He shaved as closely as a razor can.
His hair was cropped about his ears, and shorn
Above his forehead as a priest's is worn.
His legs were very long and very lean.
No calf on his lank spindles could be seen.
But he knew how to keep a barn or bin,
To play the game with auditors and win.
He knew well how to judge by drought and rain
The harvest of his seed and of his grain.
His master's cattle, swine, and poultry flock,
Horses and sheep and dairy, all his stock,
Were altogether in this Reeve's control.
And by agreement, he had given the sole
Accounting since his lord reached twenty years.
No man could ever catch him in arrears.
There wasn't a bailiff, shepherd, or farmer working
But the Reeve knew his tricks of cheating and shirking.
He would not let him draw an easy breath.
They feared him as they feared the very death.
He lived in a good house on an open space,
Well shaded by green trees, a pleasant place.
Shrewder in acquisition than his lord,
With private riches he was amply stored.
He'd learned a good trade young by work and will.
He was a carpenter of first-rate skill.
On a fine mount, a stallion, dappled gray,
Whose name was Scot, he rode along the way.
He wore a long blue coat hitched up and tied
As if it were a friar's, and at his side
A sword with rusty blade was hanging down.
He came from Norfolk, from nearby the town
That men call Bawdswell. As we rode the while,
The Reeve kept always hindmost in our file.

A Summoner in our company had his place.
Red as the fiery cherubim his face,
Pockmarked and pimpled, and his eyes were narrow.
As lecherous he was as a cock sparrow.
His brows were scabby and black, and thin his beard.
His was a face that little children feared.
Brimstone or litharge bought in any quarter,
Quicksilver, ceruse, borax, oil of tartar,
No salve nor ointment that will cleanse or bite
Could cure him of his blotches, livid white,
Or of the nobs and nubbins on his cheeks.
He loved his garlic, his onions, and his leeks.
He loved to drink the strong wine down blood-red.
Then would he bellow as if he had lost his head,
And when he had drunk enough to parch his drouth,
Nothing but Latin issued from his mouth.
He'd smattered up a few terms, two or three,
That he had gathered out of some decree—
No wonder; he heard law Latin all the day,
And everyone knows a parrot or a jay
Can cry out "Wat" or "Poll" as well as the pope;
But give him a strange term, he began to grope.
His little store of learning was paid out,
So *"Questio quod juris"* he would shout.
He was a goodhearted bastard and a kind one.
If there were better, it was hard to find one.
He'd let a good fellow, for a quart of wine,
The whole year round enjoy his concubine
Scot-free from summons, hearing, fine, or bail,
And on the sly he too could flush a quail.
If he liked a scoundrel, no matter for church law.
He would teach him that he need not stand in awe
If the archdeacon threatened with his curse—
That is, unless his soul was in his purse,
For in his purse he would be punished well.
"The purse," he said, "is the archdeacon's hell."

Of course I know he lied in what he said.
Surely a guilty man should hold in dread
The curse that damns by excommunication
While absolution brings a man salvation,
And let him heed, if higher counsels fail,
The writ remanding the accursed to jail.[1]
Within his power, and well he saw to this,
He had the young girls of the diocese.
He knew their secrets, heard their least design.
A garland big enough to be the sign
Outside an alehouse balanced on his head.
As shield he bore a great round loaf of bread.

    There was a Pardoner of Rouncivalle
With him, of blessed Mary's hospital,
But now come straight from Rome (or so said he).
Loudly he sang, "Come hither, love, to me."
The Summoner's counterbass trolled out profound;
No trumpet blew with half so vast a sound.
This Pardoner had hair as yellow as wax,
Hanging as smoothly as a hank of flax.
His locks trailed down in bunches from his head.
He let the ends about his shoulders spread,
But in thin clusters, lying one by one.
Of hood, for rakishness, he would have none,
For in his wallet he kept it safely stowed.
He traveled, as he thought, in the latest mode,
Disheveled. Save for his cap, his head was bare,
And in his eyes he glittered like a hare.
A Veronica was stitched upon his cap,
His wallet lay before him in his lap
Brimful of pardons from the very seat
In Rome. He had a voice like a goat's bleat.

[1]In this passage Chaucer says literally: "Of cursing ought each
guilty man to be afraid, for a curse will slay just as absolution saves,
and he should also beware of a *Significavit*"—a writ remanding
an excommunicated person to prison.

He had no beard and never would have a beard.
His cheek was always smooth as if just sheared.
I think he was a gelding or a mare;
But in his trade, from Berwick down to Ware,
No pardoner could beat him in the race,
For in his wallet he had a pillow case
Which he pretended was Our Lady's veil;
He said he had a piece of the very sail
St. Peter, when he fished in Galilee
Before Christ caught him, used upon the sea.
He had a latten cross embossed with stones
And in a glass he carried some pig's bones,
And with these holy relics, when he found
Some village parson grubbing his poor ground,
He'd get more money in a single day
Than in two months would come the parson's way.
Thus with his flattery and his trumped-up stock
He made dupes of the parson and his flock.
But though his conscience was a little plastic
He was in church a noble ecclesiastic.
Well could he read the Scripture or saint's story,
But best of all he sang the offertory,
For he knew well that when this song was sung,
Then he must preach, and sharpen up his tongue
To rake in cash, as well he knew the art,
And so he sang out gaily, with full heart.

    Now I have set down briefly, as it was,
Our rank, our dress, our number, and the cause
That made our sundry fellowship begin
In Southwark, at this hospitable inn
Known as the Tabard, not far from the Bell.
But what we did that night I ought to tell,
And after that our journey, stage by stage,
And the whole story of our pilgrimage.
But first, in justice, do not look askance
I plead, nor lay it to my ignorance

If in this matter I should use plain speech
And tell you just the words and style of each,
Reporting all their language faithfully.
It must be known to you as well as me
That whoso tells a story after a man
Must follow him as closely as he can.
If he relates the tale, he must be true
To every word, unless he would find new
Or else invent a thing or falsify.
Better some breadth of language than a lie!
He may not spare the truth to save his brother.
He might as well use one word as another.
In Holy Writ Christ spoke in a broad sense,
And surely his word is without offense.
Plato, if his are pages you can read,
Says let the word be cousin to the deed.
So I petition your indulgence for it
If I have cut the cloth just as men wore it,
Here in this tale, and shown its very weave.
My wits are none too sharp, you must believe.

    Our Host gave each of us a cheerful greeting
And promptly of our supper had us eating.
The victuals that he served us were his best.
The wine was potent, and we drank with zest.
Our Host cut such a figure, all in all,
He might have been a marshal in a hall.
He was a big man, and his eyes bulged wide.
No sturdier citizen lived in all Cheapside,
Lacking no trace of manhood, bold in speech,
Prudent, and well versed in what life can teach,
And with all this he was a jovial man.
And so when supper ended he began
To jolly us, when all our debts were clear.
"Welcome," he said. "I have not seen this year
So merry a company in this tavern as now,
And I would give you pleasure if I knew how.

And just this very minute a plan has crossed
My mind that might amuse you at no cost.

   "You go to Canterbury—may the Lord
Speed you, and may the martyred saint reward
Your journey! And to while the time away
You mean to talk and pass the time of day,
For you would be as cheerful all alone
As riding on your journey dumb as stone.
Therefore, if you'll abide by what I say,
Tomorrow, when you ride off on your way,
Now, by my father's soul, and he is dead,
You shall enjoy yourselves, or lop my head!
Hold up your hands, if you accept my speech."

   Our counsel did not take us long to reach.
We bade him give his orders at his will.
"Well, sirs," he said, "then do not take it ill,
But hear me in good part, and for your sport.
Each one of you, to make our journey short,
Shall tell two stories, as we ride, I mean,
Toward Canterbury; and coming home again
Shall tell two other tales he may have heard
Of happenings that some time have occurred.
And the one of you whose stories please us most,
Here in this tavern, sitting by this post,
Shall sup at our expense while we make merry
When we come riding home from Canterbury.
To cheer you still the more, I too will ride
With you at my own cost, and be your guide.
But should my judgment anyone gainsay,
He'll foot the bill we run up on the way.
If you agree, no need to stand and reason.
Tell me, and I'll be stirring in good season."

   This thing was granted, and we swore our pledge
To take his judgment on our pilgrimage,
His verdict on our tales, and his advice.

He was to plan a supper at a price
Agreed upon; and so we all assented
To his command, and we were well contented.
The wine was fetched; we drank, and went to rest.
   Next morning, when the dawn was in the east,
Up sprang our Host, who acted as our cock,
And gathered us together in a flock,
And off we rode, till presently our pace
Had brought us to St. Thomas' watering place.
And there our Host began to check his horse.
"Good sirs," he said, "you know your pledge,
      of course.
Shall I remind you what it was about?
If evensong and matins don't fall out,
We'll soon find who shall tell us the first tale.
But as I hope to drink my wine and ale,
Whoever won't accept what I decide
Pays everything we spend along the ride.
Draw lots, before we're farther from the Inn.
Whoever draws the shortest shall begin.
Sir Knight," said he, "my master, choose your straw.
Come here, my lady Prioress, and draw,
And you, Sir Scholar, don't look pensive, man!
Pitch in now, everyone!" So all began
To draw the lots, and as the luck would fall
The draw went to the Knight, which pleased us all.
And when this excellent man saw how it stood,
Ready to keep his promise, he said, "Good!
Since it appears that I must start the game,
Why then, the draw is welcome, in God's name.
Now let's ride on, and listen, what I say."
And with that word we rode forth on our way,
And he, with his courteous manner and good cheer,
Began to tell his tale, as you shall hear.

The Knight's Tale

Once, as old stories tell, there was a prince
Named Theseus that in Athens ruled long since,
A conqueror in his time; for rich lands won
There was no greater underneath the sun.
He took the realm once known as Scythia
And married its brave queen, Hippolyta,
And brought her home in high festivity,
Also her younger sister, Emily.
And but for trying the most patient ear,
Make no doubt of it, I should let you hear
In full how Theseus came to overwhelm,
Together with his knights, this women's realm,
And the great battle that was thus brought on
Between Athenian and Amazon,
And how he made his conquest of the queen
And all the feasting and the marriage scene,
And how at their return a great storm broke.
But feeble are the oxen in my yoke
And large enough the field I have to plow.
These things I must forbear to tell for now.
I won't deprive another of his turn.
Each tell his tale, and let's see who can earn
His supper at the tavern for his story.

This Theseus, coming home in all his glory,
When nearly into town, became aware,
Glancing from side to side, that kneeling there
Right in the highway as his troop rode through
Was a company of women, two by two,
Each after each, and all were clad in black.
But how they shrieked, as if the sky would crack,

Such cries that not a soul in all creation
Had ever heard an equal lamentation,
And would not stop from shrieking out their pains
Till they had seized the conqueror's bridle reins.

"What company are you that so surprise
My coming home with your distracting cries?"
Theseus demanded. "Do you envy so
My honors that you utter this great woe?
Or have you been mistreated or offended?
And tell me whether it can be amended,
And why you have thus dressed yourselves in
        black."

    The eldest of them, after falling back
Into a swoon, her face so deathly white
It was in truth a pitiable sight,
Said, "Prince, whom Fortune has been pleased to
        give
Triumph, and as a conqueror to live,
Your honor and your glory no wise grieve us,
But we beseech you, pity and relieve us.
Have mercy on our grief and our distress!
Some drop of pity, in your gentleness,
On wretched women, I mean on us let fall.
For truly, Prince, not one among us all
But she has been a duchess or a queen;
Now wretches, as too plainly can be seen,
Since Fortune's fickle wheel, by which we fell,
Assures no lot it shall continue well.
And in all truth, until you should appear,
In the temple of the goddess Mercy here
This fortnight we have waited, hour by hour.
Now help us, for it lies within your power.

    "I, wretch, who weep and wail before you thus
Once was the wife of King Cappaneus
Who was destroyed at Thebes—cursed be the day!
And all of us who blacken so your way

And raise such lamentation for your pity,
We lost each one her husband at that city.
And yet old Creon, in his tyranny,
Confirmed in anger and iniquity,
Lord of the town, to show his fierce disdain
On the dead bodies of our lords there slain,
Has in a single pile their bodies tossed
And will not suffer them at any cost
Buried or burned, but as they lie unkempt
He makes his dogs go eat them in contempt."
  And with that word, they fell face down and cried,
"Pity us wretched women in your pride
And let our sorrow sink into your heart."
  This kindly prince, for all his conqueror's part,
Leaped from his horse straightway when they had
    spoken.
He felt as though his very heart were broken
To see them in such pitiable state
Who in their time had shone among the great.
He took them in his arms to give them cheer,
And drew them up, and made his good will clear,
Swearing his oath as he was a true knight
He would so give an instance of his might
And would on Creon such a vengeance wreak
That people everywhere in Greece would speak
Of how the tyrant had been richly served
As one whose death had fully been deserved.
And so at once and with no more delay
He spread his banner and rode off straightway
Toward Thebes, with all his army by his side.
Nor into Athens would he wait to ride
Nor take his ease as much as half a day,
But camped that very night well on his way,
And sent the queen to Athens, there to be
With her beautiful young sister, Emily.

The image of red Mars, with spear and shield,
Gleams from his banner on a broad white field
So that the meadows glisten all about,
And by his banner his pennon ripples out,
Of richest gold, in which was worked complete
The Minotaur that he had slain in Crete.
So rode this prince, so rode this conqueror
Among his knights, the very flower of war,
Until at Thebes they drew up to alight
Ranked in the field on which they meant to fight.
But truly, to make short work of this thing,
The tyrant Creon, who in Thebes was king,
He fought, and slew him bravely, as a knight,
In headlong battle, and put his troops to flight;
And by assault he took the town thereafter
And broke down every wall and beam and rafter,
And to the ladies he restored again
The bones of all their husbands who were slain
To do the last rites that were then in use.

   When he had taken Thebes, this prince Theseus,
All night he rested in the field at leisure
And ravaged the whole country at his pleasure.

   Ransacking the heaped bodies of the dead
After the foe had been discomfited,
The looters got to work with busy cheer
Stripping the corpses of their clothes and gear.
And so it happened in the heap they found,
Pierced through with many a grievous, bloody wound,
Two young knights, side by side, their arms the
    same.
Arcite and Palamon they were by name.
Not quite alive, and not quite dead they were.
But by their armor the heralds knew them for
Two royal Thebans, of two sisters born.
Out of the heap the looters had them torn

And had them gently carried to the tent
Of Theseus; and he promptly saw them sent
To Athens, in a prison to be kept
For life—no ransom would the prince accept.
And so rode home the laureled conqueror
To live his life out in the spoils of war,
And in a tower, in anguish and despair—
No gold can set them free—the youthful pair.

  So passes year by year and day by day,
Till once it happened, at the break of May,
That Emily, who was fairer to be seen
Than lilies rising on their stalks of green
And fresher than the May when flowers are new—
For she contended with the rose in hue—
Was dressed before the sun had shown his head,
For a May night will have no slugabed.
The season pierces every tender heart
And prods it out of slumber with a start
And says, "Arise! Do service to the spring!"
It was no wonder, then, remembering
The honors of the season, she should rise
And clothe herself, a marvel to the eyes.
Her yellow hair was braided in a tress
Behind her back, a yard long, I should guess.
In the garden, as the sun rose on the town,
As fancy pleased her, she walked up and down,
Plucked particolored flowers, white and red,
To make a delicate garland for her head,
And like an angel sang a heavenly song.
The castle tower that was so thick and strong,
The dungeon where the knights were kept for all
Their lives in prison, ran along the wall
Where Emily enjoyed the air of May.
Bright was the early sun and clear that day,
And Palamon, with reason enough to grieve,
Rose, and by custom and his jailer's leave,

Strode up and down a room at such a height
It brought the whole noble city into sight,
The garden also, with its boughs of green,
Where Emily took her pleasure in the scene.
The wretched prisoner, pacing to and fro,
Protesting to himself his heavy woe,
"That ever he had been born," he cried, "alas!"
And so it happened that his glance must pass
Right through a slit with thick bars studded well
Until on Emily his vision fell.
He paled, and cried out "Ah!" as if his heart
Had felt the sting; and Arcite, with a start,
Leaped up and said, "What made you fetch that breath?
What ails you now? You look as pale as death.
Who has offended you? For God's love, cousin,
Take it with patience that we live in prison,
For otherwise it simply cannot be.
Fortune has dealt us this adversity.
Saturn has given us our sad condition
Through evil aspect, by the stars' position,
No matter what denials may be sworn.
So stood the eternal heavens when we were born.
We must endure it; that's the long and short."
    This Palamon said sharply in retort,
"Cousin, if you so judge my situation,
Truly, you show a vain imagination.
This prison did not cause my bitter cry.
But I was wounded just now through the eye
Down to my heart, yes, wounded fatally.
The beauty of that lady whom I see
In the garden yonder roaming to and fro,
That is my cause of outcry and of woe.
Woman or goddess, I cannot well perceive;
But truly, it is Venus, I believe."
And speaking thus, he fell down on his knees
And cried out: "Venus, if indeed you please

Here in this garden by transfiguration
To show yourself to the worst wretch in creation,
Help us out of this prison to escape.
And if the eternal word my fate should shape
To die imprisoned in this luckless fashion,
Look on our lineage with some compassion
That has been brought so low by tyranny."
And with that word Arcite began to see
The garden where the lady to and fro
Was walking, and her beauty hurt him so
That if this Palamon was wounded sore,
Arcite was hurt as much as he, or more.
And with a sigh he cried out piteously:
"The freshness of her beauty suddenly
Has slain me, she who walks in yonder place.
Unless I have her mercy and her grace,
At least to see her, I may as well be dead."

This Palamon in answer frowned and said,
"You meant in earnest what I just now heard,
Or as a joke?" "In earnest, on my word.
God knows," said Arcite, "I've no mind to joke."

This Palamon wrinkled up his brows and spoke.
"It would not make your honor any greater,"
He said, "if you were false or played the traitor,
To me, your cousin, and your brother in oath,
Pledged solemnly and sworn as we are both
That never, till death itself should part us two,
For all the tortures men might put us through,
Should either of us in love forestall the other,
Nor any situation, my dear brother,
But faithfully that you should further me
As I should you, whatever the case may be.
This was the oath you swore, and so did I,
For certain, as you'll never dare deny.
You ought to help my purpose, past all doubt,
And here you treacherously set about

To love my lady, whom I serve and cherish
And ever shall, until my heart must perish.
Not you, false Arcite! Let that truth be plain.
I loved her first. To you I told my pain,
To you, my confidant, as I said before,
My brother through the solemn oath you swore,
By reason of which you owe it as a knight
To help me if it lies within your might,
Or else you are a traitor among men."
   This Arcite haughtily spoke back again.
"You should be called the traitor more than I.
Traitor you are, and let me tell you why.
By all the laws of love, I loved her first.
What can you say? You don't know yet what burst
Upon your sight, a goddess or a woman.
Your love is spiritual, and mine is human,
And so, to my sworn brother, I spoke of her.
But put it that your love was earlier:
You must have often heard the wise old saw,
'What man can give a lover any law?'
Love's law, by all the wit in my brain pan,
Is greater than any given to earthly man.
Hence man-made laws are over and over again
Broken for love, and by all ranks of men.
A man must love, although it cost his head.
He can't escape it, not though he were dead,
Whether she is a virgin, widow, or wife.
Besides, you are unlikely, all your life,
To win her favor, and no more shall I.
In prison, unransomed, we are doomed to die.
As the dogs did for the bone, so we contend.
They fought all day for nothing in the end,
For while they snarled so fiercely for their pray,
There came a kite and bore the bone away.
The old proverb holds with us: at court, my brother,
Each for himself must be the rule, no other.

Love, if you like; I love, and ever shall.
In sober truth, dear brother, that is all.
In prison we must suffer and endure
And each must bide his chance; that much is sure."

    Great was the strife and long between these two,
Which, but for time, I could describe to you.
But for the effect: it happened on a day,
To tell it all as briefly as I may,
A worthy prince, Pirithöus by name,
A childhood fellow of Prince Theseus, came
To Athens, where he often made a stay,
For no two loved each other more than they;
In truth, when one had died, as old books tell,
His fellow went and sought him down in hell.

    For many years Pirithöus had known
Arcite at Thebes, and now through him alone,
Theseus, in answer to his friendly plea,
Without a ransom, let Arcite go free,
On promise that if Arcite should be found
One instant, ever, by day or night, on ground
Where Theseus ruled, a sword should have his head.
So Arcite took his leave, and home he sped.

    How great a sorrow suffers Arcite now!
Cold through his very heart he feels death plow.
With groans and piteous cries he is distraught;
To kill himself is in his secret thought.
"Alas," he said, "if only I had never
Been brought to birth! My prison is worse than ever,
For I am doomed eternally to dwell
Not now in purgatory, but in hell.
Pirithöus, on a black day we first met!
Without you I should be in Athens yet,
In prison chained forever, but even so,
I should have been in bliss and not in woe.
The mere sight of her beauty whom I serve,
Although her grace I never may deserve,

Would well have answered and sufficed for me.
O my dear cousin, Palamon," said he,
"Yours is the triumph, truly, in this case.
You may endure content your dungeon place.
Dungeon? Not so, but rather paradise!
Yours is the lucky turn of Fortune's dice.
You have the sight of her, and I the lack.
And since false Fortune often changes tack,
And you a lusty knight whose worth is plain,
Sometime to your desire you may attain.
But I, in barren exile and despair,
No element, earth, water, fire, nor air,
Nor any creature of their composition
May help or comfort me in my condition.
I have good cause to die in hopelessness.
Farewell my life, my love, my happiness!

   "Alas, why is it common to complain
Of God or Fortune, who so often deign,
Hiding their foresight under many a guise,
To give us better than we could devise?
One man sets all his heart on gaining wealth
For which he is murdered or gives up his health.
Another from his prison cell would fly
In his own house by servants' hands to die.
Infinite mischief comes in by this door.
Man hardly knows what he is praying for.
Blind as a drunkard on his way he goes.
A drunkard has a house—that much he knows,
But what he does not know is the way thither.
On a dry road a drunken man will slither,
And as he fares, so in the world fare we.
Seeking our happiness too eagerly
We often miss the mark. Thus all may say,
But more so I, who thought that on the day
I could escape from prison, I should be
Entire and perfect in felicity,

But I am exiled from my joy instead.
Forbidden to see my love, I am but dead."
   His counterpart, this wretched Palamon,
When he perceived his fellow prisoner gone,
Grieved till the tower resounded with his din,
And on the fetters that galled him at the shin
His tears fell bitter. "You have gained the fruit,
Cousin," he said, "God knows, of our dispute.
Even now in Thebes you walk about at large
And all my woe on you is a light charge.
Since you are wise and warlike, you can gather
Our people and our kindred all together
And make so sharp a war upon this city
That by some lucky chance or by a treaty
You may possess even yet as lady and wife
Her for whose love I needs must lose my life.
The balance is all yours, by any gauge,
Rather than mine, who perish in this cage.
For I must grieve as long as I shall live
With all the pain imprisonment can give
And the added pain of love, with no relief,
Which doubles all my torment and my grief."
   With that a jealous fire so made him start
And wrung him with such fierceness at the heart
That his crazed face as pale was to behold
As boxwood or as ashes dead and cold.
   "O cruel gods, on whom it is conferred
To bind the world in your eternal word
And in your adamantine tables write
The edicts of your everlasting might,
In what esteem," he cried out, "do you hold
Man more than sheep who cower in their fold?
A man like any other beast is slaughtered,
And in a prison likewise he is quartered.
He suffers illness and misfortune's blows
And many times is innocent, God knows.

"What reason is there in this providence
That tortures and torments our innocence?
This makes my grief a still more bitter brew:
Man to his duty must be always true.
For God's sake he must put curbs on his will,
While beasts may freely all their lusts fulfill.
And when a beast is dead he has no feeling,
But man though dead must go on weeping and wailing,
Although in this world he was pinched and pained.
Beyond a doubt it has been so ordained.
I leave the answer to theology,
But in this world is found much misery.
For here a thief or serpent in the grass
Brings many a true man to an evil pass
And yet goes free to wander at his leisure,
While I must be in chains through Saturn's pleasure,
And Juno's jealous madness, who destroyed
The blood of Thebes and left it well nigh void
And cast the broken walls down waste and wide.
Now Venus kills me from the other side
For bitter jealousy and for my fear
Of him, my cousin, whom I once held dear."

The summer passes, and the nights grow long,
Doubling the pains that were already strong
Both in the lover and the prisoner.
I do not know which one was woefuler.
For Palamon faced his perpetual doom
To chains and fetters in his narrow room,
To lie in prison till he should be dead;
And Arcite, with a sentence on his head,
Must dwell forever an exile among men
And never see his lady's face again.

You lovers, here's a case to ponder on:
Which of these two, Arcite or Palamon,
Has the worse lot? For one can every day
Look on his lady while he pines away

In prison, while the other can ride free
And yet his lady never more shall see.
Judge as you like; decide it if you can,
For I shall tell my tale, as I began.

II

  One night in Thebes, when Arcite had lived through
His cruel torment for a year or two,
All in a dream he saw the winged god stand
Before him, with his sleepy wand in hand,
Mercury, with a wreath on his bright hair,
Bidding him be of hope and free from care.
The god was dressed as when he put to sleep
Argus, whose watchful task it was to keep
The lovely Io with his hundred eyes.
He spoke to Arcite thus: "You must arise
And go at once to Athens. There your grief,
For so it is ordained, shall find relief."
Arcite with that awoke and gave a start.
"Now truly, what a shrewd blow struck my heart,"
He cried. "I'll go to Athens at a breath,
Nor fail to see again for dread of death
Her whom I love and serve with all my might.
Death is no matter, dying in her sight."
  He caught up a large mirror and saw there
How changed his color was by his despair
So that he hardly knew his face his own.
He thought in Athens he might pass unknown
If he disguised his rank, and every day
Might see his lady. So he put away
His knight's attire and dressed himself instead
As a poor laborer who worked for bread,
And with a single squire who knew his case
And took a like disguise, he set his face
Toward Athens, where he came the shortest way.
So to the court he took himself one day

And proffered his services to work by hand
As any sort of drudge men might demand.
So, to be brief, he fell into a post
With Emily's own steward. He could boast
A young and mighty frame, and truth to tell
Was also wise and shrewd, and he could well
Draw water and hew wood to serve his game.
He said that Philostratus was his name,
And for a year or two he played his hand
As page in Emily's house. In all the land
No servant was so well beloved as he.
Men said it would be only charity
If Theseus raised him from his mean condition
And gave him some more honorable position.
So Theseus made him, in a little while,
Squire of his chamber; to support his style,
He furnished him with gold; and faithfully
Men brought him year by year in secrecy
His due from Thebes in revenue and rent,
Which he so quietly and wisely spent
That no man came to wonder at the source.
So for three years his life fell in this course,
His bearing such that whether in peace or war,
On no man else did Theseus set such store.

    Meanwhile, in wretched darkness, Palamon
For seven years in his dungeon cell lived on,
Wasted away by torment and distress.
Who feels the double edge of bitterness
As much as he, by love distracted so
He threatens clean out of his wits to go?
And with all this, he is a prisoner
Perpetually, not only for a year.

    But who could rhyme his pains in English rightly?
Not I; and so I pass them over lightly.

    It happened in the seventh year, in May,
The third night in the month (as old books say),

Whether it was by chance or destiny—
For if a thing is destined, it shall be—
That shortly after midnight, through a friend,
He broke from the great tower where he was penned
And fled the city as fast as he could go.
For he had lured the jailer to drink so
Of a strong potion, mixed by his design
From Theban opiates and narcotic wine,
That all the night, however men might shake him,
The jailer slept; there was no one who could wake him.
He fled as fast as he could make his way.
The short night stood upon the verge of day
When his necessity would be to hide,
And in a grove that grew there close beside
He lurked in fear; as long as it was light
He meant to hide himself, and press by night
For Thebes where he could beg his every friend
To help him war on Theseus to the end;
For he would either be deprived of life
Or win his Emily to be his wife.

   The busy lark, the herald of the day,
Sings welcome to the morning's early gray,
And fiery Phoebus rises up so bright
That the whole east is laughing with the light,
And with his beams he makes dry work and brief
Of silver drops that hang on every leaf.
Arcite, the first squire in Prince Theseus' court,
Sees the clear morning ripe for Maytime sport,
And thinking of the state of his desire
Mounts on a courser, mettlesome as fire,
And rides into the fields a mile or two,
Right toward the grove that I described to you,
To make himself a wreath of branches torn
From the honeysuckle and the fresh hawthorn.
And loud he sang, seeing the world so bright,
"May, with your flowers and green groves all alight,

Welcome, fresh May," and leaped down from his horse
With lusty heart, and quickly took his course
Into a thicket, striding hither and yon
Along a path by which this Palamon
Was hidden where he thought that none could see,
For in sore terror of his life was he.
He had no notion it could be Arcite.
God knows he had little cause to think it might.
But truly it has been said these many years,
"The meadows have their eyes, the woods have ears."
A man does well to walk an even way.
Unplanned encounters happen every day.
　　Arcite was unaware his path had led
To where his cousin could hear whatever he said,
For in the thicket Palamon sat still.
And so, when he had roved and had his fill
Of trolling out his lusty roundelay,
He fell into a study, in the way
These lovers do in their quaint changing fashion,
Now in the bud, now in the briar of passion,
Now up, now down, like a bucket in a well.
With them it's always Friday, truth to tell,
For now it shines and now the rain falls fast,
So can inconstant Venus overcast
The spirits of her people; as her day
Is full of alteration, so are they.
Friday is off-day, seldom like the week.
　　First Arcite sang, then sighed with heavy cheek.
"Alas," he said, "the day that saw my birth!
How long will Thebes be trodden to the earth
Through Juno's persecution? Now disgrace
Lies on the issue of Amphion's race
And the royal blood of Cadmus, the first man
Of Thebes, whose walls and towers he began
And in the city first was crowned a king.
I follow him, and am his true offspring,

By very lineage of the royal stock.
But now I have become a man to mock,
For him that is my mortal enemy
I serve as a mean squire, in poverty.
And Juno puts me to a still worse shame:
I dare not call myself by my true name.
Once I was Arcite; now I must be known
As Philostratus, a name not worth a bone.
Dread Mars and Juno! You have thus destroyed
All the great lineage that Thebes enjoyed.
Except for me and wretched Palamon,
Martyred in prison, all our line is gone.
And to make worse my cruel destiny
Love's fiery dart has pierced me utterly
And given me with his flame a fatal hurt.
My death was shaped before I wore a shirt!
You, Emily, have killed me with your eye.
You are the reason I am doomed to die.
My other griefs would be too small to measure
If only I could do you any pleasure."

    Palamon felt a cold sword swiftly slide
Into his heart. No longer could he hide,
But shook with rage as he heard Arcite's tale,
And from the thicket, crazed and deathly pale,
Burst out and cried, "False traitor, you are caught
Who love her for whose sake I am distraught
With so much pain and anguish! You who swore
To be my brother, the true name you bore
You've changed, and duped Prince Theseus. I, your
    foe,
Tell you you shall not love my lady so.
And though I have no weapon in this place,
But have escaped from prison by Fortune's grace,
Either you die, or give up Emily.
Choose which you will, for you shall not go free."

Scornfully Arcite heard this tale outpoured.
Fierce as a lion, he pulled out his sword.
"By God," he said, "who sits in heaven above,
Except that you are sick and crazed for love,
And have no sword or weapon at command,
You should for certain die here at my hand.
For I denounce the bond you had from me.
What, fool! You should remember love is free,
And I will love her still, for all your might.
But since you are in truth a worthy knight,
Willing in combat to decide our case,
I give my word, tomorrow in this place
With armor enough for both of us I'll be.
You take the best, and leave the worst for me.
I'll bring you meat and drink and clothes tonight,
And if it happens you can prove your right
To win in battle my lady, Emily,
Have her; she can be yours for all of me."

In love and power, as wise men declare,
Friendship can never be allowed a share.
So Palamon and Arcite fully learned.
Before the next daybreak, Arcite returned
Riding upon his horse and stark alone
With armor that he had procured unknown,
And in the grove at the moment they had set
These two knights, Palamon and Arcite, met.
Then flared and rose the color in each face
As in the hunters in the realm of Thrace
When hoping for a lion or bear they stand
Expectant in the gap, with spear in hand,
And hear him rushing through the undergrowth,
Bursting through boughs and thickets, breaking
    both,
And think, "Here comes my mortal enemy!
I'll kill him, no mistake, or he'll kill me.

For either I must slay him at the gap
Or he'll slay me, if there's the least mishap."
The knights were like such hunters in their hue,
For each well judged the other, whom he knew.

There was no "Good day," and no salutation,
But straight, without a word of hesitation,
Each of them offered help to arm the other
As cheerfully as if he were his brother.
And after that, with sharp spears poised and strong,
They thrust at each other wonderfully long.
Fiercely as frothing boars whom madness rankles,
They fought in blood up to the very ankles.

So strong is destiny, wide minister
Over the earth, and general officer
Who executes what God himself foresees,
That though incredulous of its decrees
Men swore the opposite by yea and nay,
Yet there will happen on some fated day
What has not happened in a thousand years.
For certainly our appetites and fears,
Whether of war or peace, or hate or love,
Are ruled by that prevision up above.

I have in mind Prince Theseus; his desire
Is hot for hunting, and burns with such a fire,
Especially to hunt the stag in May,
That he is never in bed at break of day,
But up and clad at dawn, ready to ride
With hounds and horn and huntsmen at his side.

Clear was the day, and Theseus with his queen,
Hippolyta, and Emily, all in green,
Are ridden out a-hunting royally
To where a grove arose conveniently,
In which there was a stag, he had been told.
Over a brook and on they ride, and hold
Their course until at last they reach the place
Where, peering through the light, with shaded face,

The Prince perceived Arcite and Palamon
As fierce as two boars fighting on and on.
Their bright swords whirled as if the lightest stroke
Were hideous enough to fell an oak.
He knew them not, nor what they meant to do,
But spurred his horse and was between the two
With drawn sword, crying, "Hold! Now for your head,
No more, each one of you! He shall be dead
Who lifts his sword to give another scar.
Tell me what manner of men or knights you are
So rash as to make here this bloody stir
Without a judge or other officer
As if you fought a fair field, royally!"
    Palamon answered unreservedly,
And said, "Prince Theseus, we deserve our death.
We are encumbered by our very breath,
Two wretched captives. What more need I say?
Give us no mercy, but proceed to slay
First me, and then my fellow, by just right.
Or slay him first, for this is that Arcite,
Exiled, unless he wished to lose his head,
And so deserves by sentence to be dead.
This is the very man who gave his name
As Philostratus when to court he came,
And now is your chief squire; and this is he
Who duped you for the love of Emily.
For since the day has come for me to die,
Let me confess in honesty that I
Am wretched Palamon, your mortal foe,
Escaped from prison, and I cherish so
The love of Emily, the fair and bright,
I am content to die here in her sight.
Wherefore I ask my sentence and my death,
But take my fellow's life in the same breath,
For it is just that we should both be slain."
    Prince Theseus answered: "This is short and plain!

Not from the rack, but your own lips proceed
Your sentences. By Mars, you die indeed!"
    The queen began to weep, and Emily,
And all the ladies in the company.
It was the greatest pity, thought they all,
That such a chance as this was should befall;
For these were men of breeding and estate,
And only love provoked this fierce debate.
They saw the bloody wounds gape wide and sore,
And they began to cry out all the more:
"Pity us women!" On bare knees they fell,
And would have kissed the prince's feet as well.
At last his mood flowed in a milder fashion,
For noble hearts run quickly to compassion.
His wrath relented on consideration
Both of their trespass and their provocation,
And though his anger for their guilt accused them,
Yet in his understanding he excused them,
For none who can, he thought, will ever fail
To further himself in love, or slip from jail.
His heart took pity on the women, too,
Whose weeping always made so much ado.
So he took counsel with his noble heart.
"Fie on the prince who plays the lion's part
Both to the contrite and the stubborn man
Who still maintains the evil he began!
Small is his wit," he told himself, "who traces
No shade of difference between such cases,
But weighs humility and pride as one."
Thus in a moment, when his wrath was done,
He spoke in full voice, with his eyes alight,
And said, "The god of love! Ah, bless my sight,
He is a god that spurns all obstacles!
He may be called a god of miracles,
For he can do, just as the whim may seize him,
With every living heart as it may please him.

Consider Palamon and Arcite here!
Out of my prison they were safe and clear,
And might have gone to live in Thebes like kings.
They know I hold their lives, and yet love brings
These his two faithful servants here to die.
This is a folly to record on high!
Who is a fool, if not a man in love?
Look, for the sake of God who sits above,
See how they bleed! Are they not well arrayed?
The god of love has generously repaid
Their service, dressing them in this red guise.
And yet they think themselves completely wise
To serve him still, whatever may befall.
But think of this, the richest point of all:
She for whose sake they held this bloody spree
Owes them as little thanks as they owe me.
By God, she knew no more of this affair
Than if she had been a cuckoo or a hare.
But everything must be tasted, hot or cold!
A man must be a fool once, young or old.
I know it from my own experience.
I've been myself a servant, long time since,
And so, because I've tasted of love's pain
And know the discord of that old refrain,
As one caught in the snare for many a session,
I utterly forgive you your transgression
Since the queen asks it, who is kneeling here,
And Emily, whose wish is also dear.
But you shall both upon your honor swear
Never in any realm of mine to dare
Make war against me, either night or day,
But be my friends as truly as you may."

They swore the oath, and graciously he said,
"In point of birth, each one of you might wed
A princess or a queen. But Emily,
For whom you held this strife and jealousy,

You understand she cannot be two wives
Although your feud went on for all your lives.
One of you or the other must play the man
And whistle for his comfort where he can.
What destiny ordains, each must fulfill.
So, if it pleases you, this is my will.
Go where you like, for each of you is free
Without a ransom or a penalty,
And fifty weeks hence, to decide your rights,
Each one of you shall bring a hundred knights
Armed for the lists. I promise without fail,
Upon my word, whoever shall prevail
And kill his adversary, or overcome
The other hundred knights and drive them from
The lists that I shall furnish in this place,
He shall wed Emily, by Fortune's grace.
And God apportion me his mercy duly
As I shall judge the issue fair and truly.
If this proposal seems to you well made,
Speak out your minds, and count yourselves repaid."

　　Whose looks but Palamon's are now alight?
Who leaps for happiness if not Arcite?
Down on their knees fall the whole company
To thank Prince Theseus, and especially
The two knights. Then they take their leave and ride
Home to the walls where Thebes lies old and wide.

III

　　I know you would all charge me with neglect
If I forgot to tell how circumspect
Was Theseus, who bestirred himself to build
Such royal lists, in workmanship so skilled,
That such a noble theater as he made
I dare say never elsewhere was displayed.
A mile about, of circular design,
Its walls were stone, its tiers rose line on line

Until the top was sixty paces high
So that no man need block his neighbor's eye.

    White to the eastward stood a marble gate
And opposite, to the westward, stood its mate.
There was no craftsman up and down the land,
If he could carve or paint or understand
Arithmetic, but Theseus offered him
His wage this theater to build and trim.
Eastward, in honor of Venus, right above
The gate, in worship of the queen of love,
He made an altar and an oratory,
And on the gate to westward, to the glory
Of Mars, he had another like it built
For which he paid in gold up to the hilt.
And on the north wall, mingling red and white,
Coral and alabaster, rich in sight,
An oratory in a turret stood
To chaste Diana, huntress of the wood.

    But for the carvings, portraits, allegories
Nobly presented in those oratories:

    In the temple of Venus, first, you might behold,
Wrought on the wall, the broken sleep, the cold
Sad sighs, the sacred tears, the lamentation,
The hot pangs of desire, the provocation
That in this life her servants must endure;
Their faith, that oaths must always reassure;
Enjoyment, Hope, Desire, Foolhardiness,
Bawdry and Riches, Youth and Loveliness,
Rape, Lies, and Charms, Expense and Flattery,
Busy Contrivances; and Jealousy
Wearing a wreath of yellow marigolds
Who sitting in her hand a cuckoo holds;
Banquets and instruments, carols and dances,
Love in as many kinds of circumstances
As ever I reckoned, and cannot mention all,
Were painted there in order on the wall.

For there appeared Cithaeron, the famed mount
Where Venus chiefly dwelt, by old account,
With all the garden in its lusty dress,
Its porter not forgotten, Idleness;
Nor young Narcissus, fair in days long done,
Nor yet the folly of King Solomon,
Medea's dread enchantments, and Circe's,
Nor yet the strength of mighty Hercules.
Thus men could see that neither wealth nor might,
Beauty nor wisdom, bravery nor sleight,
May vie with Venus, nor her rule divide.
This world, as it may please her, she will guide.

    The statue of Venus, glorious to the eye,
Was naked, floating underneath the sky,
Hidden in green waves from the navel down
That wrapped her in their bright, translucent gown.
Her right hand held a zither; on her head
She had a wreath of roses, fresh and red.
Her doves in the gentle air were flickering.
Cupid, her son, before her stood, a wing
On either shoulder; but he lacked his sight.
He held a bow, with arrows keen and bright.

    The westward shrine was painted like that place
Men know as the great temple of Mars in Thrace,
That cold realm where the god has his abode.

    First on the wall a lifeless forest showed
With gnarled and knotty trees, ruined and old,
Sharp stumps and branches, hideous to behold,
Through which a wind ran with a soughing rumble
As if they were about to burst and tumble.
And downward, in the wrinkle of a hill,
There stood the temple of Mars, of warlike will,
Wrought all of polished steel. Up to the gate
A path of terror led on long and straight,
And from the entrance came forth such a blast
It shook the gate as if it were aghast.

The walls were windowless, but on the floor
The northern light shone inward through the door
Which was of adamant, clenched both endlong
And crosswise with tough iron. To make it strong
The temple pillars were iron as thick as casks.
    There on the wall were painted the dark tasks
That Felony imagines; Anger, red
As cruel coals; the pickpurse, and pale Dread;
The smiler with the knife beneath his cloak;
The stable fired and burning in black smoke;
The treachery that murders men in bed,
And open war in which grim gashes bled;
Sharp-threatening Feud, with bloody knife still hot.
A mournful whickering filled that sorry spot.
The killer of himself was also there;
His own heart's blood had spattered on his hair;
The nail through the victim's temple driven at night;
Death with his cold lips gaping to the light.
In midmost of the temple sat Mischance.
Madness was laughing in a crazy dance.
The slit-throat corpse flung where the leaves are dense;
A thousand slain, and not by pestilence;
The tyrant with his prey seized and constrained;
The town destroyed, where not a thing remained;
The burning ships fanned by the tempest's breath;
The huntsman by the wild bear hugged to death;
The sow that eats the child in his very cradle,
The cook, scalded for all of his long ladle;
All turns of life that Mars rules for his part:
The teamster ridden over by his cart
Lying under the wheel; the trades Mars owns,
The barber, and the butcher with his bones,
The smith whose anvil sharpens many a sword.
And Conquest sat there in a tower as lord
With the keen blade that waited over his head
Hanging upon a subtly woven thread.

Armed in a chariot stood the grim god Mars,
A statue poised beneath a pair of stars,
Puella and Rubeus, whose intimations
The geomancers use in divinations.
And in the chariot crouched a wolf before him
With fiery eyes, who mouthed a man and tore him.

Within Diana's temple, last of all,
Hunting and chastity adorned the wall:
Callisto, whom the eye of Jove found fair,
And whom Diana turned into a bear
And then was made the lodestar in the sky;
Actaeon, changed into a stag, whose eye
Had seen Diana to her wood-bath going
Naked; his hounds devoured him unknowing;
And Daphne, turned into a laurel tree
Lest the sun god should have her chastity.

High on a stag this goddess had her seat
With little dogs running about her feet,
And underneath her sandal was a moon;
Waxing it was, but would be waning soon.
Her statue was arrayed in beads of green
With quiver and bow; in front of her was seen
A woman in travail, and she seemed to call,
"Help me, Diana! Your help is best of all."
He painted to the life whose colors told
This story, and they cost a deal of gold.

Complete at last the noble theater stood,
And Theseus found it wonderfully good.
The day approached when the two knights should bring
Their companies of a hundred to the ring
There to decide in arms their lovers' rights.
Each made for Athens with his hundred knights,
And verily, it seemed to many a man
That never since the time the world began
Was greater prowess found among so few.
All those who hoped to shine in the world's view

Or longed in chivalry to leave a name
Pleaded to have their part in that great game,
And happy was the man who got his place,
For if tomorrow brought a similar case
I need not tell you that each lusty knight
Who is a lover and a man of might,
Whether it be in England or elsewhere,
Would curse himself unless he could be there.
A fair fight for a lady, you'll agree,
God bless us! That's a lusty sight to see!
    Each took the arms he fancied would prevail.
One wore a breastplate, one a coat of mail,
One had a Prussian shield, and one a targe,
One swung an iron mace, heavy and large,
One had an ax, as taste or whim took hold.
The newest fashion turns out to be old.
    With Palamon came Lycurgus, king of Thrace.
Black was his beard and manly was his face.
The pigment of his eyes gleamed in his head
In hue between the yellow and the red.
Fierce as a griffin he looked round about
Beneath his heavy eyebrows, coarse and stout.
His thighs were big, his muscles hard and strong,
His shoulders broad, his arms well-turned and long.
High up, as the fashion was in his cold land,
On a gold chariot he took his stand;
Four bulls in the traces plodded, all of white;
And with its rough claws gilded golden bright,
Over his arms and gear he chose to wear,
Coal-black with age, the skin of a great bear.
His long hair was combed down behind his back
And shone like a raven's feather, glistening black.
Stout as an arm his golden coronet
With diamonds and bright rubies thickly set.
Behind his chariot many a white wolfhound
Came loping, leashed and with their muzzles bound,

Twenty or more, each big as any steer,
That he might hunt the lion or the deer.
A hundred lords came with him in his troop
And all well armed, a grim, stouthearted group.

With Arcite rode, as the old stories say,
Emetreus, king of India, on a bay
Caparisoned in figured cloth of gold,
Over his gear a Tartar coat; each fold
With large pearls was embroidered, round and white.
His saddle was of forged gold, beaten bright.
A little mantle from his shoulder spread
Brimful of fiery rubies, glittering red.
His hair in ringlets was allowed to run,
Yellow and crisp, and shining like the sun.
His lips were full, bright citron was his eye,
His nose was aquiline, his color high.
His face was lightly freckled yellow and black,
His gaze a lion's ready to attack.
His manly beard had well begun to spring,
His voice was like a trumpet thundering;
Some five and twenty years he might have been.
He wore a wreath of laurel, fresh and green,
And on his wrist he carried for delight
A perching falcon, tame and lily white,
While leoprads ran about him, likewise tame.
So with a hundred knights, well armed, he came.
On Sunday all these lords, true to their time,
Rode into Athens near the hour of prime.

The minstrelsy, the honors of the feast,
The royal gifts to greatest and to least
That Theseus offered, as a prince's way is,
And who sat first or last upon the dais,
Which of the ladies was most ravishing
Or which among them could best dance or sing,
Or who most feelingly could speak of love;
What falcons sat on perches up above,

What hounds were lying on the floor below,
These matters, for the tale's sake, I forgo.

That night, before the dawn began to spring,
When Palamon could hear the first lark sing,
In Venus' hour he rose to dedicate
His heart to her, and at the eastern gate
Within her shrine prayed thus upon his knee:
"For the love you bore Adonis, hear my plea,
Fairest of fair, Jove's daughter, Vulcan's wife,
My lady whom I serve with all my life,
Venus, have mercy on a lover's part
And take my poor petition to your heart!
Alas," he said, "I have no tongue to tell
The bitter pains and torments of my hell.
I am confused; my lips can only say,
'Pity a lover, you who know love's way.'
Solace the pains that pierce me deep and sore
And I will be your servant evermore
To the limit of my might, and faithfully
Will wage your battle against chastity.
I do not ask tomorrow the victor's glory
As for mere fame or but to make a story
For prowess to be bruited up and down.
I would have Emily to be my own.
Mars is the god of arms; but you above
So shine that you can bring me to my love.
But if it should not be your will, then here
Let Arcite run my heart through with a spear.
I shall not care, when I have lost my life,
If Arcite has my lady for his wife."

When Palamon had prayed thus earnestly
And made his sacrifice punctiliously,
After a time the statue of Venus shook
And made a sign, an omen that he took
With glad heart, though it came with some delay.
The third hour after he had gone away,

Up rose the sun, and up rose Emily,
And hied her to the shrine of chastity,
Diana's temple. The maids who with her came
Had incense, clothes, and horns of mead, and flame;
Nothing left out that sacrifice required.
Soon with twin flames the altar had been fired,
And Emily washed in water from a well.
But of her ceremonies I dare not tell
Except in general, though it would be sport
To give these doings a complete report.
To him that means well it should bring no charge,
But then a man who wants to be at large
Should speak discreetly of a pagan rite.
Her hair, unbraided, shone combed out and bright,
She wore a coronal made from the oak
Called evergreen, and thus at last she spoke
When she had done her service, as was told
By Theban Statius in his books of old:
   "Chaste huntress of the wild woods fresh and green,
And in the realm below, dark Pluto's queen,
To whom are open earth and sea and sky,
Goddess of maidens, well you know that I
Desire to be a maiden all my life,
And never to be a man's love nor his wife.
Among your followers I have kept my place,
A maid, in love with hunting and the chase
And to go walking in the greenwood wild
And not to be a wife and be with child;
For nothing will I have to do with man.
Now help me, lady, since you may and can.
Let me with Palamon, who loves me sore,
And Arcite, too, be done forevermore.
Let peace and fellowship between them flow,
And from my heart divert their ardor so
That all their busy love and hot desire,
Their burning torment and unhappy fire

Be quenched, or solaced in some other place.
But if you will not do me such a grace,
Or if the destiny I must fulfill
Compels me to wed either against my will,
Then let me have the one who most wants me.
Behold, goddess of perfect chastity,
The bitter tears that down my cheeks now fall.
You are a maid, and keeper of us all.
Let none my virgin honesty invade,
And I will serve you all my life, a maid."
   The altar fires burned clear, with quiet motion,
While Emily was thus at her devotion.
But then her eyes perceived a startling sight.
One of the flames died down, and lost its light,
And then rekindled; but when that was done
The other fire was wholly quenched and gone,
And from it as it died a whistling came
As from a wet log thrown into the flame,
And from the tip of the expiring wood
Ran out, in many drops, an ooze of blood.
She knew not what the omen signified,
But almost mad with terror, wept and cried.
And thereupon Diana, bow in hand,
Appeared and said, "Child, you must understand
What destiny the high gods have conferred
On you, and fixed by their eternal word.
To one you shall be wedded of these two
That have endured such bitter pains for you.
But which one it shall be I may not tell.
I can remain no longer. So farewell,
But let the fires that on my altar flare
Love's pending fortune in this case declare."
Her arrows clashed as she was vanishing
And shook their quiver till it seemed to ring.
"Alas, what is all this?" cried Emily.
"In your protection, goddess, utterly

I place myself," she said, and went her way.
    Arcite as well, when next the hour of day
Belonged to Mars, walked to his temple there
On the western gate, and thus he made his prayer:
    "Strong god, whom men in the cold realm of Thrace
Honor, and who in every land and place
Hold in your grip the bridle of all war,
Accept my youthful sacrifice, and for
That very heat and pain of fierce desire
With which you once yourself burned in the fire
And using the fair young Venus to fulfill,
Had her fresh beauty in your arms at will,
Though with one misadventure you both met
When the sly Vulcan caught you in his net
And found you lying with his wife, alas!
By your pains judge and pity those that pass
Through me; as yours were bitter, mine are so.
I am young and lacking wisdom, as you know,
And as I think, with love afflicted more
Than ever any living soul before,
Since she who has thus cast me down the brink
Is heedless whether I should swim or sink.
My one hope is to win her in this place,
And well I know without your help or grace
No strength of mine has power to prevail.
Then in the battle do not let me fail,
But let me have the triumph in this story.
Mine be the blood and labor, yours the glory!"
    The doors clanged, and the fires burned so bright
The altar filled the temple with its light.
The ground gave out sweet odors; Arcite cast
More incense on the fire, and then at last
The statue of mailed Mars began to ring,
And with that sound he heard a murmuring
That faintly spoke the dim word "Victory!"
For which he honored Mars, and joyously

Went homeward to his inn, the ritual done,
As blithely as a bird in the bright sun.
  At once, in the heavens that rule us from above,
Venus, the queen of beauty and of love
Made such a strife with Mars, mighty in arms,
That Jove was busy quelling their alarms;
Till aged Saturn, the pale god and cold,
Who knew the turns of fortune from of old,
Found in his long experience an art
To satisfy them all in every part.
Age has the advantage, true words have admitted,
For age may be outrun but not outwitted.
Age has both wisdom and experience.
And so, to pacify their virulence,
Old Saturn, though it ran against his bent,
Found means to make both partisans content.
  "My orbit has so wide a course to turn,
Venus," he said, "dear daughter, none can spurn
My power, and no man's might avail with me.
Mine are the drownings in the pallid sea,
Mine are the prison and the dungeon-cote,
Stranglings are mine, and hangings by the throat;
The secret poisoning, the grumbling crowd,
The murmur of rebellion growing loud;
Mine is the ruin of the lofty halls,
The falling in of towers and of walls
On carpenters or miners; mine the stroke
When Samson hugged the pillars till they broke;
Such ills as are not feverish but cold,
Dark treason, turns and chances from of old;
My aspect is the father of pestilence.
Now do not weep; I shall use diligence
To see that Palamon, to please your whim,
Shall have his lady as you promised him.
Though Mars shall help his servant, none the less
You two must sometimes live in quietness

Despite your differences of disposition
Which give us quarrels without intermission.
Now put an end to tears. I shall fulfill
Your pleasure, ready to serve you at your will."

IV

Great was the feast in Athens on that day,
And then besides, the lusty month of May
Made every living heart so well content
That all of Monday, hour by hour, they spent
In the pleasures of the tourney or the dance
Or Venus and her holy ordinance.
But they went promptly to their rest at night
To get up early and witness the great fight.
At morning, when the day began to spring,
Came noise of harness and the clattering
Of horses in the stables all about,
And to the palace ambled many a rout
Of lords in every sort of finery,
Goldsmithing rich and strange, embroidery,
Bright helmets, clanging shields. The armorers go
Among the bustle, hurrying to and fro
With file and hammer. The steed snorts and sidles
And flecks of white foam spatter golden bridles.
Yeomen on foot with short staves press along.
Pipe, trumpet, clarinet, drum skirl through the
    throng,
Such as in battle blow a bloody sound.
By threes and tens men choke the palace ground,
Proving the merits of each rival knight.
"*He* looks a fierce one." "*He's* the one to fight."
Some held with the black beard, some with the thick-
    haired.
Long after sunrise they argued and compared.
Wakened by minstrelsy, great Theseus kept
Within the palace chamber where he slept

Till both the knights, honored in equal sort,
Were brought at length before him to the court.
Then Theseus to a window made his way,
While people pushed to hear what he might say,
And sat like a throned god while a herald cried
For silence. When he felt the crowd subside
And saw that all the tumult had grown still,
The herald thus proclaimed the prince's will:

   "It would be carnage, and offense to right,
If noble blood in this affair should fight
To the mortal finish; wherefore, lest they die,
Prince Theseus has resolved to modify
His first intent. On forfeit of his life
Let none take missile, battle-ax, or knife
Into the lists, nor short sword by his side.
Only a single tilt each knight shall ride
With sharp-ground spear against his opposite;
Then he may parry on foot, if he thinks fit.
Whoever is wounded or is overmatched,
He shall on no condition be dispatched,
But brought to the stake ordained on either side;
Thither he shall be dragged and there abide.
And if either of the chief antagonists
Is taken or slain, all fighting in the lists
Shall end; the tourney shall no longer last.
God speed you all! Go forth, and lay on fast.
With long swords and with maces fight your fill.
Be on your way; this is your prince's will."

   The people raised their voice in such a cry
Their shout of exultation reached the sky.

   "God bless a prince so kindly and so good
He does not want to see a waste of blood!"
The pipes began to skirl, the whole throng rolled
Off through the city hung with cloth of gold.

   In style the prince took up his reins to ride,
These Theban knights one upon either side;

Next after them the queen, and Emily,
And then by rank came the whole company.
They clattered through the city street by street
And reached the lists, where Theseus took his seat,
High up and richly furnished, with the queen
And Emily, the center of the scene,
And other ladies round them. Then the throng
Pushed to their seats and shoved their way along,
And Arcite, with his banner rippling red,
His hundred knights through the west entrance led,
The gate of Mars, while through the eastern gate
Palamon at the same moment rode in state
Under the banner of Venus, glistening white,
Leading his equal hundred for the fight.
In all the world, in every realm and nation,
So balanced, without shade of variation,
So matched in prowess, age, and noble birth,
Two companies were never seen on earth.
In two fair lines, drawn up in seemly style,
They ranged themselves; then, to prevent all guile,
Their names were read, each one. The gates were barred,
The clamor rose, "Lay on, young knights, fight hard!"
The heralds gave up riding to and fro,
And now loud clarion and trumpet blow.
There is no more to say but east and west
In went each spear, set stoutly in its rest;
In went the sharp spur to the horse's side.
There men saw who knew how to joust and ride.
Shafts shiver on thick shields, and like a stone
The smote man feels the blow on his breastbone.
Up fly the spent spears twenty feet in air.
Out swords come, bright as silver in the glare.
They hack and hew the helmets to a shred.
Blood bursts out, and in sickly streams flows red.
They maul men's bones with maces heavy and strong.
One cuts a passage in the thickest throng.

Steeds stumble under riders; down go all,
And underfoot a man rolls like a ball.
A knight with truncheon is fighting on his feet,
Another hurls a rider from his seat.
One through the body hurt, his captors take
And drag him, though he struggles, to the stake.
There, as the promise was, he must abide.
Another is dragged off from the opposing side,
And Theseus halts them now and then for ease,
To rest themselves and drink, if they should please.

   Often that day these Thebans met in fight
And each unhorsed and hurt his fellow knight.
No tiger in Gargaphia, robbed by men
Of the tiny whelp she had hidden in some glen,
So cruel on the scent as Arcite was
To wreak on Palamon his jealous cause.
No lion in the wastes of Benmarin,
Hunted or mad with hunger, ever was in
Such thirst of blood or tracked his quarry so
As Palamon to slay Arcite, his foe.
Their sides were bleeding and their helmets hacked.

   But sometime comes an end to every act.
Before the sun sank in the evening breeze,
Emetreus, the great king, found means to seize
This Palamon, who struggled with Arcite,
And deep in the flesh he made his long sword bite.
Then twenty men lay hold on him and take
The unyielding victim with them to the stake,
And in the attempt to rescue Palamon
The mighty King Lycurgus is borne down,
And King Emetreus, for all his strength,
So Palamon hit him, to a full sword's length
Is lifted from his saddle. But they take
Palamon willy-nilly to the stake.
His hardy heart can give him no help now.
Conquered, he must abide by his own vow.

Who grieves but Palamon, no more to fight?
The prince, as soon as he had seen this sight,
Cried out to those who fought, "Ho! It is done.
No more. Arcite of Thebes has fairly won,
As I am true judge, helping neither side.
My sister Emily shall be his bride."
The people's clamor swept from wall to wall
With such a joy it seemed the lists would fall.

What can fair Venus now do up above?
What says the goddess? What does the queen of love
But weep so for the wanting of her will
The lists with brimming tears are like to fill?
"Truly," she said, "I am shamed on every side."

But Saturn spoke. "Peace, daughter," he replied.
"Mars is content. His knight has been rewarded.
Soon you shall see your own desire accorded."

The heralds, the trumpets, and the minstrelsy
Are all in joy for Arcite's victory.
But listen! Be more quiet while I tell
How on the sudden a miracle befell.

Taking his helmet off to show his face,
This Arcite rode the length of the great place
Looking at Emily, where she sat up high,
And she returned his look with friendly eye
(For women, whatsoever tastes they savor,
Speaking in general, follow Fortune's favor),
And she was all his cheer, and he gladhearted.

Out of the ground a hellish Fury started
By Pluto sent (such was old Saturn's plan),
For terror of which his frightened horse began
To swerve, and then fell foundering in a heap.
Quicker than Arcite could recover and keep
His seat, he was pitched over on his head
So roughly that he lay there as though dead.
His ribs were broken by his saddlebow,
He was as black as coal or as a crow

So rushed the blood to his congested face.
Quickly they raised and bore him from the place
And took him to the palace, deep in gloom.
They cut his armor from him, and in a room
Put him to bed, still clear in memory
And always crying out for Emily.

The prince, though this mishap had chanced to fall,
Had no desire to disappoint them all.
Besides, men said that Arcite would not die;
He would recover from his malady.
Another thing they took for a great gain,
That no one in the tourney had been slain.
As for their hurts and wounds and broken arms,
One recommended salves, another charms.
And so the prince, whose will was for the best,
Honored and comforted his every guest,
And for the visiting lords, as was but right,
Conducted revels all the livelong night.
Three days he feasted them, and then attended
While they rode out of town, their mission ended,
And every man turned home the shortest way.
There was no more but "Farewell and good day."

The breast of Arcite swells, the bitter sore
That fills his heart increases more and more.
The clotted blood, despite all medical skill,
Festers, remaining in the tissue still.
No cupping nor bloodletting gives him aid,
Nor any drink of herbs, however made.
The venom is past all virtue to expel.
The passage of his lungs begins to swell.
The poison and the festering congest
His every muscle downward through his chest.
No measure helps him, in his hope to live,
Upward emetic, downward laxative.
All organs in that region are disrupted
And nature there is totally corrupted.

When Nature leaves the victim in the lurch,
Doctor, good-by! Go bear the man to church!
This is the long and short: Arcite must die,
And so he calls at last for Emily
And Palamon, and when they had drawn near,
These were the words he spoke for them to hear:
   "Nowise the woeful spirit in my heart
May speak one point of all my sorrow's smart
To you, my lady, for I love you most.
But I bequeath the service of my ghost
To you above all creatures who are cast
Into this world, since my life may not last.
Ah, for the grief, the pains both sharp and strong
That for your sake I suffered, and so long!
Alas, for death! Alas, my Emily!
Alas, this parting of our company!
Alas, queen of my heart! Alas, my wife,
My heart's love, and the ender of my life!
What is this world? What do men ask to have?
Now with his love, now in his cold grave,
Alone, without a soul for company.
Farewell, my lovely foe, my Emily!
Now softly take me in your arms, and pay,
For love of God, good heed to what I say.
   "I have with Palamon, my cousin here,
Had strife and rancor many a jealous year
For love of you. Yet God so pity me,
In speaking of a lover, truthfully,
For honor, kindred, knighthood, I know none
So worthy to be loved as Palamon
Who serves you now, and will do all his life.
And if you ever should become a wife,
Forget not Palamon, that worthy man."
And with the final word his speech began
To fail; the cold of death began to creep
From feet to breast with overcoming sleep.

The strength ebbed from him till it left no more
Than thought, with which his heart beat sick and sore,
And even thought failed when the heart felt death.
His eyes dusked over, and his sinking breath
Fluttered, and yet it seemed he still could see
His lady; his last word was "Emily!"
His spirit changed its mansion, and went there
Where never I was; I cannot tell you where.
Theology is past my slim resources.
I do not find the soul's fate in my sources,
And all those views I do not care to tell
Divines hold on the question where souls dwell.
Arcite is cold; Mars take him to his peers!

      Infinite are the sorrows and the tears
Of young and old. Such weeping never filled
The town of Troy, when Hector, newly killed,
Was carried home. Alas, the pity there,
Flaying of cheeks, and tearing out of hair!
"With Emily," the shrieking women cry,
"And gold enough, why did he have to die?"

      No one could comfort Theseus but his old
Father Aegeus, to whom the world had told
The story of its endless transformations.
He had seen its ups and downs and its mutations,
Joys after griefs, griefs after ecstasies,
And proffered examples and analogies.

      "Just as no man has ever died," said he,
"Who did not live his life in some degree,
Just so no man has lived and eaten bread
In all the world but some day he is dead.
This world is but a thoroughfare of woe,
And we are pilgrims, passing to and fro.
Death is the healing of each wordly sore."
Of such sort was his comfort, and much more.

      Theseus, with all his busy care and stir,
Thought now where they might build the sepulcher,

And in the end he was resolved upon
The place where both Arcite and Palamon
Had in their jealous combat first been seen.
There in the very grove, pleasant and green,
Where Arcite had complained of love's hot fire
He meant to burn him on a funeral pyre.
He gave command to cut the old oaks low
And lay the wood in billets in a row.
Next he procured a bier, and had it dressed
In cloth of gold, the richest he possessed.
In the same clothing he arrayed Arcite,
Save that upon his hands were gloves of white
And on his head a wreath of laurel green
And in his hand a sharp sword, bright and keen.
He laid him, face uncovered, on the bier,
And wept so it was pitiable to hear.
Then that he might be seen of one and all,
When it was day he brought him to the hall.

There Palamon came, his hair unkempt and slack,
Sprinkled with ashes, and clad all in black,
And wretchedest of that whole company,
Outweeping all the others, Emily.

The foremost of the Greeks, with sorry cheer,
High on their shoulders lifted up the bier
And bore it slowly, with weeping eyes and red,
Through the chief street, where black cloth had been
    spread.
Duke Theseus and Aegeus, grave and old,
Bore in their hands vessels of finest gold
Well filled with honey and milk, with blood and
    wine.
Palamon with his followers next in line;
And after that came Emily, in her hand
Fire for the rites long practiced in that land.

The rich appurtenance of their undertaking,
The form and labor of their fire-making,

I shall not tell at length; the pyre was high
So that its green top seemed to brush the sky.
First many loads of straw to catch the flames,
Then birch, oak, box, ash, trees of many names
Above the straw: elm, linden, chestnut, beech,
Maple and thorn to tempt the fire's reach.
You will not hear from me how all the trees
Were felled, nor how the local deities,
Nymphs, fauns, and hamadryads and the rest,
Ran up and down, scattered and dispossessed,
Nor how the beasts and wood birds, one and all,
Fled terrified when the trunks began to fall;
Nor how the ground stood all aghast and bright,
Affronted with the unfamiliar light;
Nor how Arcite among the garlands lay,
The flowers, incense, myrrh, and rich array;
How Emily swooned when men had made the fire,
Nor what she said, nor what was her desire;
Nor what the gems and weapons that men cast
Into the fire when it burned high and fast,
Nor how the Greek knights rode in a huge rout,
Keeping the fire to leftward, thrice about
With loud cries and thrice more with clanging spears,
And thrice the women shrieked above their tears;
Nor how the ashes of Arcite burned cold,
Nor how the Greeks all night their wake-feast hold,
Nor how they keep the funeral games appointed,
Who wrestled best, naked, with oil anointed;
Read these old books, if you have time to spend,
For I shall bring my long tale to an end.

By lapse and natural process of the years,
The Greeks forgot their mourning and their tears,
Abandoned by a general consent.
Then, I recall, occurred a parliament
That with its other business had in view
The obedience that Athenians thought due

From Thebes; and Theseus, thinking of this end,
Ordered his officers that they should send
For Palamon, who came, not knowing why,
In black, and with his sorrow in his eye.
The prince called Emily, seated them in place,
And when a hush fell, with a thoughtful face
He sighed, and held his peace a moment still,
And then he soberly declared his will.

"The Prime Mover, when he forged the chain of love
That binds us to the cause of things above,
Great was his purpose, and high was his intent,
And in that act he well knew what he meant,
For by the means of that fair chain he bound
The fire, the air, the water, and the ground
And fixed the limits they may not exceed.
That same Prince and First Mover has decreed
To all life in this wretched world below
A day beyond which none of us may go,
Although we may abridge our natural term.
This truth we need no learning to confirm;
Experience proves it, and I cite it here
Only to make my resolution clear.
Thus by the order of things men comprehend
This Mover suffers neither change nor end.
For any man, unless he is a fool,
Knows well that every part comes from the whole;
For nature did not take its origin
From part or parcel, but all things begin
With what is perfect and immutable
And thence descending, grow corruptible.
Thus by his ordinance, in wise progression
Species of all sorts live but in succession
And not eternally. This is no lie
As anyone can see with his own eye.

"Consider the oak, so long a-nourishing
From when the acorn first began to spring,

And with so long a life, as we may see,
Yet withered in the end is the great tree.

"Consider how the stone we tread each day
Is wasting as it lies there in the way.
The broadest river time at last will drain
And cities that wax great at length will wane.
So you may see that all things have an end.

"Thus man and woman also, foe and friend,
In either term, in youth or else in age,
Must die, the king as truly as the page;
One in his bed, and one in the deep sea,
One in the open field, their ends agree.
There is no help; we go the common way.
All things must die, it is but truth to say.
It cannot profit any soul alive
Against this everlasting law to strive.

"Thus it is wisdom, as it seems to me,
To make a virtue of necessity
And take that well which we cannot eschew,
The more so as it is our common due.
Whoever grumbles, he takes folly's side
And is a rebel to the world's great guide.
And certainly a man is honored most
If in his flower he gives up the ghost,
When steadfast and secure in his good name
He spares himself and all his friends from shame;
His friends should be more grateful for his death
When in full honor he gives up his breath
Than when old age has made his prowess pale
And all his honors a forgotten tale.

"The opposite doctrine is but willfulness.
Why do we grumble, why this heaviness
Because good Arcite, in his highest hour,
Took leave, with all his honors in full flower,
Out of the dreary prison of this life?
Why grumble here his cousin and his wife

About his welfare who loved them so well?
Can Arcite thank them? God in his wisdom tell!
His soul and themselves also they offend,
And yet their lusts and whims they cannot mend!

   "What is the gist of this long argument
But that for woe I counsel merriment
And that we thank great Jove for all his grace?
And so, before departing from this place,
I urge that from two sorrows, long and sore,
We make one perfect joy forevermore.
Consider! Where grief struck most deeply in,
That is the point at which we shall begin.

   "Sister," he said, "this is my full intent
With all the advice here of my parliament.
This gentle Palamon, your own true knight,
Who serves you with his will and heart and might,
And ever has since first he saw your face,
You shall take pity on him in your grace,
Accept him for your husband and your lord.
Lend me your hand. We all are in accord.
Show us what womanly pity you have to give!
What, the man is a king's nephew, as I live,
But were he a knight with nothing but his gear,
Since he has served you now this many a year
And borne for you so great adversity,
You should consider that, it seems to me.
Justice by noble mercy is outshone."

   Then Theseus turned to knightly Palamon.
"I fancy it will take but little prayer
To settle your consent to this affair.
Come near, and take your lady by the hand."
And so their marriage was agreed and planned
In the full presence of the parliament
And by their counsel and encouragement.
Thus, after his long trial, joyously
Has Palamon at last gained Emily,

And God, who all this breadth of world has wrought,
Send him the love that he has dearly bought!
Now all is for the best with Palamon,
In health, in wealth, his stint of sorrow done.
For Emily loves him with such tenderness
And he serves her with such a gentleness
No word of jealousy can intervene
To grieve them, nor suspicion come between.
I have told how Palamon won Emily.
Now God save all this excellent company!

Prologue to the Miller's Tale

When the Knight finished, no one, young or old,
In the whole company, but said he had told
A noble story, one that ought to be
Preserved and kept alive in memory,
Especially the gentlefolk, each one.
Our good Host laughed, and swore, "The game's begun,
The ball is rolling! This is going well.
Let's see who has another tale to tell.
Come, match the Knight's tale if you can, Sir Monk!"
    The Miller, who by this time was so drunk
He looked quite bloodless, and who hardly sat
His horse, was never one to doff his hat
Or stand on courtesy for any man.
Like Pilate in the Church plays he began
To bellow. "Arms and blood and bones," he swore,
"I know a noble yarn to square the score
With the Knight's tale, one that will leave us quits."
Our host could see that ale had bleared his wits.
"Robin," he said, "hold on a minute, brother.
Some better man shall come first with another.

Let's do this right. You tell yours by and by."
    "God's soul," the Miller told him, "that won't I!
Either I'll speak, or go on my own way."
    "The devil with you! Say what you have to say,"
Answered our Host. "You are a fool. Your head
Is overpowered."
                    "Now," the Miller said,
"Everyone listen! But first I will propound
That I am drunk, I know it by my sound.
If I can't get my words out, put the blame
On Southwark ale, I ask you, in God's name!
I'll tell you a holy legend of the life
A carpenter lived at one time with his wife
And how a student put horns on his head."
    The Reeve replied. "Stifle your noise," he said.
"Forget your ignorant drunken bawdiness.
It is a sin and great foolishness
To injure any man by defamation
And to give women such a reputation.
Tell us of other things; you'll find no lack."
    Promptly this drunken Miller answered back:
"Oswald, my brother, true as babes are suckled,
The man who has no wife, he is no cuckold.
I don't say for this reason that you are.
There are plenty of faithful wives, both near and far,
Always a thousand good for every bad,
And you know this yourself, unless you're mad.
I see you are angry with my tale, but why?
You have a wife; no less, by God, do I.
But I wouldn't, for the oxen in my plow,
Shoulder more than I need by thinking how
I may myself, for aught I know, be one.
I'll certainly believe that I am none.
A husband mustn't be curious, for his life,
About God's secrets or about his wife.

If she gives him plenty and he's in the clover,
No need to worry about what's left over."
   The Miller, to make the best of it I can,
Refused to hold his tongue for any man,
But told his tale like any low-born clown.
I am sorry that I have to set it down,
And all you people, for God's love, I pray,
Whose taste is higher, do not think I say
A word with evil purpose; I must rehearse
Their stories one and all, both better and worse,
Or play false with my matter, that is clear.
Whoever, therefore, may not wish to hear,
Turn over the page and choose another tale;
For small and great, he'll find enough, no fail,
Of things from history, touching courtliness,
And virtue too, and also holiness.
If you choose wrong, don't lay it on my head.
You know the Miller couldn't be called well bred.
So with the Reeve, and many more as well,
And both of them had bawdy tales to tell.
Reflect a little, and don't hold me to blame.
There's no sense making earnest out of game.

The Miller's Tale

There used to be a rich old oaf who made
His home at Oxford, a carpenter by trade.
He took in boarders, and with him used to live
A student who knew what study has to give,
But he was poor, and let his fancies turn
To astrology; that was his whole concern,

And he had smattered up some propositions
By means of which he could predict conditions
If people asked him at a given hour
Whether to look for sunshine or for shower,
Or want to know whatever might befall,
Events of all sorts, I can't count them all.

He was known as handy[1] Nicholas, this student.
Well versed in love, he knew how to be prudent,
Going about unnoticed, sly, and sure.
In looks no girl was ever more demure.
Lodged at this carpenter's, he lived alone;
He had a room there that he made his own,
Festooned with herbs, and he was sweet himself
As licorice or ginger. On a shelf
Above his bed's head, neatly stowed apart,
He kept the trappings that went with his art,
His astrolabe, his books—among the rest,
Thick ones and thin ones, lay his *Almagest*—
And the counters for his abacus as well.
Over his cupboard a red curtain fell
And up above a pretty zither lay
On which at night so sweetly would he play
That with the music the whole room would ring.
"Angelus to the Virgin" he would sing
And then the song that's known as "The King's
      Note."
Blessings were called down on his merry throat!
So this sweet scholar passed his time, his end
Being to eat and live upon his friend.

This carpenter had newly wed a wife
And loved her better than he loved his life.
He was jealous, for she was eighteen in age;
He tried to keep her close as in a cage,

[1]Chaucer's word is *hendē*, implying, I take it, both *ready to hand*
and *ingratiating*. Nicholas was a Johnny-on-the-spot and also had
a way with him.

For she was wild and young, and old was he
And guessed that he might smack of cuckoldry.
His ignorant wits had never chanced to strike
On Cato's word, that man should wed his like;
Men ought to wed where their conditions point,
For youth and age are often out of joint.
But now, since he had fallen in the snare,
He must, like other men, endure his care.

    Fair this young woman was, her body trim
As any mink, so graceful and so slim.
She wore a striped belt that was all of silk;
A piece-work apron, white as morning milk,
About her loins and down her lap she wore.
White was her smock, her collar both before
And on the back embroidered all about
In coal-black silk, inside as well as out.
And like her collar, her white-laundered bonnet
Had ribbons of the same embroidery on it.
Wide was her silken fillet, worn up high,
And for a fact she had a willing eye.
She plucked each brow into a little bow,
And each one was as black as any sloe.
She was by far a prettier sight to see
Than the new blossoms on a spring pear tree,
And softer than the wool of an old wether.
Down from her belt there hung a purse of leather
With silken tassels and with studs of brass.
No man so wise, wherever people pass,
Who could imagine in this world at all
A wench like her, the pretty little doll!
Far brighter was the dazzle of her hue
Than a coin struck in the Tower, fresh and new.
As for her song, it twittered from her head
Sharp as a swallow perching on a shed.
And she could skip and sport as a young ram
Or calf will gambol, following his dam.

Her mouth was sweet as honey-ale or mead
Or apples in the hay, stored up for need.
She was as skittish as an untrained colt,
Slim as a mast and straighter than a bolt.
Her simple collar bore a big brooch-pin
Wide as a shield's boss underneath her chin.
High up along her legs she laced her shoes.
She was a pigsney, she was a primrose
For any lord to tumble in his bed
Or a good yeoman honestly to wed.
    Now sir, and again sir, this is how it was:
A day came round when handy Nicholas,
Her husband gone to Oseney, well away,
Began to fool with this young wife, and play.
These students always have a wily head.
He caught her in between the legs, and said,
"Sweetheart, unless I have my will with you
I'll die for stifled love, by all that's true,"
And held her by the haunches, hard. "I vow
I'll die unless you love me here and now,
Sure as my soul," he said, "is God's to save."
    She shied just as a colt does in the trave,
And turned her head hard from him, this young wife,
And said, "I will not kiss you, on my life.
Why, stop it now," she said, "stop, Nicholas,
Or I will cry out 'Help, help,' and 'Alas!'
Be good enough to take your hands away."
    "Mercy," this Nicholas began to pray,
And spoke so well and poured it on so fast
She promised she would be his love at last,
And swore by Thomas à Becket, saint of Kent,
That she would serve him when she could invent
Or spy out some good opportunity.
"My husband is so full of jealousy
You must be watchful and take care," she said,
"Or well I know I'll be as good as dead.

You must go secretly about this business."
    "Don't give a thought to that," said Nicholas.
"A student has been wasting time at school
If he can't make a carpenter a fool."
And so they were agreed, these two, and swore
To watch their chance, as I have said before.
When Nicholas had spanked her haunches neatly
And done all I have spoken of, he sweetly
Gave her a kiss, and then he took his zither
And loudly played, and sang his music with her.

    It happened to the parish church one day
To do Christ's work this good wife made her way,
And as she went her forehead cast a glow
As bright as noon, for she had washed it so
It glistened when she finished with her work.

    Serving this church there was a parish clerk
Whose name was Absolom, a ruddy man
With goose-gray eyes and curls like a great fan
That shone like gold on his neatly parted head.
His tunic was light blue and his nose red,
And he had patterns that had been cut through
Like the windows of St. Paul's in either shoe.
He wore above his tunic, fresh and gay,
A surplice white as a blossom on a spray.
A merry devil, as true as God can save,
He knew how to let blood, trim hair, and shave,
Or write a deed of land in proper phrase,
And he could dance in twenty different ways
In the Oxford fashion, and sometimes he would sing
A loud falsetto to his fiddle string
Or his guitar. No tavern anywhere
But he had furnished entertainment there.
Yet if a man broke wind, he winced a bit,
And spoke with delicacy, no word unfit.

    This Absolom, so jolly and so gay,
Went about with a censer each saint's day

Censing the parish women one and all.
Many the doting look that he let fall,
And specially on this carpenter's young wife.
To look at her, he thought, was a good life,
She was so trim, so fit for lechery.
If she had only been a mouse, and he
A cat, I think he would have made short work
Of catching her. This jolly parish clerk
Had such a heartful of love-hankerings
He would not take the women's offerings;
No, no, he said, it would not be polite.

  The moon, when darkness fell, shone full and bright,
And Absolom, always ready for love's sake
With his guitar to be up and awake,
Made toward the carpenter's, brisk and amorous,
And went along until he reached the house
A little after the cocks began to crow.
Under a casement he sang sweet and low,
"Dear lady, by your will, be kind to me,"
And strummed on his guitar in harmony.
This lovelorn singing woke the carpenter
Who said to his wife, "What, Alison, don't you hear
Absolom singing under our bedroom wall?"

  "Yes, God knows, John," she answered, "I hear it all."

  What would you like? In this way things went on
Till jolly Absolom was woebegone
For wooing her, awake all night and day.
He combed his curls and made himself look gay.
He swore to be her slave and used all means
To court her with his gifts and go-betweens.
He sang and quavered like a nightingale.
He sent her sweet spiced wine and seasoned ale,
Cakes that were piping hot, mead sweet with honey,
And since she was town-bred, he proffered money.
For some are won by wealth, and some no less
By blows, and others yet by gentleness.

Sometimes, to keep his talents in her gaze,
He acted Herod in the mystery plays
High on the stage. But what can help his case?
For she so loves this handy Nicholas
That Absolom is living in a bubble.
He has nothing but a laugh for all his trouble.
She leaves his earnestness for scorn to cool
And makes this Absolom her proper fool.
For this is a true proverb, and no lie:
"It always happens that the nigh and sly
Will make the absent suffer." So 'tis said,
And Absolom may rage or lose his head
But just because he was farther from her sight
This nearby Nicholas got in his light.

    Now hold your chin up, handy Nicholas,
For Absolom may wail and sing "Alas!"
One Saturday when the carpenter had gone
To Oseney, Nicholas and Alison
Agreed that he should use his wit and guile
This simple jealous husband to beguile,
And if it happened that the game went right
She would sleep in his arms the livelong night,
For this was his desire and hers as well.
At once, with no more words, this Nicholas fell
To working out his plan. He would not tarry,
But quietly to his room began to carry
Both food and drink to last him out a day,
Or more than one, and told her what to say
If her husband asked her about Nicholas.
She'd say she had no notion where he was;
She hadn't laid eyes on him all day long;
He must be sick, or something must be wrong;
No matter how her maid had called and cried
He wouldn't answer, whatever might betide.

    This was the plan, and Nicholas kept away,
Shut in his room, for that whole Saturday.

He ate and slept or did as he thought best
Till Sunday, when the sun was going to rest,
This carpenter began to wonder greatly
Where Nicholas was and what might ail him lately.
"Now, by St. Thomas, I begin to dread
All isn't right with Nicholas," he said.
"He hasn't, God forbid, died suddenly!
The world is ticklish these days, certainly.
Today I saw a corpse to church go past,
A man that I saw working Monday last!
Go up," he told his chore-boy, "call and shout,
Knock with a stone, find what it's all about
And let me know."

        The boy went up and pounded
And yelled as if his wits had been confounded.
"What, how, what's doing, Master Nicholas?
How can you sleep all day?" But all his fuss
Was wasted, for he could not hear a word.
He noticed at the bottom of a board
A hole the cat used when she wished to creep
Into the room, and through it looked in deep
And finally of Nicholas caught sight.
This Nicholas sat gaping there upright
As though his wits were addled by the moon
When it was new. The boy went down, and soon
Had told his master how he had seen the man.

The carpenter, when he heard this news, began
To cross himself. "Help us, St. Frideswide!
Little can we foresee what may betide!
The man's astronomy has turned his wit,
Or else he's in some agonizing fit.
I always knew that it would turn out so.
What God has hidden is not for men to know.
Aye, blessed is the ignorant man indeed,
Blessed is he that only knows his creed!

So fared another scholar of the sky,
For walking in the meadows once to spy
Upon the stars and what they might foretell,
Down in a clay-pit suddenly he fell!
He overlooked that! By St. Thomas, though,
I'm sorry for handy Nicholas. I'll go
And scold him roundly for his studying
If so I may, by Jesus, heaven's king!
Give me a staff, I'll pry up from the floor
While you, Robin, are heaving at the door.
He'll quit his books, I think."

                          He took his stand
Outside the room. The boy had a strong hand
And by the hasp heaved off the door at once.
The door fell flat. With gaping countenance
This Nicholas sat studying the air
As still as stone. He was in black despair,
The carpenter believed, and hard about
The shoulders caught and shook him, and cried
    out
Rudely, "What, how! What is it? Look down at us!
Wake up, think of Christ's passion, Nicholas!
I'll sign you with the cross to keep away
These elves and things!" And he began to say,
Facing the quarters of the house, each side,
And on the threshold of the door outside,
The night-spell: "Jesu and St. Benedict
From every wicked thing this house protect . . ."

   Choosing his time, this handy Nicholas
Produced a dreadful sigh, and said, "Alas,
This world, must it be all destroyed straightway?"

   "What," asked the carpenter, "what's that you say?
Do as we do, we working men, and think
Of God."

            Nicholas answered, "Get me a drink,

And afterwards I'll tell you privately
Of something that concerns us, you and me.
I'll tell you only, you among all men."

This carpenter went down and came again
Bearing a draft of strong ale, a full quart.
As soon as each of them had drunk his part
Nicholas shut the door and made it fast
And sat down by the carpenter at last
And spoke to him. "My host," he said, "John dear,
Swear now by all that you hold sacred here
That not to any man will you betray
My confidence. What I'm about to say
Is Christ's own secret. If you tell a soul
You are undone, and this will be the toll:
If you betray me, you shall go stark mad."

"Now Christ forbid it, by His holy blood,"
Answered this simple man. "I don't go blabbing.
No, though I say it myself, I don't like gabbing.
Speak up just as you like, I'll never tell,
Not wife nor child, by Him that harrowed hell."

"Now, John," said Nicholas, "this is no lie.
I have discovered through astrology
And studying the moon that shines so bright
That Monday next, a quarter through the night,
A rain will fall, and such a mad, wild spate
That Noah's flood was never half so great.
This world," he said, "in less time than an hour
Shall drown entirely in that hideous shower.
Yes, every man shall drown and lose his life."

"Alas," the carpenter answered, "for my wife!
Alas, my Alison! And shall she drown?"
For grief at this he nearly tumbled down,
And said, "But is there nothing to be done?"

"Why, happily there is, for anyone
Who'll take advice," this handy Nicholas said.
"You mustn't expect to follow your own head.

For what said Solomon, whose words were true?
'Proceed by counsel, and you'll never rue.'
If you will act on good advice, no fail,
I'll promise, and without a mast or sail,
To see that she's preserved, and you and I.
Haven't you heard how Noah was kept dry
When, warned by Christ beforehand, he discovered
That the whole earth with water should be covered?"

"Yes," said the carpenter, "long, long ago."

"And then again," said Nicholas, "don't you know
The grief they all had trying to embark
Till Noah could get his wife into the Ark?[1]
That was a time when Noah, I dare say,
Would gladly have given his best black wethers
    away
If she could only have had a ship alone.
And therefore do you know what must be done?
This demands haste, and with a hasty thing
People can't stop for talk and tarrying.

"Start out and get into the house right off
For each of us a tub or kneading-trough,
Above all making sure that they are large,
In which we'll float away as in a barge.
And put in food enough to last a day.
Beyond won't matter; the flood will fall away
Early next morning. Take care not to spill
A word to your boy Robin, nor to Jill
Your maid. I cannot save her, don't ask why.
I will not tell God's secrets, no, not I.
Let it suffice, unless your wits are mad,
To have as good a grace as Noah had.
I'll save your wife for certain, never doubt it.
Now go along, and make good time about it.

[1] A stock comic scene in the mystery plays, of which the carpenter would have been an avid spectator.

"But when you have, for her and you and me,
Brought to the house these kneading-tubs, all three,
Then you must hang them under the roof, up high,
To keep our plans from any watchful eye.
When you have done exactly as I've said,
And put in snug our victuals and our bread,
Also an ax to cut the ropes apart
So when the rain comes we can make our start,
And when you've broken a hole high in the gable
Facing the garden plot, above the stable,
To give us a free passage out, each one,
Then, soon as the great fall of rain is done,
You'll swim as merrily, I undertake,
As paddles the white duck behind her drake.
Then I shall call, 'How, Alison! How, John!
Be cheerful, for the flood will soon be gone.'
And 'Master Nicholas, what ho!' you'll say.
'Good morning, I see you clearly, for it's day.'
Then we shall lord it for the rest of life
Over the world, like Noah and his wife.

"But one thing I must warn you of downright.
Use every care that on that selfsame night
When we have taken ship and climbed aboard,
No one of us must speak a single word,
Nor call, nor cry, but pray with all his heart.
It is God's will. You must hang far apart,
You and your wife, for there must be no sin
Between you, no more in a look than in
The very deed. Go now, the plans are drawn.
Go, set to work, and may God spur you on!
Tomorrow night when all men are asleep
Into our kneading-troughs we three shall creep
And sit there waiting, and abide God's grace.
Go along now, this isn't the time or place
For me to talk at length or sermonize.
The proverb says, 'Don't waste words on the wise.'

You are so wise there is no need to teach you.
Go, save our lives—that's all that I beseech you!"
    This simple carpenter went on his way.
Many a time he said, "Alack the day,"
And to his wife he laid the secret bare.
She knew it better than he; she was aware
What this quaint bargain was designed to buy.
She carried on as if about to die,
And said, "Alas, go get this business done.
Help us escape, or we are dead, each one.
I am your true, your faithful wedded wife.
Go, my dear husband, save us, limb and life!"
    Great things, in all truth, can the emotions be!
A man can perish through credulity
So deep the print imagination makes.
This simple carpenter, he quails and quakes.
He really sees, according to his notion,
Noah's flood come wallowing like an ocean
To drown his Alison, his pet, his dear.
He weeps and wails, and gone is his good cheer,
And wretchedly he sighs. But he goes off
And gets himself a tub, a kneading-trough,
Another tub, and has them on the sly
Sent home, and there in secret hangs them high
Beneath the roof. He made three ladders, these
With his own hands, and stowed in bread and cheese,
A jug of good ale, plenty for a day.
Before all this was done, he sent away
His chore-boy Robin and his wench likewise
To London on some trumped-up enterprise,
And so on Monday, when it drew toward night,
He shut the door without a candlelight
And saw that all was just as it should be,
And shortly they went clambering up, all three.
They sat there still, and let a moment pass.
    "Now then, 'Our Father,' mum!" said Nicholas,

And "Mum!" said John, and "Mum!" said Alison,
And piously this carpenter went on
Saying his prayers. He sat there still and straining,
Trying to make out whether he heard it raining.

　　The dead of sleep, for very weariness,
Fell on this carpenter, as I should guess,
At about curfew time, or little more.
His head was twisted, and that made him snore.
His spirit groaned in its uneasiness.
Down from his ladder slipped this Nicholas,
And Alison too, downward she softly sped
And without further word they went to bed
Right where the carpenter slept on other nights.
There were the revels, there were the delights!
And so this Alison and Nicholas lay
Busy about their solace and their play
Until the bell for lauds began to ring
And in the chancel friars began to sing.

　　Now on this Monday, woebegone and glum
For love, this parish clerk, this Absolom
Was with some friends at Oseney, and while there
Inquired after John the carpenter.
A member of the cloister drew him away
Out of the church, and told him, "I can't say.
I haven't seen him working hereabout
Since Saturday. The abbot sent him out
For timber, I suppose. He'll often go
And stay at the granary a day or so.
Or else he's at his own house, possibly.
I can't for certain say where he may be."

　　Absolom all at once felt jolly and light,
And thought, "Time now to be awake all night,
For certainly I haven't seen him making
A stir about his door since day was breaking.
Don't call me a man if when I hear the cock
Begin to crow I don't slip up and knock

On the low window by his bedroom wall.
To Alison at last I'll pour out all
My love-pangs, for at this point I can't miss,
Whatever happens, at the least a kiss.
Some comfort, by my word, will come my way.
I've felt my mouth itch the whole livelong day,
And that's a sign of kissing at the least.
I dreamed all night that I was at a feast.
So now I'll go and sleep an hour or two,
And then I'll wake and play the whole night through."

When the first cockcrow through the dark had come
Up rose this jolly lover Absolom
And dressed up smartly. He was not remiss
About the least point. He chewed licorice
And cardamom to smell sweet, even before
He combed his hair. Beneath his tongue he bore
A sprig of Paris like a truelove knot.
He strolled off to the carpenter's house, and got
Beneath the window. It came so near the ground
It reached his chest. Softly, with half a sound,
He coughed, "My honeycomb, sweet Alison,
What are you doing, my sweet cinnamon?
Awake, my sweetheart and my pretty bird,
Awake, and give me from your lips a word!
Little enough you care for all my woe,
How for your love I sweat wherever I go!
No wonder I sweat and faint and cannot eat
More than a girl; as a lamb does for the teat
I pine. Yes, truly, I so long for love
I mourn as if I were a turtledove."

Said she, "You jack-fool, get away from here!
So help me God, I won't sing 'Kiss me, dear!'
I love another more than you. Get on,
For Christ's sake, Absolom, or I'll throw a stone.
The devil with you! Go and let me sleep."

"Ah, that true love should ever have to reap

So evil a fortune," Absolom said. "A kiss,
At least, if it can be no more than this,
Give me, for love of Jesus and of me."

"And will you go away for that?" said she.

"Yes, truly, sweetheart," answered Absolom.

"Get ready then," she said, "for here I come,"
And softly said to Nicholas, "Keep still,
And in a minute you can laugh your fill."

This Absolom got down upon his knee
And said, "I am a lord of pure degree,
For after this, I hope, comes more to savor.
Sweetheart, your grace, and pretty bird, your favor!"

She undid the window quickly. "That will do,"
She said. "Be quick about it, and get through,
For fear the neighbors will look out and spy."

Absolom wiped his mouth to make it dry.
The night was pitch dark, coal-black all about.
Her rear end through the window she thrust out.
If fared no better or worse with Absolom
Than with his mouth to kiss her naked bum
Before he had caught on, a smacking kiss.

He jumped back, thinking something was amiss.
A woman has no beard, he was well aware,
But what he felt was rough and had long hair.

"Alas," he cried, "what have you made me do?"

"Te-hee!" she said, and banged the window to.

Absolom backed away a sorry pace.

"You've bearded him!" said handy Nicholas.
"God's body, this is going fair and fit!"

This luckless Absolom heard every bit,
And gnawed his mouth, so angry he became.
He said to himself, "I'll square you, all the same."

But who now scrubs and rubs, who chafes his lips
With dust, with sand, with straw, with cloth and chips,
If not this Absolom? "The devil," says he,
"Welcome my soul if I wouldn't rather be

Revenged than have the whole town in a sack!
Alas," he cries, "if only I'd held back!"
His hot love had become all cold and ashen.
He didn't have a curse to spare for passion.
The moment when he kissed her on the ass,
That was the cure to make his sickness pass!
He cried as a child does after being whipped;
He railed at love. Then quietly he slipped
Across the street to a smith who was forging out
Parts that the farmers needed round about.
He was busy sharpening colter and plowshare
When Absolom knocked as though without a care.
   "Undo the door, Jervice, and let me come."
   "What? Who are you?"
                    "It is I, Absolom."
   "Absolom, is it! By Christ's precious tree,
Why are you up so early? Lord bless me,
What's ailing you? Some gay girl has the power
To bring you out, God knows, at such an hour!
Yes, by St. Neot, you know well what I mean!"
   Absolom thought his jokes not worth a bean.
Without a word he let them all go by.
He had another kind of fish to fry
Than Jervice guessed. "Lend me this colter here
That's hot in the chimney, friend," he said. "Don't fear.
I'll bring it back right off when I am through.
I need it for a job I have to do."
   "Of course," said Jervice. "Why, if it were gold
Or coins in a sack, uncounted and untold,
As I'm a rightful smith, I wouldn't refuse it.
But, Christ's foot! how on earth do you mean to
     use it?"
   "Let that," said Absolom, "be as it may.
I'll let you know tomorrow or next day,"
And took the colter where the steel was cold
And slipped out with it safely in his hold

And softly over to the carpenter's wall.
He coughed and then he rapped the window, all
As he had done before.

                              "Who's knocking there?"
Said Alison. "It is a thief, I swear."
    "No, no," said he. "God knows, my sugarplum,
My bird, my darling, it's your Absolom.
I've brought a golden ring my mother gave me,
Fine and well cut, as I hope that God will save me.
It's yours, if you will let me have a kiss."
    Nicholas had got up to take a piss
And thought he would improve the whole affair.
This clerk, before he got away from there,
Should give *his* ass a smack; and hastily
He opened the window, and thrust out quietly,
Buttocks and haunches, all the way, his bum.
Up spoke this clerk, this jolly Absolom:
"Speak, for I don't know where you are, sweetheart."
    Nicholas promptly let fly with a fart
As loud as if a clap of thunder broke,
So great he was nearly blinded by the stroke,
And ready with his hot iron to make a pass,
Absolom caught him fairly on the ass.
    Off flew the skin, a good handbreadth of fat
Lay bare, the iron so scorched him where he sat.
As for the pain, he thought that he would die,
And like a madman he began to cry,
"Help! Water! Water! Help, for God's own heart!"
    At this the carpenter came to with a start.
He heard a man cry "Water!" as if mad.
"It's coming now," was the first thought he had.
"It's Noah's flood, alas, God be our hope!"
He sat up with his ax and chopped the rope
And down at once the whole contraption fell.
He didn't take time out to buy or sell

Until he hit the floor in a dead swoon.
   Then up jumped Nicholas and Alison
And in the street began to cry, "Help, ho!"
The neighbors all came running, high and low,
And poured into the house to see the sight.
The man still lay there, passed out cold and white,
For in his tumble he had broken an arm.
But he himself brought on his greatest harm,
For when he spoke he was at once outdone
By handy Nicholas and Alison
Who told them one and all that he was mad.
So great a fear of Noah's flood he had,
By some delusion, that in his vanity
He'd bought himself these kneading-troughs, all three,
And hung them from the roof there, up above,
And he had pleaded with them, for God's love,
To sit there in the loft for company.
   The neighbors laughed at such a fantasy,
And round the loft began to pry and poke
And turned his whole disaster to a joke.
He found it was no use to say a word.
Whatever reason he offered, no one heard.
With oaths and curses people swore him down
Until he passed for mad in the whole town.
Wit, clerk, and student all stood by each other.
They said, "It's clear the man is crazy, brother."
Everyone had his laugh about this feud.
So Alison, the carpenter's wife, got screwed
For all the jealous watching he could try,
And Absolom, he kissed her nether eye,
And Nicholas got his bottom roasted well.
God save this troop! That's all I have to tell.

Prologue to the Reeve's Tale

When people had laughed about this frivolous case
Of Absolom and handy Nicholas,
Different ones had different things to say,
But mostly laughed, accepting it as play.
And at the story I saw no man grieve
Unless it were but one, Oswald the Reeve,
Since carpentry had been his craft by training.
He found some anger in his heart remaining.
He grumbled, and was somewhat piqued with it.
"My life," he said, "I could pay you every bit
With a proud miller and the bait he nibbled,
If I took any pleasure in being ribald.
But I am old. Age blunts my taste for fun.
I live on fodder now; grass time is done.
This white top that I have spells my long cares;
My heart, too, fails as plainly as my hairs.
We're medlars, 'open-arses,' that's our curse,
We old men; as that fruit keeps getting worse
Till finally it rots in hay or mold,
Even so it is with us as we grow old.
Until we are rotten we are never ripe.
We still keep dancing while the world will pipe.
We find our will sticks ever on this nail:
We have a white head matched with a green tail
Just as a leek has; though our powers grow tame,
Our will yearns after folly just the same.
We talk, when we have lost the power to do.
In our old ashes the raked fire shows through.

   "We have, as I'll point out, four coals, no less:
Boasting, lying, anger, covetousness.

Along with age these four sparks always go,
For while our limbs may stiffen and turn slow,
Desire will never fail us, that's the truth.
And I myself have always a colt's tooth
For all the years that now are past and done
Since first my tap of life began to run.
For at my very birth, beyond a doubt,
Death drew the tap of life and let it out,
And ever since the tap has run away
Till almost empty is the keg today.
The stream of life falls to the bottom rim.
Well may the happy tongue lift up a hymn
To griefs outlived that long ago it bore!
With old folk, there is dotage, and no more."

   Our lord the Host, as soon as he had heard
The Reeve's discourse, put in his kingly word.
He said, "What does it come to, all this wit?
Why should we talk all day of Holy Writ?
The devil taught a reeve to preach, no fail,
Or a cobbler how to doctor or to sail.
Don't waste our time. Tell what you have to say.
It's half past seven. Here's Deptford in our way,
Greenwich is yonder, with many a scoundrel in it.
If you've a tale, it's high time to begin it."

   "Now, sirs, I beg you," said Oswald the Reeve,
"That none of you will be upset or grieve
If I should take him down from his high horse.
It's always proper to answer force with force.
This drunken Miller here has told us all
About a carpenter who took a fall,
Perhaps in scorn, since I myself am one.
With leave, I'll pay him back before I'm done.
I'll speak his low talk, just as he has spoken.
I pray to God he gets his neck well broken.
In my eye he can see what mote there is,
But what he can't see is the beam in his."

The Reeve's Tale

At Trumpington, near Cambridge, a brook flows;
Across this brook, moreover, a bridge goes,
And on the said brook stands a mill as well,
And sober truth is all this that I tell.
A miller lived there once for many a day
Who dressed up like a peacock. He could play
The bagpipes, wrestle, shoot his bow, and fish,
Mend nets, and lathe a wooden cup or dish.
He wore a long knife always at his belt;
Keen as a sharpened sword its edges felt.
A fancy dagger too he kept upon him,
And no man dared to put a finger on him.
He kept a Sheffield blade inside his hose.
He had a round face and a flattened nose.
His skull had no more hair than a bald ape.
He went to market looking for a scrape,
And anyone who was bold enough to lay
A hand on him he swore he'd soon repay.
He was for fact a thief of corn and meal,
And sly at that, well versed in how to steal.
He was christened Simon; Simkin by nickname.
As for his wife, from noble kin she came.
Her father was the parson of the town,
And handsome was the dowry he paid down,
For Simkin with his blood would be allied.
She was brought up in a convent; in his pride
Simkin refused to take a wife, he said,
Unless she were a maiden and well bred,
To keep up his position as a yeoman.
Proud as a jay she was and pert, this woman.

They made a sight together, did this pair.
On saints' days he would march in front of her,
The muffler of his hood tied round his head
While she came after in a cape of red,
And Simkin sported long hose of the same.
No one dared speak to her except as "Dame,"
And none so hardy walking by the way
Who dared make love or even so much as play,
Unless he would be killed, with Simkin's wife,
For fear of Simkin's cutlass or his knife.
These jealous men are dangerous, as we know;
At least they want their wives to think them so.
She suffered a smirch by being a priest's daughter,
And so she was as snotty as ditch water,
Hoity-toity and down-her-nose to spare.
A lady ought to carry herself with care,
She thought, what for the duty of maintaining
Her kinship and her stock of convent training.

    Between them they produced a daughter, grown
To twenty or so, and save for her alone
No other children except one, a mere
Babe in the cradle, of some half a year.
She was a plump, well-rounded wench, this lass,
Her nose was flat, her blue eyes clear as glass,
Her buttocks broad, her breasts were round and high.
But she had lovely hair, and that's no lie.

    This parson, seeing that the girl was fair,
Had it in mind to name her as his heir,
Both of his goods and dwelling in addition.
He made her marriage hard, for his ambition
Was to bestow her, hand and property,
On blood that came of worthy ancestry.
The things that are Holy Church's must be spent
On blood that Holy Church owns by descent;
He would not leave his holy blood in the lurch
Although he might devour the Holy Church.

A heavy toll this miller took, past doubt,
Of wheat and barley all the land about.
He cheated the great college worst of all
That stands in Cambridge, King's or Soler Hall,
For he was given their malt and wheat to grind.

They happened, on a certain day, to find
Their steward sick, and in a stupor lying.
They thought for certain that he must be dying,
And so this miller stole both meal and corn
More than he ever had since he was born
A hundredfold; he thieved it courteously
Before, but now he stole outrageously.
The provost stormed and raised a great affair,
But all this gave the miller little care.
He talked big, swearing, "Not so," on his oath.

Two poor young students at that time were both
Residing in this hall of which I speak.
They loved their fun, and they were full of cheek,
And merely for a jaunt they busily
Begged the provost to let them go and see
Their corn ground at the mill. Each bet his neck
The miller wouldn't cost them half a peck
Whether by force or sleight he tried to thieve.
At last the provost granted them his leave.

John was the name of one, Alan the other.
Their birthplace was the same, a town called Strother,
Far to the north, I cannot tell you where.[1]

Alan gathered his stuff for this affair,
And got a horse to put the grain sack on.
So off went Alan the student, off went John,

---

[1]Chaucer may intend his listeners to think of an actual town of his time named Strother, and of a family of that name identified with it. The speech of the students, as the tale goes on, is sprinkled with snatches of northern dialect, an effect it would be difficult to transpose into modern English.

Each with a sword and buckler by his side.
John knew the way, he did not need a guide,
And at the mill the grain sack down he set.
Alan spoke first. "Simkin," he said, "well met!
How are your lovely daughter and your wife?"

"Alan!" said Simkin. "Welcome, on my life,
And also John. What are you doing here?"

"Simkin," said John, "without a slave, no fear,
A man slaves for himself, or he's a fool.
Necessity, say the learned, knows no rule.
Our steward, I expect, will soon be dead
His molars ache so steadily in his head.
That's why I'm here, and Alan too. We've come
To grind our corn, and then to carry it home.
Help us get off as quickly as may be."

"Just as you want it," Simkin said. "Trust me.
What will you do while this is going on?"

"By God, right by the hopper," answered John,
"I'll stand, and see just how the corn goes in.
I've never watched yet, by my father's kin,
The way the hopper jiggles to and fro."

"Is that," said Alan, "what you're going to do?
I'll be down underneath then, by my hide,
And notice how the grain comes down the slide
Into the trough. That's what I'll do for sport,
For, John, the fact is that I'm of your sort,
I am as bad a miller as you can be."

The miller smiled at their simplicity,
And thought, "So that's it, that's their stratagem!
They fancy no one can hornswoggle them.
But yet I'll let them have some dust in the eye
For all the sleight in their philosophy.
The better the trap, no matter how sly they make
    it,
The more I'll pilfer when I'm ready to take it.

Instead of flour I'll give them only bran.
'The greatest scholar is not the wisest man,'
As one time to the wolf remarked the mare.
For all their cunning a fig is what I care."
 Out through the doorway he slipped quietly
When he perceived his time, in secrecy,
And up and down he looked until he found
The students' horse, where it was standing bound
Behind the mill beneath a clump of trees.
Up to the horse as easy as you please
He went, and stripped the bridle off, and when
The horse was loose he started for the fen
Where there were wild mares running, and thundered
   in,
"Wehee," whinnying on through thick and thin.
 This miller came back, not a word he spoke,
But with the students he began to joke
And worked until the corn was all well ground.
And when the meal was in the sack and bound
This John goes out and finds no horse at all.
"Help! Help!" and "God's bones!" he began to
   call.
"Our horse is gone! Come out here, Alan, man!
Step on your feet! Get going, if you can!
Our provost's palfrey lost—here's a fine deal!"
 This Alan, he forgot both corn and meal.
His husbandry was wholly put to rout.
"What, where was he heading?" he began to shout.
 The miller's wife came leaping in on the run.
"Off to the fen," she said, "your horse has gone
With the wild mares, as fast as he can go,
And no thanks to the hand that tied him so.
He should have put a better knot in the reins."
 "Alas," this John said, "Alan, for Christ's pains,
Put down your sword, and I'll put mine down too.
A roe can't run, by God, the way I do.

He can't shake both of us, he won't be able.
God's heart, why didn't you put him in the stable?
God, Alan, you're a fool! Look what you've done!"

Hell bent away these hapless scholars run
Straight toward the fen, Alan, and with him John.
The miller, when he saw that they were gone,
Took of their flour half a bushel or so
And told his wife to knead it into dough.
"I think these students had their fears," he said,
"But a miller can beat a scholar, head for head,
For all his knowledge. Let them go their way!
Look, where they go! Yes, let the children play.
They'll work before they catch him, I'll be bound!"

These luckless students ran and thrashed around
With "Whoa! Whoa! Stand! This way! Behind, keep
      clear!
You go and whistle, and I'll hold him here!"
To cut it short, until the very night
They could not, though they worked with all their
      might,
Lay hands upon their nag, he ran so fast,
Until they caught him in a ditch at last.

Weary and wet as a cow is in the rain
Alan, and with him John, came back again.
"A curse," said John, "on the day that I was born!
Now we'll be in for ribbing and for scorn.
Our meal is stolen, men will call us 'fool,'
Yes, both the provost and our friends at school,
And specially the miller, damn the day."

With Bayard the horse in hand along the way
Back to the mill, thus John moaned in his ire.
He found the miller sitting by his fire,
For it was night. No farther could they go,
But begged him for the love of God to show
Some comfort and some shelter for their penny.

The miller answered them, "If there is any,

Such as it is, you two shall have your part.
My house is small, but with your scholar's art
You can by syllogisms make a place
A mile wide out of twenty feet of space.
See if there's room in this place for us each,
Or as your way is, puff it up with speech."

"Now, by St. Cuthbert, always a bright word,
Simon," said John. "Well answered! I have heard
'A man must always take one of two things,
Such as he finds, or else such as he brings.'
But specially, and this I beg you most,
Get us some meat and drink, make cheer, good
    host,
And we will pay in full, you understand.
A man can't lure a hawk with empty hand.
Look, here's our silver, ready to be spent."

His daughter off to town the miller sent
For ale and bread, and roasted them a goose,
And tied their horse, no more to wander loose.
In his own room he made them up a bed
With sheets and Chalon blankets neatly spread
Not more than ten or twelve feet from his own.
His daughter in the same room slept alone,
All by herself, in another bed close by.
It was the best that could be done—and why?
There were no roomier quarters, that was clear.
They talked and ate their supper with good cheer,
And pulled hard on the strong ale, as seemed best.
And when the midnight came, they went to rest.

This miller was well oiled by now. His head,
He had drunk so much, was pale instead of red.
He hiccups, and his voice comes through his nose
As if he had a cold. To bed he goes,
And with him goes his wife, jolly and gay,
Light in the head and frisking like a jay

So well her merry whistle had been wet.
Under the footboard of their bed they set
The cradle, where the child could nurse and rock.
And when they finish all that's in the crock
The daughter goes to bed; when she is gone
To bed goes Alan and to bed goes John.
And that was all—they did not need a drug.

   This sleeping miller had so plied the jug
He snorted like a horse, nor did he mind
What might be happening to his tail behind.
His wife kept up a counterbass in style.
You could have heard them snore for half a mile.
The wench snored with them, too, for company.

   Alan, who listened to this melody,
Poked John and said, "Are you sleeping through this
    row?
Have you ever heard such music before now?
Here's a fine service to wind up the day
Between them all! I hope they burn away
With itch. Did ever such a racket rend
A poor man's ears? The best of a bad end
I'll give them, though. I see I'll have no rest
All the long night; no matter, it's for the best.
For, John, by all the wealth of church or bench,
If I can work it, I'm going to lay that wench.
The law itself some easement offers us,
For John, there is a maxim that goes thus:
If in one point of law a man's aggrieved,
Then in some other he shall be relieved.
Our corn is stolen; that we can't gainsay,
And we've been in a bad fix this whole day.
Now since my loss is past all cancellation,
I will accept instead some compensation.
By the soul of God," he said, "it shall be so."

   "Alan," this John replied, "think twice! You know

This miller is a dangerous man," he said.
"And if he wakes and jumps up out of bed
He may do both of us an injury."

"I hold him," Alan answered, "a mere flea."
He rose, and toward the wench began to creep.
This wench lay stretched out flat and fast asleep.
He got so near she could not bat an eye
Before it was too late to raise a cry.
To cut the story short, they were at one.
Now make hay, Alan, and we'll turn to John.

This John lay quiet for a moment or so.
He brooded to himself, and nursed his woe.
"This is a wicked prank, and no escape.
I see that I'm no better than an ape.
My pal, here, for his troubles and his harms
Has got the miller's daughter in his arms.
He took a chance, and now his needs are fed
While like a sack of chaff I lie in bed.
People will joke about this exploit soon,
And I'll pass for a fool and a poltroon.
I'll rise and take my chance too, come what may,
For 'nothing venture, nothing have,' they say."
He rose, and to the cradle cautiously
He went, and picked it up, and quietly
He put it by his bed's foot on the floor.

Soon after this the good wife ceased to snore.
She went out for a leak, and coming back,
She missed the cradle. She felt first on one tack,
Then on another, but cradle there was none.
"Mercy," she said, "I've almost been undone!
I almost got into the students' bed.
Eh, bless me, then I would have been ill sped!"
And on she gropes until her fingers find
The cradle and the bed, and in her mind
She had no thought of anything but good,
For there right by the bed the cradle stood,

And since the night was dark, she could not see,
But by the student crawled in trustfully,
And lay quite still, and would have gone to sleep.
Presently John the student, with a leap,
Pitched into this good woman. Year in, year out,
She had not had for long so merry a bout,
For hard and deep he went; he thrust like mad.

    Such was the jolly life these students had
Until the cocks were tuning up their choir
For the third time. Alan began to tire
As dawn came near, for he had worked all night.
"Molly," he whispered, "it will soon be light.
I can't stay any longer at your side.
But sweetheart, always, though I walk or ride,
I am your own forever, till I die."

    "Now, darling, go," said Molly, "and good-by.
But wait, I'm going to tell you something still.
On the way home, as you go past the mill,
Stop at the door, and there, right in behind,
A good half-bushel loaf of bread you'll find.
Kneaded it was and baked from your own meal,
The very same I helped my father steal.
And now God keep you safe, sweetheart, God keep—"
And she was almost in a state to weep.

    Alan got up. "Before it's day, I ought
To crawl in with my crony here," he thought,
And promptly felt the cradle with his hand.
"I'm all turned round, I don't know where I stand.
My head is fuzzy with my work tonight.
By God, I haven't got my bearings right.
The cradle makes it certain I've gone wrong.
Here's where the miller and his wife belong,"
And as the devil would have it, groped his way
Straight to the bed in which the miller lay,
And in with John, or so he thought, he eased him,
And lay down by the miller instead, and seized him

Around the neck, and speaking softly, said:
"Wake up, you John, wake up, you dull swine's head!
Listen, for Christ's soul, to some noble sport,
For, by St. James, although it has been short,
Flat on her back, three times in this one night,
I've rolled the miller's daughter, while for fright,
You lay here!"

        "Have you so," the miller said,
"False thief? God's dignity, you shall be dead!
Traitor! You dared abuse a daughter of mine,
False scholar, and she comes of such a line?"
And he seized Alan by the Adam's-apple,
And Alan desperately began to grapple
With him, and let him have it on the nose,
And down the miller's chest a red stream flows
And on the floor, with nose smashed and teeth broke
They heave and roll like two pigs in a poke,
And up they get and down again they go
Till on a stone the miller stubbed his toe
And took a backward tumble on his wife,
Who had no notion of this frenzied strife,
For she had quickly dozed off with this John
Who had not slept all night for what went on;
But with the fall her eyes popped open wide,
And "Holy cross of Bromholm, help!" she cried.
"Into thy hands, O Lord—on thee I call!
Wake, Simon! Fiends and devils on me fall!
My ribs are burst. Help! I'm as good as dead.
Someone is on my belly and my head.
Help, Simkin, for the wicked students fight!"
  This John sprang up as quickly as he might
And here and there along the walls he fumbled
To find a staff; and out she also tumbled
And knew the right nooks better than he could,
And by the wall she found a stick of wood,

And saw a tiny glimmering of light
Where through a crack the moon was shining bright,
And by this glint of light she saw the two,
But could not tell for certain who was who
Except for something pale that she made out.
Seeing this thing of white, she had no doubt
It was a nightcap that the student wore.
Closer and closer with her stick she bore,
Thinking to hit this Alan a good bop,
And fetched the miller one on his bald top.
He went down with a yelp, "Ow, I am dying!"
These students beat him up and left him lying,
And quickly dressed and got their meal and horse
And set out promptly on their homeward course,
And at the mill they found, as Molly had said,
Well-baked, their good half-bushel loaf of bread.

  So this proud miller got himself a beating,
And lost his labor, what with all his cheating,
And paid for every bit they had to sup,
Alan and John, who soundly beat him up.
His wife got hers, so did his daughter too.
This comes of the cheating that false millers do!
True are the words of this old proverb still:
"Let him not look for good whose works are ill,"
For tricked himself shall every trickster be.
And now may God, throned high in majesty,
Bring us, both great and small, into His glory!
Thus I have paid the Miller with my story.

Prologue to the Cook's Tale

For joy the cook of London, all the while
The Reeve was telling of the students' guile,
Felt just as though his back were being scratched.
"Christ's blood," he said, "this miller was dispatched
To a shrewd end for hospitality!
King Solomon in his tongue said prudently,
'Not every man into your household bring,'
For offering shelter is a ticklish thing.
Before he offers privacy and room,
A man should have some notion as to whom!
Now God, I pray you, give me grief and care
If ever since my name was Roger Ware[1]
I heard of a miller better set to work!
A wicked joke he suffered in the murk!

   "We mustn't, God forbid, stop now; that's clear.
And therefore if you will vouchsafe to hear
A tale from me, who am only a poor man,
I'll tell you a little prank, as well as I can,
That happened in our city."

                      Our Host said,
"Tell, Roger, and make it good, for you have bled
The juice from many a pasty, and you have sold
Many a pie that has been hot and cold
Twice over, and you have received Christ's curse
From many a pilgrim who has fared the worse
From parsley you have served with fatted goose,
For in your shop there's many a fly goes loose.

---

[1]The name, or names, "Roger Ware of London, Cook" and "Roger Knight de Ware, Cook," appear in legal records of Chaucer's time.

Now tell on, Roger. You have a noble name!
And don't be angry; take it as a game.
By way of sport a true word may be said!"

    "Right you are," answered Roger, "by my head!
But as the Flemings say, 'True jest, no jest.'
So, Harry Bailly, take it for the best
Yourself; don't let my tale get under your skin
Although it deals with the keeper of an inn.
I'll wait a while and let you cool your wits.
Before we part, I promise, we'll be quits."
He laughed to show that he was in good cheer,
And then he told his tale, as you shall hear.

    [Chaucer finished only fifty-odd lines of the Cook's
Tale, which, had it been completed, would evidently have
belonged to the same genre as the Miller's Tale and
Reeve's Tale. After the opening sequence, Knight's Tale,
Miller's Tale, Reeve's Tale, and the fragment of the
Cook's Tale, a gap occurs. The reader should always
remember that Chaucer did not even approach complet-
ing the whole design he set himself in *The Canterbury
Tales*. The next fragment, by current scholarly arrange-
ment, draws attention to the Lawyer.]

   ঙ৯ঙ৯ ঙ৯ঙ৯ ঙ৯ঙ৯ ঙ৯ঙ৯ ঙ৯ঙ৯ ঙ৯ঙ৯ ঙ৯ঙ৯ ঙ৯ঙ৯ ঙ৯ঙ৯ ঙ৯ঙ৯

The Words of the Host to the Company

Our Host became aware that the bright sun
A quarter of his daily arc had run
Above the horizon, and half an hour and more;
And though not deeply versed in learned lore
He knew at least it was the eighteenth day
Of April, that is harbinger to May;
And noticed that the shadow of each tree
Had stretched out till it had the same degree

Of length as the upright body from which it fell;
And therefore by the shadow he could tell
That Phoebus, who was shining clear and bright,
Had climbed to forty-five degrees in height;
And for that day and in that latitude
It was ten o'clock, he was driven to conclude,
And suddenly he swung his horse around.

"Now sirs," he said, "to one and all I sound
A warning: this day is a quarter gone.
What, for the love of God and of St. John,
Lose just as little time as ever you may.
Time, sirs, is always ebbing, night and day,
And slips from us, with the hidden hours we take
To sleep, and with our heedlessness awake,
Even as the stream that never turns again
Descending from the mountain to the plain.
As Seneca and many wise men hold,
Lost time is more to be bewailed than gold.
'We can regain,' he says, 'lost property,
But loss of time destroys us utterly.'
It will not come again, for hope or dread,
Once gone, no more than Malkyn's maidenhead
When she has lost it in her wantonness.
We mustn't rot this way in idleness.

"Sir Lawyer, as you hope to win a cause,
Tell us a story, as your promise was.
By free consent you are subject to abide
Judgment in this case as I shall decide.
Discharge your promise now to everyone,
And then at least your duty will be done."

"Host," he replied, "so be it. I assent.
To break a promise is not my intent.
A promise is a debt. I'll gladly pay
My full pledge; that's the best that I can say.
The laws we give to others, by all right,
We ought to keep ourselves, and not to slight.

So says the book. Yet none the less I find
I have no profitable tale in mind
But Chaucer, though he's ignorant enough,
And though his rhyme and meter are but rough,
Has told it in such English as he can
Long since, a fact well known to many a man.
And if he has not told a story, brother,
In one book, he has told it in another!
More lovers have been blessed with his attentions,
One or another place, than Ovid mentions
In his *Epistles,* that are very old.
Why should I tell a tale already told?
Of Ceyx and Alcione when young
He told the tale, and since then he has sung
Of all these noble women and lovers too,
If you will look his good-sized volume through,
The Legend, as it's called, of Cupid's Saints.
There may be found, with their true love's complaints,
Lucrece, deep-wounded; Thisbe of Babylon;
Phyllis turned to a tree for Demophon;
Dido drawing her sword for the falsity
Of her Aeneas; and Hermione,
And Deianeira and Hypsipyle,
And Ariadne's island in the sea;
Leander for the sake of Hero drowned;
The tears of Helen, and the woe profound
Briseis suffered, and you, Laodamia;
Your cruelty is there too, Queen Medea,
Your little children hanging by the throat
For your false Jason! And he takes full note,
Penelope, Hypermnestra, and Alcestis,
That your true womanhood among the best is!
But Chaucer writes no word—in truth, not he—
Of such a foul example as Canace
Who sinfully loved her brother. And say I,
On each and every such foul story, fie!

Nor does he speak of Apollonius
Of Tyre, in which the King Antiochus
Bereft his daughter of her maidenhead,
Throwing her on the pavement. Never was read
A tale more horrible. Chaucer, therefore,
Taking full counsel with himself, forbore
To write in any tale of his narration
Such an unnatural abomination![1]
Nor will I undertake one, if I may!
  "But for my tale, what shall I do this day?
I would not be like those Pierides
(You'll find them in the *Metamorphoses*)
Changed into magpies when they aped the Muses.
But none the less, a fig for all excuses!
Although my plain fare follows his sublime.
I'll speak in prose, and let him have his rhyme."
  With this the Lawyer, in his serious way,
Began his tale, as you shall hear straightway[2]

Prologue to the Lawyer's Tale

O poverty, sharp state of hard misfortune!
With thirst, with cold, with hunger sorely tried!
Such is your shame no help will you importune,
Yet if you ask for none, your needs gape wide
And of themselves lay bare what you would hide.

[1] Chaucer is taking a dig at his contemporary, Gower, who did tell the "accursed" stories in question.

[2] It looks as though Chaucer had originally meant the Lawyer to tell a story in prose, but the Lawyer's Tale as in fact we have it is an elaborate and formal narrative in the seven-line rhyme-royal stanza.

For very need you must, whatever you would,
Borrow or beg or steal your livelihood!

You blame Christ, and you cry out bitterly
He misapportions worldly wealth; you fall
In envy of your neighbor, sinfully;
You say that you have little, and he has all.
"Sometime for certain he will hear the call
Of reckoning," you say, "when on the coals
His tail burns for not helping needy souls."

Give ear to the pronouncements of the wise:
"Better be dead than live poor and abject!"
"You are a thing your neighbor will despise!"
Be poor, and say good-by to all respect!
On still another wise man's words reflect:
"Evil are all the poor man's days," they warn.
Take care, then, lest you fall upon that thorn!

If you are poor, you have your brother's hate,
And all your friends will give you a wide berth.
O you rich merchants, prosperous of estate,
You prudent people, men of wealth and worth,
You never throw a loser! There's no dearth
Of sevens in your bag, you lords of chance!
Come Christmas, you can lead a merry dance!

From sea and land alike your gain accrues.
You know, you men of wisdom, all the lore
Of kingdoms. You are fathers of the news
And rumors, whether it be of peace or war.
Right now I should not have a tale in store
But that a merchant, dead this many a year,
Told me a story once that you shall hear.

[This prologue is no doubt intended to be characteristic of the Lawyer in its formality and sententiousness. Certainly it is characteristic of Chaucer. The conventional purple of the rhetoric suggests an earlier manner than the best realistic dialogue and detail of Chaucer's full maturity; but the purple is thin and fades quickly in favor of proverbs, dice, humor, and hard worldly wisdom.

The Lawyer's Tale itself is a sustained piece of elaborate rhetoric, likely enough first written before he conceived *The Canterbury Tales* and later adapted and brought into the plan. It purports to be an historical account of Constance, daughter of the Roman emperor, but belongs to a cycle current in folklore and known as the story of the "calumniated wife." Constance is married to the sultan of Syria, who, with his "barons and lieges," is converted as a condition of the contract. At the wedding banquet, by the machinations of the sultan's mother, the sultan and the other converts are killed. Constance is put alone in a boat with clothes, money, and provisions. She prays to the cross of Christ:

> O shining altar, happy, holy cross,
> Red with the Lamb's blood, mercifully free,
> That washed the world of the old iniquity,
> From the fiend keep me, and from his talons keep,
> That day when I shall perish in the deep!

Constance in her ship is driven to heathen Northumbria, in England, where she converts the local constable and his wife, Hermengyld, who protect her. A knight falls in love with Constance, and when she will not yield kills Hermengyld and accuses Constance of the murder. She is exculpated by a miracle when in King Alla's court the knight is struck dead in the act of swearing her guilt on a "British book of the Gospels." Constance marries Alla, and again becomes the victim of treachery by a royal husband's mother. Donegild, Alla's mother, sends false word to the king, while he is fighting the Scots, that Constance has given birth to a monster. She then forges an order that Constance be cut adrift again in the same boat. After further trials and divine interpositions, Constance is finally reunited with her father the emperor, her husband Alla, and their son. The Lawyer's tone is fervently edifying; Chaucer's poetry frequently responds with beautiful and genuine accent to the occasions for piety with which the story provides him. But on the whole the story interested and excited the Host more, perhaps, than it would most modern readers.]

Epilogue to the Lawyer's Tale

Promptly our Host, when the Lawyer's tale was done,
Rose in his stirrups. "Good people, everyone,
This was the kind of story that we need!
God's bones," he said, "Sir Parish Priest, proceed,
Give us a tale, as you said you would before.
You learned men, I see, have much in store
Of profit to us, by God's dignity!"

    At this the Parson answered him, "Bless me!
What ails the man, so sinfully to swear?"

    Our Host replied, "Oho, a Jankin there?
I smell a Lollard[1] in the wind," said he.
"Good people," said our Host, "listen to me!
Just wait, for, by God's passion, we shall hear
Some kind of sermon from this Lollard here."

    "No, by my father's soul, he shall not preach,
Nor gloss a text," the Shipman said, "nor teach!
We all believe in the great God," said he.
"This man will stir up some perplexity,

---

[1] A name applied to the followers of John Wycliffe. "Jankin" was a contemptuous name for a priest.

Or sow tares in the clean field of our corn.
And therefore, Host, before he starts, I warn,
In my own jolly person I shall tell
A story, and clank you all so merry a bell
That none will sleep in this whole company.
But I'll not talk about philosophy
Nor phislyas[1] nor highbrow terms of law.
There is but little Latin in my craw."

[The Shipman's Prologue or Lawyer's Epilogue is a fragment of uncertain position in *The Canterbury Tales*. It may not have been meant for the Shipman. It was very likely Chaucer's intention to cancel it in his progressive rearrangements of his unfinished work. Since it is good Chaucer and carries on the interplay among the pilgrims, it ought not to be lost.

The story that now stands in the manuscripts as the Shipman's Tale was itself probably first meant for one of the other pilgrims, very likely the Wife of Bath. The speaker remarks at the outset that wives are expensive, and that "the innocent husband, although he is the one who pays, has to clothe *us* richly for his own vanity," a remark hardly consistent with the Shipman as narrator. The tale itself, though amusing in plot, does not represent Chaucer at quite his liveliest execution of scene and suspense. It concerns a merchant, "who was rich, and on that account considered wise." The merchant has a wife and a friend who is a monk, "Don John," an "outrider," like the Monk in the Prologue, permitted to range beyond the cloister on visits of inspection to monastic properties. The wife, in a private conversation with Don John, accuses her husband of stinginess and begs him to lend her a hundred francs. Don John quietly borrows the sum from

[1]The word "phislyas" remains unexplained. Manuscript copyists may have garbled the term Chaucer intended, or Chaucer may have deliberately put a nonsense word or a mangled form of some actual word in the speaker's mouth to suggest his want of education.

the merchant and is rewarded with the wife's favor while her husband is away on a business journey to Bruges. When the time for repayment comes, the monk tells the merchant that he has left the hundred francs with his wife to be returned. The merchant has to be content with her protest that she will repay him in other ways. "You have slacker debtors than I!" He begs her for the future to take better care of property that he leaves in her charge.

> And so I end my tale, and may God send
> Credit enough to serve us to life's end!]

The Words of the Host to the Shipman and Prioress

"Well told, by the Lord's body!" said our Host.
"Long may you voyage up and down the coast,
Noble Sir Skipper, and anchor in the roads!
God give this monk bad years, a thousand loads!
Aha, good people! Look out for such a scrape!
This monk, he turned the man into an ape,
And, by St. Augustine, his wife as well!
Let no more monks come in, wherever you dwell!
    "But on now. Let us look about and see
Who shall speak next among this company."
Then courteously as if he were a maid,
"My lady Prioress, were I not afraid,"
He said, "that I might trouble you or grieve,
My thought would be this, always by your leave,
That next among us it is you who should
Tell us a tale, if so be that you would.
Will you vouchsafe to do so, lady dear?"
    "Gladly," she said, and told as you shall hear.

Prologue to the Prioress's Tale

"O Lord, our Lord, how marvelously thy name
Is spread abroad through this wide world," said she.
"Not only are thy praise and precious fame
Wrought on the earth by men of dignity,
But children's mouths proclaim thine excellency,
For often the mere suckling at the breast
Thy bounty and thy praise will manifest.

"Wherefore in praise, after my best endeavor,
Of thee and the white lily that in her hour
Brought thee to birth, and is a maid forever,
A story shall I tell, though with no power
To increase her honor, she the unsoiled flower
Who in herself is honor; they are one;
Soul's blessing, and root of mercy, next her Son.

"O Mother and Maiden both, in mercy lavish,
O bush unburned, burning in Moses' sight,
That down from the very Deity didst ravish
Through thy humility in thee to alight
The Spirit that cheered thy heart, when by his might
The Father's wisdom was conceived in thee,
Help me to tell it to thy dignity!

"Lady, thy bounty and thy regalness,
Thy virtue and thy great humility
There is no tongue nor knowledge can express,
For often, Lady, before men pray to thee
Thou comest first in thy benignity

And through thy prayers thou makest the way clear
To guide us to thy Son, to thee so dear.

"So weak, O happy Queen, is all my art
To show forth thine exceeding worthiness
I cannot bear the weight upon my heart,
But as a child of twelve months' age or less
Who scarcely can a single word express,
Just so I fare, and so to thee I pray
Direct this song of you that I shall say."

The Prioress's Tale

In a great city of Asia, right among
Good Christian people, once there used to be
A ghetto, kept by a local lord who wrung
Foul profit from it, and wretched usury,
Hateful to Christ and to his company.
And through the street men freely rode or went;
At either end was nothing to prevent.

A little school of Christian people stood
Down at the farther end, in which there were
A crowd of children, born of Christian blood,
That in the school sat learning year by year
The kind of lessons that were usual there;
They learned to sing and read, that is to say,
As little children do in their small way.

Among these children was a widow's son
Of seven years, who off to school would fare
Each day, his little studies just begun;
And when he saw the image anywhere

Of Christ's dear mother, it was his custom there,
As he was taught, to kneel down and repeat
His *Ave* as he went along the street.

Her little son this widow had so taught
Our blessed Lady to honor and to please,
A lesson that in nowise he forgot,
For to a good child learning comes with ease.
But when I think of matters such as these,
St. Nicholas always stands before my gaze,
Who honored Christ even in his earliest days.

And as this little child sat studying
His little book, his primer, he could hear
The children at their books of anthems sing
The *Alma Redemptoris*. He drew as near,
Step after step, as he could get for fear,
And listened word by word and note by note
Until he knew the opening verse by rote.

What all this Latin meant he could not say,
For he was tender in his years, and young.
But he began to beg a friend one day
To tell him what it meant in his own tongue,
Or why this anthem was so often sung.
To explain all this and set his mind at ease
He begged him many times on his bare knees.

His friend, who was an older boy than he,
Answered, "This song, as I have heard them say,
Was made about our blessed Lady, she
Most gracious ever, to honor her, and pray
That she will be our help in our last day.
But this is all the light I have to throw;
I'm studying music; grammar I hardly know."

"And was this song made up in reverence
Of Christ's dear mother?" said this innocent one.
"Now certainly, with all my diligence,
I'll learn it before Christmastide is gone.
Punish me when my primer isn't done
Or beat me thrice an hour though they do,
To honor our Lady I'll learn it all right through."

Homebound, his schoolmate taught him privately
Each day, until he knew it all by rote,
And then he sang it well and openly,
Word after word, and true to every note!
Twice every day the song came from his throat;
Schoolward and homeward he would not forget,
For on the mother of Christ his mind was set.

This little child, as I have said, throughout
The ghetto passing, never would forego
To lift his voice, and happily to shout
"O alma redemptoris," both to and fro.
The sweetness of Christ's mother had pierced so
Into his heart that for her grace to pray
He could not stop from singing on his way.

The serpent, our first foe, who has his nest
Of hornets in Jews' hearts, puffed up and said,
"O Hebrew people, is it for the best
That a mere boy, just as he likes, should tread
Your street, and bring contempt upon your head,
And sing to such a purpose, for a cause
That is against the reverence of your laws?"

From this time on the cursed Jews conspired
This innocent boy out of the world to chase.
A murderer for their purposes they hired

Who in an alley had a secret place,
And as he went by at his childish pace,
This Jew seized on him, and held him fast, and slit
His neck, and threw his body in a pit.

Into a privy they threw the boy, I say,
A place in which these Jews purged their entrails.
O cursed people, unchanged since Herod's day,
What think you that your foul design avails?
Murder will out, for certain; it never fails,
The more so where the honor of God's name
May spread! The blood cries on your deed of shame!

O martyr, wedded to virginity,
Now may you sing, while following evermore
The white celestial Lamb, of whom—said she—
St. John the Evangelist in Patmos bore
His witness, saying that they who go before
This Lamb of God, singing a song all fresh,
Are such as knew no woman in the flesh.

Waiting and watching all the livelong night
This widow sat, poor soul, but nothing brought
Her little child; and hence, when it grew light,
Her face all pale with fear and anxious thought,
She looked for him at school, and elsewhere sought,
Until at least she learned that he had passed
Along the ghetto, and was seen there last.

With mother's pity in her breast enclosed,
She went, as if she were half out of mind,
To every spot where it could be supposed
She had some likelihood her child to find,
And to Christ's mother, who is meek and kind
She cried, and so at last it came about
Among the cursed Jews she sought him out.

She asked and pleaded with a piteous eye,
And every Jew that lived in all that place
She questioned whether her child had not come by.
They answered, "No"; but Jesus by his grace
So moved her mind that soon she found the trace,
For at the spot, seeking her child, she cried
Where in the pit they had thrown him, close beside.

O great God, whose perfection is extolled
By praise of innocents, here shows thy might!
This gem of chastity, this emerald
And ruby of martyrdom, unstained and bright,
Where, with his throat cut, he lay prone and slight,
The *Alma Redemptoris* began to sing
So loud that the whole place began to ring!

The Christians in amazement, as they went
Along the street, came wondering at this thing.
And quickly for the magistrate they sent.
He came without a moment's tarrying,
And praised the Lord Christ, who is heaven's king,
His mother also, honor of mankind.
The Jews he told them then to take and bind.

They gathered up this child, and solemnly
Toward a near abbey set out to convey
His body in procession, mournfully,
While still he sang his song along the way.
Swooning beside the bier his mother lay.
Scarcely could all the people who were there
This second Rachel from his body tear.

The magistrate at once put every Jew
To death with torment and with shamefulness.
He spared not one that of this murder knew.
He would not palter with such wickedness.

"He that deserves ill, he shall have no less,"
And so he ordered that wild horses draw
Their flesh, and then he hanged them by the law.

Upon his bier, before the altar placed,
This martyr lay while mass was being said,
And then the abbot and his monks made haste
To bury him; and while their fingers shed
The drops of water, though he lay as dead,
Still the child spoke, sprinkled with holy water,
And sang *"O alma redemptoris mater!"*

At this the abbot, who was a holy man,
As monks are holy, or at least should be,
Pleaded with this young martyr, and began
To implore him, saying, "Dear child, enlighten me,
By virtue of the Holy Trinity,
How you can sing thus, when to my poor eye
Your throat is cut, unless my senses lie."

"My throat is cut clear down to the neck-bone,"
This child said. "Such is the nature of mankind
I should have died long since by that alone.
But it is written in books, as you may find,
That Christ will have his glory kept in mind,
And for the worship of his mother dear
I still may sing *'O alma,'* loud and clear.

"As well as I knew how, the sweet renown
Of Christ's dear mother, mercy's well and spring,
I loved, and when the time came to lay down
My life, she came to me and bade me sing
This anthem in my hour of perishing;
And then it seemed that after I had sung
She laid a grain of pearl upon my tongue.

"And so I sing, and sing I must, indeed,
In honor always of that blessed Maid,
Until some hand has taken away the seed
Of pearl that here upon my tongue she laid.
'My little child,' she said, 'be not afraid,
For I will come for you when they have taken
This grain away; you shall not be forsaken.' "

This holy monk, as it befitted most,
This abbot caught his tongue and took the grain,
And quietly the child gave up the ghost.
But when this miracle had been made plain,
The abbot's tears ran down like salty rain,
And flat he fell, face downward on the ground,
And lay as still as if he had been bound.

The monks upon the stone floor also lay,
Weeping, and praising her that men hold dear,
Christ's mother; and then they rose and went their way,
And carried off this martyr from his bier;
And in a tomb of marble white and clear
Enclosed his little body, young and sweet.
Where he is now, God grant that we may meet!

Young Hugh of Lincoln, you who were also
Murdered by Jews accursed, notoriously,
For it was but a little while ago,
Pray for us, in our fitful errancy,
We sinful folk, that God will mercifully,
In honor of her that Christ our Saviour bore,
Multiply mercy to us evermore!

꙰ ꙰ ꙰ ꙰ ꙰ ꙰ ꙰ ꙰ ꙰ ꙰

Prologue to "Sir Topaz"

This miracle so sobered every man
That it was truly wonderful to see,
Until our good Host presently began
To joke, and for the first time looked at me.
"What kind of creature have we here?" said he.
"Eyes always on the ground, I see, by habit.
I think you must be looking for a rabbit.

"Come here, look up, give us a cheerful eye!
Now sirs, make way. Let this man have a place.
He's shaped around the middle as well as I,
A puppet for any woman to embrace
In a fond arm, so small, so fair of face!
Judging by looks, I'd say that he's an elf,
Riding along there always by himself!

"Make yourself heard, as others here have made.
Tell us a merry story." "Host, although
You may regard yourself as ill repaid,"
I answered, "not a story do I know
Except a rhyme that I learned long ago."
"Good," he replied. "His manner makes it clear
This is some exquisite thing that we shall hear."

[Chaucer's tale of "Sir Thopas" is a parody of the old
ballads and romances. The literary features that he bur-
lesques ought to be sufficiently obvious. Sir Thopas would
do well enough as a parody of some strains that the
Romantic poets and their successors cultivated. People
who listen to ballads on discs will not be unfamiliar with

some of the rhyme tags and turns of conventional rhetoric
that Chaucer makes fun of, not without an affectionate
ear for their music and their charm even while he reduces
them to absurdity. Chaucer added to the amusement of
his contemporaries by representing his hero as one of
the Flemish knights whose pretensions to fashionable
chivalry were ridiculed at the English court.]

Sir Topaz

Listen, my lords, and with consent
I'll tell you a tale of merriment
    As welcome as ever was
Of a noble knight on prowess bent
In combat and in tournament.
    His name was Sir Topaz.

Born was he in a far country,
In Flanders, over across the sea,
    Poperyng was the place;
His father a man of high degree
Who was the lord of that country
    By birth and by God's grace.

This child became a doughty knight.
As fine wheat bread his face was white,
    His lips were red as a rose;
Like scarlet dye his cheeks were bright;
I tell you, and with truth I write,
    He had a shapely nose.

Well could he hunt for the wild deer
And hawk beside the river clear

His goshawk gray on his wrist.
He was an archer without peer,
And as for wrestling, far or near,
    Never the prize he missed.

Saffron his hair, his beard the same
That clear down to his girdle came,
    His shoes of Cordovan leather;
Of Bruges his brown hose bore the name
His robe, of stuff like scarlet flame,
    Cost plenty altogether!

Many a maiden bright in her bower
Pines for him as a paramour
    When sleep should guard her bed.
No lecher he, but chaste and pure,
Though sweeter than the bramble flower
    Whose haws are round and red.

Now it befell upon a day,
As tell you truthfully I may,
    Sir Topaz forth would ride.
He mounted on his dapple gray
And with a slim lance took his way,
    A long sword by his side.

Into the woods his course he pressed
In which was many a wild beast,
    In truth, both buck and hare,
And as he rode, by north, by east,
He met, or nearly met at least,
    A deal of woe and care.

There herbs and herblets deck the dale,
Ginger and licorice, without fail,
    And gillyflowers by scores,

And nutmeg good to season ale,
Whether the same be fresh or stale,
  Or put in chests indoors.

There sing these birds, none will gainsay,
Such as the woodpecker and jay,
  So merry a sound to hear.
The throstle too poured out his lay,
And the wood dove on a flowering spray,
  She sang both loud and clear.

All when he heard the throstle sing
Sir Topaz fell in love-longing,
  And like a madman rode he.
So sweated his steed with galloping
That he was wet enough to wring;
  His good sides were all bloody.

Then soon this knight so weary was
For galloping over the soft grass,
  His high heart in a pother,
That down he laid him in that place
To do his horse a little grace,
  And gave him some good dry fodder.

"Bless me now, O Saint Marie!
What ails this love to pounce on me
  And bind me till I hurt?
I dreamed all night in a fantasy
An elf queen should my mistress be
  And sleep beneath my shirt.

"I'll love an elf queen, for so 'tis;
No earthly woman worthy is
    As mate for me to take
      In town;

All other women I forsake
And to an elf queen off I'll make
    Over both dale and down."

He climbed his saddle flesh and bone
And galloped over stile and stone
    An elf queen forth to see,
Till long he had ridden and long had gone
And found in a region lost and lone
    The land of Faërie
      So wild;
For in that country there was none
Who dared to come to him, not one,
    Though woman it be or child.

Until a giant grim and gaunt
Appeared, by name Sir Elephant,
    A man of dangerous deed.
"Now, knight, by the great god Termagant,
Deliver yourself from this my haunt
    Or I will slay your steed
      With mace.
        Here is the queen of Faërie
        With tabor and flute and minstrelsy.
        Her dwelling is this place."

[Chaucer did not finish "Sir Thopas"; he did not even recount the impending combat between the knight and Sir Olifaunt. Little will be lost by allowing the Host to interrupt him somewhat earlier than he does in Chaucer's text.]

The Host's Interruption of "Sir Topaz"

"No more," our Host said, "for God's dignity!
No more of this, for you have rendered me
So weary of your downright silliness
That as I pray the Lord my soul to bless,
Your filthy nonsense makes my poor ears ache!
This is pure doggerel. The devil take,
I tell you, such a rhyme as this," said he.

    "Why so?" I answered. "Why break in on me
More than another man, and stop me so
From offering you the best rhyme that I know?"

    "By God," said he, "since plainly, in a word,
Your filthy rhyming isn't worth a turd!
You're doing nothing at all but wasting time!
Sir, one word for it: you shall no longer rhyme.
Alliterate for us, let's see how that goes,
Or let us have at least a thing in prose
In either a merry or edifying vein."

    "Gladly," I answered him, "by God's dear pain!
I'll let you hear a little thing in prose
To satisfy your taste, as I suppose,
Or you are hard to please if it should fail!
It is a virtuous and a moral tale,
Though different people different versions know
And variously tell, as I shall show.

    "Consider: you know that each Evangelist
Who tells us of the sufferings of Christ
Does not say all things as his fellows do;
Their meaning none the less is wholly true,
And all of them are in accord in sense
Though in their records we find difference.

For some of them say more and some say less
The pity of his passion to express.
I speak of Mark and Matthew, Luke and John;
Beyond a doubt their meaning is all one.
And so, milords, bear with me, I beseech,
And if you think I deviate in my speech,
As for example if a larger store
Of proverbs than you may have heard before
Within this little treatise here I scatter,
To heighten the point and substance of my matter,
And though the selfsame words I may not say
That you have heard, to all of you I pray
Do not reproach me; for in gist and sense
You will not find a shade of difference
From the small book I follow as I write
This merry tale. And therefore do not slight
My words, but hear out what I have to say,
And do not interrupt my tale, I pray."

[Chaucer's "little thing in prose," a translation from
the French of the "little treatise" known as the "Book
of Melibeus and Dame Prudence," occupies twenty-four
double-columned pages in Robinson's text. It would be
found anything but a "merry tale" by modern readers;
it belongs to a time when edification and entertainment
had not parted company. The story exalts the wisdom
and patience of Dame Prudence, wife of Melibeus, and
especially the virtue of forgiveness, which Prudence in-
duces her husband to practice toward his enemies when
they repent. "For doubtless," to quote the concluding
words, "if we are sorry and repent of the sins and tres-
passes which we have committed in the sight of our
Lord God, he is so magnanimous and merciful that he
will forgive us our sins, and bring us to the bliss that
has no end."]

Epilogue to the Tale of Melibeus

When I had told this little tale of mine
Of Melibeus, and Prudence the benign,
Our Host declared, "As I'm a Christian man,
I swear by the body of St. Madrian
I'd rather than a barrel of good ale
That Godelief, my wife, had heard this tale!
This patience, she has heard of no such fad,
Such as this wife of Melibeus had.
By God's bones, when I set about to drub
My servants, she brings out the biggest club,
And 'Kill the dogs,' she cries, 'kill the last one,
And break them, break their backs and every bone!'
And if a neighbor in church will not incline
And make his bow to this good wife of mine
Or is so bold as not to give her place,
When she comes home she throws it in my face,
And cries, 'You false poltroon, avenge your wife!
God's bones, I see I'll have to take your knife
And you shall have my distaff and go spin!'
Night, day, or anytime, she will begin:
'Alas, that ever my fate,' she'll say, 'took shape
To marry a milksop and a cowardly ape
That anyone at all can overbear.
Stand up for your wife's rights? You wouldn't dare!'
    "That's how I live, unless I want to fight,
And out the door I take myself, come night,
Or otherwise I'm lost, that is unless
I'd be a wild lion for foolhardiness.
She'll make me wipe some neighbor off the slate
One of these days, and leave me to my fate,

For I'm a dangerous man with knife in hand
Even though I lack the courage to withstand
My wife. She has big arms, as he shall learn,
Upon my word, who does her an ill turn.
But let us drop this matter for the present.
   "And now, Milord the Monk," he said, "look pleasant,
For you shall tell a tale, by all that's true!
Look, Rochester stands yonder, in full view.
Keep the ball rolling, don't break up our game.
But, my good Lord, I do not know your name.
Milord Don John? Don Thomas can it be,
Or else Don Alban? And what family
Do you belong to by your father's kin?
I swear to God you have a handsome skin!
You crop in noble pastures," said our Host.
"You are no penitent, no shrunken ghost.
You are an officer, a commanding man,
Some cellarer, some worthy sacristan,
As I'm a Christian! By the day of doom,
You live a lord's life when you are at home!
No novice you, no threadbare cloisterer;
You are a wise and wily governor,
And judging by your bone and flesh, I'd say
A man who has also lived well in his day.
Confusion, I pray God, be visited
On the man who put religion in your head!
You would have made a lusty cock, all right.
Given a license equal to your might
To procreate with all your inclination,
You would have multiplied your generation!
What are you doing, wearing a monk's cope?
God give me grief, but if I were the pope
Not only you but every lusty man
Should have a wife, according to my plan,
Shaved crown or not. For the whole world is forlorn!

The church from procreation takes the corn;
We laity are thin husks to rely on.
A puny tree will yield a puny scion.
Our offshoots are so spindling and so slender
On this account, they hardly can engender,
And that's the reason that our wives assay
You monkish men, for you can better pay
The dues of Venus than we of feeble loin,
For God knows you don't pay them in small coin!
But don't be angry, though I joke this way.
True words are spoken in jest, Milord, they say."

   This worthy Monk took it all patiently,
And said, "I will proceed as diligently
As ever I can, always in decency,
To tell you a story, or two of them, or three,
And if you care to listen, I'll relate
St. Edward's life; or first I will narrate
Some tragedies, such as I have to tell.
I have a hundred of them in my cell.
By tragedy is meant a kind of story,
Such as old books preserve, of how from glory
And the renown of high prosperity
From time to time men tumble wretchedly
And end forlorn; and they are done in verse
Of six feet as a rule—hexameters
Men call them. Many are in prose as well,
Or various forms; this is enough to tell.

   "Now listen, if it pleases you to hear.
But first I ask you, though I do not steer
Always in proper order through these things,
Each in his time, popes, emperors, or kings,
As men in written histories may find,
But put them some before and some behind
As I recall them now, although confused,
I pray you let my ignorance be excused."

[The Monk proceeds to relate the fall from eminence and power of Lucifer, Adam, Samson, Hercules, Nebuchadnezzar, Belshazzar, Xenobia, King Peter of Cyprus; Chaucer's own contemporary, Bernabo Visconti; Ugolino of Pisa, for whom Chaucer's source is Dante; Nero, Holofernes; Antiochus Epiphanes, king of Syria; Alexander the Great, Julius Caesar, and Croesus. The last stanza from the tragedy of Croesus contains one of Chaucer's memorable images, and will serve to illustrate the eight-line stanza in which the Monk's tale is composed.

    Thus hanged at last was Croesus, the proud king,
    His royal throne to him of no avail.
    Tragedy is no other kind of thing,
    Nor can lament in singing nor bewail,
    Except that Fortune ever will assail
    With unexpected stroke realms that are proud;
    For when men trust in her, then will she fail
    And cover up her bright face with a cloud.]

The Knight's Interruption of the Monk's Tale

"Stop!" cried the Knight. "No more of this, good sir!
You have said plenty, and much more, for sure,
For only a little such lugubriousness
Is plenty for a lot of folk, I guess.
I say for me it is a great displeasure,
When men have wealth and comfort in good measure,
To hear how they have tumbled down the slope.
The opposite is a solace and a hope
As when a man begins in low estate
And climbs the ladder and grows fortunate,
And stands there firm in his prosperity.
That is a welcome thing, it seems to me,

And of such things it would be good to tell."

"Well said," our Host declared. "By St. Paul's bell,
You speak the truth; this Monk's tongue is too loud.
He told how fortune covered with a cloud—
I don't know what-all; and of tragedy
You heard just now, and it's no remedy,
When things are over and done with, to complain.
Besides, as you have said, it is a pain
To hear of misery; it is distressing.
Sir Monk, no more, as you would have God's blessing.
This company is all one weary sigh.
Such talking isn't worth a butterfly,
For where's the amusement in it, or the game?
And so, Sir Monk, or Don Pierce by your name,
I beg you heartily, tell us something else.
Truly, but for the jingling of your bells
That from your bridle hang on every side,
By Heaven's King, who was born for us and died,
I should long since have tumbled down in sleep,
Although the mud had never been so deep,
And then you would have told your tale in vain;
For certainly, as these learned men explain,
When all his hearers turn their backs away
It doesn't matter what a man may say.
I know well I shall have the essence of it
If anything is told here for our profit.
A tale of hunting, sir, pray share with us."

"No," said the Monk, "I'll not be frivolous.
Another shall tell a tale, as I have told."

Then spoke our Host, with a rude voice and bold,
And said to the Nun's Priest, "Come over here,
You priest, come hither, you Sir John, draw near!
Tell us a thing to make our spirits glad.
Be cheerful, though the jade you ride is bad.
What if your horse is miserable and lean?
If he will carry you, don't care a bean!

Keep up a joyful heart, and look alive."
  "Yes, Host," he answered, "as I hope to thrive,
If I weren't merry, I know I'd be reproached."
And with no more ado his tale he broached,
And this is what he told us, every one,
This precious priest, this goodly man, Sir John.

The Nun's Priest's Tale

Once a poor widow, aging year by year,
Lived in a tiny cottage that stood near
A clump of shade trees rising in a dale.
This widow, of whom I tell you in my tale,
Since the last day that she had been a wife
Had led a very patient, simple life.
She had but few possessions to content her.
By thrift and husbandry of what God sent her
She and two daughters found the means to dine.
She had no more than three well-fattened swine,
As many cows, and one sheep, Moll by name.
Her bower and hall were black from the hearth-flame
Where she had eaten many a slender meal.
No dainty morsel did her palate feel
And no sharp sauce was needed with her pottage.
Her table was in keeping with her cottage.
Excess had never given her disquiet.
Her only doctor was a moderate diet,
And exercise, and a heart that was contented.
And if she did not dance, no gout prevented;
No apoplexy had destroyed her head.
She never drank wine, whether white or red.
She served brown bread and milk, loaves white or black,
Singed bacon, all this with no sense of lack,

And now and then an egg or two. In short,
She was a dairy woman of a sort.
  She had a yard, on the inside fenced about
With hedges, and an empty ditch without,
In which she kept a cock, called Chanticleer.
In all the realm of crowing he had no peer.
His voice was merrier than the merry sound
Of the church organ grumbling out its ground
Upon a saint's day. Stouter was this cock
In crowing than the loudest abbey clock.
Of astronomy instinctively aware,
He kept the sun's hours with celestial care,
For when through each fifteen degrees it moved,
He crowed so that it couldn't be improved.
His comb, like a crenelated castle wall,
Red as fine coral, stood up proud and tall.
His bill was black; like polished jet it glowed,
And he was azure-legged and azure-toed.
As lilies were his nails, they were so white;
Like burnished gold his hue, it shone so bright.
This cock had in his princely sway and measure
Seven hens to satisfy his every pleasure,
Who were his sisters and his sweethearts true,
Each wonderfully like him in her hue,
Of whom the fairest-feathered throat to see
Was fair Dame Partlet. Courteous was she,
Discreet, and always acted debonairly.
Companionable, she bore herself so fairly
Since she could boast of being seven nights old
The heart of Chanticleer was in her hold
As if she had him locked up, every limb.
He loved her so that all was well with him.
It was a joy, when up the sun would spring,
To hear them both together sweetly sing,
"My love has gone to the country, far away!"
For as I understand it, in that day

The animals and birds could sing and speak.
   Now as this cock, one morning at daybreak,
With each of the seven hens that he called spouse,
Sat on his perch inside the widow's house,
And next him fair Dame Partlet, in his throat
This Chanticleer produced a hideous note
And groaned like a man who is having a bad dream;
And Partlet, when she heard her husband scream,
Was all aghast, and said, "Soul of my passion,
What ails you that you groan in such a fashion?
You're always a sound sleeper. Fie, for shame!"
   And Chanticleer awoke and answered, "Dame,
Take no offence, I beg you, on this score.
I dreamt, by God, I was in a plight so sore
Just now, my heart still quivers from the fright.
Now God see that my dream turns out all right
And keep my flesh and body from foul seizure!
I dreamed I was strutting in our yard at leisure
When there I saw, among the weeds and vines,
A beast, he was like a hound, and had designs
Upon my person, and would have killed me dead.
His coat was not quite yellow, not quite red,
And both his ears and tail were tipped with black
Unlike the fur along his sides and back.
He had a small snout and a fiery eye.
His look for fear still makes me almost die.
This is what made me groan, I have no doubt."
   "For shame! Fie on you, faint heart!" she burst out.
"Alas," she said, "by the great God above,
Now you have lost my heart and all my love!
I cannot love a coward, as I'm blest!
Whatever any woman may protest,
We all want, could it be so, for our part,
Husbands who are wise and stout of heart,
No blabber, and no niggard, and no fool,
Nor frightened of every weapon or sharp tool.

No braggart either, by the God above!
How dare you say, for shame, to your true love
That there is anything you ever feared?
Have you no man's heart, when you have a beard?
Alas, and can a nightmare set you screaming?
God knows there's only vanity in dreaming!
Dreams are produced by such unseemly capers
As overeating; they come from stomach vapors
When a man's humors aren't behaving right
From some excess. This dream you had tonight,
It comes straight from the superfluity
Of your red choler, certain as can be,
That causes people terror in their dreams
Of darts and arrows, and fire in red streams,
And of red beasts, for fear that they will bite,
Of little dogs, or of being in a fight;
As in the humor of melancholy lies
The reason why so many a sleeper cries
For fear of a black bull or a black bear
Or that black devils have him by the hair.
Through other humors also I could go
That visit many a sleeping man with woe,
But I will finish as quickly as I can.

"Cato, that has been thought so wise a man,
Didn't he tell us, 'Put no stock in dreams'?
Now, good sir, when we fly down from our beams,
For God's sake, go and take a laxative!
On my salvation, as I hope to live,
I give you good advice, and no mere folly:
Purge both your choler and your melancholy!
You mustn't wait or let yourself bog down,
And since there is no druggist in this town
I shall myself prescribe for what disturbs
Your humors, and instruct you in the herbs
That will be good for you. For I shall find
Here in our yard herbs of the proper kind

For purging you both under and above.
Don't let this slip your mind, for God's own love!
Yours is a very choleric complexion.
When the sun's in the ascendant, my direction
Is to beware those humors that are hot.
Avoid excess of them; if you should not,
I'll bet a penny, as a true believer,
You'll die of ague, or a tertian fever.
A day or so, if you do as I am urging,
You shall have worm-digestives, before purging
With fumitory or with hellebore
Or other herbs that grow here by the score;
With caper-spurge, or with the goat-tree berry
Or the ground-ivy, found in our yard so merry.
Peck 'em up just as they grow, and eat 'em in!
Be cheerful, husband, by your father's kin!
Don't worry about a dream. I say no more."

    "Madame," he answered, "thanks for all your lore.
But still, to speak of Cato, though his name
For wisdom has enjoyed so great a fame,
And though he counseled us there was no need
To be afraid of dreams, by God, men read
Of many a man of more authority
Than this Don Cato could pretend to be
Who in old books declare the opposite,
And by experience they have settled it,
That dreams are omens and prefigurations
Both of good fortune and of tribulations
That life and its vicissitudes present.
This question leaves no room for argument.
The very upshot makes it plain, indeed.

    "One of the greatest authors that men read
Informs us that two fellow travelers went,
Once on a time, and with the best intent,
Upon a pilgrimage, and it fell out
They reached a town where there was such a rout

Of people, and so little lodging space,
They could not find even the smallest place
Where they could both put up. So, for that night,
These pilgrims had to do as best they might,
And since they must, they parted company.
Each of them went off to his hostelry
And took his lodging as his luck might fall.
Among plow oxen in a farmyard stall
One of them found a place, though it was rough.
His friend and fellow was lodged well enough
As luck would have it, or the destiny
That governs all us creatures equally.
And so it happened, long before the day,
He had a dream as in his bed he lay.
He dreamed that his parted friend began to call
And said, 'Alas, for in an ox's stall
This night I shall be murdered where I lie.
Come to my aid, dear brother, or I die.
Come to me quickly, come in haste!' he said.
He started from his sleep, this man, for dread,
But when he had wakened, he rolled back once more
And on this dream of his he set no store,
Dismissing it as a vain thing, unconcerned.
Twice as he slept that night the dream returned,
And still another and third time his friend
Came in a dream and said, 'I have met my end!
Look on my wounds! They are bloody, deep, and wide.
Now rise up early in the morningtide
And at the west gate of the town,' said he,
'A wagon with a load of dung you'll see.
Have it arrested boldly. Do as bidden,
For underneath you'll find my body hidden.
My money caused my murder, truth to tell,'
And told him each detail of how he fell,
With piteous face, and with a bloodless hue.
And do not doubt it, he found the dream was true,

For on the morrow, as soon as it was day,
To where his friend had lodged he made his way.
No sooner did he reach this ox's stall
Than for his fellow he began to call.

"Promptly the stableman replied, and said,
'Your friend is gone, sir. He got out of bed
And left the town as soon as day began.'

"At last suspicion overtook this man.
Remembering his dreams, he would not wait,
But quickly went and found at the west gate,
Being driven to manure a farmer's land
As it might seem, a dung cart close at hand
That answered the description every way,
As you yourself have heard the dead man say.
And he began to shout courageously
For law and vengeance on this felony.
'My friend was killed this very night! He lies
Flat in this load of dung, with staring eyes.
I call on those who should keep rule and head,
The magistrates and governors here,' he said.
'Alas! Here lies my fellow, done to death!'

"Why on this tale should I waste further breath?
The people sprang and flung the cart to ground
And in the middle of the dung they found
The dead man, while his murder was still new.

"O blessed God, thou art so just and true,
Murder, though secret, ever thou wilt betray!
Murder will out, we see it day by day.
Murder so loathsome and abominable
To God is, who is just and reasonable,
That he will never suffer it to be
Concealed, though it hide a year, or two, or three.
Murder will out; to this point it comes down.

"Promptly the magistrates who ruled that town
Have seized the driver, and put him to such pain.
The stableman as well, that under strain

Of torture they were both led to confess
And hanged by the neck-bone for their wickedness.
"Here's proof enough that dreams are things to dread!
And in the same book I have also read,
In the next chapter that comes after this—
I don't speak idly, by my hope of bliss—
Two travelers who for some reason planned
To cross the ocean to a distant land
Found that the wind, by an opposing fate,
Blew contrary, and forced them both to wait
In a fair city by a harborside.
But one day the wind changed, toward eventide,
And blew just as it suited them instead.
Cheerfully these travelers went to bed
And planned to sail the first thing in the morning.
But one of them received a strange forewarning.
A marvel it was, for while asleep he lay
He dreamed a curious dream along toward day.
He dreamed that a man appeared at his bedside
And told him not to sail, but wait and bide.
'Tomorrow,' he told the man, 'if you set sail,
You shall be drowned. I have told you my whole tale.'
He woke, and of this warning he had met
He told his friend, and begged him to forget
His voyage, and to wait that day and bide.
His friend, who was lying close at his bedside,
Began to laugh, and told him in derision,
'I am not so flabbergasted by a vision
As to put off my business for such cause.
I do not think your dream is worth two straws!
For dreams are but a vain absurdity.
Of apes and owls and many a mystery
People are always dreaming, in a maze
Of things that never were seen in all their days
And never shall be. But I see it's clear
You mean to waste your time by waiting here.

I'm sorry for that, God knows; and so good day.'
With this he took his leave and went his way.
But not the half his course had this man sailed—
I don't know why, nor what it was that failed—
When by an accident the hull was rent
And ship and man under the water went
In full view of the vessels alongside
That had put out with them on the same tide.
Now then, fair Partlet, whom I love so well,
From old examples such as these I tell
You'll see that none should give too little heed
To dreams; for I say seriously, indeed,
That many a dream is too well worth our dread.

    "Yes, in St. Kenelm's life I have also read—
He was the son of Cynewulf, the king
Of Mercia—how this Kenelm dreamed a thing.
One day, as the time when he was killed drew near,
He saw his murder in a dream appear.
His nurse explained his dream in each detail,
And warned him to be wary without fail
Of treason; yet he was but seven years old,
And therefore any dream he could but hold
Of little weight, in heart he was so pure.
I'd give my shirt, by God, you may be sure,
If you had read his story through like me!

    "Moreover, Partlet, I tell you truthfully,
Macrobius writes—and by his book we know
The African vision of great Scipio—
Confirming dreams, and holds that they may be
Forewarnings of events that men shall see.
Again, I beg, look well at what is meant
By Daniel's story in the Old Testament,
Whether *he* held that dreams are vanity!
Read also about Joseph. You shall see
That dreams, or some of them—I don't say all—
Warn us of things that afterward befall.

Think of the king of Egypt, Don Pharaoh;
Of his butler and his baker think also,
Whether they found that dreams have no result.
Whoever will search through kingdoms and consult
Their histories reads many a wondrous thing
Of dreams. What about Croesus, Lydian king—
Didn't he dream he was sitting on a tree,
Which meant he would be hanged? Andromache,
The woman who was once great Hector's wife,
When the day came that he must lose his life,
The very night before his blood was spilled
She dreamed of how her husband would be killed
If he went out to battle on that day.
She warned him; but he would not heed nor stay.
In spite of her he rode out on the plain,
And by Achilles he was promptly slain.
But all that story is too long to tell,
And it is nearly day. I must not dwell
Upon this matter. Briefly, in conclusion,
I say this dream will bring me to confusion
And mischief of some sort. And furthermore,
On laxatives, I say, I set no store,
For they are venomous, I'm sure of it.
I do not trust them! I like them not one bit!
   "Now let's talk cheerfully, and forget all this.
My pretty Partlet, by my hope of bliss,
In one thing God has sent me ample grace,
For when I see the beauty of your face,
You are so scarlet-red about the eye,
It is enough to make my terrors die.
For just as true as *In principio*
Mulier est hominis confusio—
And Madame, what this Latin means is this:
'Woman is man's whole comfort and true bliss'—
Feeling you soft at night, and I beside you,
Although it's true, alas, I cannot ride you

Because our perch is built so narrowly,
I am then so full of pure felicity
That I defy whatever sort of dream!"
    And day being come, he flew down from the beam
And with him his hens fluttered, one and all;
And with a "cluck, cluck" he began to call
His wives to where a kernel had been tossed.
He was a prince, his fears entirely lost.
Before the morning reached the hour of prime
He'd trodden Partlet for the twentieth time.
Grim as a lion he strolled to and fro,
Strutting about well up on either toe;
He would not deign to set foot on the ground.
"Cluck, cluck," he said, whenever he had found
A kernel, and his wives came running all.
Thus royal as a monarch in his hall
I leave to his delights this Chanticleer,
And presently the sequel you shall hear.
    After the month in which the world began,
The month of March, when God created man,
Had passed, and when the season had run through
Since March came in just thirty days and two,
It happened that Chanticleer, in all his pride,
His seven hens parading at his side,
Lifted his eyes, beholding the bright sun,
Which in the sign of Taurus had then run
Twenty and one degrees and somewhat more,
And knew by instinct, not by learned lore,
It was the hour of prime. He raised his head
And crowed with lordly voice. "The sun," he said,
"Forty and one degrees and more in height
Has climbed the sky. Partlet, my world's delight,
Hear all these birds, how happily they sing,
And see the pretty flowers, how they spring.
With solace and with joy my spirits dance!"
But suddenly he met a sore mischance,

For in the end joys ever turn to woes.
Quickly the joys of earth are gone, God knows,
And could a rhetorician's art indite it,
He'd be on solid ground if he should write it
In a chronicle, as true notoriously!
Now every wise man, listen well to me.
This story is as true, I undertake,
As is the book of Lancelot of the Lake
On which the women set so great a store.
Now to my matter I will turn once more.

    A sly iniquitous fox, with black-tipped ears,
Who had lived in the neighboring wood for some three
      years,
His fated fancy swollen to a height,
Had broken through the hedges that same night
Into the yard where in his pride sublime
Chanticleer with his seven wives passed the time.
Quietly in a bed of herbs he lay
Till it was past the middle of the day,
Waiting his hour on Chanticleer to fall
As gladly do these murderers, one and all,
Who lie in wait, concealed, to murder men.
O murderer, lurking traitorous in your den!
O new Iscariot, second Ganelon,
False hypocrite, Greek Sinon, who brought on
The utter woe of Troy and all her sorrow!
O Chanticleer, accursed be that morrow
When to the yard you flew down from the beams!
That day, as you were well warned in your dreams,
Would threaten you with dire catastrophe.
But that which God foresees must come to be,
As there are certain scholars who aver.
Bear witness, any true philosopher,
That in the schools there is great altercation
On this point, which has kept in disputation
A hundred thousand scholars, man for man.

I cannot sift it down to the pure bran
As can the sacred Doctor, Augustine,
Boëthius, or Bishop Bradwardine,
Whether God's high foreknowledge so enchains me
I needs must do a thing as it constrains me—
"Needs must"—that is, by plain necessity;
Or whether a free choice is granted me
To do it or not do it, either one,
Though God must know all things before they are
    done;
Or whether his foresight nowise can constrain
Except contingently, as some explain;
I will not labor such a high concern.
My tale is of a cock, as you shall learn,
Who took his wife's advice, to his own sorrow,
And walked out in the yard that fatal morrow.
Women have many times, as wise men hold,
Offered advice that left men in the cold.
A woman's counsel brought us first to woe
And out of Paradise made Adam go
Where he was living merrily and at ease.
But since I don't know whom I may displease
By giving women's words an ill report,
Pass over it; I only spoke in sport.
Books tell of it that you can read or skim in.
You'll soon discover what they say of women.
I'm telling you the cock's words, and not mine.
Harm in no woman at all can I divine.

    Happily bathing where the sand was dry
Lay Partlet, with her sisters all near by,
And Chanticleer, as regal as could be,
Sang merrily as the mermaid in the sea.
Physiologus the bestiary declares
Truly that they can sing the merriest airs.
And so it happened, as he fixed his eye
Among the herbs upon a butterfly,

He caught sight of this fox who crouched there low.
He felt no impulse then to strut or crow,
But cried "cucock!" and gave a fearful start
Like one who has been frightened to the heart.
A beast by instinct, should he chance to see
His opposite, at once desires to flee
Even the first time that it meets his eye.

   This Chanticleer, no sooner did he spy
The fox than promptly enough he would have fled.
But "Where are you going, kind sir?" the fox said.
"Are you afraid of me, who am your friend?
Truly, I'd be a devil from end to end
If I should mean you harm or villainy.
I have not come to invade your privacy.
In truth, the only reason that could bring
This visit of mine was just to hear you sing.
Beyond a doubt, you have as fine a voice
As any angel who makes heaven rejoice.
For feeling in your music you excel
Boëthius or any who sing well.
Milord your father once—and may God bless
His soul—your noble mother too, no less,
Have been inside my house, to my great ease,
And verily sir, I should be glad to please
You also. But for singing, I declare
As I enjoy my eyes, that precious pair,
I never heard a man save you so sing
As did your father when the night took wing.
Straight from the heart, in truth, came all his song.
To make his voice more resonant and strong
He'd strain until he shut his either eye,
So loud and lordly would he make his cry,
And stand up on his tiptoes therewithal
And stretch his neck till it grew long and small.
He had such excellent discretion, too,
That either his singing, all the region through,

Or else his wisdom, no one could surpass.
I've read the tale in *Don Burnel the Ass*,
In verse, of how once on a time a cock
Was hit on the leg by a priest who threw a rock
When he was young and foolish; and for this
He caused the priest to lose his benefice.
But no comparison, in all truth, lies
Between your sire, so prudent and so wise,
And that shrewd cock, for all his subtlety.
Sing, sir! Show me, for holy charity,
If you can match your father, that wise man!"

 Blind to all treachery, Chanticleer began
To beat his wings, like one who cannot see
The traitor, ravished by his flattery.

 Alas, you lords, about your court there slips
Many a flatterer with deceiving lips
Who pleases more abundantly, I fear,
Than he who speaks the plain truth to your ear.
Read in Ecclesiastes, you will see
What flatterers are. Lords, heed their treachery!

 This Chanticleer stood tiptoe at full height.
He stretched his neck, he shut his eyelids tight,
And he began to crow a lordly note.
The fox, Don Russell, seized him by the throat
At once, and on his back bore Chanticleer
Off toward his den that in the grove stood near,
For no one yet had threatened to pursue.

 O destiny, that no man may eschew!
Alas, that Chanticleer flew from the beams!
Alas, that Partlet took no stock in dreams!
And on a Friday happened this mischance!

 Venus, whose pleasures make the whole world dance,
Since Chanticleer was ever your true servant,
And of your rites with all his power observant
For pleasure rather than to multiply,
Would you on Friday suffer him to die?

Geoffrey, dear master of the poet's art,
Who when your Richard perished by a dart
Made for your king an elegy so burning,
Why have I not your eloquence and learning
To chide, as you did, with a heart so filled,
Fridays? For on a Friday he was killed.
Then should I show you how I could complain
For Chanticleer in all his fright and pain!

In truth, no lamentation ever rose,
No shriek of ladies when before its foes
Ilium fell, and Pyrrhus with drawn blade
Had seized King Priam by the beard and made
An end of him—the *Aeneid* tells the tale—
Such as the hens made with their piteous wail
In their enclosure, seeing the dread sight
Of Chanticleer. But at the shrillest height
Shrieked Partlet. She shrieked louder than the wife
Of Hasdrubal, whose husband lost his life
When Roman hands burned Carthage, and her state
Of torment and of frenzy was so great
She willfully chose the fire for her part,
Leaped in, and burned herself with steadfast heart.

Unhappy hens, you shrieked as when for pity,
While tyrant Nero put to flames the city
Of Rome, rang out the shriek of senators' wives
Because their husbands had all lost their lives;
This Nero put to death these innocent men.
But I will come back to my tale again.

Now this good widow and her daughters heard
These woeful hens shriek when the crime occurred,
And sprang outdoors as quickly as they could
And saw the fox, who was making for the wood
Bearing this Chanticleer across his back.
"Help, help!" they cried. They cried, "Alas! Alack!
The fox, the fox!" and after him they ran,
And armed with clubs came running many a man.

Ran Coll the dog, and led a yelping band;
Ran Malkyn, with a distaff in her hand;
Ran cow and calf, and even the very hogs,
By all the frenzied barking of the dogs
And men's and women's shouts so terrified,
Ran till it seemed their hearts would burst inside;
They squealed like fiends in the pit, with none to still
    them.
The ducks quacked as if men were going to kill them.
The geese for very fear flew over the trees.
Out of the beehive came the swarm of bees.
Ah! Bless my soul, the noise, by all that's true,
So hideous was that Jack Straw's retinue
Made never a hubbub that was half so shrill
Over a Fleming they were going to kill
As people made that day over the fox.
They brought brass trumpets, and trumpets made of box,
Of horn, of bone, on which they blew and squeaked,
And those who were not blowing whooped and shrieked.
It seemed as if the very heavens would fall!
    Now hear me, you good people, one and all!
Fortune, I say, will suddenly override
Her enemy in his very hope and pride!
This cock, as on the fox's back he lay,
Plucked up his courage to speak to him and say.
"God be my help, sir, but I'd tell them all,
That is, if I were you, 'Plague on you fall!
Go back, proud fools! Now that I've reached the wood,
I'll eat the cock at once, for all the good
Your noise can do. Here Chanticleer shall stay.'"
    "Fine!" said the fox. "I'll do just what you say."
The cock, as he was speaking, suddenly
Out of his jaws lurched expeditiously,
And flew at once high up into a tree.
And when the fox saw that the cock was free,

"Alas," he said, "alas, O Chanticleer!
So far as I have given you cause for fear
By seizing you and bearing you away,
I've done you wrong, I am prepared to say.
But, sir, I did it with no ill intent.
Come down, and I shall tell you what I meant.
So help me God, it's truth I'll offer you!"

    "No, no," said he. "We're both fools, through and
       through.
But curse my blood and bones for the chief dunce
If you deceive me oftener than once!
You'll never again by flattery persuade me
To sing and wink my eyes, by him that made me.
For he that willfully winks when he should see,
God never bless him with prosperity!"

    "Ah," said the fox, "with mischief may God greet
The man ungoverned, rash, and indiscreet
Who babbles when to hold his tongue were needful!"

    Such is it to be reckless and unheedful
And trust in flattery. But you who hold
That this is a mere trifle I have told,
Concerning only a fox, or a cock and hen,
Think twice, and take the moral, my good men!
For truly, of whatever is written, all
Is written for our doctrine, says St. Paul.
Then take the fruit, and let the chaff lie still.
Now, gracious God, if it should be your will,
As my Lord teaches, make us all good men
And bring us to your holy bliss! Amen.

ᷚᷚᷚ ᷚᷚᷚ ᷚᷚᷚ ᷚᷚᷚ ᷚᷚᷚ ᷚᷚᷚ ᷚᷚᷚ ᷚᷚᷚ ᷚᷚᷚ ᷚᷚᷚ

Epilogue to the Nun's Priest's Tale

"Sir Chaplain," said our good Host, "by St. Paul's,
A blessing on your britches and your balls!
This was a merry tale of Chanticleer.
But, on my word, if you were secular,
You'd make a cock to tread the hens all right!
If with your strength you have the appetite,
You'd need some hens, according to my view;
Seven times seventeen, I think, would be too few.
Look at the sinews on this gentle priest,
What a big neck, and what a span of chest!
He peers round like a sparrowhawk in eye.
His cheeks need no brazil-wood for a dye
Or coccus grain brought in from Portugal.
Now, sir, good luck go with you for your tale!"
    And after this, with his usual good cheer,
Our Host spoke to another, as you shall hear.

[To what other pilgrim the Host spoke is impossible
to determine. Chaucer may have been laying the ground-
work for a link which he did not live to write, or the con-
cluding couplet may even be an attempt by some copyist
to patch up Chaucer's unfinished plan.

    The next group of stories presented here is not ex-
plicitly linked with any of the other Canterbury Tales.
But the group makes a coherent sequence within itself.
G. L. Kittredge viewed it as a panel, interrupted by
comic byplay, of medieval doctrine and controversy on
marriage, and called it the "Marriage Group."]

Prologue to the
Wife of Bath's Tale

"Experience, though all authority
Was lacking in the world, confers on me
The right to speak of marriage, and unfold
Its woes. For, lords, since I was twelve years old
—Thanks to eternal God in heaven alive—
I've married at church door no less than five
Husbands, provided that I can have been
So often wed, and all were worthy men.
But I was told, indeed, and not long since,
That Christ went to a wedding only once
At Cana, in the land of Galilee.
By this example he instructed me
To wed once only—that's what I have heard!
Again, consider now what a sharp word,
Beside a well, Jesus, both God and man,
Spoke in reproving the Samaritan:
'Five husbands thou hast had'—this certainly
He said to her—'and the man that now hath thee
Is not thy husband.' True, he spoke this way,
But what he meant is more than I can say
Except that I would ask why the fifth man
Was not a husband to the Samaritan?
To just how many could she be a wife?
I've never heard this number all my life
Determined up to now. For round and round
Scholars may gloze, interpret, and expound,
But plainly, this I know without a lie,
God told us to increase and multiply.
That noble text I can well understand.
My husband—this too I have well in hand—

Should leave both father and mother and cleave to me.
Number God never mentioned, bigamy,
No, nor even octogamy; why do men
Talk of it as a sin and scandal, then?
    "Think of that monarch, wise King Solomon.
It strikes me that *he* had more wives than one!
To be refreshed, God willing, would please me
If I got it half as many times as he!
He had a gift, and one of God's own giving,
For all his wives! There isn't a man now living
Who has the like. By all that I make out
On the first night this king had many a bout
With each, he was so thoroughly alive.
Blessed be God that I have married five,
And always, for the money in his chest
And for his nether purse, I picked the best.
In divers schools ripe scholarship is made,
And various practice in all kinds of trade
Makes perfect workmen, as the world can see.
Five husbands have had turns at schooling me.
Welcome the sixth, whenever I am faced
With yet another. I don't mean to be chaste
At all costs. When a spouse of mine is gone,
Some other Christian man shall take me on,
For then, says the Apostle, I'll be free
To wed, in God's name, where it pleases me.
To marry is no sin, as we can learn
From him; better to marry than to burn,
He says. Why should I care what obloquy
Men heap on Lamech and his bigamy?
Abraham was, by all that I can tell,
A holy man; so Jacob was as well,
And each of them took more than two as brides,
And many another holy man besides.
Where, may I ask, in any period,
In plain words can you show Almighty God

Forbade us marriage? Point it out to me!
Or where did he command virginity?
The Apostle, when he speaks of maidenhood,
Lays down no law. This I have understood
As well as you, milords, for it is plain.
Men may advise a woman to abstain
From marriage, but mere counsels aren't commands.
He left it to our judgment, where it stands.
Had God enjoined us all to maidenhood
Then marriage would have been condemned for good.
But truth is, if no seed were ever sown,
In what soil could virginity be grown?
Paul did not dare command a thing at best
On which his Master left us no behest.
　"But now the prize goes to virginity.
Seize it whoever can, and let us see
What manner of man shall run best in the race!
But not all men receive this form of grace
Except where God bestows it by his will.
The Apostle was a maid, I know; but still,
Although he wished all men were such as he,
It was only *counsel* toward virginity.
To be a wife he gave me his permission,
And so it is no blot on my condition
Nor slander of bigamy upon my state
If when my husband dies I take a mate.
A man does virtuously, St. Paul has said,
To touch no woman—meaning in his bed.
For fire and fat are dangerous friends at best.
You know what this example should suggest.
Here is the nub: he held virginity
Superior to wedded frailty,
And frailty I call it unless man
And woman both are chaste for their whole span.
　"I am not jealous if maidenhood outweighs
My marriages; I grant it all the praise.

It pleases, them, these virgins, flesh and soul
To be immaculate. I won't extol
My own condition. In a lord's household
You know that every vessel can't be gold.
Some are of wood, and serve their master still.
God calls us variously to do his will.
Each has his proper gift, of all who live,
Some this, some that, as it pleases God to give.

    "Virginity is a high and perfect course,
And continence is holy. But the source
Of all perfection, Jesus, never bade
Each one of us to go sell all he had
And give it to the poor; he did not say
That all should follow him in this one way.
He spoke to those who would live perfectly,
And by your leave, lords, that is not for me!
The flower of my best years I find it suits
To spend on the acts of marriage and its fruits.

    "Tell me this also: why at our creation
Were organs given us for generation,
And for what profit were we creatures made?
Believe me, not for nothing! Ply his trade
Of twisting texts who will, and let him urge
That they were only given us to purge
Our urine; say without them we should fail
To tell a female rightly from a male
And that's their only object—say you so?
It won't work, as experience will show.
Without offense to scholars, I say this,
That they were made for both these purposes,
That we may both be cleansed, I mean, and eased
Through intercourse, where God is not displeased.
Why else in books is this opinion met,
That every man should pay his wife his debt?
Tell me with what a man should hope to pay
Unless he put his instrument in play?

They were supplied us, then, for our purgation,
But they were also meant for generation.
   "But none the less I do not mean to say
That all those who are furnished in this way
Are bound to go and practice intercourse.
The world would then grant chastity no force.
Christ was a maid, yet he was formed a man,
And many a saint, too, since the world began,
And yet they lived in perfect chastity.
I am not spiteful toward virginity.
Let virgins be white bread of pure wheat-seed.
Barley we wives are called, and yet I read
In Mark, and tell the tale in truth he can,
That Christ with barley bread cheered many a man.
In the state that God assigned to each of us
I'll persevere. I'm not fastidious.
In wifehood I will use my instrument
As freely by my Maker it was lent.
If I hold back with it, God give me sorrow!
My husband shall enjoy it night and morrow
Whenever it pleases him to pay his debt.
A husband, though—I've not been thwarted yet—
Shall always be my debtor and my slave.
From tribulation he shall never save
His flesh, not for as long as I'm his wife!
I have the power, during all my life,
Over his very body, and not he.
For so the Apostle has instructed me,
Who bade men love their wives for better or worse.
It pleases me from end to end, that verse!"
   The Pardoner, before she could go on,
Jumped up and cried, "By God and by St. John,
Upon this topic you preach nobly, Dame!
I was about to wed, but now, for shame,
Why should my body pay a price so dear?
I'd rather not be married all this year!"

"Hold on," she said. "I haven't yet begun.
You'll drink a keg of this before I'm done,
I promise you, and it won't taste like ale!
And after I have told you my whole tale
Of marriage, with its fund of tribulation—
And I'm the expert of my generation,
For I myself, I mean, have been the whip—
You can decide then if you want a sip
Out of the barrel that I mean to broach.
Before you come too close in your approach,
Think twice. I have examples, more than ten!
'The man who won't be warned by other men,
To other men a warning he shall be.'
These are the words we find in Ptolemy.
Go read them right there in his *Almagest*."

"Now, Madame, if you're willing, I suggest,"
Answered the Pardoner, "as you began,
Continue with your tale, and spare no man.
Teach us young men your practice as our guide."

"Gladly, if it will please you," she replied.
"But first I ask you, if I speak my mind,
That all this company may be well inclined,
And will not take offense at what I say.
I only mean it, after all, in play.

"Now, sirs, I will get onward with my tale.
If ever I hope to drink good wine or ale,
I'm speaking truth: the husbands I have had,
Three of them have been good, and two were bad.
The three were kindly men, and rich, and old.
But they were hardly able to uphold
The statute which had made them fast to me.
You know well what I mean by this, I see!
So help me God, I can't help laughing yet
Thinking of how at night I made them sweat,
And I thought nothing of it, on my word!
Their land and wealth they had by then conferred

On me, and so I safely could neglect
Tending their love or showing them respect.
So well they loved me that by God above
I hardly set a value on their love.
A woman who is wise is never done
Busily winning love when she has none,
But since I had them wholly in my hand
And they had given me their wealth and land,
Why task myself to spoil them or to please
Unless for my own profit and my ease?
I set them working so that many a night
They sang a dirge, so grievous was their plight!
They never got the bacon, well I know,
Offered as prize to couples at Dunmow
Who live a year in peace, without repentance!
So well I ruled them, by my law and sentence,
They gladly brought me fine things from the fair,
Happy whenever I spoke with a mild air,
For God knows I could chide outrageously.

   "Now judge if I could do it properly!
You wives who understand and who are wise,
This is the way to throw dust in their eyes.
There isn't on the earth so bold a man
He can swear false or lie as a woman can.
I do not urge this course in every case,
Just when a prudent wife is caught off base;
Then she should swear the parrot's mad who tattled
Her indiscretions, and when she's once embattled
Should call her maid as witness, by collusion.
But listen, how I threw them in confusion:

   " 'Sir dotard, this is how you live?' I'd say.
'How can my neighbor's wife be dressed so gay?
She carries off the honors everywhere.
I sit at home. I've nothing fit to wear.
What were you doing at my neighbor's house?
Is she so handsome? Are you so amorous?

What do you whisper to our maid? God bless me,
Give up your jokes, old lecher. They depress me.
When I've a harmless friend myself, you balk
And scold me like a devil if I walk
For innocent amusement to his house.
You drink and come home reeling like a souse
And sit down on your bench, worse luck, and preach.
Taking a wife who's poor—this is the speech
That you regale me with—costs grievously,
And if she's rich and of good family,
It is a constant torment, you decide,
To suffer her ill humor and her pride.
And if she's fair, you scoundrel, you destroy her
By saying that every lecher will enjoy her;
For she can't long keep chastity intact
Who is from every side at once attacked.
    " 'Some want us for our wealth, so you declare,
Some for our figure, some think we are fair,
Some want a woman who can dance or sing,
Some want kindness, and some philandering,
Some look for hands and arms well turned and small.
Thus, by your tale, the devil may take us all!
Men cannot keep a castle or redoubt
Longer, you tell me, than it can hold out.
Or if a woman's plain, you say that she
Is one who covets each man she may see,
For at him like a spaniel she will fly
Until she finds some man that she can buy.
Down to the lake goes never a goose so gray
But it will have a mate, I've heard you say.
It's hard to fasten—this too I've been told—
A thing that no man willingly will hold.
Wise men, you tell me as you go to bed,
And those who hope for heaven should never wed.
I hope wild lightning and a thunderstroke
Will break your wizened neck! You say that smoke

And falling timbers and a railing wife
Drive a man from his house. Lord bless my life!
What ails an old man, so to make him chide?
We cover our vices till the knot is tied,
We wives, you say, and then we trot them out.
Here's a fit proverb for a doddering lout!
An ox or ass, you say, a hound or horse,
These we examine as a matter of course.
Basins and also bowls, before we buy them,
Spoons, spools, and such utensils, first we try them,
And so with pots and clothes, beyond denial;
But of their wives men never make a trial
Until they are married. After that, you say,
Old fool, we put our vices on display.
" 'I'm in a pique if you forget your duty
And aren't forever praising me for beauty
Or aren't at all hours doting on my face
And calling me "fair dame" in every place,
Or fail to give a feast on my birthday
To keep my spirits fresh and make me gay,
Or if all proper courtesies aren't paid
My nurse, and equally my chambermaid,
My father's kin with all his family ties—
You say so, you old barrelful of lies!
   " 'Yet just because he has a head of hair
Like shining gold, and squires me everywhere,
You have a false suspicion in your heart
Of Jenkin, our apprentice. For my part
I wouldn't have him if you died tomorrow!
But tell me this, or go and live in sorrow:
That chest of yours, why do you hide the keys
Away from me? It's my wealth, if you please,
As much as yours. Will you make a fool of me,
The mistress of our house? You shall not be
Lord of my body and my wealth at once!
No, by St. James himself, you must renounce

One or the other, if it drives you mad!
What do you gain by spying? You'd be glad
To lock me up, I think, inside your chest.
"Enjoy yourself, and go where you think best,"
You ought to say; "I won't hear tales of malice.
I know you for a faithful wife, Dame Alice."
A woman loves no man who keeps close charge
Of where she goes. We want to be at large.
Blessed above all other men was he,
The wise astrologer, Don Ptolemy,
Who has this proverb in his *Almagest:*
"Of all wise men his wisdom is the best
Who does not care who has the world in hand."
Now by this proverb you should understand,
Since you have plenty, it isn't yours to care
Or fret how richly other people fare,
For by your leave, old dotard, you for one
Can have all you can take when day is done.
The man's a niggard to the point of scandal
Who will not lend his lamp to light a candle;
His lamp won't lose although the candle gain.
If you've enough, you ought not to complain.

" 'You say, too, if we make ourselves look smart,
Put on expensive clothes and dress the part,
We lay our virtue open to disgrace.
And then you try to reinforce your case
By saying these words in the Apostle's name:
"In chaste apparel, with modesty and shame,
So shall you women clothe yourselves," said he,
"And not in rich coiffure or jewelry,
Pearls or the like, or gold, or costly wear."
Now both your text and rubric, I declare,
I will not follow as I would a gnat!

" 'You told me once that I was like a cat,
For singe her skin and she will stay at home,
But if her skin is smooth, the cat will roam.

No dawn but finds her on the neighbors calling
To show her skin, and go off caterwauling.
If I am looking smart, you mean to say,
I'm off to put my finery on display.

" 'What do you gain, old fool, by setting spies?
Though you beg Argus with his hundred eyes
To be my bodyguard, for all his skill
He'll keep me only by my own free will.
I know enough to blind him, as I live!

" 'There are three things, you also say, that give
Vexation to this world both south and north.
You add that no one can endure the fourth.
Of these catastrophes a hateful wife—
You precious wretch, may Christ cut short your life!—
Is always reckoned, as you say, for one.
Is this your whole stock of comparison,
And why from all your parables of contempt
Can luckless helpmates never be exempt?
You also liken woman's love to hell,
To barren land where water will not dwell.
I've heard you call it an unruly fire;
The more it burns, the hotter its desire
To burn up everything that burned will be.
You say that just as worms destroy a tree
A wife destroys her spouse, as they have found
Who get themselves in holy wedlock bound.'

"By these devices, lords, as you perceive,
I got my three old husbands to believe
That in their cups they said things of this sort,
And all of it was false; but for support
Jenkin bore witness, and my niece did too.
These innocents, Lord, what I put them through!
God's precious pains! And they had no recourse,
For I could bite and whinny like a horse.
Though in the wrong, I kept them well annoyed,
Or oftentimes I would have been destroyed!

First to the mill is first to grind his grain.
I was always the first one to complain,
And so our peace was made; they gladly bid
For terms to settle things they never did!

"For wenching I would scold them out of hand
When they were hardly well enough to stand.
But this would tickle a man; it would restore him
To think I had so great a fondness for him!
I'd vow when darkness came and out I stepped,
It was to see the girls with whom he slept.
Under this pretext I had plenty of mirth!
Such wit as this is given us at our birth.
Lies, tears, and needlework the Lord will give
In kindness to us women while we live.
And thus in one point I can take just pride:
I showed myself in the end the stronger side.
By sleight or strength I kept them in restraint,
And chiefly by continual complaint.
In bed they met their grief in fullest measure.
There I would scold; I would not do their pleasure.
Bed was a place where I would not abide
Feeling my husband's arm across my side
Till he agreed to square accounts and pay,
And after that I'd let him have his way.
To every man, therefore, I tell this tale:
Win where you're able, all is up for sale.
No falcon by an empty hand is lured.
For victory their cravings I endured
And even feigned a show of appetite.
And yet in old meat I have no delight;
It made me always rail at them and chide them,
For though the pope himself sat down beside them
I would not give them peace at their own board.
No, on my honor, I paid them word for word.
Almighty God so help me, if right now
I had to make my last will, I can vow

For every word they said to me, we're quits.
For I so handled the contest by my wits
That they gave up, and took it for the best,
Or otherwise we should have had no rest.
Like a mad lion let my husband glare,
He finally got the worst of the affair.

"Then I would say, 'My dear, you ought to keep
In mind how gentle Wilkin looks, our sheep.
Come here, my husband, let me kiss your cheek!
You should be patient, too; you should be meek.
Of Job and of his patience when you prate
Your conscience ought to show a cleaner slate.
He should be patient who so well can preach.
If not, then it will fall on me to teach
The beauty of a peaceful wedded life.
For one of us must give in, man or wife,
And since men are more reasonable creatures
Than women are, it follows that *your* features
Ought to exhibit patience. Why do you groan?
You want my body yours, and yours alone?
Why, take it all! Welcome to every bit!
But curse you, Peter, unless you cherish it!
Were I inclined to peddle my *belle chose*,
I could walk out dressed freshly as a rose.
But I will keep it for your own sweet tooth.
It's your fault if we fight. By God, that's truth!'

"This was the way I talked when I had need.
But now to my fourth husband I'll proceed.

"This fourth I married was a roisterer.
He had a mistress, and my passions were,
Although I say it, strong; and altogether
Stubborn and young I was, and pert in feather.
If anyone took up his harp to play,
How I could dance! I sang as merry a lay
As any nightingale when of sweet wine
I'd drunk my draft. Metellius, the foul swine,

Who beat his spouse until he took her life
For drinking wine, if I had been his wife,
He'd never have frightened me away from drinking!
But after a drink, Venus gets in my thinking,
For just as true as cold engenders hail
A thirsty mouth goes with a thirsty tail.
Drinking destroys a woman's last defense
As lechers well know by experience.

   "But, Lord Christ, when it all comes back to me,
Remembering my youth and jollity,
It tickles me to the roots. It does me good
Down to this very day that while I could
I took my world, my time, and had my fling.
But age, alas, that poisons everything
Has robbed me of my beauty and my pith.
Well, let it go! Good-by! The devil with
What cannot last! There's only this to tell:
The flour is gone, I've only chaff to sell.
Yet I'll contrive to keep a merry cheek!
But now of my fourth husband I will speak.

   "My heart was, I can tell you, full of spite
That in another he should find delight.
I paid him for this debt; I made it good.
I furnished him a cross of the same wood,
By God and by St. Joce—in no foul fashion,
Not with my flesh; but I put on such passion
And rendered him so jealous, I'll engage
I made him fry in his own grease for rage!
On earth, God knows, I was his purgatory;
I only hope his soul is now in glory.
God knows it was a sad song that he sung
When the shoe pinched him; sorely was he wrung!
Only he knew, and God, the devious system
By which outrageously I used to twist him.
He died when I came home from Jerusalem.
He's buried near the chancel, under the beam

That holds the cross. His tomb is less ornate
Than that where King Darius lies in state
And which the paintings of Appelles graced
With subtle work. It would have been a waste
To bury him lavishly. Farewell! God save
His soul and give him rest! He's in his grave.
   "And now of my fifth husband let me tell.
God never let his soul go down to hell
Though he of all five was my scourge and flail!
I feel it on my ribs, right down the scale,
And ever shall until my dying day.
And yet he was so full of life and gay
In bed, and could so melt me and cajole me
When on my back he had a mind to roll me,
What matter if on every bone he'd beaten me!
He'd have my love, so quickly he could sweeten me.
I loved him best, in fact; for as you see,
His love was a more arduous prize for me.
We women, if I'm not to tell a lie,
Are quaint in this regard. Put in our eye
A thing we cannot easily obtain,
All day we'll cry about it and complain.
Forbid a thing, we want it bitterly,
But urge it on us, then we turn and flee.
We're chary of what we hope that men will buy.
A throng at market makes the prices high;
Men set no value on cheap merchandise,
A truth all women know if they are wise.
   "My fifth, may God forgive his every sin,
I took for love, not money. He had been
An Oxford student once, but in our town
Was boarding with my good friend, Alison.
She knew each secret that I had to give
More than our parish priest did, as I live!
I told her my full mind, I shared it all.
For if my husband pissed against a wall

Or did a thing that might have cost his life,
To her, and to another neighbor's wife,
And to my niece, a girl whom I loved well,
His every thought I wouldn't blush to tell.
And often enough I told them, be it said.
God knows I made his face turn hot and red
For secrets he confided to his shame.
He knew he only had himself to blame.

   "And so it happened once that during Lent,
As I did often, to Alison's I went,
For I have loved my life long to be gay
And to walk out in April or in May
To hear the talk and seek a favorite haunt.
Jenkin the student, Alice, my confidante,
And I myself into the country went.
My husband was in London all that Lent.
I had the greater liberty to see
And to be seen by jolly company.
How could I tell beforehand in what place
Luck might be waiting with a stroke of grace?
And so I went to every merrymaking.
No pilgrimage was past my undertaking.
I was at festivals, and marriages,
Processions, preachings, and at miracle plays,
And in my scarlet clothes I made a sight.
Upon that costume neither moth nor mite
Nor any worm with ravening hunger fell.
And how so? It was kept in use too well.

   "Now for what happened. In the fields we walked,
The three of us, and gallantly we talked,
The student and I, until I told him he,
If I became a widow, should marry me.
For I can say, and not with empty pride,
I've never failed for marriage to provide
Or other things as well. Let mice be meek;
A mouse's heart I hold not worth a leek.

He has one hole to scurry to, just one,
And if that fails him, he is quite undone.
    "I let this student think he had bewitched me.
(My mother with this piece of guile enriched me!)
All night I dreamed of him—this too I said;
He was about to kill me flat in bed;
My very bed in fact was full of blood;
But still I hoped it would result in good,
For blood betokens gold, as I have heard.
It was a fiction, dream and every word,
But I was following my mother's lore
In all this matter, as in many more.
    "Sirs—let me see; what did I mean to say?
Aha! By God, I have it! When he lay,
My fourth, of whom I've spoken, on his bier,
I wept of course; I showed but little cheer,
As wives must do, since custom has its place,
And with my kerchief covered up my face.
But since I had provided for a mate,
I did not cry for long, I'll freely state.
And so to church my husband on the morrow
Was borne away by neighbors in their sorrow.
Jenkin, the student, was among the crowd,
And when I saw him walk, so help me God,
Behind the bier, I thought he had a pair
Of legs and feet so cleanly turned and fair
I put my heart completely in his hold.
He was in fact some twenty winters old
And I was forty, to confess the truth;
But all my life I've still had a colt's tooth.
My teeth were spaced apart; that was the seal
St. Venus printed, and became me well.
So help me God, I was a lusty one,
Pretty and young and rich, and full of fun.
And truly, as my husbands have all said,
I was the best thing there could be in bed.

For I belong to Venus in my feelings,
Yet have the heart of Mars in all my dealings.
From Venus come my lust and appetite,
From Mars I get my courage and my might,
Born under Taurus, while Mars stood therein.
Alas, alas, that ever love was sin!
I yielded to my every inclination
Through the predominance of my constellation;
This made me so I never could withhold
My chamber of Venus, if the truth be told,
From a good fellow; yet upon my face
Mars left his mark, and in another place.
Never, so may Christ grant me intercession,
Have I yet loved a fellow with discretion,
But always I have followed appetite,
Let him be long or short or dark or light.
I never cared, as long as he liked me,
What his rank was or how poor he might be.
      "What should I say, but when the month ran out,
This jolly student, always much about,
This Jenkin married me in solemn state.
To him I gave land, titles, the whole slate
Of goods that had been given me before;
But my repentance afterward was sore!
He wouldn't endure the pleasures I held dear.
By God, he gave me a lick once on the ear,
When from a book of his I tore a leaf,
So hard that from the blow my ear grew deaf.
Stubborn I was as a lioness with young,
And by the truth I had a rattling tongue,
And I would visit, as I'd done before,
No matter what forbidding oath he swore.
Against this habit he would sit and preach me
Sermons enough, and he would try to teach me
Old Roman stories, how for his whole life
The man Sulpicius Gallus left his wife

Only because he saw her look one day
Bareheaded down the street from his doorway.
  "Another Roman he told me of by name
Who, since his wife was at a summer's game
Without his knowledge, thereupon forsook
The woman. In his Bible he would look
And find that proverb of the Ecclesiast
Where he enjoins and makes the stricture fast
That men forbid their wives to rove about.
Then he would quote me this, you needn't doubt:
'Build a foundation over sands or shallows,
Or gallop a blind horse across the fallows,
Let a wife traipse to shrines that some saint hallows,
And you are fit to swing upon the gallows.'
Talk as he would, I didn't care two haws
About his proverbs or his stale old saws.
Set right by him I never meant to be.
I hate the man who tells my faults to me,
And more of us than I do, by your pleasure.
This made him mad with me beyond all measure.
Under his yoke in no case would I go.
  "Now, by St. Thomas, I will let you know
Why from that book of his I tore a leaf,
For which I got the blow that made me deaf.
  "He had a book, *Valerius,* he called it,
And Theophrastus, and he always hauled it
From where it lay to read both day and night
And laughed hard at it, such was his delight.
There was another scholar, too, at Rome,
A cardinal, whose name was St. Jerome;
He wrote a book against Jovinian.
The book included too Tertullian,
Chrysippus, Trotula, Abbess Héloïse
Who lived near Paris; it contained all these,
Bound in a single volume, and many a one
Besides; the Parables of Solomon

And Ovid's *Art of Love*. On such vacation
As he could snatch from worldly occupation
He dredged this book for tales of wicked wives.
He knew more stories of their wretched lives
Than those told of good women in the Bible.
No scholar ever lived who did not libel
Women, believe me; to speak well of wives
Is quite beyond them, unless it be in lives
Of holy saints; no woman else will do.
Who was it painted the lion, tell me who?
By God, if women had only written stories
Like wits and scholars in their oratories,
They would have pinned on men more wickedness
Than the whole breed of Adam can redress.
Venus's children clash with Mercury's;
The two work evermore by contraries.
Knowledge and wisdom are of Mercury's giving,
Venus loves revelry and riotous living,
And with these clashing dispositions gifted
Each of them sinks when the other is uplifted.
Thus Mercury falls, God knows, in desolation
In Pisces, which is Venus' exaltation.
And Venus falls when Mercury is raised.
Thus by a scholar no woman can be praised.
The scholar, when he's old and cannot do
The work of Venus more than his old shoe,
Then sits he down, and in his dotage fond
Writes that no woman keeps her marriage bond!

"But now for the story that I undertook—
To tell how I was beaten for a book.

"Jenkin, one night, who never seemed to tire
Of reading in his book, sat by the fire
And first he read of Eve, whose wickedness
Delivered all mankind to wretchedness
For which in his own person Christ was slain
Who with his heart's blood bought us all again.

'By this,' he said, 'expressly you may find
That woman was the loss of all mankind.'

"He read me next how Samson lost his hair.
Sleeping, his mistress clipped it off for fair;
Through this betrayal he lost both his eyes.
He read me then—and I'm not telling lies—
How Deianeira, wife of Hercules,
Caused him to set himself on fire. With these
He did not overlook the sad to-do
Of Socrates with *his* wives—he had two.
Xantippe emptied the pisspot on his head.
This good man sat as patient as if dead.
He wiped his scalp; he did not dare complain
Except to say 'With thunder must come rain.'

"Pasiphaë, who was the queen of Crete,
For wickedness he thought her story sweet.
Ugh! That's enough, it was a grisly thing,
About her lust and filthy hankering!
And Clytemnestra in her lechery
Who took her husband's life feloniously,
He grew devout in reading of her treason.
And then he told me also for what reason
Unhappy Amphiaraus lost his life.
My husband had the story of *his* wife,
Eriphyle, who for a clasp of gold
Went to his Grecian enemies and told
The secret of her husband's hiding place,
For which at Thebes he met an evil grace.
Livia and Lucilia, he went through
Their tale as well; they killed their husbands, too.
One killed for love, the other killed for hate.
At evening Livia, when the hour was late,
Poisoned her husband, for she was his foe.
Lucilia doted on her husband so
That in her lust, hoping to make him think
Ever of her, she gave him a love-drink

Of such a sort he died before the morrow.
And so at all turns husbands come to sorrow!
   "He told me then how one Latumius,
Complaining to a friend named Arrius,
Told him that in his garden grew a tree
On which his wives had hanged themselves, all three,
Merely for spite against their partnership.
'Brother,' said Arrius, 'let me have a slip
From this miraculous tree, for, begging pardon,
I want to go and plant it in my garden.'
   "Then about wives in recent times he read,
How some had murdered husbands lying abed
And all night long had let a paramour
Enjoy them with the corpse flat on the floor;
Or driven a nail into a husband's brain
While he was sleeping, and thus he had been slain;
And some had given them poison in their drink.
He told more harm than anyone can think,
And seasoned his wretched stories with proverbs
Outnumbering all the blades of grass and herbs
On earth. 'Better a dragon for a mate,
Better,' he said, 'on a lion's whims to wait
Than on a wife whose way it is to chide.
Better,' he said, 'high in the loft to bide
Than with a railing wife down in the house.
They always, they are so contrarious,
Hate what their husbands like,' so he would say.
'A woman,' he said, 'throws all her shame away
When she takes off her smock.' And on he'd go:
'A pretty woman, unless she's chaste also,
Is like a gold ring stuck in a sow's nose.'
Who could imagine, who would half suppose
The gall my heart drank, raging at each drop?
   "And when I saw that he would never stop
Reading all night from his accursed book,
Suddenly, in the midst of it, I took

Three leaves and tore them out in a great pique,
And with my fist I caught him on the cheek
So hard he tumbled backward in the fire.
And up he jumped, he was as mad for ire
As a mad lion, and caught me on the head
With such a blow I fell down as if dead.
And seeing me on the floor, how still I lay,
He was aghast, and would have fled away,
Till I came to at length, and gave a cry.
'You'd kill me for my lands? Before I die,
False thief,' I said, 'I'll give you a last kiss!'
      "He came to me and knelt down close at this,
And said, 'So help me God, dear Alison,
I'll never strike you. For this thing I've done
You are to blame. Forgive me, I implore.'
So then I hit him on the cheek once more
And said, "Thus far I am avenged, you thief.
I cannot speak. Now I shall die for grief.'
But finally, with much care and ado,
We reconciled our differences, we two.
He let me have the bridle in my hand
For management of both our house and land.
To curb his tongue he also undertook,
And on the spot I made him burn his book.
And when I had secured in full degree
By right of triumph the whole sovereignty,
And he had said, 'My dear, my own true wife,
Do as you will as long as you have life;
Preserve your honor and keep my estate.'
From that day on we'd settled our debate.
I was as kind, God help me, day and dark,
As any wife from India to Denmark,
And also true, and so he was to me.
I pray the Lord who sits in majesty
To bless his soul for Christ's own mercy dear.
And now I'll tell my tale, if you will hear."

"Dame," laughed the Friar, "as I hope for bliss,
It was a long preamble to a tale, all this!"

"God's arms!" the Summoner said, "it is a sin,
Good people, how friars are always butting in!
A fly and a friar will fall in every dish
And every question, whatever people wish.
What do you know, with your talk about 'preambling'?
Amble or trot or keep still or go scrambling,
You interrupt our pleasure."

                             "You think so,
Sir Summoner?" said the Friar. "Before I go,
I'll give the people here a chance or two
For laughs at summoners, I promise you."

"Curse on your face," the Summoner said, "curse me,
If I don't tell some stories, two or three,
On friars, before I get to Sittingborne,
With which I'll twist your heart and make it mourn,
For you have lost your temper, I can see."

"Be quiet," cried our Host, "immediately,"
And ordered, "Let the woman tell her tale.
You act like people who've got drunk on ale.
Do, Madame, tell us. That is the best measure."

"All ready, sir," she answered, "at your pleasure,
With license from this worthy Friar here."

"Madame, tell on," he said. "You have my ear."

꧁ ꧁ ꧁ ꧁ ꧁ ꧁ ꧁ ꧁ ꧁ ꧁

The Wife of Bath's Tale

In the old days when King Arthur ruled the nation,
Whom Welshmen speak of with such veneration,
This realm we live in was a fairy land.
The fairy queen danced with her jolly band

On the green meadows where they held dominion.
This was, as I have read, the old opinion;
I speak of many hundred years ago.
But no one sees an elf now, as you know,
For in our time the charity and prayers
And all the begging of these holy friars
Who swarm through every nook and every stream
Thicker than motes of dust in a sunbeam,
Blessing our chambers, kitchens, halls, and bowers,
Our cities, towns, and castles, our high towers,
Our villages, our stables, barns, and dairies,
They keep us all from seeing any fairies,
For where you might have come upon an elf
There now you find the holy friar himself
Working his district on industrious legs
And saying his devotions while he begs.
Women are safe now under every tree.
No incubus is there unless it's he,
And all they have to fear from him is shame.

It chanced that Arthur had a knight who came
Lustily riding home one day from hawking,
And in his path he saw a maiden walking
Before him, stark alone, right in his course.
This young knight took her maidenhead by force,
A crime at which the outcry was so keen
It would have cost his neck, but that the queen,
With other ladies, begged the king so long
That Arthur spared his life, for right or wrong,
And gave him to the queen, at her own will,
According to her choice, to save or kill.

She thanked the king, and later told this knight,
Choosing her time, "You are still in such a plight
Your very life has no security.
I grant your life, if you can answer me
This question: what is the thing that most of all
Women desire? Think, or your neck will fall

Under the ax! If you cannot let me know
Immediately, I give you leave to go
A twelvemonth and a day, no more, in quest
Of such an answer as will meet the test.
But you must pledge your honor to return
And yield your body, whatever you may learn."

    The knight sighed; he was rueful beyond measure.
But what! He could not follow his own pleasure.
He chose at last upon his way to ride
And with such answer as God might provide
To come back when the year was at the close.
And so he takes his leave, and off he goes.

    He seeks out every house and every place
Where he has any hope, by luck or grace,
Of learning what thing women covet most.
But he could never light on any coast
Where on this point two people would agree,
For some said wealth and some said jollity,
Some said position, some said sport in bed
And often to be widowed, often wed.
Some said that to a woman's heart what mattered
Above all else was to be pleased and flattered.
That shaft, to tell the truth, was a close hit.
Men win us best by flattery, I admit,
And by attention. Some say our greatest ease
Is to be free and do just as we please,
And not to have our faults thrown in our eyes,
But always to be praised for being wise.
And true enough, there's not one of us all
Who will not kick if you rub us on a gall.
Whatever vices we may have within,
We won't be taxed with any fault or sin.

    Some say that women are delighted well
If it is thought that they will never tell
A secret they are trusted with, or scandal.
But that tale isn't worth an old rake handle!

We women, for a fact, can never hold
A secret. Will you hear a story told?
Then witness Midas! For it can be read
In Ovid that he had upon his head
Two ass's ears that he kept out of sight
Beneath his long hair with such skill and sleight
That no one else besides his wife could guess.
He loved her well, and trusted her no less.
He begged her not to make his blemish known,
But keep her knowledge to herself alone.
She swore that never, though to save her skin,
Would she be guilty of so mean a sin,
And yet it seemed to her she nearly died
Keeping a secret locked so long inside.
It swelled about her heart so hard and deep
She was afraid some word was bound to leap
Out of her mouth, and since there was no man
She dared to tell, down to a swamp she ran—
Her heart, until she got there, all agog—
And like a bittern booming in the bog
She put her mouth close to the watery ground:
"Water, do not betray me with your sound!
I speak to you, and you alone," she said.
"Two ass's ears grow on my husband's head!
And now my heart is whole, now it is out.
I'd burst if I held it longer, past all doubt."
Safely, you see, awhile you may confide
In us, but it will out; we cannot hide
A secret. Look in Ovid if you care
To learn what followed; the whole tale is there.

  This knight, when he perceived he could not find
What women covet most, was low in mind;
But the day came when homeward he must ride,
And as he crossed a wooded countryside
Some four and twenty ladies there by chance
He saw, all circling in a woodland dance,

And toward this dance he eagerly drew near
In hope of any counsel he might hear.
But the truth was, he had not reached the place
When dance and all, they vanished into space.
No living soul remained there to be seen
Save an old woman sitting on the green,
As ugly a witch as fancy could devise.
As he approached her she began to rise
And said, "Sir knight, here runs no thoroughfare.
What are you seeking with such anxious air?
Tell me! The better may your fortune be.
We old folk know a lot of things," said she.

"Good mother," said the knight, "my life's to pay,
That's all too certain, if I cannot say
What women covet most. If you could tell
That secret to me, I'd requite you well."

"Give me your hand," she answered. "Swear me true
That whatsoever I next ask of you,
You'll do it if it lies within your might
And I'll enlighten you before the night."

"Granted, upon my honor," he replied.

"Then I dare boast, and with no empty pride,
Your life is safe," she told him. "Let me die
If she, the queen, won't say the same as I.
Let's learn if the haughtiest of all who wear
A net or coverchief upon their hair
Will be so forward as to answer 'no'
To what I'll teach you. No more; let us go."
With that she whispered something in his ear,
And told him to be glad and have no fear.

When they had reached the court, the knight declared
That he had kept his day, and was prepared
To give his answer, standing for his life.
Many the wise widow, many the wife,
Many the maid who rallied to the scene,
And at the head as justice sat the queen.

Then silence was enjoined; the knight was told
In open court to say what women hold
Precious above all else. He did not stand
Dumb like a beast, but spoke up at command
And plainly offered them his answering word
In manly voice, so that the whole court heard.

    "My liege and lady, most of all," said he,
"Women desire to have the sovereignty
And sit in rule and government above
Their husbands, and to have their way in love.
This is what most you want. Spare me or kill
As you may like; I stand here by your will."

    No widow, wife, or maid gave any token
Of contradicting what the knight had spoken.
He should not die; he should be spared instead;
He well deserved his life, the whole court said.

    The old woman whom the knight met on the green
Sprang up at this. "My sovereign lady queen,
Before your court has risen, do me right!
I taught, myself, this answer to the knight,
For which he pledged his honor in my hand,
Solemnly, that the first thing I demand,
He'd do it, if it lay within his might.
Before the court I ask you, then, sir knight,
To take me," said the woman, "as your wife,
For well you know that I have saved your life.
Deny me, on your honor, if you can."

    "Alas," replied this miserable man,
"That was my promise, it must be confessed.
For the love of God, though, choose a new request!
Take all my wealth, and let my body be."

    "If that's your tune, then curse both you and me,"
She said. "Though I am ugly, old, and poor,
I'll have, for all the metal and the ore
That under earth is hidden or lies above,
Nothing, except to be your wife and love."

"My love? No, my damnation, if you can!
Alas," he said, "that any of my clan
Should be so miserably misallied!"

All to no good; force overruled his pride,
And in the end he is constrained to wed,
And marries his old wife and goes to bed.

Now some will charge me with an oversight
In failing to describe the day's delight,
The merriment, the food, the dress at least.
But I reply, there was no joy nor feast;
Nothing but sorrow and sharp misery.
He married her in private, secretly,
And all day after, such was his distress,
Hid like an owl from his wife's ugliness.

Great was the woe this knight had in his head
When in due time they both were brought to bed.
He shuddered, tossed, and turned, and all the while
His old wife lay and waited with a smile.
"Is every knight so backward with a spouse?
Is it," she said, "a law in Arthur's house?
I am your love, your own, your wedded wife.
I am the woman who has saved your life.
I've never done you anything but right.
Why do you treat me this way the first night?
You must be mad, the way that you behave!
Tell me my fault, and as God's love can save,
I will amend it, truly, if I can."

"Amend it?" answered this unhappy man.
"It never can be amended, truth to tell.
You are so loathsome and so old as well,
And your low birth besides is such a cross
It is no wonder that I turn and toss.
God take my woeful spirit from my breast!"

"Is this," she said, "the cause of your unrest?"

"No wonder!" said the knight. "It truly is."

"Now sir," she said, "I could amend all this

Within three days, if it should please me to,
And if you deal with me as you should do.
   "But since you speak of that nobility
That comes from ancient wealth and pedigree,
As if *that* constituted gentlemen,
I hold such arrogance not worth a hen!
The man whose virtue is pre-eminent,
In public and alone, always intent
On doing every generous act he can,
Take him—he is the greatest gentleman!
Christ wills that we should claim nobility
From him, not from old wealth or family.
Our elders left us all that they were worth
And through their wealth and blood we claim high birth,
But never, since it was beyond their giving,
Could they bequeath to us their virtuous living;
Although it first conferred on them the name
Of gentlemen, they could not leave that claim!
   "Dante the Florentine on this was wise:
'Frail is the branch on which man's virtues rise'—
Thus runs his rhyme—'God's goodness wills that we
Should claim from him alone nobility.'
Thus from our elders we can only claim
Such temporal things as men may hurt and maim.
   "It's plain enough that true nobility
Is not bequeathed along with property,
For many a lord's son does a deed of shame
And yet, God knows, enjoys his noble name.
But he, though scion of a noble house
And elders who were wise and virtuous,
Who will not follow his elders, who are dead,
But leads, himself, a shameful life instead,
He is not noble, be he duke or earl.
It is the churlish deed that makes the churl.
And therefore, my dear husband, I conclude
That though my ancestors were rough and rude,

Yet may Almighty God confer on me
The grace to live, as I hope, virtuously.
Call me of noble blood when I begin
To live in virtue and to cast out sin.

   "As for my poverty, at which you grieve,
Almighty God in whom we all believe
In willful poverty chose to lead his life,
And surely every man and maid and wife
Can understand that Jesus, heaven's king,
Would never choose a low or vicious thing.
A poor and cheerful life is nobly led;
So Seneca and others have well said.
The man so poor he doesn't have a stitch
Who thinks himself repaid, I count as rich.
He that is covetous, he is the poor man,
Pining to have the things he never can.
It is of cheerful mind, true poverty.
Juvenal says about it happily:
'The poor man as he goes along his way
And passes thieves is free to sing and play.'
Poverty is a good we loathe, a great
Reliever of our busy worldly state,
A great amender also of our minds
As he that patiently will bear it finds.
And poverty, for all it seems distressed,
Is a possession no one will contest.
Poverty, too, by bringing a man low,
Helps him the better God and self to know.
Poverty is a glass where we can see
Which are our true friends, as it seems to me.
So, sir, I do not wrong you on this score;
Reproach me with my poverty no more.

   "Now, sir, you tax me with my age; but, sir,
You gentlemen of breeding all aver
That men should not despise old age, but rather
Grant an old man respect, and call him 'father.'

"If I am old and ugly, as you have said,
You have less fear of being cuckolded,
For ugliness and age, as all agree,
Are notable guardians of chastity.
But since I know in what you take delight,
I'll gratify your worldly appetite.

"Choose now, which of two courses you will try:
To have me old and ugly till I die
But evermore your true and humble wife,
Never displeasing you in all my life,
Or will you have me rather young and fair
And take your chances on who may repair
Either to your house on account of me
Or to some other place, it well may be.
Now make your choice, whichever you prefer."

The knight took thought, and sighed, and said to her
At last, "My love and lady, my dear wife,
In your wise government I put my life.
Choose for yourself which course will best agree
With pleasure and honor, both for you and me.
I do not care, choose either of the two;
I am content, whatever pleases you."

"Then have I won from you the sovereignty,
Since I may choose and rule at will?" said she.

He answered, "That is best, I think, dear wife."

"Kiss me," she said. "Now we are done with strife,
For on my word, I will be both to you,
That is to say, fair, yes, and faithful too.
May I die mad unless I am as true
As ever wife was since the world was new.
Unless I am as lovely to be seen
By morning as an empress or a queen
Or any lady between east and west,
Do with my life or death as you think best.
Lift up the curtain, see what you may see."

And when the knight saw what had come to be

And knew her as she was, so young, so fair,
His joy was such that it was past compare.
He took her in his arms and gave her kisses
A thousand times on end; he bathed in blisses.
And she obeyed him also in full measure
In everything that tended to his pleasure.

    And so they lived in full joy to the end.
And now to all us women may Christ send
Submissive husbands, full of youth in bed,
And grace to outlive all the men we wed.
And I pray Jesus to cut short the lives
Of those who won't be governed by their wives;
And old, ill-tempered niggards who hate expense,
God promptly bring them down with pestilence!

Prologue to the Friar's Tale

This Friar, this noble beggar, all the while
Glared at the Summoner in a threatening style,
But for the moment, out of courtesy,
He had not spoken an incivility.
At last he broke his silence to the Wife.
"Madame," he said, "God give you a good life!
You've touched here on hard points of disputation
That give the schoolmen's wits great agitation.
You've spoken of many things right well, I say.
But, Madame, as we ride along our way,
We only need to carry on our game.
Leave questions of authority, in God's name,
To schools and preachers of divinity!
If it will entertain this company,
I'll tell you to what end a summoner fell.
By God, by the name itself you know right well

That no good of a summoner can be spoken.
May no one present smell an evil token!
A summoner is a bearer of vexation
Running about with writs for fornication
Who's beaten up at the edge of every town."

"Ah, sir," our Host said, "keep your anger down.
Remember your position. Be polite.
In company we cannot have a fight.
On with your tale, and let the Summoner be."

"No," said the Summoner, "let him say to me
Whatever he likes, for when it comes my lot,
By God, I'll pay him back to the last jot!
I'll tell him what an honor it is to be
A flattering friar, a beggar such as he,
And also many another sort of crime
I need not mention at the present time.
I'll teach him what his business is, I will!"

"No more of this," our Host replied. "Be still!
On with your story, my good master dear,"
He told the Friar, who spoke as you shall hear.

~~~~~~

The Friar's Tale

In my part of the country recently
Lived an archdeacon, of high family,
Who boldly used the power of his station
Relentlessly to punish fornication,
Witchcraft and sorcery and bawdiness,
Blackmail and slander and unfaithfulness,
And broken contracts, wills, and testaments,
Churchwardens careless about sacraments,
And usury and simony also,
But chiefly lechers knew him to their woe.

He made them sing if they were brought to court!
He stiffly chided those whose tithes were short
Should anyone betray them or complain.
No pocketbook escaped him without pain!
For thin tithes or a slender offering
He taught his people piteously to sing!
Before the bishop caught them with his hook
Their names were entered in the archdeacon's book,
Who by the fines within his jurisdiction
Had power to keep their purses in constriction.
  He had a summoner ready at his side,
As clever a tool as England could provide,
For on the sly he kept a corps of spies
Who well could teach him where to find a prize.
He let a lecher or two go safe and sound
To learn where twenty others could be found.
These scandals, though this Summoner here become
Mad as a hare, I'll tell them all and some.
They can't fine us or threaten us with conviction.
Over us friars they have no jurisdiction,
And never shall they have, their whole lives through.
—"Peter! The women in the brothels too
Are put beyond our charge," the Summoner cried.
  "Keep still, and go to the devil," our Host replied.
"Bad luck go with you! Let him tell his tale.
No matter how the Summoner may rail,
Speak up, spare nothing, sir. Go right ahead."
  —This summoner had pimps (the Friar said)
As ready as any falcon in the land,
Offered his lure, to come right to his hand.
They found out secrets for him left and right.
Their friendship had not sprung up overnight!
They served as his informers on the sly.
Great was the profit that he got thereby,
Greater than the archdeacon ever guessed.
Without a writ, this ignorant man oppressed

And summoned, upon pain of Christ's own curse,
Innocents who were glad to fill his purse
Or at a tavern buy him sumptuous meals.
He was, like Judas, the sort of thief who steals
No matter how small is the treasury.
The archdeacon had but half his loyalty.
To give him his full praise, and not to skimp,
He was a thief, a summoner, and a pimp.
He had wenches also in his retinue,
And whether it was Sir Robert or Sir Hugh
Or Jack or Rafe, any who paid a call
And slept with them, they went and told him all.
The wench and he were perfectly agreed.
He'd fetch a forged writ ready at his need
And summon them to the chapter; then his plan
Was to dismiss the wench and skin the man.
Then he would say, "For your sake, friend, I aim
Out of our black book here to scratch your name.
There's nothing more for you to worry about.
Count me your friend, when I can help you out."
For it would be past cunning to describe
In two years all his ways of getting a bribe.
No hunting dog in the whole world, far or near,
Can tell a stricken from a scatheless deer
With nose infallible as this summoner's
For lechers, paramours, or adulterers,
And since his income all came from that source
He fixed his whole mind on it with full force.

This summoner, always on the hunt for prey,
Was riding with a trumped-up charge one day
To summon an old widow, a poor hag,
Hoping to add her small bribe to his swag,
And through a woodland as he took his course
He saw before him a yeoman on a horse
Who bore a bow with arrows bright and keen.
Over his shoulders fell a coat of green,

He wore a black-fringed hat upon his head.
   "Well overtaken, sir," the summoner said.
   "Well met to all good fellows," he replied.
"Where through this greenwood do you mean to ride?
Is it a long way that you have to go?"
   The summoner promptly answered and said, "No,
I have a debt close by here to collect."
   "Are you a bailiff?" "Yes, as you suspect."
He did not dare to give his trade its name
And say he was a summoner, for shame.
   The yeoman said, "Now that's good luck, dear brother.
You are a bailiff, and I am another.
But as a stranger here, I well may need
Your help and friendship, if you are agreed.
I've gold and silver; visit in our shire
And you shall have it all, if you desire."
   "Much thanks," the summoner said, and then they both
Clasped hands, one with the other, and took an oath
To be sworn brothers to their final day,
And rode well pleased together on their way.
   This summoner, who was as full of words
As full of cruelty are these butcher birds
And always prying, "Brother, could you give,"
He said, "some notion of just where you live,
In case I want to look you up some day?"
   The yeoman answered suavely, "Far away
In the north country is my dwelling, brother.
I hope to see you there some time or other.
Before we part, I'll make the way so clear
That you can't miss my house, you needn't fear."
   "Now, brother," said the summoner, "while we ride
Along our way, perhaps you will confide
Some of your tricks to me. Speak without sham,
Seeing you are a bailiff, as I am.
Tell me how best to work this trade I'm in,
And do not spare for conscience nor for sin,

But tell me how you do it, as a brother."
    "As I'm an honest man," replied the other,
"I'll tell you the true story of it all.
The wages of my work are only small,
My master is a strict one, hard to please,
The office that I hold gives little ease,
Hence by extortion I contrive to live.
In fact I take whatever men will give.
Somehow, by cunning or by violence,
From year to year I win my maintenance.
That is my story, if I'm not to lie."
    "Truth is," the summoner answered, "so do I.
Before God, I'll take anything that's not
Either too heavy for me or too hot.
Whatever I manage to take in on the sly
Gives me no pricks of conscience, no, not I!
I couldn't live except for my extortion.
Shrift for that sin will never be my portion!
I've no remorse for such pranks as I've done.
A curse on these confessors, every one!
We are a pair, by God, two of the same.
But, my dear brother, let me have your name,
We are well met," the summoner said. Meanwhile
The yeoman had begun somewhat to smile.
    "You really want me," he replied, "to tell?
I am a fiend; my dwelling is in hell.
I ride about this country trafficking
To find out who will give me anything.
My gains are all ill gotten, every cent.
And see how you ride with the same intent,
To pick up profits, you don't scruple how!
I do the same, for I would go right now
To the world's limit in the hope of prey."
    "Bless me!" the summoner said. "What's that you say?
I took you for a yeoman! What I see
Is certainly a man's shape, just like me.

Have you a form and figure where you dwell?
Do you still keep your shape down there in hell?"

"No, as to that," he said, "we are without
Body or form down there, but going about
Here on the earth, we can put on a shape
Whenever we want, whether of man or ape.
The likeness of an angel I can wear,
And it's no wonder; though you squint and stare
A lousy juggler can delude your sight,
And I, believe me, have far greater sleight."

"Why," said the summoner, "do you stalk your game
In various forms, not always in the same?"

"We try to fashion for ourselves a shape
That gives our prey the least chance to escape."

"What makes you toil so, in and out of season?"

"Ah, dear sir summoner, there's many a reason,"
Answered the fiend. "But all things have their time.
The hours are short, the morning is past prime,
And still I have earned nothing for today.
I'll turn my thoughts to profit, if I may.
We hardly need beyond this point compare
Our minds, for brother, your wit is all too bare
And easily seen through, as I could show.
But since you ask me why we labor so,
Sometimes we are only tools who must fulfill
God's purposes, and execute his will
Upon his creatures, just as he may please,
In various forms, by various agencies.
Without him, certainly, we have no force
If he is pleased to stand athwart our course.
At our request, we sometimes have his leave
Only the flesh and not the soul to grieve—
Job, for example, whom we tortured so.
Sometimes we are permitted to work woe
On both, that is, the body and the soul,
And sometimes we are suffered to control

Only the spirit, and vex that with unrest,
And not the body; and all is for the best,
For if a man repels us in temptation,
Then that becomes a cause of his salvation
Although we never intended thus to make him
Safe and secure, but rather meant to take him.
Sometimes we act as servants even to men—
A fiend did to St. Dunstan—or as when
The apostles long ago made use of me."

   "But tell me," said the summoner, "honestly,
All these new bodies into which you go,
Are they physical, like men's?" The fiend said, "No.
We feign them sometimes, and sometimes we arise
In the bodies of the dead before men's eyes
And speak to them as reasonably and well
As to the witch of old spoke Samuel.
(Yet some men will maintain it wasn't he;
I have no use for you divinity!)
One thing I warn you, though, and I'm not fooling:
You'll see how we are formed, you'll have your schooling
Where you shall find your every last concern
Answered in full. You will not need to learn
From me, for by your own experience
You'll qualify to lecture with more sense
On all these points than Vergil himself could do
When he was living, or than Dante too.
Now let's be cheerful. I'll keep you company,
Brother, until you turn your back on me."

   "Never," the summoner said, "though it turned out
That you were Satan himself! For all about
I am well known as a yeoman, and we both
Are now sworn brothers. I'll stand by my oath,
And so let's mind our trade. Take what men give,
You your part and I mine, and so we'll live,
And either of us who has more than the other,
Let him be honest and share it with his brother."

"Agreed," the devil answered. They rode on,
And as they neared the entrance to the town
To which the summoner meant to make his way,
They came upon a wagonload of hay.
The cart was stuck, the going was so bad.
The driver lashed and shouted as if mad,
"You, Scot! You, Badger! You'd hold back for stones?
The devil with you," he shouted, "skin and bones!
I mean it, sure as you were ever foaled.
The trouble I've had with you, it can't be told.
The devil take the lot, horse, cart, and hay!"

The summoner thought, "Here's a good trick to play,"
And innocently toward the fiend drew near
And whispered, "Listen, brother, don't you hear
The driver's words? Take it, he's given you
Both hay and cart and his three horses, too."

"Not so," the devil answered, "not a bit.
Trust me, he doesn't mean a word of it.
Ask him yourself, if you don't credit me,
Or wait a minute or two, and you will see."

The driver lashed his horses on the croup,
And in the traces they began to stoop.
"Git," yelled the driver, "pull, and Jesus bless
You and his handiwork, greater and less!
By God, that was the way to do it, boy!
My cart's out of the mud now, by St. Loy!
That was well pulled. God save you, good old gray!"

"You hear that?" said the fiend. "What did I say?
You ought to understand from this, dear brother,
The fool said one thing, but he meant another.
We might as well be on our way; it's clear
That I won't pick up any booty here."

When they were past the town, the summoner said,
"A hag lives here who'd sacrifice her head
To save a cent, or be almost as glad.
But I'll have twelve pence, though it drives her mad,

Or else I'll summon her. She'll pay my price,
Though God knows I can't tax her with a vice.
But since you can't support yourself, I see,
In these parts, take a lesson here from me."

    He knocked upon the woman's gate. "Come out,
Old hag," he said. "You have a priest, no doubt,
Or else a friar inside with you somewhere."

    "Bless me!" the woman said. "Who's knocking there?
God save you! What do you want with me, good sir?"

    "I have a writ here," said the summoner.
"On penalty of Christ's curse, take care to be
Tomorrow morning at the archdeacon's knee
To answer to his court for certain things."

    "Now, Lord," she said, "Christ Jesus, king of kings,
So help me, but, good sir, I can't obey.
I have been sick, and that for many a day.
I cannot walk so far, nor even ride,
But I'd be dead for the pain here in my side.
May I not ask my accusers to prefer
A charge in writing, good sir summoner,
And answer by a proxy?"

                    "That could be,"
The summoner answered. "Pay me now, let's see,
Twelve pence, and I can call it an acquittal.
The profit that I make will be but little.
The profits go to my master, not to me.
Pay up, I must ride on immediately.
Give me the twelve pence now, I cannot tarry."

    "Twelve pence!" she cried. "Now sainted Lady Mary
Keep me from tribulation and from sin,
But though I had the world itself to win
There's no such sum as twelve pence in my hold.
You know right well that I am poor and old.
Make known your charity through me, a wretch!"

    "If that's your tune," he said, "the foul fiend fetch
My soul if you get off with my consent."

"Alas," she said, "God knows I'm innocent!"

"Give me the twelve pence, or by sweet St. Anne
I'll carry away," he said, "your brand-new pan
To meet a debt you've owed since long ago.
You cuckolded your husband, as you know,
And I myself paid out your compensation."

"You lie," the widow said. "By my salvation,
I have never yet, as widow or as wife,
Been summoned to your court in all my life,
Nor in my body have I been untrue.
I give the devil, with his rough, black hue,
Your body, and with it he can have my pan!"

When in these terms he heard her curse the man,
Upon her knees, the devil said to her,
"Good mother Mabel, does your heart concur
In this? Is it your real wish, and no lie?"

"The devil take him sooner than he can die,
And pan and all, unless he will repent!"

"That, you old heifer, is far from my intent,"
The summoner said. "That's what I'll never do,
Repent for anything I've had from you.
I wish I had your smock and every rag!"

"Now don't be angry, brother! Through this hag
Your body and this pan are mine by right,"
The devil said. "You'll be in hell tonight,
Where you can study our secrets to infinity
And learn more than a master of divinity."
With this the devil seized him; body and soul
He was borne off in this foul fiend's control
And went to the heritage that summoners find.
And God who in his image made mankind
Save us and guide us, ever and again
And help these summoners to become good men!

Lords (said the Friar), I could have filled your ear,
If given leisure by this Summoner here,
Straight from the words of Christ and Paul and John

And of our other doctors, many a one,
With tortures that would make your spirits wince,
Although there is no tongue that can evince,
Not though I took a thousand years to tell,
The miseries of that cursed house of hell.
But that we may escape that cursed place,
Watch ever, and pray Jesus in his grace
Deliver us from the lion in the way,
Satan the tempter, who lies in wait to slay
The innocent. Be ready to oppose
The fiend who would enslave you; thus dispose
Your hearts. He cannot tempt you past your might,
For Christ will be your champion and your knight.
And pray that all these summoners repent
Before the devil takes them off hell bent!

Prologue to the Summoner's Tale

The Summoner in his stirrups rose tiptoe,
His heart inflamed against the Friar so
That like an aspen he was quivering.
   "Lords," he burst out, "I only ask one thing.
I beg, for courtesy, since you have heard
This lying Friar to his last false word,
Give me the right to tell my tale as well.
He is acquainted, so he brags, with hell,
And that, before God, is but little wonder.
Friars and fiends are never far asunder.
There was a friar once, as you've heard tell,
Who was carried in a vision down to hell,
And as an angel led him here and there,
Showing the torments, he could see nowhere

A single friar, though other wretched folk
Were plentiful. So finally he spoke
And asked the angel, 'Sir, have we such grace,
We friars, that all of us escape this place?'
   " 'Not so, there are millions here,' the angel said,
And straightway down to Satan himself he led
The friar, and told him, 'Satan has a tail
Broader by far than any barge's sail.
Hold up your tail, Satan,' commanded he.
'Expose your anus, let the friar see
The spot where friars nestle in this place.'
And in less time than a half-furlong race,
Just as a swarm of bees comes from the hive
Out of the devil's arse there came a drive
Of twenty thousand friars in a rout
And all through hell they buzzed and swarmed about
And came again as fast as they had gone
And in his arse they crept back, every one.
He clapped his tail shut on them and lay still.
This friar, after he had looked his fill
On all the torments of this sorry place,
His spirit was restored him, by God's grace,
And found his body, but when he was awake,
All he could do for fear was shiver and shake.
Try as he would, he still saw in his mind
The devil's arse, the birthright of his kind.
This is what waits for them, and I'm no liar!
God save you all, except this cursed Friar!"

The Summoner's Tale

Lords, there's a place—in Yorkshire, as I guess—
A marshy country known as Holderness
In which a friar used to go about
Preaching, and begging too, you needn't doubt.
And in a church this friar preached one day,
Rousing the people specially to pay
For trentals,[1] and to give, for God's sweet sake,
Their substance where it might be used to make
Houses of worship, not to let it go
Where it would all be wasted, or bestow
Their charity where there is no need to give,
On church foundations well endowed to live
In comfort—God be thanked! "Trentals," he said,
"From punishment deliver souls now dead,
The souls of friends, alike both old and young—
Yes, and although in haste they may be sung,
Don't think the priest is being frivolous.
He's only allowed each day to sing one mass.
Deliver them speedily!" he cried. "Let out
The souls! It is hard enough being clawed, no doubt,
With awls or meathooks, or to burn or bake.
Be quick and give at once, for Christ's sweet sake!"
When people in church had given what they intended,
Then with his *qui cum patre* off he wended.
He wouldn't stay, but with his robe tucked high
And scrip and staff, began to poke and pry
In every house, begging for meal or corn.
His fellow had a staff well tipped with horn,

[1] Masses, in sets of thirty, for the dead.

A pair of tables made of ivory,
A stylus that was polished handsomely,
And stood there with his tables, entering
The names of all who gave them anything
As though to say prayers for them by and by.
"Give us a bushel of wheat or malt or rye,
A little cake for God, a sliver of cheese;
We have no choice, give us whatever you please,
Just a God's ha'penny or an offering penny,
A little of your pork, if you have any;
Give us a scrap of blanket, worthy dame,
Dear sister—look, I am writing down your name.
Bacon or beef, whatever you can find."
    A sturdy rascal trailed along behind
Who was their porter, carrying a sack;
Each gift they got, he laid it on his back.
And when the friar out the door had gone
He always scraped the names off, every one,
That he had written earlier on his tables.
He stuffed them up with flimflam and with fables.
    —"Now there you lie, you Summoner!" said the Friar.
    "Hush up!" our Host said, "by the holy choir!
For Christ's dear mother, go on, spare nothing at all."
    "As I'd be saved," the Summoner said, "I shall."
    —From house to house he went along his round
Until he reached a house where he had found
Welcome above a hundred other places.
Sick lay the man who had done him these good graces;
Bedridden, prostrate on a couch he lay.
    "Now God be with us! Thomas, friend, good day,"
Began the friar, speaking pleasantly.
"Thomas, God bless you! Many a time," said he,
"This bench has been a welcome thing to feel.
Here I have eaten many a cheerful meal."
And from the bench he drove away the cat,
And laying down his staff and scrip and hat

Seated himself at ease and settled down.
His fellow had gone walking off toward town
And with the porter he was on his way
To lodgings where he planned that night to stay.

   "Well, my dear master," said the ailing man,
"How have you been the while since March began?
I haven't seen you these two weeks or more."

   "God knows," he said, "I've labored long and sore,
And your salvation is my special care.
For that I've offered many a precious prayer.
Our other friends, God bless them too, I pray!
I have been at mass at your own church today
And gave them a sermon out of my small wit—
Not all drawn from the text of Holy Writ;
The text may leave you often at a loss
And so I'll teach you wholly by the gloss.
A glorious role the art of glossing plays,
For as we scholars put it, 'The letter slays.'
I taught them that they should be charitable,
And spend their wealth where it is reasonable.
I saw our good wife there—ah, where is she?"

   "Out in the yard, I think, most probably."
Answered his host. "She will be coming soon."

   "Ah, you are welcome, master, by St. John!"
The woman greeted him as she came in.
"Now tell me honestly, how have you been?"

   Up from the bench the friar rose politely
And in his arms embraced his hostess tightly,
And chirping like a sparrow, kissed her sweetly,
And said, "Right well, as one who is completely
Your servant—God be thanked, who soul and life
Bestowed on you! I saw no other wife
In the whole church as fair, so may I be
Saved from perdition!"

                   "Ah, sir," answered she,
"May God amend my faults! You are welcome, though."

"Thanks, Madame. I have always found it so.
But with your pardon, I have things to discuss
With Thomas, if you won't be piqued with us.
These curates can't conduct a probing session
And tenderly bring a conscience to confession;
They're negligent and careless in their shrift.
But preaching is my labor and my gift
And study of Paul's words and Peter's pen.
I live to fish for souls of Christian men,
To yield Christ Jesus what is his by debt.
On spreading his holy word my heart is set."

"Now, by your leave, dear master," answered she.
"Rebuke him well, for the Holy Trinity!
Though he can have whatever he desires,
His temper is as foul as a pismire's.
I cover him at night and make him warm
And put my leg across him or my arm.
He only groans as the boar does in our sty.
I get no pleasure out of him, not I,
Except his groans; I please him in no way."

"Thomas, *je vous dis!* Thomas, *sans doute* I say,
This is the devil's work, this must be mended.
God has forbidden anger. He is offended
By rage, of which I'll say a word or so."

"Now sir," the woman said, "before I go,
What will you have to eat? I'll set about it."

"Madame," he said, "*je vous dis*, do not doubt it,
If from a capon I had just the liver,
And some of your soft bread, only a sliver,
And then a roast pig's head—but for my sake
I'd have no creature killed—then I'd partake
Of homely plenty with you—enough and quite.
I am a man whose sustenance is light.
My spirit finds its nurture in the Bible,
And my poor flesh is so inured to trouble
And wakefulness, my stomach is destroyed.

I speak in friendship; do not be annoyed
At feelings I so openly disclose.
To very few would I do so, God knows."
   "Now sir," she said, "one word, and I am done.
A little after you had left our town,
Within these two weeks past, my child has died."
   "I saw his death revealed," the friar replied.
"At home, as I was in our dormitory,
I saw him, in a vision, borne to glory
Not half an hour after he was dead,
God teach me truth! So also did the head
Of our infirmary, and our sacristan—
True friars for these fifty years, who can
Now celebrate at last their jubilee
And walk alone, not two by two, thanks be
To God who lends us life! I rose up quickly,
While down my cheeks the tears were running
     thickly,
And all our convent. With no clamoring bells
We chanted the *Te Deum,* nothing else,
Save that to Christ I offered then and there
Thanks for his revelation, in a prayer.
For trust me, you good people, on this score:
Our prayers are more effectual, and more
Is open to us of Christ's hidden things
Than laymen see, although they may be kings.
We live in poverty and abstinence,
And laymen live in luxury and expense,
Their foul delights, their meat and drink and waste.
We hold the lusts of this world in distaste.
Dives and Lazarus lived differently,
And their rewards were different; for he
That means to pray must fast, and must be clean,
Foster his soul, and make his body lean.
We follow the apostle; clothes and food
Are good enough for us though far from good.

The cleanness and the fasting of us friars
Renders acceptable to Christ our prayers."

[The Summoner's Tale, after this account of how the
friar swept the cat from the bench and made himself at
home, continues to reveal at great length the friar's
hypocrisy and greed. The friar preaches to Thomas first
on his own favorite theme, the sin of gluttony, then
on Thomas's particular sin of anger, embellishing both
themes with a profusion of "old examples" and authori-
ties. Finally the friar gets down to the practical business
of begging, and Thomas is exasperated beyond control.
The denouement of the story makes use of a situation
current in medieval anecdote. Thomas promises the friar
a gift if he on his side will promise to divide it equally
with his fellows. The friar puts his hand where Thomas
directs and receives a "reverberation of air" of the same
kind that Nicholas bestowed on Absolom in the Miller's
Tale. The problem of dividing this gift into equal shares
is solved by a squire at the table of a neighboring lord to
whom the friar rushes off in dudgeon. The squire receives
"a new gown" for his ingenuity, and the friar's humilia-
tion is complete. The whole is good Chaucer, but the
Pardoner's Prologue and Tale together make a far more
impressive and dramatic example of the exposure of the
methods of a hypocritical preacher.]

᭙᭙ ᭙᭙ ᭙᭙ ᭙᭙ ᭙᭙ ᭙᭙ ᭙᭙ ᭙᭙ ᭙᭙ ᭙᭙

Prologue to and Conclusion
of the Student's Tale

"You ride, Sir Oxford Student," our Host said,
"As shy and quiet as a girl just wed
Sits at the table. I haven't heard you say
A single word, not even one all day.
You're deep in some sly turn of reasoning,

That's plain. But there's a time for everything
As Solomon says. For God's sake, show more cheer!
It's not the time nor place to study here.
Tell us some tale or other, make it gay!
To any game a man agrees to play
He ought to lend himself with full assent.
But don't preach to us, as friars do in Lent,
Bringing old sins to mind to make us weep,
Nor tell a tale that will put us all to sleep.
Tell some adventure or some merry trick.
Your tropes and terms and flowers of rhetoric,
Save them till you have something to express
In high style, as in letters men address
To kings, for instance. Talk in a plain way
For now, and let us take in what you say."

   "Host," said the Student, "I am in your hands.
You rule us for the present; your demands
I shall obey in reason, without fail.
And I will undertake to tell a tale
I learned in Padua from a worthy clerk,
So proved both by his words and by his work.
Now he is dead and coffined, nailed away;
As for his soul, God give it rest, I pray!
His name was Francis Petrarch, laurel-crowned.
By his sweet tongue all Italy was found
Illumined by the light of poetry,
As by Lignaco in philosophy,
Or law, or other forms of art as well.
But death, that will not suffer us to dwell
Longer on earth than the twinkling of an eye,
Has slain them both, and so we all shall die.

   "But to keep on, and speak as I began
A little further of this worthy man
From whom I learned the tale you'll hear, he chose,
Before the story proper, to compose
A prelude in high style, in which he speaks

Of Piedmont and Saluzzo, and the peaks
Known as the Apennines, high hills to see,
That form the boundaries of West Lombardy.
Of Monte Viso specially he writes,
Where in a little spring upon its heights
The Po first rises, and eastward from its source
Flows toward Aemilia, swelling in its course
To Ferrara and to Venice. That would make
A long account for me to undertake,
And seems in truth, by all I can observe,
Irrelevant, except as it may serve
As prelude to the tale he means to tell.
This is the tale, which you may hear as well."

[The Oxford Student's tale of patient Griselda, the
inconceivably submissive wife of Walter, Marquis of
Saluzzo, was given literary currency by Boccaccio in his
Decameron. Chaucer derived it from Petrarch's Latin
translation, in combination with one or more French ver-
sions. "In its ultimate origin," says Robinson, "the story
of Griselda is doubtless a fairy tale." I have merely sum-
marized the story itself, but have rendered in full the
Student's conclusion, with its ironical compliment to the
Wife of Bath, and his "song," or "Chaucer's Envoy" as
the copyists label it.

Walter, besought by his people to marry, chooses Gri-
selda, daughter of Janicula the poorest man in a poor
village. Though this maiden, says Chaucer, was of tender
age, a mature and steadfast heart was enclosed in the
breast of her virginity. She fostered her poor old father,
and would never be idle until she slept. She declares her-
self unworthy of marrying Walter, but swears that she
will never deliberately disobey him in act or thought,
though it cost her life. After the marriage, she increases
in excellence, and is beloved by Walter's people.

Presently Walter begins to be obsessed by the notion
of testing her steadfastness in submission. He removes
from her successively a daughter and a son, on the plea

that the people resent her origin and do not want descendants of Janicula to succeed to Walter's title. Griselda thinks her children are to be killed, but makes no complaint and alters in no respect her conduct toward her husband. She only asks the "sergeant" who takes the children to bury their bodies where beasts and birds of prey will not rend their tender flesh. Walter, in the meanwhile, has provided for their secret bringing up at other courts.

Griselda's final test begins when Walter announces that he intends to put her aside and marry another wife. To this end he has managed to secure "counterfeit Papal bulls." Griselda says that she came naked from her father's house (Walter could not receive her in the clothes she was wearing and had provided others) and naked she would like to return. But she begs a smock in order that the womb in which his children had lain might not be seen bare as she walked back. "Do not let me go on my way like a worm. Remember, my dear lord, that I was your wife, though unworthy."

But more is to come. Griselda is summoned back to prepare Walter's house for the wedding. She sets tables, makes beds, and drives the servants to hurry with their sweeping and shaking. She is then called on to praise the new bride; but who should this turn out to be but her own grown daughter! The whole pretense is dropped, Walter is satisfied with his proofs of his wife's submission, mother and children are reunited, and Griselda resumes her wifehood, profoundly thanking her husband because he has preserved her son and daughter.]

This tale is written, not that it were good
For wives to follow such humility,
For that could not be borne, although they would;
But that each man, whatever his station be,
Should stand as steadfast in adversity
As did Griselda; therefore Petrarch wrote
This tale, with high style and exalted note.

For since to mortal man a wife could show
Griselda's patience, how much more we ought
To take all that God sends us here below
With good grace; for he tests what he has wrought,
And yet he tempts no man his blood has bought,
As in the Epistle of St. James we read.
He tests men daily, that is true indeed,

And suffers us, for virtue's exercise,
By the sharp scourges of adversity
Often to be hard whipped; not in this wise
To learn our will, for in all certainty
Before we breathed he knew our frailty.
All for our best is each stroke he may give;
In virtuous patience then we ought to live.

But one word, lords, before my tale is done.
It would be hard to turn up nowadays
As many as three Griseldas in a town,
For put them now to such tests and assays,
Their gold is so alloyed in vicious ways
With brass that though the coin be fair, its blend
Would sooner break in two than yield or bend.

Now, for the love of this good Wife of Bath,
Whose life may God maintain and long protect
Supreme and lofty in that noble path
She treads with all the members of her sect—
Shame, if her practice fell into neglect!—
It's time to trade our earnestness for play.
Listen! I'll say a song that goes this way:

Chaucer's Envoy

Dead is Griselda, she and her patience lie
Buried as one in her Italian vale,
Wherefore in open hearing thus I cry:
Husbands, be not so rash as to assail
The patience of your wives, hoping to find
Griseldas, for in truth you stand to fail!

You wives, with meek Griseldas do not vie!
Your nimble tongues let no submission nail,
And let no scholar in his reason try
To write of you so marvelous a tale,
Lest Chichevache,[1] who eats meek wives and kind,
Should fatten upon you her lean entrail!

Ape Echo, never still beneath the sky,
Whose ready answers are not known to fail.
Be not a fool for innocence, put by
Submission, take command, and proudly sail.
Engrave this lesson deeply on your mind
Since to the general good it may avail.

You archwives, strong as camels, take the high
And overpowering hand against the male.
You little wives, be eager and be spry
As Indian tigers, though you may be frail.
Follow my counsel, and as millwheels grind
So let your voices rattle on and rail.

[1]Chichevache, the "lean cow," fed only on submissive wives
and got little to eat. Bicorne ate patient husbands, and got a more
plentiful diet.

Neither with fear nor deference mollify
Your husband; though he arms himself in mail
Your shafts of crabbed eloquence will fly
Into his plated breast and turn him pale.
In jealous tortures wrap him up and bind
And make him sleep on bare ground like a quail.

If you are fair, keep well in people's eye
Your face and clothes; if plain, redress the scale
By spending freely. Never mope or sigh;
Make friends, and do not let their love grow stale.
Light as a linden leaf, put care behind,
And let your husband gnash his teeth and wail.

Prologue to the Merchant's Tale

"Weeping and wailing, care and other sorrow
I know sufficiently, by night and morrow,"
The Merchant said, "and others also know
If they are married men. To prove it so,
I'll tell you that it happens thus with me.
I have a wife, the worst one there could be,
For though the fiend were yoked with her, I swear
She'd overmatch him, and have strength to spare.
Why in detail should I expose to view
Her bitter malice? She's a perfect shrew!
There is a wide and mighty opposition
Between Griselda's wonderful submission
And the exceeding cruelty of my wife.
Could I untie the knot, for all my life
I never again would tumble in the snare.
We married men, we live in grief and care,
And by St. Thomas, whoever tries it out
Will find I speak the truth, beyond a doubt.

The greater part I cannot tell at all.
What, God forbid that such a thing befall!
Ah, good Sir Host, I've been a husband now
Two months, no more than that, and yet I vow
That men without a helpmeet all their lives,
Though people pierced them to the heart with knives,
Could not, no matter how they tried, relate
A quantity of sorrow half so great
As I could tell of my wife's cursedness."

    "Well then, Sir Merchant," said our Host, "God bless
Your soul, you know so much about that art,
Speak up, I beg, and let us hear a part."

    "Gladly," he answered, "but of my own sore,
For misery of heart, I'll say no more."

The Merchant's Tale

In Lombardy once lived a prosperous knight
Who had satisfied his fleshly appetite
On women sixty years without a wife,
As do these fools of irreligious life.
But turning sixty, whether in devotion
Or merely in his dotage, he took the notion
To be a married man, and settle down.
He labored at all hours, searching the town
For prospects, praying that he might not miss,
By the Lord's will, his taste of wedded bliss,
Hoping to live within that holy plan
In which God first united woman and man.

    "No other life," he said, "is worth a bean.
Wedlock is happy, spotless, and serene,
So much so that it is a heaven on earth."
So said this wise old knight, this man of worth.

And certainly, as true as God is king,
To bring a wife home is a glorious thing,
Especially when a man is old and white;
She's then the very savor of delight.
Then should he take a wife both young and fair
On whom he can beget himself an heir.
Then all his days in joy and solace pass,
While bachelors can only sing "Alas!"
When they encounter some catastrophe
In their amours, mere childish vanity.
Building on quicksand, they will find for sure
Quicksand it is when taken for secure.
A married life is ordered and content.
Who is so faithful and obedient
As wife to mate, or who else can there be
To tend him, sick or well, so anxiously,
Loving and serving him with tireless breath
Although he lies bedridden till his death?
And yet some scholars hold this isn't so!
One such is Theophrastus, but what though
It pleases him to lie? "Don't wed," says he,
"With any notions of economy
Or hope of cutting down household expense.
A faithful servant shows more diligence
In keeping your possessions than your wife,
For she'll lay claim to half of them for life.
God help me, if you have ill health to bear,
Real friends or servants give you better care
Than she whose policy it is to wait
Until she can inherit your estate.
And if you take a wife to warm your bed
The chances are that you'll be cuckolded."
This saying and a hundred that are worse
The man writes, on his bones God send a curse!
But take no stock in all such vanity;
Scout Theophrastus, and pay heed to me!

A wife is God's gift; furniture and rent,
Money and jewels, lands and rights are lent
Only at Fortune's pleasure; one and all
They pass, no more than shadows on a wall.
A wife remains; far longer in your house
Than you may want her lasts the enduring spouse.
    A marriage is a solemn sacrament.
Destruction on a man sits imminent
Who has no helpmeet; he is desolate—
I speak of people in the secular state—
And why? My words aren't idle. We are taught
That woman as man's helpmeet was first wrought.
When God made Adam and the work was done,
Seeing him belly-naked and alone,
God said, according to his gracious plan,
"Let us now make a helpmeet for this man
Like to himself," and so he fashioned Eve.
Here by established proof you may perceive
A wife is man's support, above all price,
His comfort and his earthly paradise.
So pliant and so virtuous is she
They cannot help but live in unity.
One flesh they are, and one flesh, as I guess,
Has but one heart in joy or in distress.
A wife! Ah, holy mother of God! How can
Affliction ever touch a married man?
It's more than I or any tongue can do
To tell the happiness between these two!
If poor, she helps him work; she spares him waste;
All that her husband likes is to her taste.
She never answers "No" when he says "Yes."
"Do this," says he; "All ready, sir," she says.
Any man worth a cabbage all his life
Ought to thank God on bare knees for his wife.
A man will never be hoodwinked nor fooled
If by his wife's advice he is well schooled,

For women are so faithful and so wise
A prudent man will do as they advise.
Taught by his mother's counsel, Jacob won
His father's blessing, though the younger son,
Wrapping his neck in kid-skin. Judith kept
God's people safe; while Holofernes slept,
Through wise forethought, she slew him with a nail.
Nabal, her spouse, was saved by Abigail
From being slain. And think how Esther freed
The people of God from misery at their need
And through good counsel saw that Mordecai
By Ahausuerus was exalted high.
There's no superlative degree in life,
Says Seneca, above a humble wife.

   Allow your wife her tongue, as Cato urges.
She shall command, and you must bear her scourges.
And yet she will obey for courtesy.
She'll be your mistress of economy.
A sick man, when he has no wife to keep
His house in order, well may wail and weep.
Be warned—this is the fruit of my research—
And love your wife as Christ has loved his church.
Loving yourself, you love your wife; no man
Will hate his flesh, but nurse it while he can.
And so my bidding is, cherish your wife
If ever you hope to prosper in this life.
A wife and husband take the safer way
For worldly people, whatever wits may say,
So firmly knit that no harm can betide,
Especially upon the woman's side.

   This knight, this January of whom I told,
Considered both that he was growing old
And that in marriage with a true helpmeet
Is virtuous life, tranquil and honey-sweet,
And for his friends he one day duly sent
To let them know the drift of his intent.

With serious face he let his mind unfold.
"My friends," he said, "I am growing white and old.
I'm almost, God knows, on the final brink,
And somewhat of my soul I ought to think.
My body I have foolishly expended;
Now, bless the Lord, my folly will be mended.
I mean, in fact, to be a married man,
And that with all the promptness that I can.
I'll have a maid of tender years and fair,
No more than twenty. Make it your first care,
I beg; I'll look about, but you can spy
A proper match more readily than I,
Since there are more of you. But of one thing
I warn you, my good friends. I will not bring
An old wife home, that's certain. For old fish
And young flesh, by the adage, are my dish.
A pike is better than a pickerel,
And better than old beef is tender veal.
A woman kept for thirty years in storage
Is only bean-straw and exhausted forage.
Old widows, too, of such craft are possessed
That I could never live with them in rest.
Scholars grow subtle, taught in various schools;
Women of much instruction are no fools,
They are half-scholars; a young thing we can guide,
As warm wax by the fingers can be plied;
Wherefore I will not have, and for this cause,
An old wife; on this point we needn't pause.
If it should happen she couldn't give me pleasure,
Then I'd be driven to a desperate measure;
To lechery and adultery I'd fly
And go straight to the devil when I die.
She would conceive no child, and it would be
Far worse than if my hounds had eaten me
If my estate—I say this to you all—
Should lapse and in the hands of strangers fall.

"I am not in my dotage, be it said.
I know the reasons why a man should wed.
If he can't always keep to a chaste life,
Religiously he ought to take a wife
For procreation, honoring God above,
Not for indulgence only, or for love;
And those who wed to give the flesh its due
The sin of lechery by this means eschew;
Or they may also wed to help each other
In trouble, as a sister should a brother,
And live together in holy chastity.
But sirs, with pardon, that is not for me!
For this, thank God, is a boast that I can make:
My limbs are stout enough to undertake
Whatever it's proper that a man should do.
I best can tell what I am equal to!
Although my hair is white, it sits on me
Like bloom before the fruit upon a tree.
A tree in blossom is neither dry nor dead,
And I feel nowhere white but on my head.
My heart and all my limbs are still as green
As laurel all year round, whenever seen.
And now, since you have heard my full intention,
Accede to it, I beg, without dissension."

His friends at once were eager to unfold
Their various views and cases from of old,
But as in every friendly disputation
The question always ends in altercation,
A strife sprang up between the knight's two brothers.
Placebo was the name of one; the other's
Justinus. "You had little need, it's clear,
To ask advice of any of us here,"
Placebo said, "but that you would not shun
The wise word that we have from Solomon:
'Do everything by counsel, and the event
Will never bring you reason to repent.'

Despite his word, God never give me rest
If I don't think your own design is best.
I've been a court man, though unworthily,
And stood about in noble company,
Yet never contradicted them; and why?
I'm well aware milord knows more than I.
Whatever he says, for settled truth I take it.
I say the same, or as near as I can make it.
A counselor who thinks that his advice
Outweighs his lord's is a fool at any price.
Lords are no fools, as you today have shown.
By God, there isn't a man in the whole town,
Nor Italy, who could have spoken better!
Christ will approve your counsel to the letter.
It shows a high heart, truly, and a bold
In any man who is getting to be old
To marry a young thing. By my father's kin,
You're fastening your heart on a fine pin,
A pretty one! Do just as you may please,
For my best judgment with your own agrees."

    "Brother, you've had your word. Listen, I pray,"
Justinus answered, "to what I have to say.
Seneca tells us we should understand
To whom we give our chattels or our land
And if I ought to know on every score
To whom I give my chattels, how much more
I ought to know to whom I give away
My body, and for good! It's no child's play
To take a wife without investigation.
It ought to be your earnest occupation
To find out whether she is wise or lazy,
Sober or drunk or shrewish or man-crazy,
Rich, poor, or wasteful; and though it is a folly
To look for anything unblemished wholly
In this world, man or beast, a wife who had
A few more virtuous qualities than bad

Ought to suffice. But that takes time to learn.
For I, God knows, have felt the salt tears burn
In secret, since I married. Praise who will
A husband's life, I find it has its fill
Of cost and care, and lean is its reward.
And yet my neighbors, all with one accord,
Especially the womenfolk, contrive
To say I have the truest wife alive
And meekest. But I best know where the shoe
Pinches my foot. Do as you want to do
For all of me; and yet I say beware
How you embark on marriage, if she's fair
And young especially. The youngest man
Among us will be doing all he can
By keeping his wife his own. You won't, trust me,
Please her for three years, or for less than three,
That is to say, to her full satisfaction.
A wife imposes many a strict exaction.
I hope, with all this, that you aren't offended."

    "Well," answered January, "have you ended?
Rubbish, your Seneca and your proverbs!
Pedantic stuff, not worth a sack of herbs!
Wiser than you support me, as you've heard,
In my intention. Placebo, what's your word?"

    "I hold it is a cursed man," said he,
"Who puts up bars to wedlock, certainly."
With that they rose as quickly as they could,
Agreed that he should marry when he would.

    Strange fantasies and deep preoccupation
About his marriage seized the imagination
Of January. His mind was thronged at night,
As one who had set a mirror, polished bright,
At midpoint in a crowded marketplace,
With many a fair shape, many a pretty face.
So all the maidens of the neighborhood

Passed through his thoughts; one choice at first seemed
    good
For beauty, and one enjoyed a wide acclaim
For truth and kindness; one had a bad name,
Though rich. But love is blind, it cannot see;
At last, upon his own authority,
He made his choice, and as he lay in bed
He pictured to himself in heart and head
How fresh her beauty was, her age how tender,
Her waist how small, her arms how long and slender,
Her prudent conduct and her gentleness,
Her womanly bearing and her faithfulness.
And when his mind was fixed on her and fettered,
He thought his choice could never have been bettered.
Another summons to his friends he sent,
And asked them first to make no argument
Against his purpose. He said there lived in town
A girl whose beauty was of great renown,
And even though she had been humbly bred
Her youth and beauty were enough, he said,
And he would take this girl to be his wife
In peace and holiness to live his life.
  "One point," he said, "still makes my conscience
    wince.
No man has perfect joy, I've heard long since,
Both here on earth and also up in heaven.
Shun though he will the sins, the deadly seven,
And every branch of that accursed tree,
Yet there is such complete felicity
In marriage and its comforts are so great,
I find myself now, in my aging state,
Appalled lest I should lead so merry a life,
So delicate and free from every strife,
That I shall have my paradise right here.
And since true paradise is bought so dear,

Through stern repentance and through tribulation,
How should I, when I live in such elation
As married men all do, come to that bliss
In which Christ lives eternal? Tell me this."

   "If that is the sole obstacle you see,"
Replied Justinus, "then it well may be
That by God's mercy you'll repent before
You've even led your wife to the church door!
What, God sees to it that his grace is sent
A married man, to help his soul repent,
Far oftener than to a single man!
And hence—I give the best advice I can—
Do not despair! In the upshot of the story
She may turn out to be your purgatory!
She may become God's means of grace, his whip,
And then your soul straight up to heaven will skip
Faster than any arrow from a bow.
I hope hereafter you will come to know
That marriage, in its great felicity,
If you will use its pleasures moderately
And keep from other species of temptation,
Will prove no fatal hindrance to salvation.
On marriage, this great project you have planned,
The Wife of Bath, if you can understand,
Has said much well, and said it in small space.
And now good-by. God keep you in his grace."

   His brothers, when they saw that it must be,
With all the shrewdness of legality
Contracted that this girl, whose name was May,
Should promptly wed this January. The day
Arrived at last when off to church they went,
There to receive the holy sacrament.
Wearing his stole, the priest instructed her
To be as Sarah and Rebecca were,
Faithful and wise. He said the usual prayers
And signed them with the cross, and asked that theirs

Might be a union such as God would bless,
And made all safe enough with holiness.
And thus they have been married solemnly.
   Gay is the palace; from all Italy
The daintiest food and music have been brought.
Nor Orpheus nor Amphion could have wrought
Such melodies; so loud they were to hear
That Joab never trumpeted so clear,
Nor Theodamas with the fate of Thebes in doubt.
Bacchus in every nook was pouring out
The wine, and Venus smiled both left and right,
For January had become her knight
And meant to show that no one could disparage
His prowess whether in liberty or marriage.
With wedding torch in hand she danced along
Before the bride and the whole blissful throng.
You, Martianus, poet who celebrated
Those nuptials when Philology was mated
With Mercury, with the songs that then were sung
By the nine muses, too feeble is your tongue
To write this merry wedding on your page
When tender youth was matched with stooping age!
   The bride sat so becomingly and well
That to behold her seemed a kind of spell.
Queen Esther viewed with no such downcast cheek
Ahasuerus, nor with eye so meek;
And January, whenever he saw her face,
Like one entranced, stood ravished in his place.
But in his heart he threatened that, come night,
He'd strain her to him with more appetite
Than Paris did his Helen. None the less,
Knowing he must offend her tenderness,
He pitied her. "Would God," he said, "O fair
And tender flesh, that you might fully bear
My sharp and keen desire! But that I did
All I desire to do, may God forbid!

Would it were night, and night were never done,
And would to God these people were all gone!"
He took whatever measures he could take,
In a sly fashion, for politeness' sake,
To hurry them from the table; and at last
They rose and danced and drank, and then they cast
Spices about the house, and every man
Was merry but one, a squire named Damian
Who'd carved for January many a day.
He was so ravished by the lady May
He was beside himself, for with her brand
Venus so hurt him he could scarcely stand.
He sought his bed as fast as he knew how.
I have no more to say of him for now.
I leave him there to weep and to complain
Till the young May takes pity on his pain.

   O perilous flames that in the bedstraw glow
Called into service by a household foe!
False steward, servant sly and treacherous,
From your acquaintance God deliver us
As from a subtle adder in the breast!
O January, drunken and possessed
By your desire, behold how Damian,
Your own squire and your humble serving man,
Intends to work on you an injury!
God help you spy this household enemy,
For in this world no peril can befall
Worse than a foeman in your very hall!

   The sun's diurnal arc has run its turn.
No longer may his body now sojourn
Upon the horizon in that latitude.
Night, with its mantle that is dark and rude,
Spreads through the hemisphere and all about,
And now the lusty company sets out,
And taking leave, with thanks on every side,
Home to their houses cheerfully they ride.

Then the time came when hasty January
Desired to go to bed; he would not tarry.
He drank spiced wines and cordials, and partook
Of sundry aphrodisiacs from the book
De Coitu, composed by Constantine,
The accursed monk. Of many that were fine
He had a plentiful supply on call,
And no distaste for eating one and all.
"For love of God, as soon as it can be,"
He told his friends, "without discourtesy,
Empty the house!" At length the bride was led,
No stone more silent, to the marriage bed,
And by the priest the bed was duly blessed,
And all the people from the chamber pressed,
And January needed no advice
To seize his youthful May, his paradise.
He fondles her, he kisses her right often;
But little had a fresh trim done to soften
His bristling beard, as harsh as dogfish skin
And sharp as briar. "Alas, that I must sin
Against your tenderness before I'm through,"
He said. "Yet think! No laborer can do
His task at once both well and hastily.
With leisure this will all go perfectly.
How long we frolic is our own affair.
In wedlock we are joined as a true pair,
And blessed be the yoke that we are in,
For acts of marriage do not count as sin.
A man can do no sin with his own wife,
Nor trespass on himself with his own knife.
The law itself has given us leave to play."
And so he labored till the break of day,
And took a sop in wine, and sat up straight,
And sang aloud in bed, and kissed his mate,
And squawked and jabbered on like a magpie,
While as he sang the skin hung slack and dry

About his neck. But God knows in her heart
What May thought as he played his coltish part
In shirt and nightcap, his neck wrinkled lean.
She did not think his antics worth a bean.

   "The day has come," he said at last. "I'll take
My rest now, for I cannot stay awake,"
And down he laid his head and slept till prime.
And later, at what he thought a fitting time,
January arose; but youthful May
Remained within her room till the fourth day,
A custom brides observe, and for the best;
For every laborer sometime must have rest
Or else he could not hope to stay alive;
Bird, beast, or man, no creature would survive.

   This Damian meanwhile, sick with Venus' fire,
So burned that he was dying for desire,
And secretly he set about to borrow
A pen-case, and set down his tale of sorrow
As a complaint in form, or as a lay
To the fresh beauty of his lady May,
And putting his life to risk, for better or worse,
He pinned it next his heart in a silk purse.

   When the young May had let the fourth day pass
From noon to noon, then, after the high mass,
At dinner in the hall she took her place.
Fresh as a summer's morning was her face.
It chanced that January, that kindly man,
Bethought himself of absent Damian.
"Mother of God," he said, "how can it be
That Damian isn't here to carve for me?
What, is he ill?" The other squires were quick
To excuse him on the ground that he was sick;
Nought else, they said, could keep him from his charge.

   "This troubles me no little. By and large,"
Said January, "I never expect to meet
A squire so wise, trustworthy, and discreet.

A pity it would be if he should die!
He is an excellent man. But by and by,
When we have finished dinner, I shall pay
A visit to him, and so too shall May,
To give him comfort." For this generous word
The knight was blessed by everyone who heard.
"Madame," he said, "be sure that you and all
Your women, after dinner, go and call
On Damian. Say that I will come as well
As soon as I have rested for a spell.
But hurry," he told her. "I can hardly bide
The time till you are sleeping by my side."

   With her attendant women the young May
Went presently to the room where Damian lay.
She sat down by his bedside, full of cheer,
And Damian, when he saw the way was clear,
Slipped the purse in her hand, and sighed, and said,
"Mercy! Do not expose me! I am dead
If what is in this purse should come to light."
She hid the purse as quickly as she might
Within her bosom; there let it safely stay
While back to January she makes her way!

   He on the bedside comfortably was seated.
With many a kiss his youthful bride he greeted,
Then all at once lay down to sleep. She feigned
A need to go where we are all constrained
To go at sundry times. By this invention
She gave to Damian's billet due attention,
And tearing it to pieces at the last,
The shreds in the privy secretly she cast.

   Who now is in a study but fair May?
Beside old January down she lay,
Who slept until he woke up with a cough,
And wanted her to take her clothing off,
For he desired of her, he said, some pleasure
To which her clothes were not a helpful measure.

Whether or not she liked it, she obeyed.
But lest the more fastidious should upbraid,
Just what he did I do not dare to tell,
Or whether she thought it paradise or hell.
I leave them at their work while the day flies
Till the bell for evensong, when they must rise.

    Whether it was predestined or by chance,
Or that the planets did not look askance
But stood at that time in benign array—
Since all things have their time, the learned say—
For any woman to obtain her love,
I cannot answer. The great God above,
Who knows that nothing is without a cause,
Let him judge of the matter! But truth was
That in her youth and freshness the fair May
Took an impression from that very day
So full of pity for this Damian
That from her heart she cannot drive the man.
"I do not care whom this thing may offend,"
She thought, "for here I promise to the end
To love him best of any soul alive."

    How nobly generosity can thrive
In women, when their minds are left alone!
Some tyrant, with a heart as hard as stone,
Might well have let him perish in his place
Rather than take him kindly to her grace,
Rejoicing in the cruelty of her pride,
Heedless that she became a homicide!
Not so this gentle May, for on her part,
Since pity soonest fills a noble heart,
She wrote to him and granted him her grace;
Nothing remained, she said, but time and place;
And when the road was clear, this gentle May
Called upon Damian again one day,
Under his pillow slyly thrust her letter,
And squeezed his hand, and told him to get better.

Up on his feet was Damian by the morrow.
Quite vanished were his sickness and his sorrow.
He preened and primped himself and combed his hair,
And went to January with an air
As humble as a dog beneath the stick.
He was so pleasant and so politic
That all who spoke of him spoke only good,
And fully in his lady's grace he stood.

Some scholars tell us that the only true
Felicity is pleasure; to this view,
In noble fashion, as became a knight,
January subscribed with all his might.
His house, his way of life, were like a king's.
He had a garden, among other things,
Walled in with stone, and truly I suppose
That he who wrote the *Romance of the Rose*
Could tell its beauty only in small part,
Nor could Priapus summon up the art,
Though god of gardens, to describe how cool
Amid the garden lay the flowering pool
Under a laurel that was always green.
Many a time came Pluto and his queen,
Proserpina, with all their faërie throng
About this pool, dancing and making song.

Old January here so loved to be
That no one was allowed to touch the key
Except himself; he carried early and late
A silver latchkey to the wicket gate,
And in the summer thither he would go
With May his wife, and no one else to know,
And anything that wasn't done in bed
He accomplished in the garden plot instead.
So this old January and youthful May
Lived in this fashion many a merry day.
But worldly satisfactions will take wing
From January and every living thing!

O stroke of chance, O Fortune mutable,
Like the deceiving scorpion inscrutable
With flattery in his eye, death in his tail!
O brittle joy, your venom will not fail,
Strange monster, that in hues of steadfast glow
Can paint your gifts, deceiving high and low!
Old January, whom you first received
As your full friend, why have you now bereaved
Of both his eyes? This noble man, alas,
In mid prosperity sees his pleasure pass,
For he is blind, and that quite suddenly,
And with this loss the fire of jealousy
So burns his heart that in his grief and pain
He wishes both his wife and he were slain.
He wanted her to himself in death and life,
Neither a mistress nor again a wife,
But dressed in black, and in her widowed state
Sole as the turtledove without a mate.

But when he had fretted for a month and raged,
His grief at last began to be assuaged.
He bore in patience his adversity,
Except for his outrageous jealousy
Which would not suffer his wife, for love or honor,
To take a step without his hand upon her;
And this brought many a tear to the young May
And grief to Damian; neither night nor day
Could he speak words of purpose to her ear
Unless old January was there to hear.
But back and forth between them letters went
And each by signs knew what the other meant.

O January, what would it avail
If you could see as far as ships can sail?
For in the end it is no worse to be
Deluded blind than when a man can see.
Argus, although he had a hundred eyes,
Was yet deceived, and so to their surprise

Have others been who never could suppose
That they would find themselves hoodwinked, God
    knows!
  The youthful May, despite his jealousy,
In warm wax made a double of the key
That January kept, by which he went
Into the garden; and knowing her intent,
Damian took the wax and made from it
As slyly as he could a counterfeit.
This key portends a marvel, it is clear,
Which, if you want to listen, you shall hear.
  Ovid, God knows the truth of what you say
So nobly: where is the ruse that in some way
Love will not find, though long and arduous?
Remember Thisbe and her Pyramus!
Though strictly kept apart, yet after all
They made their plans by whispering through a
    wall,
A stratagem that no one could have guessed.
  It happened that January became obsessed,
Through his wife's egging on, again to pay
A visit to his garden. The eighth day
Of June had come when "Up," he said, "my love!
Come forth now, for your eyes are like a dove!
Winter is past, and all his wet rains dried.
The voice of the turtle is heard in the land. My bride,
My shining spouse, come forth now, and be mine!
The garden is enclosed. Fairer than wine
Your breasts are to behold, my chosen wife,
In whom I have found no blemish all my life!"
  Such were the old lascivious words he said.
She signaled Damian to go on ahead,
And with his key he slipped in through the gate
And quietly under a bush sat down to wait.
Then January, as blind as any stone,
With May in hand, thinking they were alone,

Entered his garden, fresh and fair. Behind them
He banged the wicket so that none should find them.
   "You are the soul," he said, "that I best love,
For by the Lord who sits in heaven above
I should far rather die upon a knife
Than do you any wrong, my own true wife!
Remember how I chose you, not for greed,
God is my witness, but pure love, indeed.
And though I may be old and cannot see,
Yet for the love of God be true to me!
Three things you have to gain by being true:
The love of Christ, the honor that is due
A faithful wife, and my estate entire.
Have the agreement drawn as you desire;
It is all yours, and I will have this done
Before the setting of tomorrow's sun,
So may God bring my soul at last to bliss!
And now in covenant let me ask a kiss,
And do not blame the jealous watch I keep
For you are printed on my heart so deep
That knowing I am old and you are fair
Makes absence from you more than I can bear
For very love, and this is past all doubt.
Now kiss me, wife, and then we'll stroll about."
   At this the youthful May began to weep.
"I have a soul as well as you to keep,"
She answered. "Let me perish on that day,
So help me God, and in the foulest way
A woman can, when I do such a shame
To all my kind, or sully so my name
As to be false; and should I prove so black,
Then have me stripped and put me in a sack
And in the nearest river let me drown.
I am gently bred, no woman of the town.
Why do you speak this way? But ever untrue
You men are; your reproofs are ever new.

You don't know how to wear a trustful face,
But doubt us and accuse us of disgrace."
    With this she looked and saw where Damian
Was sitting under his bush, and she began
To cough and with her fingers stealthily
She motioned him to climb up in a tree
That stood charged with its fruit, and up he went.
He knew well what her every signal meant
And was acquainted with her mind far better
Than her own husband was, for in a letter
She'd told him how the business should proceed
And given him all the instructions he would need.
And so I leave him perched in his pear tree
While January and May stroll merrily.
    Bright was the day and blue the firmament,
And Phoebus flowed down, golden in descent,
To gladden every flower with balminess.
He was in Gemini, as I should guess,
Only a little from his declination
In Cancer, which is Jupiter's exaltation.
And it so happened, that bright morningtide,
That in the garden, at the farther side,
Pluto, who is the king of Faëry,
And many a lady in his company,
Was sitting on a turf-bench fresh and green
Together with Proserpina, his queen,
Whom he had ravished once upon a day
And in his grisly chariot fetched away
While she was gathering flowers in a mead
On Aetna, as in Claudian you may read.
    "Wife," Pluto said, "this no one can deny;
Experience daily thrusts on every eye
The myriad treasons women do to man.
There are ten thousand notable tales I can
Relate of your sly fickleness and stealth.
O Solomon, first in wisdom and in wealth,

Remembrance of your words ought not to fail!
Thus did he praise the virtues of the male:
'Among a thousand men I have found one,
But among women I have yet found none.'
So says the king who knows your wickedness!
Jesus, the son of Sirach, as I guess,
Speaks of you too with little deference.
An itch and a corrupting pestilence
This very day upon your bodies light!
Do you not see this honorable knight?
Because, alas, he is blind and old of limb,
His own man is about to cuckold him.
See where he sits, the lecher, in the tree!
But I propose now, in my majesty,
In justice to this old, blind, worthy knight,
To give him back again his lost eyesight
Just when his wife intends to wrong his name.
He'll know that she's a harlot, to the shame
Of her and all who may be like her, too."

    "So?" said Proserpina. "That's what you'll do?
Then by my mother's soul, I'll undertake
To give her, and all women for her sake,
An answer adequate to save their faces
If they are taken in embarrassing cases.
I shall see to it that no woman dies
For lack of answer; though with both his eyes
A man had seen a thing, yet we shall swear,
Outface, and weep, and scold, and overbear
And by our boldness find means to excuse us
And put to rout the people who accuse us
Until you men look gullible as geese.
What do I care for your authorities?
I know well that this Jew, this Solomon,
Found women who were fools, and more than one.
But though he found no woman true and good,
Plenty of other men have lived who could

Discover women who were virtuous.
Witness those women dwelling in Christ's house!
By martyrdom they proved their constancy.
But don't be in a pet, true though it be
He said he found no woman who was good.
Accept it as it should be understood.
In God alone, he meant, may we behold
The sovereign goodness, God who sits threefold.
Come, for the sake of God, who is but one,
Why do you make so much of Solomon?
What though his life was rich and glorious?
What though he made a temple, God's own house?
He made one also to false gods, this king.
How could he do a more forbidden thing?
He was, however you whitewash his name,
A lecher and idolater all the same.
The true God in his old age he forsook.
God spared him for his father's sake, the book
Informs us, or he'd sooner have expired,
This rich old Solomon, than he desired.
The slanders that you publish, lie for lie,
On women, are not worth a butterfly!
I am a woman, and for woman's sake
Must speak, or swell and perish of heartbreak;
For since he said our tongues are doomed to rail,
I'll answer those who slander us, never fail!"

  "Good madame, don't be angry any more,"
Said Pluto. "I give up! But since I swore
To give this man his sight, as I had planned,
I warn you fairly that my word must stand.
I am a king; lies would discredit me."

  "And I," she said, "a queen of Faëry!
I shall provide her answer, never doubt it.
And now let's have no further words about it."

  Meanwhile in the garden with his lovely May
Old January was piping like a jay,

"You are my love, and other I have none."
They walked about the pathways, one by one,
Until they came again to the pear tree
Where Damian was sitting watchfully
Among the leaves that hung so fresh and green.
   "Alas," May sighed, "for love of heaven's queen,
I must have some of the small pears I see
Or I shall perish, for so desperately,
As I can tell you, a woman in my plight
May crave fruit that unless her appetite
Is soothed she well may die."
                              "Alas the time!
Had I a servant here, one who could climb!
Alas, that I have lost my sight!" he cried.
   "Indeed, yes, but for all that," she replied.
"Although I know you've little faith in me,
If you would put your arms around the tree,
I could, by setting my foot upon your back,
Climb well enough."
                    "My heart's blood should not lack,"
He said, "if it would help you." Down he bent;
She clambered on his back and up she went.
Ladies, I am a rude and ignorant man;
I cannot use fine phrases. Damian
Pulled up her smock and suddenly pitched in.
And Pluto, when he saw this act of sin,
At once restored to January his sight
And made him see as well as ever he might.
And when he had regained his sight once more
There never was man so glad on any score;
But with his thoughts fixed always firm and fast
Upon his wife, up in the tree he cast
His opening glance, where Damian had addressed
Young May in a manner not to be expressed
Unless I were to speak indecorously.
He let out such a yell of agony

As does a mother seeing her child die.
"Stop! Help! For God's love!" he began to cry.
"Outrageous woman, what is this you do?"
    And promptly she replied, "Sir, what ails you?
Be patient and of reasonable mind!
I have only helped you see when you were blind.
So may my soul be saved, I tell no lies!
I found out that the way to heal your eyes,
The sovereign remedy to make you see,
Was wrestling with a man up in a tree.
God knows I did it with the best intent."
    "Wrestle!" he answered. "Yes, but in it went!
He did it to you, I saw it with my eyes.
May I be hanged if it was otherwise!"
    "My medicine is false, then! Could you see,
You never would have used such words to me.
You have a glimmer only, not true sight."
    "I see," he said, "as well as ever I might,
With both my eyes, thank God; and God forbid it,
But on my word, it seemed to me he did it."
    "You're in a daze, a daze, good sir," said she.
"This is my thanks for helping you to see!
Alas, that ever I tried to be so kind!"
    "Well, then," he said, "let it all slip from mind.
Come down, my love. If I have spoken amiss,
I am sorry for it, as I hope for bliss.
But by my father's soul, I could well see,
Or so I thought, how Damian in that tree
Lay by you, and your smock lay on your breast!"
    "Well, sir," she answered, "think as you think best.
But, sir, a man who wakens out of sleep
Is hardly able all at once to keep
His mind on things or see without mistakes.
He has to wait until he truly wakes.
So with a man long blinded it will be.
He cannot all at once expect to see

When first his sight returns as he will do
When he has had his eyes a day or two.
Until your vision settles for a while,
There's many an object likely to beguile
Your eyesight. Do take care, for by heaven's king,
A man may fancy he perceives a thing
That's nowise what it seems at the first view,
And he that misconceives will misconstrue."
   With this she sprang down lightly from the tree.
Who now rejoices if it is not he?
Stroking her softly, and with many a kiss,
Back to his palace he leads her home in bliss.
And so I end my tale of January.
God bless us, and his holy mother, Mary.

Epilogue to the Merchant's Tale

"God's mercy! From a wife like that, I pray,"
Our Host declared, "God keep me well away!
You see what kind of sleights and subtleties
There are in women! They are busy as bees
Fooling us innocent men in age or youth,
And in a pinch they'll always waive the truth.
On that the Merchant's tale has set the seal.
I have a wife, and there's no blade of steel,
Although she's poor, more faithful and more true;
But she's a telltale and a noisy shrew
And has a heap of other faults as well.
No matter! These aren't things it helps to tell.
But do you know? This much I will confide:
Bitter is my remorse at being tied
To such a woman. I'd be a fool to try
And reckon all her faults. The reason why?

My wife would promptly hear a full report
From some among us. Traffic of this sort
Women know how to carry on for fair.
Who it would be I hardly need declare.
Besides, to count her vices, every one,
Exceeds my wit, and so my tale is done."

~~~ ~~~ ~~~ ~~~ ~~~ ~~~ ~~~ ~~~ ~~~ ~~~

Epilogue to the Squire's Tale

[Next in the marriage group comes the Squire's Tale, which Chaucer did not finish. It breaks off at the beginning of Part Three after some 660 lines. Since we have only a fragment, and since the tale is of a kind widely familiar through *The Arabian Nights*, I have not attempted a version here, but have merely summarized the opening situation.

Cambuscan, king of Tartary, has an elder son, Algarsyf, a younger son, Cambalo, and a daughter, Canacee. On his birthday feast, when he had reigned twenty years, a strange knight enters, and with a bearing such that "Gawain, with his courtliness of another age, if he had come again from Faëry, could not have improved on his speech by a word," he presents Cambuscan, on behalf of the king of Arabia and India, with a steed of brass capable of transporting the rider in a single day to any place he might choose, and of flying as high as an eagle. He presents also to Canacee a mirror in which impending mischance can be foreseen and the characters of friends and foes distinguished. He gives her also a ring that enables the wearer to understand the language of any bird and the healing properties of all herbs. His presents include a sword the edge of which will bite through any armor, while the flat of the blade will cure the wounds inflicted by the edge.

It was this unfinished tale that prompted Milton, in "Il
Penseroso," to write his famous recollection of Chaucer:

> Or call up him that left half told
> The story of Cambuscan bold,
> Of Camball, and of Algarsife,
> And who had Canace to wife
> That owned the virtuous ring and glass,
> And of the wondrous horse of brass
> On which the Tartar king did ride.

Apparently the Squire's Tale, like the stories of the
Friar and the Summoner, was to form an interlude in
the discussion of marriage. The Franklin returns to the
theme.]

"Well done, and nobly, Squire," the Franklin said.
"I praise the wit you carry in your head.
Considering that your age is still so scant,
You speak so feelingly that I would grant,
For my part, if you live, there's no one here
Likely in eloquence to prove your peer.
God give you luck, sir! May it never desert you,
And may God help you to persist in virtue!
What you have said gives great delight to me.
I have a son, and by the Trinity
I'd rather than a parcel of good land
Should tumble right this moment in my hand,
That he could be a man of such discretion
As you are! Where's the value in possession
Unless a man is virtuous, I would know?
I've chided with my son, and shall do so,
For not applying himself to virtuous ends.
He plays at dice, he gambles and he spends,
And loses all he has; that is his way.
And he would rather pass the time of day
With servants than surrender to the leading

Of worthy men who would teach him sense and breed-
      ing."
   "Straw for your breeding!" said our Host. "You know,
      sir,
That each of you must tell a tale or so, sir,
Or go back on your word."
                           "Indeed I do.
Don't blame me if I speak a word or two,"
The Franklin answered, "with the Squire, here."
   "Tell on, begin. Let nothing interfere."
   "Gladly, Sir Host," he said. "I will obey
As best I can. Listen to what I say,
And if, as may God grant, it pleases you,
Then I can rest assured my tale will do."

Prologue to the Franklin's Tale

The old chivalric Bretons in their days
Wrote various romances, known as "lays,"
In rhyme, in their original Breton tongue.
These lays to the sound of instruments were sung,
Or read if the company were so inclined;
And one of these old lays I have in mind,
Which I will say with what good will I can.
But, sirs, because I am an ignorant man,
Here at the very outset, I beseech,
Forgive me for the rudeness of my speech.
The study of rhetoric never was my care;
The things I say, they must be plain and bare.
I never on Parnassus slept; I know
Nothing of Marcus Tullius Cicero.
The only colors I can recognize
Grow in the fields, or come from paints or dyes;

All other hues I find remote and strange.
Colors of rhetoric are beyond my range.
To all such matters my responses fail;
But if you like, you may listen to my tale.

ல்லை ல்லை ல்லை ல்லை ல்லை ல்லை ல்லை ல்லை ல்லை ல்லை

The Franklin's Tale

Once in Armorica, or Brittany,
There lived a knight who labored busily
To serve a lady as best he could devise.
Many an exploit and great enterprise
He undertook before she would be won,
For she was fair as any under the sun
And came of kindred of so high a sphere
That scarcely had this knight the heart for fear
To tell his pain. At last his worthiness,
And most of all his mild submissiveness,
Upon her secret heart contrived to bring
So deep a pity for his suffering
That she was ready with her full accord
To take him for her husband and her lord,
In lordship such as men have over their wives.
And in the greater bliss to lead their lives
He pledged her by his free will as a knight
That he would never, by darkness or daylight,
Against her will assert his sovereignty
Or put on the least show of jealousy,
But rather obey her will in all he could
As any lover with his lady should,
Except that his authority in name
He would preserve; that he must do for shame.
  She thanked him, and with great humility
She answered him, "Sir, since you offer me

A free rein, as you generously do,
May God forbid that ever, between us two,
Through fault of mine there should be any strife.
Sir, I will be your true, your humble wife,
I swear, until my heart bursts in my breast."
So they were both at ease, and lived in' rest.

For one thing, sirs, in safety I dare say:
One friend must let another have his way
Or not for long will friends keep company.
Love will not be constrained. Authority
No sooner comes than with a clap of wing,
Farewell! Love's god is gone. Love is a thing
As any spirit free. All women crave
Freedom by nature, not like some bond-slave
To be held in subjection; and so too,
Should I confess the whole truth, we men do.
In love, the most forbearing man does best.
He has the advantage over all the rest.
Great merit lies in patience, every way,
For it can conquer, as the learned say,
Points that assertiveness can never gain.
At every word a man may not complain.
Learn to forbear, or else, as our lives go,
You'll learn as much whether you will or no.
There's not a living soul, be sure of this,
Who sometimes does not do or speak amiss.
Anger or sickness or the stars' position,
Wine, woe, or change of bodily condition,
Cause many an act of haste or word of spite.
No man can be avenged for every slight.
To all who have a touch of self-command
The time must tell whether to yield or stand.

This worthy knight, wise in such ways as these,
Pledged her his patience for a life of ease,
And she on her side undertook to swear
No fault of hers would give him cause for care.

Both wise and humble was this true accord.
And so she took her servant and her lord,
In love her servant and her lord in marriage.
He lord and servant both? But why disparage
His state as service? It was high above,
For he had both his lady and his love,
His lady as she long had been, and now
His wife too, as the laws of love allow.
And in this comfort, that defies all telling,
He took her home, near Penmark, to his dwelling.

   A year and more they dwelt together thus,
Until this knight, known as Arveragus,
Resolved to go and live a year or two
In England, for the exploits he might do
In arms; on such an honorable part,
For all its arduousness, he set his heart.

   But now to speak of Dorigen, his wife,
Who loved her husband as her heart's own life.
She sighed and mourned his absence past all measure,
As wives do nobly when it gives them pleasure.
She could not sleep, she fasted and complained,
And longing for his presence so constrained
Her heart that all the world seemed bleak and bare.
Her friends, who were acquainted with her care,
Gave her such consolation as friends may,
Haranguing her, and urging night and day
That she was killing herself quite needlessly,
And every kind of comfort there can be
They plied her with and proffered early and late
To make her give up her unhappy state.

   Little by little, as everybody knows,
A man may chisel stone until it shows,
In time, some figure graven on its face;
And so in time her boundless grief gave place,
And what with hope and reason's ministration
She took the imprint of their consolation.

Arveragus, in the midst of all her care,
Sent letters home to tell of his welfare
And promised quickly to come back again
Or else his heart would break for Dorigen.

Her friends saw that her grief began to slake,
And on their knees they begged her, for God's sake,
To join their company, to stroll and play
And drive her gloomy fantasies away;
And finally she granted their request,
Seeing that her consent was for the best.

Her castle stood on ground close by the sea,
And walking with her friends for company
And looking out from where the cliffs rose high
She saw the barges and the ships pass by
Sailing their course, wherever they chose to go.
But this became a portion of her woe,
For often to herself, "Alas," said she,
"Is there no single ship of all I see
Will bring my lord home? Were we not apart,
All healed would be my bitterness of heart."

Or on the cliffside she would sit and think
At other times, and look down from the brink;
But when she saw the ledges black and drear,
She scarcely could support herself for fear,
And sinking down with cold sighs on the turf
She piteously stared at the white surf.
"Eternal God," she said, "whose providence
Governs the world, in your omnipotence
You make no idle thing, as men declare.
But, Lord, these grisly ledges, black and bare,
That rather in their fiendish desolation
Seem a foul chaos than a fair creation
By such a perfect God, steadfast and wise,
Why have you wrought this work that so defies
All reason? By it, whether west or east,
Is fostered neither man nor bird nor beast.

Not good but harm comes of it, to my thought.
Do you not see the deaths these rocks have wrought?
A hundred thousand bodies of mankind,
Lord, they have slain and banished out of mind,
Yet of your work so fair a part was man
You made him in your likeness. By your plan
It seemed you felt great partiality
Toward man at first; but then how can it be
That you create our means of overthrow,
And means that bring no good, but only woe?
Well do I know the learned are content
To prove all for the best by argument,
For reasons, as they say, beyond my knowing.
But may the God who set the wind to blowing
Keep my lord safe! On that point I will rest
And let the learned argue what is best!
But these black rocks, Lord, that you deigned to make,
In hell I would they were sunken for his sake!
These ledges kill my very heart for fear."
So she would say, with many a piteous tear.

   Her friends perceived it gave her no relief
To ramble by the sea, but rather grief,
And so they took her elsewhere for diversion.
They went on many a countryside excursion
To springs and rivers that were thought entrancing.
They played chess and backgammon and went dancing.
One morning, well provisioned for the day,
They set out for a garden; it was May,
May that had painted with his gentle showers
This garden with all hues of leaves and flowers;
And men had laid it out by artifice
With such a skill that, as I hope for bliss,
No garden was so fair at any price
Unless it were, for certain, paradise.
The odor of the flowers, fresh to sight,
Might well have made the lowest heart feel light

That ever was born into this world, unless
Disease or great grief ruled it to excess,
Delight so filled the place at every glance.

After their dinner they began to dance
And sing, save Dorigen, who still forlorn
Within her heart could never cease to mourn,
Not seeing him among the dancers go
Who was her husband and her love also.

Now in this dance, among the other men,
A squire danced in view of Dorigen
Jollier in appearance and more gay,
Or so I judge, than the very month of May.
He sang, he danced, better than any man
Who is or has been since the world began.
And if to picture him I could contrive,
He was among the handsomest men alive,
Young, strong, and full of courage, rich and wise,
And well regarded. Briefly, to disguise
No truth, this lusty squire, all quite unknown
To Dorigen herself, loved her alone
Above all creatures. But he did not dare
To tell his pain; he had fallen in despair.
Cupless, he drank his grief; he dared not say
A word except in songs. He would betray
Somewhat in them, in general, how he burned,
Saying he loved, and found love unreturned,
And made upon this theme, in sundry ways,
Complaints and songs, rondels and virelays.
His grief, he said, he did not dare to tell,
But languished as a fury does in hell.
He said that he would die as Echo did
For her Narcissus, all her passion hid.
These were the only clues he dared to chance,
Except perhaps that sometimes at a dance
It may well be he looked into her face
In such style as a man who pleads for grace.

But she knew nothing at all of his intent.
And yet before the company all went,
While they were in the garden, it befell,
Since he was one of whom the world spoke well,
A neighbor, too, whom she had known before,
That they began to talk; and more and more
He approached his purpose with her, saying thus,
This handsome squire, known as Aurelius:
"Madame," he said, "if I might hope to please
Your heart, by God who made the earth and seas,
I wish that day that your Arveragus
Went on his voyage, I, Aurelius,
Had gone whence I should never again return,
For well I know that all in vain I burn.
My one reward is but my breaking heart.
Madame, take pity on my sorrow's smart!
A word of yours can slay me or can save.
Here at your feet would God I found my grave!
I have no time to spend on further breath.
Have mercy, sweet, or you will cause my death!"
  She looked, with these words, at Aurelius.
"Is this your drift?" she said. "Do you speak thus?
Never before have I known what you meant,
But now, Aurelius, I see your intent.
By the very God who gave me soul and life,
Never shall I become an untrue wife
In word or work; with all my strength of wit
I will be his to whom I have been knit.
That's all the answer you shall get from me."
But afterward she told him jokingly,
"Aurelius, by Almighty God above,
I promise you that I will be your love,
Since your complaint is pitiable, I see,
That day when from the length of Brittany
You move the rocks and ledges, without fail,
And leave no stone to stop a coasting sail,

I say, when you have made the coast so clean
Of rocks there's not a stone left to be seen,
Then I will love you best of any man.
This pledge I'll keep as well as ever I can."

"Is there no other grace in you?" said he.

"No, by the Lord," she answered, "who made me!
I know all this will never come about.
This folly in your heart, go cast it out!
What pleasure can a man take in his life
Falling in love with someone else's wife
Who has her body freely at his will?"

Aurelius felt his heart with sorrow fill.

"This is impossible," he said, "and I,
Madame, at once and horribly must die."

Home to his house he went in mortal hurt.
He saw that it was past him to avert
His death; he felt his heart already cold.
On bare knees sinking, he began to hold
His hands toward heaven, and quite out of his head
Implored the gods, not knowing what he said.

"Lord of all growing things, who in your power
Give times and seasons to each herb and flower
According to your station in the sky,
Phoebus," he said, "look with a pitying eye
On me, Aurelius, wretched and forlorn,
Whose death, Lord, by his lady has been sworn.
For I know well that if you so incline
You best can help this failing heart of mine,
Save for my lady. Vouchsafe that I may say,
Phoebus, what help I need, and in what way.

"Your sister, the fair Luna—she, I mean,
The goddess of the ocean and its queen,
(Though Neptune is the ocean's deity,
Yet empress over him in turn is she)—
You well know, Lord, that just as her desire
Is to be quickened and lighted by your fire

For which she follows you so busily,
Even so the sea desires naturally
To follow her, the goddess over all
Oceans and rivers also, great and small.
Wherefore, Lord Phoebus, this is my petition:
When next she faces you in opposition,
In Leo, pray her by her grace to hide
Five fathoms deep beneath a great flood tide
The highest rock on the coast of Brittany.
Lord Phoebus, do this miracle for me!
Then truly to my lady may I say:
'Now keep your promise, the rocks are all away!'
Implore your sister for two years to run
Her journey at the same pace as the sun;
Then, facing you, she will be full and bright
Always, and spring tide will last day and night.
Let flood tide last two years! If in this way
She will not make my lady mine, then pray
That she will sink each last rock underground
Into her own dark realm, where she is bound
To Pluto, and on bare feet I will seek
Your Delphian temple. The tears upon my cheek
See, and take pity! Do not look askance."
With this he swooned and fell down in a trance.

His brother took him up, and to his bed
Brought him, distracted both in heart and head,
And there, for my part, I will let him lie
And choose, himself, whether to live or die.

In welfare and great honor through the sea,
As if he were the flower of chivalry,
Arveragus, with other worthy men,
Came safely home. O happy Dorigen,
Who took her husband in her arms once more,
The lusty knight, the worthy man of war,
Who loved her as he loved his own heart's life.
He nourished no suspicions of his wife;

If in his absence someone had undertaken
To talk love to her, it left his faith unshaken.
For questions such as these he had no leisure.
He jousted, danced, and labored for her pleasure.
And so I leave them in their bliss to dwell,
And of the sick Aurelius I will tell.

   Wasting with grief Aurelius lay bound
Two years before he could set foot on ground.
To no one could he have a hope of turning
For help except his brother, a man of learning,
The only living soul who had ever heard
His toil and trouble, even by a word,
For he had kept his love more tightly hid
Than Pamphilus for Galatea did.
To outward view his breast looked whole and clean,
But in his heart the arrow rankled keen,
And wounds, as well you know, that seem to heal
Are dangerous, unless the surgeon's steel
Can reach the arrow. His brother, by good chance,
Recalled at last that when he was in France,
At Orleans—as in every nook and cranny
Young students like to delve for the uncanny
And lore that leads them well out of their way—
While he was studying, he saw one day
A book of natural magic, which a friend
Who was at Orleans for another end,
The study of law, had left in spite of all
Upon his desk. He started to recall
This book, that spoke much of the operations
Founded upon the eight and twenty stations
Belonging to the moon—such stuff as that,
Nonsense in our own day not worth a gnat,
For Holy Church forbids, in our belief,
That through such folly we should come to grief.

   His heart began to dance for very glee
Remembering this book. "Immediately,

My brother," he told himself, "shall find his cure,
For there are sciences, of that I'm sure,
That can produce such triumphs of illusion
As these magicians work to men's confusion.
Magicians, I've heard tell, have brought a barge
Into a banquet hall to row at large
On water, or a lion with grim head,
Or made flowers grow, or grapes both white and red,
Or made a castle rise of mortar and stone,
And at a chosen moment—*poof*, it's gone,
Though it appeared to everybody's sight.
My thought is this: at Orleans, if I might
Discover an old school friend who had in mind
The mansions of the moon, or another kind
Of natural magic, he could save my brother.
For by illusion, one way or another,
A learned clerk could make men seem to see
That all the frowning rocks in Brittany
Were gone, and ships were sailing close to shore,
And make the spell last for a week or more.
And then my brother in his love could feast,
Or breaking her word, she would be shamed, at least."
    Why should I make a longer tale of this?
He gave his brother such a hope of bliss
That up he got from bed without delay
And started off toward Orleans. On their way,
Only a little distance from the town,
They noticed a young student, sole alone,
Approaching them, and at the point of meeting
He gave them both a cheerful Latin greeting,
And then he said a marvelous thing: "I know
Why you have come here," and they could not go
Another step, had they been so inclined,
Before he told them all they had in mind.
    About his friends of student days long sped
Aurelius' brother asked him; they were dead,

The student answered him, at which he wept.
   Down from his horse's back Aurelius leapt
And went home to his house with this magician.
The luxuries placed at their disposition
Aurelius never had seen in all his days.
Before they supped, their host put on displays
Of deer-thronged parks and great stags antlered
   high,
The tallest that were ever seen with eye.
Aurelius watched a hundred killed by hounds
Or bleeding bitterly with arrow wounds.
He saw, when the deer had vanished into air,
Some falconers by a river flowing fair,
And by their hawks he watched a heron slain.
He saw knights who were jousting on a plain,
He saw his lady, as a final pleasure,
Dancing, and saw himself, too, dance the measure.
And when the master who had wrought this spell
Saw it was time, he clapped hands, and farewell!
The revels were all gone, and left no trace.
Yet from the house they had never moved a pace,
But sat still in his study, where on shelves
He kept his books, and none except themselves
To watch these marvels.
               He called out to inquire,
"Is supper ready?"
              "Sir," replied his squire,
"Whenever you like."
              "We'll sup, then. That is best,
For even a lover sometimes needs his rest."
   Then they discussed what his reward should be
For removing all the rocks of Brittany
From the Gironde to the outlet of the Seine.
He set a stiff price, swearing by God's pain
No less than a thousand pounds would do; that sum
Was hardly enough, he said, to make him come.

Aurelius answered, "Tush, a thousand pound!
This whole wide world, that men believe is round,
I'd offer it to you, were I lord of it.
We've driven a bargain, yes, our minds are knit.
You shall be paid to the last pound, no less.
But take care that you don't, for laziness,
Keep us from starting out at once tomorrow."

"Agreed," he said, "or else God give me sorrow."

Aurelius went to bed when he desired
And slept most of the night, for partly tired
And partly with his new hope of relief,
His woeful heart found respite from its grief.
And on the morrow, as soon as it was day,
To Brittany they took the nearest way.

According to the books that I remember,
This happened in the season of December,
Frosty and cold. Phoebus in coppery hue,
He that in Cancer shone so hot and new,
Like burnished gold, with beams that flowed out bright,
In Capricorn was driven to alight
Where he looked old and pale enough, past doubt.
Rain, sleet, and bitter frost had put to rout
Green things in yards and gardens. January
Sat by the fire with forked beard making merry
And from his ox-horn drinking down the wine.
Before him stood the flesh of the tusked swine,
And "Noël!" shouted every lusty man.

Aurelius, in all points that a host can,
Ministered to his guest with deference,
And begged him to exert all diligence
To save him from his sorrow and his smart,
Or with a sword he swore to pierce his heart.

The scholar felt such pity for this man
That night and day he did what cunning can
To learn a time when he could try conclusions
And bring forth such a prodigy of illusions

By means of his celestial jugglery—
I have no knowledge of astrology
Nor of its terms—that she and all would say
The rocks had vanished marvelously away
From Brittany, or sunk beneath the ground.
The most propitious time at last he found.
The hour of moonrise and the lunar station
That best accorded with his operation
He knew, and all his data were complete
To work his superstition and deceit,
Such as men practiced in that heathenish day.
He had no further reason for delay,
And through his magic, for a week or more,
It seemed that all the rocks had quit the shore.

    Aurelius, when he knew he had to meet
No obstacle, fell at his master's feet.
"Grateful am I, sad wretch," he said, "to you,
And grateful to my lady Venus, too,
For this deliverance." And he set out
To visit the temple, where he had no doubt
That he would see his lady, and when he thought
The time was ripe, humbly, with heart distraught
By fear, he greeted her, this woeful man.

    "My lady, whom I love as best I can,
And most would dread of all earth to displease,
But that for you I have so lost all ease
That dead before your feet I must fall down,
You never should know why I am woebegone.
But truly I must die or else complain!
You kill me for no fault through very pain.
But though to save me you would never have stirred,
Take care before you break faith with your word.
Repent before you slay me for my love.
For, Madame, by the very God above,
You know well that your promise was not light.
Not that I challenge anything of right

From you, my lady, but only through your grace;
Yet in a garden yonder—you know the place—
You are well aware of what you promised me,
And in my hand you pledged it, fair and free,
To love me best—God knows you told me this,
Although I am unworthy of such bliss.
Madame, it is your honor I defend
More than my heart's life, though right now it end.
I have done just as you commanded me,
And if you are willing, you may go and see.
Do as you think best; keep your pledge in mind.
Dead or alive, in the garden you will find
My body, in which state is yours to say—
But certainly, the rocks are all away."

He took his leave. Astonished in her place
She stood, no drop of blood in all her face.
She had not dreamt she would fall in such a trap.
"Alas, that this should happen! It is a gap
In nature's order. Never had I thought,"
She cried, "that such a marvel could be wrought
Or such a prodigy be possible!"
And home she went, a creature sorrowful.
To walk was almost more than she could do.
She wept and swooned for a whole day or two
So that it might have moved the hardest eye.
But there was none to whom she could tell why,
For out of town Arveragus had gone.
She spoke alone, within her heart withdrawn,
With pale face and with grief instead of cheer,
And uttered her complaint, as you shall hear:

"Fortune, of you," she said, "must I complain,
For binding me unwitting in your chain,
From which I see no means to help me fly
Except to be dishonored or to die.
One of these two I am compelled to choose,
But none the less I should far rather lose

My life than in my body suffer shame,
Know myself false, or forfeit my fair name.
By death, for certain, I could pay my score,
And has not many a faithful wife before
And many a maiden, caught in such a mesh,
Destroyed herself rather than soil her flesh?

"Yes, true it is; these stories bear me out:
When thirty tyrants, at a drinking bout
In Athens, had slain Phidon, in their spite
They haled his daughters in, for foul delight,
Naked, and on the pavement made them dance
In their sire's blood—God look on them askance!
And these unhappy maidens in their dread,
Rather than lose each one her maidenhead,
Managed somehow to leap into a well
And there to drown themselves, as old books tell.

"Again, from Lacedaemon were required
No less than fifty maids who were desired
By the Messenians for their lechery,
And not one maiden in the company
But she was slain, and with a good intent
Chose rather to be slaughtered than consent
That she should lose by force her maidenhead.
Of death, then, why should I feel any dread?

"Aristoclides, in his tyranny,
Would have defiled Stymphalis, but that she,
After her father had been slain one night,
Straight to Diana's temple took her flight
And with her hands clung to the statue there.
She would not leave it, and no man could tear
Her hands away or make her move a pace
Till she was slaughtered in the very place.

"Now since these maidens with such scorn refused
By man's foul pleasures to be thus abused,
A wife far more should kill herself outright
Than be defiled by their lewd appetite.

What shall I say of Hasdrubal's true wife
Who at the siege of Carthage took her life?
For when she saw the Romans had the town,
She took her children, and with them all leaped down
Into the fire, and chose to die by flame
Rather than let a Roman do her shame.
Did not Lucrece, whom Tarquin took by force,
At Rome find refuge in the same recourse?
She killed herself, thinking it merely shame
To go on living when she had lost her name.
The seven maidens of Miletus, too,
Destroyed themselves for dread lest the Gauls do
An outrage to them. A thousand tales and more
I could recall, I think, upon this score.
The wife of Abradates, when he died,
Into his wounds allowed her blood to glide,
And said, 'At least my body shall remain,
If I have any choice, without a stain.'

    "Think of Alcestis, what a wife was she!
And what says Homer of good Penelope?
All Greece knows of her long-tried faithfulness.
And of chaste Portia I can say no less.
Without her Brutus, whom she swore to give
Her heart whole and entire, she could not live.

    "What more examples need I multiply?
Seeing so many have preferred to die
Rather than suffer foul iniquity,
I will conclude the better part for me
Is to destroy myself than be shamed thus.
I will be faithful to Arveragus
Or else I will contrive some way to die."[1]

    So Dorigen complained, with sorrowing eye,

[1] I have somewhat abbreviated and altered Dorigen's "complaint," omitting a number of examples to which Chaucer makes only general allusion, and transposing her pledge of faithfulness to the end of the speech.

A day or two, until, on the third night
Arveragus came home and saw her plight
And asked her why it was she wept so sore.
But Dorigen at this wept all the more.

"Alas," she cried, "that ever I was born!
Thus have I said, and thus too have I sworn—"
And told him all that you have heard me say.

Her husband answered in the friendliest way,
And cheerfully, "There is nothing further, then?"

"No, no, by God's own truth," said Dorigen.
"This is too much—I speak under God's will."

"Now, wife," he said, "let things that sleep lie still.
All may be well, who knows, this very day.
But you must keep your promise, that I say.
I'd rather be stabbed for very love of you
Than see you to your promised word untrue.
Truth is the highest thing within man's keeping—"
But as he said this word he burst out weeping,
And charged her, "I forbid, on pain of death,
That for as long a time as you draw breath
You let this thing be known to any man—
I will endure my grief as best I can—
Or wear a downcast look, lest people guess
That you have borne a blow or a distress."

He called a squire from among his men,
Also a maid, and "Go with Dorigen
To such a place," he told them. They set out
In ignorance what this errand was about.

Now many of you may well think, in all fact,
That he was a lewd fellow in this act,
Willing to risk his wife to such a fate.
But hear the tale! Before you judge her, wait.
She may have better luck than you have guessed.
Hark to the tale, then judge as you think best.

This amorous Aurelius chanced to meet
Dorigen in the town's most crowded street,

Bound for the garden. Full of his intent,
He greeted her and asked her where she went.
Distractedly, as if she were half mad,
She said, "To the garden, as my husband bade,
To keep my promise there, alas, alas!"
    Aurelius felt a great compassion pass
Into his heart, and wondering at this turn,
Pitied her, and her worthy knight's concern
That she should keep the promise she had spoken,
So loth he was to see his wife's word broken.
On all sides it seemed better to this squire
For pity's sake to abandon his desire
Rather than act so base and mean a part,
Against all generous chivalry of heart.
And so, in a few words, he answered thus:
    "Madame, say to your lord, Arveragus,
That since I can perceive his nobleness
Toward you, and since I see your great distress,
I should far rather suffer woe forever
Than the great love between you mar or sever.
Into your hand, with every surety paid,
Whatever bond or promise you have made,
Madame, I now release, and give my word
Never to charge you with a pledge deferred,
And take my leave of the best and truest wife
Whom ever yet I met in all my life.
But what they promise let all wives take care!
Let them remember Dorigen, and beware!
Thus can a squire perform a generous act
As well as a knight can, and that for fact!"
    She thanked Aurelius kneeling on bare knees,
And went home to her husband, well at ease,
And told him all that you have heard me say.
It was enough, be certain, to repay
Arveragus beyond my power to tell.
Why longer on this matter should I dwell?

Arveragus and Dorigen his wife
In sovereign happiness took up their life.
No difference nettled them or came between.
He cherished her as though she were a queen,
She, true forever after, as before.
Of these two you shall hear from me no more.

Aurelius, who had lost his whole outlay,
Wished that his eyes had never seen the day.
"Alas," he said, "I promised to confer
A thousand pounds on this philosopher,
Pure gold, true weight! What am I now to do?
I see that I am ruined, through and through.
There's nothing for it but to go and sell
My whole estate, and beg. I cannot dwell,
Shaming my kinfolk, longer in this place
Unless I can induce him to show grace.
I'll ask him, though, if he will let me pay
Year after year, by given month and day,
And thank his bounty for the privilege.
I won't play false with him, I'll keep my pledge."

From such funds as his coffers chanced to hold
He carried the magician sums of gold,
Perhaps five hundred pounds' worth, at the most,
And begged for time. "Master, I dare to boast,"
He said, "that I have never failed a promise yet.
You may be sure that I shall pay my debt
However I fare, however I may be hurt,
Though I'm reduced to begging in my shirt.
But if you would consent, on surety,
To give me a respite, say two years or three,
Then I could manage. If not I must sell
All that my father left me, truth to tell."

"Have I not done for you as I agreed?"
Asked the magician soberly. "Indeed,
Truly and well," Aurelius replied.

"Have you not had your lady?" "No," he sighed.

"What is the reason? Tell me if you can."
And thereupon Aurelius began:
"Arveragus, for very knightliness,
Would rather have died," he said, "in his distress
Than see his wife her promised word undo."
He told him Dorigen's reluctance, too,
How loth she was to be a faithless wife,
How she would rather have given up her life,
How guilelessly, since she had never heard
Of such illusions, she had pledged her word.
"For this I pitied her, and just as he
Freely and nobly sent his wife to me,
I sent her freely back in the same way,
And so it stands; I have no more to say."

The magician, hearing this, replied, "Dear brother,
Each of you acted nobly toward the other.
You are a squire, Arveragus a knight,
Yet God forbid but that a scholar might
In his turn also do a generous act
As well as any of you, in sober fact!
Sir, I forgive your debt to the last pound
As if you had just now popped out of the ground
And never until this moment heard of me!
You shall not pay a penny, but go free,
In spite of all my toil and all my art.
You've lodged and fed me well, and for my part
It is enough. God bless you, and good day."
And so he took his horse and rode away.

Now, sirs, here is a nice case to be tried:
Which of them was most generous? You decide
Before we farther on our journey go.
My tale is done; I have told you all I know.

[One of the manuscript fragments of *The Canterbury Tales* consists of the Second Nun's Prologue and Tale (a life of St. Cecilia) and the Canon's Yeoman's Prologue

and Tale. "At Boughton under Blean forest," as Chaucer
relates, a man clothed in black above a white surplice
overtook the pilgrims, his horse in such a lather it could
hardly keep going. He was accompanied by a Yeoman,
who, in conversation with the Host, began to hint more
and more directly at the profession of his master, the
Canon, who was obviously an alchemist. The Yeoman
describes how they live among thieves in the alleys on the
edge of a town, how they borrow money under pretense
that they can make "two pounds out of one," and how
they always fail in their effort to produce gold by trans-
mutation. The Canon draws near while the Yeoman is
revealing his secrets, and tells him not to say a word
more. The Host commands the Yeoman to keep right
on speaking, and when the Canon sees that he cannot
control the situation, he quickly rides away. The Yeoman
then launches into his tale, which is a series of anecdotes
exposing the cheats and sleights of a canon who practiced
alchemy. (Not the Canon who has just ridden away, as
the Yeoman keeps insisting!) The description of the
canon's tricks is in Chaucer's best colloquial manner, and
the tale is historically valuable; but it is full of alchemical
jargon, and an attempt at a modern version would make
thorny going.

Another manuscript fragment consists of the Physi-
cian's Tale and the Pardoner's Prologue and Tale. Since
Chaucer did not complete *The Canterbury Tales* and
therefore did not give them any final arrangement, I have
not hesitated to put the Pardoner's Tale at a climactic
point toward the end, although editors of Chaucer's text
would place it earlier. It is a folk tale, current through-
out the world in various forms, and certainly one of
Chaucer's finest and best-told stories. Nothing in *The
Canterbury Tales*, indeed, is better than Chaucer's
whole presentation of the Pardoner and his methods
of preaching.

The Physician tells the story of the Roman "knight"
Virginius, his beautiful and virtuous daughter Virginia,
and the unjust magistrate Apius, who, in lust for the

girl, plotted with a scoundrel named Claudius to trump
up a claim that she was really the daughter of Claudius
and had been stolen from the cradle. Apius rules in favor
of Claudius before Virginius can state his case, and thus
Virginia is apparently delivered into the magistrate's
power. Virginius confronts his daughter with the choice
between death and shame, and after asking a little time
to bewail her fate, she asks him to "smite softly with
his sword," and swoons. Virginius cuts off her head and
sends it to the false judge. This tale deeply affects the
Host, whose taste for tragedy the interrupted Monk's
Tale has already shown to be limited.]

The Words of the Host to the Physician and the Pardoner

"Help, by Christ's nails and blood!" our Host began,
Swearing as though beside himself. "This man
Was a false rascal and false judge as well!
The shamefulest death that ever tongue can tell
Fall on such judges and all who give them aid!
And yet this guiltless girl was slain. She paid,
Alas, for all her beauty far too dearly.
Hence men may see, I say, and but too clearly,
The gifts that Fortune and that Nature give
Bring death to many a soul that else might live.
Her beauty was her death, I dare well say.
Alas, she died in such a piteous way!
In both the gifts I spoke of now men find
Harm oftener than profit, to my mind.
But in all truthfulness, my master dear,
This was a pitiable tale to hear.
No matter, let it pass, it's all the same.

God save your gentle flesh and your whole frame,
Also your urinals and thundermugs,
Your hippocras and all your other drugs,
And every box of pills that you possess
I pray God and our Lady Mary bless!
You're a man of dignity, if I can tell it,
Yes, by St. Ronyan, proper as a prelate!
Have I said well? I cannot speak in form,
But well I know you took my heart by storm.
You almost made me have a heart attack.
God's bones! Without a pill to bring it back,
Or else a drink of moist and corny ale,
Or unless I hear right off some merry tale,
This girl has cost my heart, for pity of her.
Now my fine friend," he said, "you Pardoner,
Be quick, tell us a tale of mirth or fun."

    "St. Ninian!" he said, "it shall be done,
But at this tavern here, before my tale,
I'll just go in and have some bread and ale."

    The proper pilgrims in our company
Cried quickly, "Let him speak no ribaldry!
Tell us a moral tale, one to make clear
Some lesson to us, and we'll gladly hear."

    "Just as you wish," he said. "I'll try to think
Of something edifying while I drink."

Prologue to the Pardoner's Tale

"In churches," said the Pardoner, "when I preach,
I use, milords, a lofty style of speech
And ring it out as roundly as a bell,
Knowing by rote all that I have to tell.

My text is ever the same, and ever was:
Radix malorum est cupiditas.[1]

"First I inform them whence I come; that done,
I then display my papal bulls, each one.
I show my license first, my body's warrant,
Sealed by the bishop; it would be abhorrent
If any man made bold, though priest or clerk,
To interrupt me in Christ's holy work.
And after that I give myself full scope.
Bulls in the name of cardinal and pope,
Of bishops and of patriarchs I show.
I say in Latin some few words or so
To spice my sermon; it flavors my appeal
And stirs my listeners to greater zeal.
Then I display my cases made of glass
Crammed to the top with rags and bones. They pass
For relics with all the people in the place.
I have a shoulder bone in a metal case,
Part of a sheep owned by a holy Jew.
'Good men,' I say, 'heed what I'm telling you:
Just let this bone be dipped in any well
And if cow, calf, or sheep, or ox should swell
From eating a worm, or by a worm be stung,
Take water from this well and wash its tongue
And it is healed at once. And furthermore
Of scab and ulcers and of every sore
Shall every sheep be cured, and that straightway,
That drinks from the same well. Heed what I say:
If the good man who owns the beasts will go,
Fasting, each week, and drink before cockcrow
Out of this well, his cattle shall be brought
To multiply—that holy Jew so taught
Our elders—and his property increase.

" 'Moreover, sirs, this bone cures jealousies.

[1] Covetousness is the root of evil.

Though into a jealous madness a man fell,
Let him cook his soup in water from this well,
He'll never, though for truth he knew her sin,
Suspect his wife again, though she took in
A priest, or even two of them or three.

" 'Now here's a mitten that you all can see.
Whoever puts his hand in it shall gain,
Sowing his land, increasing crops of grain,
Be it wheat or oats, provided that he bring
His penny or so to make his offering.

" 'There is one word of warning I must say,
Good men and women. If any here today
Has done a sin so horrible to name
He daren't be shriven of it for the shame,
Or any woman, young or old, is here
Who has cuckolded her husband, be it clear
Such sinners neither have the power nor grace
To offer to my relics in this place.
But any who is free of such dire blame,
Let him come up and offer in God's name
And I'll absolve him through the authority
That by the pope's bull has been granted me.'

"By such hornswoggling I've won, year by year,
A hundred marks[1] since being a pardoner.
I stand in my pulpit like a true divine,
And when the people sit I preach my line
To ignorant souls, as you have heard before,
And tell skullduggeries by the hundred more.
Then I take care to stretch my neck well out
And over the people I nod and peer about
Just like a pigeon perching on a shed.
My hands fly and my tongue wags in my head
So busily that to watch me is a joy.
Avarice is the theme that I employ

---

[1] A substantial sum, considering the purchasing power of money in Chaucer's time.

In all my sermons, to make people free
In giving pennies—especially to me.
My mind is fixed on what I stand to win
And not at all upon correcting sin.
I do not care, when they are in the grave,
If souls go berry-picking that I could save.
Truth is that evil purposes determine,
And many a time, the origin of a sermon:
Some to please people and by flattery
To gain advancement through hypocrisy,
Some for vainglory, some again for hate.
For when I daren't fight otherwise, I wait
And give him a tongue-lashing when I preach.
No man escapes or gets beyond the reach
Of my defaming tongue, supposing he
Has done a wrong to my brethren or to me.
For though I do not tell his proper name,
People will recognize him all the same.
By sign and circumstance I let them learn.
Thus I serve those who have done us an ill turn.
Thus I spit out my venom under hue
Of sanctity, and seem devout and true!

   "To put my purpose briefly, I confess
I preach for nothing but for covetousness.
That's why my text is still and ever was
Radix malorum est cupiditas.
For by this text I can denounce, indeed,
The very vice I practice, which is greed.
But though that sin is lodged in my own heart,
I am able to make other people part
From avarice, and sorely to repent,
Though that is not my principal intent.

   "Then I bring in examples, many a one,
And tell them many a tale of days long done.
Plain folk love tales that come down from of old.
Such things their minds can well report and hold.

Do you suppose, while I have power to preach
And take in silver and gold for what I teach
I'll ever live in willful poverty?
No, no, that's not my thinking, certainly.
I mean to preach and beg in sundry lands.
I won't do any labor with my hands,
Nor live by making baskets. I don't intend
To beg for nothing; that is not my end.
I won't ape the apostles; I must eat,
I must have money, wool, and cheese, and wheat,
Though taken from the meanest wretch's tillage
Or from the poorest widow in a village,
Yes, though her children starved for want. In fine,
I mean to drink the liquor of the vine
And have a jolly wench in every town.
But, in conclusion, lords, I will get down
To business: you would have me tell a tale.
Now that I've had a drink of corny ale,
By God, I hope the thing I'm going to tell
Is one that you'll have reason to like well.
For though myself a very sinful man,
I can tell a moral tale, indeed I can,
One that I use to bring the profits in
While preaching. Now be still, and I'll begin."

The Pardoner's Tale

There was a company of young folk living
One time in Flanders, who were bent on giving
Their lives to follies and extravagances.
In taverns and in brothels they held dances
With lutes and harps. They diced away the hours,
And also ate and drank beyond their powers,

Through which they paid the devil sacrifice
In his own temple with their drink and dice,
Their abominable excess and dissipation.
They swore oaths that were worthy of damnation;
Grisly it was to listen when they swore.
The blessed body of our Lord they tore—
The Jews, it seemed to them, had failed to rend
His body enough—and each laughed at his friend
And fellow in sin. To encourage their pursuits
Came comely dancing girls, peddlers of fruits,
Singers with harps, bawds and confectioners
Who are the very devil's officers
To kindle and blow the fire of lechery
That is the follower of gluttony.

    Witness the Bible, if licentiousness
Does not reside in wine and drunkenness!
Recall how drunken Lot, unnaturally,
With his two daughters lay unwittingly,
So drunk he had no notion what he did.

    Herod, the stories tell us, God forbid,
When full of liquor at his banquet board
Right at his very table gave the word
To kill the Baptist, John, though guiltless he.

    Seneca says a good word, certainly.
He says there is no difference he can find
Between a man who has gone out of his mind
And one who carries drinking to excess,
Only that madness outlasts drunkenness.
O gluttony, first cause of mankind's fall,
Of our damnation the cursed original
Until Christ bought us with his blood again!
How dearly paid for by the race of men
Was this detestable iniquity!
This whole world was destroyed through gluttony.

    Adam our father and his wife also
From paradise to labor and to woe

Were driven for that selfsame vice, indeed.
As long as Adam fasted—so I read—
He was in heaven; but as soon as he
Devoured the fruit of that forbidden tree
Then he was driven out in sorrow and pain.
Of gluttony well ought we to complain!
Could a man know how many maladies
Follow indulgences and gluttonies
He'd keep his diet under stricter measure
And sit at table with more temperate pleasure.
The throat is short and tender is the mouth,
And hence men toil east, west, and north, and south,
In earth, and air, and water—alas to think—
Fetching a glutton dainty meat and drink.

This is a theme, O Paul, that you well treat:
"Meat unto belly, and belly unto meat,
God shall destroy them both," as Paul has said.
When a man drinks the white wine and the red—
This is a foul word, by my soul, to say,
And fouler is the deed in every way—
He makes his throat his privy through excess.

The Apostle says, weeping for piteousness,
"I've told you of many who have come to loss—
I say it weeping. Enemies of Christ's cross,
Their belly is their God; their end is death."
O cursed belly! Sack of stinking breath
In which corruption lodges, dung abounds!
At either end of you come forth foul sounds.
Great cost it is to fill you, and great pain!
These cooks, how they must grind and pound and
        strain
And transform substance into accident[1]
To please your cravings, though exorbitant!

[1]The Pardoner makes use of a philosophical distinction here: *substance*, the real nature of a thing, as opposed to *accident*, any of its sensible qualities, such as texture or flavor.

From the hard bones they knock the marrow out.
They'll find a use for everything, past doubt,
That down the gullet sweet and soft will glide.
The spiceries of leaf and root provide
Sauces that are concocted for delight,
To give a man a second appetite.
But truly, he whom gluttonies entice
Is dead, while he continues in that vice.

 O drunken man, disfigured is your face,
Sour is your breath, foul are you to embrace!
You seem to mutter through your drunken nose
The sound of "Samson, Samson," yet God knows
That Samson never indulged himself in wine.
Your tongue is lost, you fall like a stuck swine,
And all the self-respect that you possess
Is gone, for of man's judgment, drunkenness
Is the true sepulcher and annihilation.
A man whom drink has under domination
Can never keep a secret in his head.
Now steer away from both the white and red,
And most of all from that white wine keep wide
That comes from Lepe. They sell it in Cheapside
And Fish Street. It's a Spanish wine, and sly
To creep in other wines that grow nearby,
And such a vapor it has that with three drinks
It takes a man to Spain; although he thinks
He's home in Cheapside, he is far away
At Lepe. Then "Samson, Samson" will he say!

 By God himself, who is omnipotent,
All the great exploits in the Old Testament
Were done in abstinence, I say, and prayer.
Look in the Bible, you may learn it there.

 Attila, conqueror of many a place,
Died in his sleep in shame and in disgrace
Bleeding out of his nose in drunkenness.
A captain ought to live in temperateness!

And more than this, I say, remember well
The injunction that was laid on Lemuel—
Not Samuel, but Lemuel, I say!
Read in the Bible; in the plainest way
Wine is forbidden to judges and to kings.
This will suffice; no more upon these things.

Since I have shown what gluttony will do,
Now I will warn you against gambling, too;
Gambling, the very mother of low scheming,
Of lying and forswearing and blaspheming
Against Christ's name, of murder and waste as well
Alike of goods and time; and, truth to tell,
With honor and renown it cannot suit
To be a common gambler by repute.
The higher a gambler stands in power and place,
The more his name is lowered in disgrace.
If a prince gambles, whatever his kingdom be,
In his whole government and policy
He is, in all the general estimation,
Considered so much less in reputation.

Stilbon, who was a wise ambassador,
From Lacedaemon once to Corinth bore
A mission of alliance. When he came
It happened that he found there at a game
Of hazard all the great ones of the land,
And so, as quickly as it could be planned,
He stole back, saying, "I will not lose my name
Nor have my reputation put to shame
Allying you with gamblers. You may send
Other wise emissaries to gain your end,
For by my honor, rather than ally
My countrymen to gamblers, I will die.
For you that are so gloriously renowned
Shall never with this gambling race be bound
By will of mine or treaty I prepare."
Thus did this wise philosopher declare.

Remember also how the Parthians' lord
Sent King Demetrius, as the books record,
A pair of golden dice, by this proclaiming
His scorn, because that king was known for gaming.
The king of Parthia therefore held his crown
Devoid of glory, value, or renown.
Lords can discover other means of play
More suitable to while the time away.

Now about oaths I'll say a word or two,
Great oaths and false oaths, as the old books do.
Great swearing is a thing abominable,
And false oaths yet more reprehensible.
Almighty God forbade swearing at all,
Matthew be witness; but specially I call
The holy Jeremiah on this head.
"Swear thine oaths truly, do not lie," he said.
"Swear under judgment, and in righteousness."
But idle swearing is a great wickedness.
Consult and see, and he that understands
In the first table of the Lord's commands
Will find the second of his edicts this:
"Take not the Lord's name idly or amiss."
A man whose oaths and curses are extreme,
Vengeance shall find his house, both roof and beam.
"By God's own precious heart," and "By his nails"—
"My chance is seven, by Christ's blood at Hailes,[1]
Yours five and three." "Cheat me, and if you do,
By God's arms, with this knife I'll run you through!"—
Such fruit comes from the bones, that pair of bitches:
Oaths broken, treachery, murder. For the riches

---

[1] The "chance," in the game of hazard, was a number which
enabled the player rolling the dice to continue until he rolled either
a winning or losing number or until the "chance" recurred.
Chaucer's "bicchèd bonès two" are now used for craps.

At the abbey of Hailes, in Gloucestershire, some of Christ's
blood was supposed to be preserved.

Of Christ's love, give up curses, without fail,
Both great and small! —Now, sirs, I'll tell my tale.
   These three young roisterers of whom I tell
Long before prime had rung from any bell
Were seated in a tavern at their drinking,
And as they sat, they heard a bell go clinking
Before a corpse being carried to his grave.
One of these roisterers, when he heard it, gave
An order to his boy: "Go out and try
To learn whose corpse is being carried by.
Get me his name, and get it right. Take heed."
   "Sir," said the boy, "there isn't any need.
I learned before you came here, by two hours.
He was, it happens, an old friend of yours,
And all at once, there on his bench upright
As he was sitting drunk, he was killed last night.
A sly thief, Death men call him, who deprives
All people in this country of their lives,
Came with his spear and smiting his heart in two
Went on his business with no more ado.
A thousand have been slaughtered by his hand
During this plague. And, sir, before you stand
Within his presence, it should be necessary,
It seems to me, to know your adversary.
Be evermore prepared to meet this foe.
My mother taught me thus; that's all I know."
   "Now by St. Mary," said the innkeeper,
"This child speaks truth. Man, woman, laborer,
Servant, and child the thief has slain this year
In a big village a mile or more from here.
I think it is his place of habitation.
It would be wise to make some preparation
Before he brought a man into disgrace."
   "God's arms!" this roisterer said. "So that's the case!
Is it so dangerous with this thief to meet?
I'll look for him by every path and street,

I vow it, by God's holy bones! Hear me,
Fellows of mine, we are all one, we three.
Let each of us hold up his hand to the other
And each of us become his fellow's brother.
We'll slay this Death, who slaughters and betrays.
He shall be slain whose hand so many slays,
Yes, by God's dignity, before tonight!"

    The three together set about to plight
Their oaths to live and die each for the other
Just as though each had been to each born brother,
And in their drunken frenzy up they get
And toward the village off at once they set
Which the innkeeper had spoken of before,
And many were the grisly oaths they swore.
They rent Christ's precious body limb from limb—
Death shall be dead, if they lay hands on him!

    When they had hardly gone the first half mile,
Just as they were about to cross a stile,
An old man, poor and humble, met them there.
The old man greeted them with a meek air
And said, "God bless you, lords, and be your guide."

    "What's this?" the proudest of the three replied.
"Old beggar, I hope you meet with evil grace!
Why are you all wrapped up except your face?
What are you doing alive so many a year?"

    The old man at these words began to peer
Into this gambler's face. "Because I can,
Though I should walk to India, find no man,"
He said, "in any village or any town,
Who for my age is willing to lay down
His youth. So I must keep my old age still
As long a time as it may be God's will.
Nor will Death take my life from me, alas!
Thus like a restless prisoner I pass
And on the ground, which is my mother's gate,
I walk and with my staff both early and late

I knock and say, 'Dear mother, let me in!
See how I vanish, flesh, and blood, and skin!
Alas, when shall my bones be laid to rest?
I would exchange with you my clothing chest,
Mother, that in my chamber long has been
For an old haircloth rag to wrap me in.'
And yet she still refuses me that grace.
All white, therefore, and withered is my face.

  "But, sirs, you do yourselves no courtesy
To speak to an old man so churlishly
Unless he had wronged you either in word or deed.
As you yourselves in Holy Writ may read,
'Before an aged man whose head is hoar
Men ought to rise.' I counsel you, therefore,
No harm nor wrong here to an old man do,
No more than you would have men do to you
In your old age, if you so long abide.
And God be with you, whether you walk or ride!
I must go yonder where I have to go."

  "No, you old beggar, by St. John, not so,"
Said another of these gamblers. "As for me,
By God, you won't get off so easily!
You spoke just now of that false traitor, Death,
Who in this land robs all our friends of breath.
Tell where he is, since you must be his spy,
Or you will suffer for it, so say I
By God and by the holy sacrament.
You're leagued with him, false thief, in joint assent
To slay us young folk, that's clear to my mind."

  "If you are so impatient, sirs, to find
Death," he replied, "turn up this crooked way,
For in that grove I left him, truth to say,
Beneath a tree, and there he will abide.
No boast of yours will make him run and hide.
You see that oak tree? Just there you will find
This Death, and God, who bought again mankind,

Save and amend you!" So said this old man;
And promptly each of these three gamblers ran
Until he reached the tree, and there they found
Florins of fine gold, minted bright and round,
Nearly eight bushels of them, as they thought.
And after Death no longer then they sought.
Each of them was so ravished at the sight,
So fair the florins glittered and so bright,
That down they sat beside the precious hoard.
The worst of them, he uttered the first word.

"Brothers," he told them, "listen to what I say.
My head is sharp, for all I joke and play.
Fortune has given us this pile of treasure
To set us up in lives of ease and pleasure.
Lightly it comes, lightly we'll make it go.
God's precious dignity! Who was to know
We'd ever tumble on such luck today?
If we could only carry this gold away,
Home to my house, or either one of yours—
For well you know that all this gold is ours—
We'd touch the summit of felicity.
But still, by daylight that can hardly be.
People would call us thieves, too bold for stealth,
And they would have us hanged for our own wealth.
It must be done by night, that's our best plan,
As prudently and slyly as we can.
Hence my proposal is that we should all
Draw lots, and let's see where the lot will fall.
The one of us who draws the shortest stick
Shall run back to the town, and make it quick,
And bring us bread and wine here on the sly,
And two of us will keep a watchful eye
Over this gold; and if he doesn't stay
Too long in town, we'll carry this gold away
By night, wherever we all agree it's best."

One of them held the cut out in his fist

And had them draw to see where it would fall,
And the cut fell on the youngest of them all.
At once he set off on his way to town,
But the same moment after he had gone
The one who urged this plan said to the other:
"You know that by sworn oath you are my brother.
I'll tell you something you can profit by.
Our friend has gone, that's clear to any eye,
And here is gold, abundant as can be,
That we propose to share alike, we three.
But if I worked it out, as I could do,
So that it could be shared between us two,
Wouldn't that be a favor, a friendly one?"

The other answered, "How that can be done,
I don't quite see. He knows we have the gold.
What shall we do, or what shall he be told?"

"Shall it be secret, safe inside your head?
Then in short order," the first scoundrel said,
"I'll tell how we can bring this end about."

"Granted," the other told him. "Never doubt,
I won't betray you, that you can believe."

"Now," said the first, "we're two, as you perceive,
And two of us must have more strength than one.
When he sits down, get up as if in fun
And wrestle with him. While you play this game
I'll run him through the ribs. You do the same,
Using your dagger there. Then we'll be free
To split this gold just between you and me,
And all that we desire we can fulfill.
We both can roll the dice whenever we will."
Thus in agreement these two scoundrels fell
To slay the third, as you have heard me tell.

The youngest, who had started off to town,
Within his heart kept rolling up and down
The beauty of these florins, new and bright.
"O Lord," he thought, "were there some way I might

Have all this treasure to myself alone,
There isn't a man who dwells beneath God's throne
Could live a life as merry as mine should be!"
And so at last the fiend, our enemy,
Put in his head that he could gain his ends
If he bought poison to kill off his friends.
Finding his life in such a sinful state,
The devil was allowed to seal his fate.
For it was altogether his intent
To kill his friends, and never to repent.
So off he set, no longer would he tarry,
Into the town, to an apothecary,
And begged for poison; he wanted it because
He meant to kill his rats; besides, there was
A polecat living in his hedge, he said,
Who killed his capons; and when he went to bed
He wanted to take vengeance, if he might,
On vermin that devoured him by night.

The apothecary answered, "You shall have
A drug that as I hope the Lord will save
My soul, no living thing in all creation,
Eating or drinking of this preparation
A dose no bigger than a grain of wheat,
But promptly with his death-stroke he shall meet.
Die, that he will, and in a briefer while
Than you can walk the distance of a mile,
This poison is so strong and virulent."

Taking the poison, off the scoundrel went,
Holding it in a box, and next he ran
To a near street, and borrowed from a man
Three generous flagons. He emptied out his drug
In two of them, and kept the other jug
For his own drink; he let no poison lurk
In that! And so all night he meant to work
Carrying off the gold. Such was his plan,
And when he'd filled them, this accursed man
Retraced his path, still following his design,

Back to his friends with his three jugs of wine.
    But why dilate upon it any more?
For just as they had planned his death before,
Just so they killed him, and with no delay.
When it was finished, one spoke up to say:
"Now let's sit down and drink, and we can bury
His body later on. First we'll be merry,"
And as he said the words, he took a jug
That, as it happened, held the poisonous drug,
And drank, and gave his friend a drink as well,
And promptly they both died. But truth to tell,
In all that Avicenna ever wrote
He never described in chapter, rule, or note
More marvelous signs of poisoning, I suppose,
Than these two rogues presented at the close.
Thus they both perished for their homicide,
And thus the traitorous poisoner also died.

    O sin accursed above all cursedness,
O treacherous murder, O foul wickedness,
O gambling, lustfulness, and gluttony,
Traducer of Christ's name by blasphemy
And monstrous oaths, through habit and through pride!
Alas, mankind! Ah, how may it betide
That you to your Creator, he that wrought you
And even with his precious heart's blood bought you,
So falsely and ungratefully can live?

    And now, good men, your sins may God forgive
And keep you specially from avarice!
My holy pardon will avail in this,
For it can heal each one of you that brings
His pennies, silver brooches, spoons, or rings.
Come, bow your head under this holy bull!
You wives, come offer up your cloth or wool!
I write your names here in my roll, just so.
Into the bliss of heaven you shall go!
I will absolve you here by my high power,
You that will offer, as clean as in the hour

When you were born —Sirs, thus I preach. And now
Christ Jesus, our souls' healer, show you how
Within his pardon evermore to rest,
For that, I will not lie to you, is best.

But in my tale, sirs, I forgot one thing.
The relics and the pardons that I bring
Here in my pouch, no man in the whole land
Has finer, given me by the pope's own hand.
If any of you devoutly wants to offer
And have my absolution, come and proffer
Whatever you have to give. Kneel down right here,
Humbly, and take my pardon, full and clear,
Or have a new, fresh pardon if you like
At the end of every mile of road we strike,
As long as you keep offering ever newly
Good coins, not counterfeit, but minted truly.
Indeed it is an honor I confer
On each of you, an authentic pardoner
Going along to absolve you as you ride.
For in the country mishaps may betide—
One or another of you in due course
May break his neck by falling from his horse.
Think what security it gives you all
That in this company I chanced to fall
Who can absolve you each, both low and high,
When souls, alas, from bodies chance to fly!
By my advice, our Host here shall begin,
For he's the man enveloped most by sin.
Come, offer first, Sir Host, and once that's done,
Then you shall kiss the relics, every one,
Yes, for a penny! Come, undo your purse!

"No, no," said he. "Then I should have Christ's curse!
I won't do such a thing for love or riches!
You'd make me kiss a piece of your old britches
And for a saintly relic make it pass
Although it had been tinctured by your ass.
By the true cross that in the Holy Land

St. Helen found, I wish I had in hand
Your balls instead of relics! I'll be bound,
Just cut 'em off, I'll help you carry 'em round.
I'll have them both enshrined in a hog's turd!"
  The Pardoner did not answer; not a word,
He was so angry, could he find to say.
  "Now," said our Host, "I will not try to play
With you, nor any other angry man."
  Immediately the worthy Knight began,
Seeing that all the people laughed, "No more,
This has gone far enough. Now as before,
Sir Pardoner, be gay, look cheerfully,
And you, Sir Host, who are so dear to me,
Come, kiss the Pardoner, I beg of you,
And Pardoner, draw near, and let us do
As we've been doing, let us laugh and play."
And so they kissed, and rode along their way.

Prologue to the Manciple's Tale

Do you not know where stands a little town
Under Blean forest, called Bob-up-and-down,
That lies along the Canterbury way?
There our good Host began to joke and play,
And said, "What, sirs, Dobbin is in the mire![1]
Isn't there anyone, for prayer or hire,
Who'll wake our fellow riding there behind?
He's ready for a thief to rob and bind.
Cock's bones! Look how he's nodding in his course!
Look, he's about to tumble from his horse!

[1]The words "Dun is in the mire" were used to begin a game in which the smallest possible number of people, beginning with two, tried to remove a log from the room.

Is he a cook of London, curse him, he?
Bring him up here, he knows his penalty.
He'll have to tell a story now, I say,
Although it isn't worth a bundle of hay.
God help your soul, you Cook! Come to, take
    warning!
What ails you, sleeping this way in the morning?
Have you had fleas in bed, or are you tight,
Or have you worked out on some wench all night
Until you don't know how to lift your head?"

    This Cook, so pale he showed no streak of red,
Answered our Host, "As I've a soul to bless,
I feel, I don't know why, such heaviness
I'd rather sleep, in the state in which I've fallen,
Than have the best wine in Cheapside, a whole gallon."

    "Well," said the Manciple, "if it would ease
Your plight, Sir Cook, and if it won't displease
Any who ride here in this company,
And if our Host will grant the courtesy,
I will, for now, excuse you from your tale.
For in all truth, your countenance is pale,
Also your eyes are badly bleared, I think,
And this I know, your breath gives off a stink
Sour enough to show that you aren't well.
I will not flatter you; it's truth I tell.
See how he yawns at us, this drunken clown,
As if he meant to swallow us all down.
Clamp down your jaws, or by your father's kin
The devil himself will put his hell's foot in!
Curse on your breath, it will infect us all.
Fie! Such a stinking swine may ill befall!
This lusty man's a warning, sirs, that's plain.
Sweet sir, will you go tilting at the vane?[1]
You have the perfect build for that, I think.

---

[1]The object of this form of jousting was to hit the vane on one
end of a pivoting bar without being caught by the bag or club
that swung on the other.

You are an ape, you've had so much to drink;
Men play with straws when they have reached that
    stage."
These words reduced the Cook to a mute rage.
He nodded hard for lack of words to say,
And the horse pitched him off, and there he lay
Until men got him up by hook or crook.
Here was a feat of chivalry by a cook!
Alas, he should have stuck to pot and ladle!
Before he was again propped in his saddle
There was a lot of shoving to and fro.
It cost no small amount of care and woe
To lift this sorry, pale, unwieldy ghost.

    The Manciple was cautioned by our Host.
Who said, "Since drink is now in domination
Over this man, I fear, by my salvation,
That he would make a crude job of his tale.
For whether it's wine, or old or musty ale
That he's been drinking, he talks through his nose.
He snorts, and has a cold. With all his woes,
He has enough and more to do right now,
He and his nag, to keep out of the slough.
And if again in the saddle he grows dizzy
And tumbles from his horse, we'll all be busy
Boosting his corpse up in his sodden state.
He doesn't matter; tell on, he can wait.

    "Yet, Manciple, you go too far, I think,
Scolding him openly for his vice of drink.
Some day it well may happen that this Cook
Will pay you with a leaf from your own book.[1]
He'll speak of little things, I mean, amounts
That he will quarrel with in your accounts.
That, put to proof, would hurt your dignity."

    "True, that would be a great catastrophe,"

[1]Chaucer. "Another day he may *reclaim* you and bring you to *lure*"—terms of falconry.

The Manciple said. "He'd have me in a snare!
And I'd far rather pay him for his mare
Than have him picking fights with me and striving.
I won't offend him, by my hopes of thriving!
For all I said, it was in fun I spoke.
And you know what? You'll see a first-rate joke.
I have a draft of wine, a noble grape,
Here in a gourd. This Cook shall not escape.
He'll take a drink, if I can work it so.
I'll bet my life the fellow won't say no."

   And sure enough, alas, if I'm to keep
A true account of things, the Cook drank deep
Out of this vessel. He had drunk before
Enough and plenty; why did he need more?
And after burbling in this horn, the Cook
Returned it with a marvelous happy look,
And thanked the Manciple as best he could.

   Our Host laughed wondrous loud. "Now for our good,
Wherever we go," he said, "we ought to carry
Good drink along. I see it's necessary,
For it turns rancor and grief, however strong,
To love and concord, and heals many a wrong.
O great god Bacchus, blessings on your name
Who can so transform earnest into game!
Honor and thanks be to your deity!
But on this matter no more words from me.
Manciple, speak, and tell your tale, I pray."

   "Well, sir," he answered, "hear what I have to say."

[The Manciple's Tale, not among Chaucer's most impres-
sive performances, relates that Phoebus Apollo, "while he
was living down here on this earth," had a beloved wife
and a white crow, which he taught to speak. The crow
informed Phoebus of the infidelity of his wife. Phoebus
killed his wife; then, deciding that the crow had been a
"traitor," plucked his white feathers, deprived him of song

and speech, and "slung him out of doors to the devil; and
for this reason all crows are black."]

Prologue to the Parson's Tale

Just as the Maniciple his tale had ended
The sun from the south line had so far descended
That if my eye can judge such things as these,
His height was short of twenty-nine degrees.
The time was four o'clock, as I should guess,
For eleven feet, or little more or less,
My shadow stretched, a length to which the light
Would have apportioned my six feet of height
At that degree of the sun's elevation.
Libra, moreover, the month's exaltation,
Was steadily beginning to ascend
As we were entering at a village end.
And so our Host, at all times quick to be
The leader of our jolly company,
Spoke in this fashion: "Now, lords, every one,
A single further tale, and we are done.
You've honored all my verdicts and decrees.
We've heard, I think, from all ranks and degrees.
Almost completed now is my whole plan.
And so I pray God, good luck to the man
Who tells this last tale to us lustily.

   "Sir Priest, are you a vicar? Or do we see
A parson here? Speak truth in what you say!
But still, be what you like, don't spoil our play.
Each man but you has told his tale in turn.
What's in your wallet? Open it, let us learn,
For by your looks, if I'm the man to tell,
You ought to knit up a great matter well.

Tell us a fable, come now, for cock's bones!"
    The Parson answered in peremptory tones,
"You won't get any fable told by me!
For Paul, in writing to St. Timothy,
Reproves those who abandon truthfulness
To deal in fables and such wretchedness.
Why should my fist sow chaff when if I please
I'm able to sow wheat with equal ease?
And so I say, if you will be content
With virtuous matter, of a moral bent,
And count yourselves with such a theme sufficed,
I shall be more than glad, in honor of Christ,
To give you such due pleasure as I can.
But I must warn you, I'm a Southern man.
I can't alliterate, pounding along by letter,
'Rim, ram, ruff.' And I hold rhyme little better!
I won't deceive you. I'll tell a tale in prose,
A merry one, if you desire, to close
This feast and leave our fabric firmly knit.
And Jesus in his mercy send me wit
On this our journey that I may show you all
That perfect, glorious pilgrimage men call
The heavenly Jerusalem, and the way
To enter on it. Vouchsafe to me, I pray,
Your will and pleasure, and if it will avail,
I shall begin at once upon my tale.
    "And yet I put this meditation of mine
To the correction, both by word and line,
Of learned men; for I myself, trust well,
Am ignorant of texts; I try to tell
Only the gist. So with all due subjection
I say, therefore, I speak under correction."
    Our company was not slow in complying.
To end, it seemed, with something edifying
Was only the right and proper thing to do,
Also to give him place and hear him through;
And so we told our Host that he should say

We all begged for his tale without delay.
    Our Host as ever had words for us all.
"Now to your lot, Sir Priest, good fortune fall!
Tell us your meditation, but to my thinking
You ought to hurry, for the sun is sinking.
Speak fruitfully, and that in little space,
And may God help you do well, by his grace!
Tell what you like, we'll gladly give you ear."
    And with these words he said as you shall hear.

[The Parson's merry tale in prose, which knits up all
the feast, occupies over forty double-columned pages in
Robinson's text, and consists of "a sermon on Penitence,
in which is embodied a long treatise, originally separate,
on the Deadly Sins."

"At the end of the Parson's Tale," says Robinson,
"in every ms. which has that tale complete, stands the
so-called Retractation of the author." Naturally enough,
the genuineness of Chaucer's "retractations" has been
challenged. Every reader must make his own guess wheth-
er Chaucer wrote them or not, and if he did whether
they constitute an expression of unqualified repentance
for much of his greatest work. Whatever the decision,
these lines of prose deserve a place in any volume that
seeks even partially to represent what has come down to
us as the text of Chaucer.]

ↄ৯৫২ ↄ৯৫২ ↄ৯৫২ ↄ৯৫২ ↄ৯৫২ ↄ৯৫২ ↄ৯৫২ ↄ৯৫২ ↄ৯৫২ ↄ৯৫২

Chaucer's Retractation

IIERE TAKETH THE MAKER OF THIS BOOK HIS LEAVE

Now pray I to all those who hear this little treatise or
read it,[1] that if there be anything in it that pleases them,

---

[1]The reference is to the Parson's Tale, which the retractations
immediately follow.

that they thank our Lord Jesus Christ for it, from whom proceeds all wit and all goodness. And if there be anything that displeases them, I pray them also that they attribute it to my want of skill, and not to my purpose, which would gladly have said better if I had had skill. For our book says, "All that is written is written for our doctrine," and that is my intent. Wherefore I beseech you humbly, for the mercy of God, that you pray for me that Christ have mercy on me and forgive me my sins; and especially for my translations and writings that concern worldly vanities, which I renounce in my retractations; such as the book of Troilus is; the book also of Fame; the book of the XIX Ladies; the book of the Duchesse; the book of Saint Valentine's day of the Parliament of Birds; the tales of Canterbury, those that make for sin; the book of the Lion; and many another book, if they were in my remembrance, and many a song and many a lecherous lay; that Christ for his great mercy forgive me the sin. But concerning the translation of Boëthius on Consolation, and other books of the lives of saints, and homilies, and morality, and devotion, for them I thank our Lord Jesus Christ and his blessed Mother, and all the saints of heaven, beseeching them that they from henceforth to the end of my life send me grace to repent my sins, and to study toward the salvation of my soul, and grant me the grace of true penitence, confession, and satisfaction to perform in this present life, through the benign grace of him that is king of kings and priest over all priests, that bought us with the precious blood of his heart; so that I may be one of them at the day of doom that shall be saved.

TROILUS
AND
CRESSIDA

Translator's Note

The vast scheme of *The Canterbury Tales* remains un-
finished. Chaucer not only finished the *Troilus* but on
good scholarly opinion revised it at least once, though it
runs to more than eight thousand lines. It is one of the
great narratives in English and of all Chaucer's works the
greatest that is both mature and complete.

The story ostensibly forms an eddy in the Trojan war,
though it finds no place in Homer, whom Chaucer and
his age knew only by repute. Their sources for the story
of Troy were Roman and medieval, and included much
that from a classical point of view was garbled, spurious,
or invented. Homer had never heard of a love affair
between Troilus, whom he barely mentions, and a wid-
owed daughter of Calchas. That affair is as truly a medie-
val creation as the story of Tristram and Iseult. Troy, in
Chaucer, is suspiciously like London; Hector and Achilles
are medieval knights.

Chaucer took the story, which goes back to a twelfth-
century French poet, Benoit de Sainte-Maure, from the
Filostrato of Boccaccio, as he had taken the Knight's Tale
from Boccaccio's *Teseida*. But Chaucer refers to his
"author" (i.e., source) as a Latin writer, Lollius, whom
he also mentions in *The House of Fame,* apparently be-
lieving that a man so named was an authority on the
history of Troy. Chaucer expanded the *Filostrato,* altered
the action in important ways, altered even more impor-
tantly the principal characterizations, especially Pandarus,
enriched his text with matter drawn from many other
writers, and gave the whole poem the stamp of his per-
sonal style and temperament. Thus, despite the large

amount of translation in it, the *Troilus* takes rank as an original work.

Although Chaucer wrote the *Troilus* before embarking on the plan of the Canterbury pilgrimage, I have placed it after, hoping that those who read the *Tales* first will become accustomed to Chaucer's world and some of its literary and social conventions, and therefore better prepared for the *Troilus*. The Canterbury pilgrims themselves and their byplay with each other along the route exhibit Chaucer as a comic realist. Here are the people who inhabited fourteenth-century England, presented as naturally as literature can present any people of any age. The tales told by the pilgrims are another matter. They are of great variety, edifying saint's life, miracle of the Virgin, mock-heroic fable, formal medieval tragedy, Breton lay, parody, rowdy farce. If the pilgrimage itself is realistic, many of the tales are not. The pilgrimage shows us the people of medieval England as they were; the tales often show them as they *thought* they were, show the beliefs, conventions, tastes, rationalizations that colored their minds, especially the minds of the courtly circle. Dorigen, in the Franklin's Tale, will hardly strike the reader as a realistic portrait in the same way that Chaucer's portrait of the Wife of Bath is realistic. But no doubt a good many medieval ladies, whether wives or objects of *amour*, liked to think that they resembled Dorigen. Chaucer drew her character according to well-understood conventions, but conventions cannot hold sway unless for a time they satisfy some real impulse in human nature.

Any number of *The Canterbury Tales* could in one way or another furnish a commentary on the *Troilus*. But the Franklin's Tale is especially apposite. The characters live in the aura of courtly love, as in the *Troilus,* and Dorigen's "complaint" is a literary convention Chaucer uses at a number of points to express the emotions of Troilus

and Cressida. The element of convention is easier to allow
for in the Franklin's Tale simply because it never occurs
to the reader to judge that story of "natural magic, such
as men practiced in those heathenish days" by ordinary
standards of credibility. The *Troilus*, on the contrary,
at least in the main outlines of the story and in its superb
characterizations of the three principal figures, meets the
common tests of plausibility. Yet the modern reader may
find himself perplexed and reduced to fits of impatience
by much in the poem that seems exasperatingly unreal.

The reader is apt to be put off, for one thing, by
Chaucer's treatment of the emotional states of his char-
acters. Troilus particularly seems at many points to give
way to childish tantrums rather than betraying the emo-
tions of an adult. Two things are probably at work here.
As Professor F. P. Magoun suggested to me in the course
of stimulating conversations about Chaucer in which he
showed himself a liberal as well as learned critic, there
is ground for believing that worldly people in medieval
England gave unfettered expression to their feelings in a
way we do not expect of such people now. The notion of
the reticent Anglo-Saxon rests on later social changes.
This does not mean that Chaucer and his circle were
intellectually unsophisticated; it means that they might
at times have seemed emotionally unsophisticated to us,
if by emotional sophistication we mean keeping a closer
rein on the expression of intense feelings. But the second
and unquestionable point is that the "complaint" was an
established *literary* convention, and Chaucer made full
use of it. His readers or listeners enjoyed long set pieces
dilating on states of misery or rapture, embroidering them
with "old examples" and "colors of rhetoric." Often
enough the actual content of the complaints in the *Troilus*
is thoroughly characteristic of human nature. People have
always indulged in self-pity, and threatened, like Troilus,
to retaliate against a harsh fate or a reluctant mistress

by doing away with themselves. But of course ways of presenting emotional states in fiction do change. Many of the emotional monologues of Chaucer's characters, whether as long spoken harangues or as solitary discourses which they are represented as thinking or saying to themselves, would in modern fiction be presented as fantasies in their minds, or as we haphazardly say, "stream of consciousness" passages. The sense that the characters are pulling out all the emotional stops with a childlike freedom from inhibition would be lessened; the quality and content of the emotions themselves would not change as much as we might think.

The "complaint" is a subfeature of the general set of conventions within which the story of Troilus and Cressida takes place. This is the system of courtly love, now vanished from the literary and social scene along with the feudalism of which it was a part. The applicable points of the system can be picked up by any alert reader from Chaucer himself; those who wish to pursue further the historical and literary origins and development of the code should consult C. S. Lewis's *The Allegory of Love*. In Chaucer the conventions in question are not only importantly present in the *Troilus*, but are found also in *The Book of the Duchess*, the speeches of the tercels in *The Birds' Parliament*, the tale of Chanticleer and Pertelote, and in numerous other tales or passages in Chaucer's work. In the *Troilus*, the courtly-love system explains in some ways why the characters act as they do, but even more it explains why they think, feel, and express themselves as they do.

As a feudal retainer would swear fealty to his king or his liege, the lover, according to the code, swears absolute loyalty to his lady. He undertakes to obey her every command without promise of any reward except the privilege of service. If he finds favor, he pledges absolute secrecy to protect her "honor." Courtly love was held inconsistent with marriage (the Franklin rejects this view). Marriages in aristocratic medieval circles were contracts negotiated in the interests of worldly alliance; the love-craze had to find a different outlet. This is no doubt one reason why such a high price was set on secrecy to preserve the lady's reputation, a point that may somewhat baffle a later generation in which unmarried couples live openly together without stigma.

Obviously there was a large amount of equivocation in these articles of faith. If in a way courtly love idealized woman, the impulse toward idealization did not cancel the impulse toward possession. No doubt possession was commonly in view from the start. In any case the lover was held to be morally improved, indeed ennobled, by his service. Thus Troilus, when all is going well, becomes better natured, better mannered, a better soldier, free from all "vices" such as Envy, Anger, Pride, and Avarice, to use Chaucer's enumeration. It remains to add that of course the whole set of courtly-love conventions ran contrary to Christian doctrine and did not escape the condemnation of Church authorities. Much of Chaucer's irony in the poem consists of continual subtle emphasis on the irreverent parallel between the Christian system of divine love, with God at the head, and the courtly-system of profane love, with Cupid at the head, and with its supposed ennobling effect on the lover. Chaucer did not invent this parallel, but he makes the most of it, calling himself the "servant of love's servants," and thus parodying a title of the Pope, who as Christ's vicar assumed Christ's humility.

The *Troilus* has been called a tragedy of fate, and the notion that each human soul fulfills an unavoidable destiny is frequently invoked in the poem, as it is generally in Chaucer's work. So also is personified Fortune, with her turning wheel that brings about reversals from prosperity to misery and vice versa. But chance and the

·luck of the dice figure also, and while the characters are acting as opposed to reflecting they take the normal human view that choice is open to them. Destiny and fortune become entangled with theological notions derived from both Christian and Classical sources in a medley that can cause a modern reader to rub his eyes but which Chaucer's age could accept with no sense of conflict. Powers that Christianity ascribes to Providence can be freely ascribed to surrogates such as Jove or Mercury; the Christian God can be just as freely invoked in support of an oath or in the hope of salvation. (Two centuries and more later, Milton could refer to the "perfect witness of all-judging Jove.") The most sustained and reasoned passage on what can be called determinism is the long meditation in which Troilus puzzles himself over the question whether God's foreknowledge of events is consistent with freedom of the will. He concludes against free will, deciding that everything that has happened to him has happened by "necessity." This meditation comes from the *De Consolatione Philosophiae* of Boëthius, a Christian work which Chaucer had translated. (He alludes to the same dispute in the comic context of the Nun's Priest's Tale.) In the *Troilus,* the passage ends with an appeal to "Almighty Jove" to divulge the truth of the matter. The passage partly characterizes the state of mind of the young Troilus. Feeling himself helpless in the face of events, he tells himself by a natural impulse that all his misfortunes were strictly predestined. Besides its value for characterization at this point, surely Chaucer's persistent emphasis on destiny springs from another literary motive. It is a way of enhancing the reader's sense of inevitability in a tale whose ending Chaucer forecast in his opening stanzas. It would be literal-minded indeed to take the *Troilus* as a philosophic brief for determinism. Chaucer relished philosophic and theological puzzles, as he relished the dispute over dreams as foreshadowing events, but he delighted in the puzzles for their own sake rather than in committing himself to personal conclusions about them.

The frequently criticized ending of the *Troilus* finds Chaucer in a delicate situation. He has formally offended the courtly love system by writing the story of an unfaithful woman. Later he will write the *Prologue* to *The Legend of Good Women* and append the stories of the "XIX ladies," all paragons of fidelity, at least ostensibly as an assigned penance. But the *Troilus* also raises serious moral questions which did not escape Chaucer's awareness. On the worldly plane, the affair of Troilus and Cressida rests on hypocrisy. Pandarus, the good-natured, intriguing busybody, not at all scrupulous about truth in his dealings with his niece, admits that he has played the part of the procurer, protesting only that he has done so not from covetousness but friendship. Troilus invites Pandarus to choose any among his sisters and says that he would gladly perform a like service in return, a proposal hardly in keeping with his initial vows that he meant nothing but Cressida's "honor" and expected no more intimate reward than acceptance as her servant. On the ecclesiastical plane, Chaucer has written as "the servant of love's servants," knowing that the scheme of courtly love could not be reconciled with Christian doctrine. God and Jove could be interchangeable up to a point but not finally. Evidently, at the end of the *Troilus*, Chaucer felt the need, if not of an actual built-in retractation or repudiation of his work, at least of an adjustment of perspectives and an acknowledgment of his ultimate Christian allegiance.

Such an adjustment could hardly avoid inconsistencies, but Chaucer provided himself with the means to make the best of them. Throughout the poem he has kept himself present in his character as narrator. This enables him at the end to step in even more emphatically in the same character, to distance himself and the reader from the immediacy of the tale and to give it, though never losing his urbanity of touch, the tragic dimension of "all passion spent." He asks of the reader enough flexibility of response to follow him through a rapid series of changes in tone and direction of thought, which he carries out with a virtuosity that may well remind us of the Byron of *Don Juan*. Chaucer drops his story to put in a word for women betrayed by men, since he has related the opposite case. Then he addresses his own poem, its audience, its future: "Go, little book..." Then back to his story, the death of Troilus at the hands of Achilles, bluntly and summarily stated. One is a little astonished to see Troilus ascend to a suspiciously Christian-looking heaven, especially when his place in eternity is assigned to him by Mercury. But when he looks down on "this little spot of earth / Enfolded by the sea" and perceives it as vanity, one feels the tale enlarging itself against a backdrop of the instability of all human life. Chaucer is ready now for his fully Christian adjuration to young people ripe for the uncertainties of erotic attachment: "Love him that on a cross..." Then a salute to those "forms of speech old scholars and divines / Have left in verse" and a dedication, not without a note of irony, to "moral Gower" and "philosophical Strode"; then a concluding stanza of prayer derived from Dante. The reader who responds to these changes of tone will feel that Chaucer has arrived at an equilibrium appropriate to the poem itself and to Chaucer's position in a Christian society. Looked at with a more secular eye, this equilibrium may be seen as a precarious but triumphant balance among the tragic, the comic, the cynical, and the spiritual views of life.

Chaucer's tenderness toward Cressida vanishes from later treatments of the story. His Scots follower, Henryson, turns Cressida into a leper whom Troilus rides by without recognizing, though something in her look brings the thought of her into his mind. In Shakespeare's comedy she becomes a "daughter of the game," very different from Chaucer's widow in black, the "least mannish" of all creatures, timid, well bred, pliable, lamenting her helplessness and unfaithfulness.

Chaucer wrote the *Troilus* entirely in rhyme-royal stanzas. I have rendered the body of the tale in blank verse, thereby reducing it by about one half, with very little outright omission. I hope the *proems* to the first four books, some interspersed "songs," and two passages in the conclusion will help keep the reader reminded of Chaucer's original form.

Troilus and Cressida
Book 1

The double sorrow of Troilus to tell,
Who was the son of Priam, King of Troy,
The fortunes of his love, and how he fell
From woe to weal, and then again from joy,
This is my purpose; you, Tisiphone,
Help me compose these lines that grieve me so
I write them sadly, weeping as I go.

To you I call, you goddess of torment,
You cruel Fury, sorrowing ever in pain,
Help me, who am the sorrowful instrument
That, as I can, help lovers to complain.
For well it suits—the old saying is not vain—
A sorry man to have a sorry mate,
And a sad tale to go with a sad gait.

The servant of his servants, thus am I
To love's god, for I dare hope no success
In love myself, though failing I should die,
So far I am, in my unlikeliness,
From any help of his; but none the less,
If this helps any lover, by word or line,
My thanks be Love's, and let this toil be mine!

You lovers who now bathe in happiness,
If in your veins a pitying drop there be,
Reflect upon the outlived heaviness
That you have suffered, and the adversity
Of other folk; remember feelingly
How you, too, Love dared sometimes to displease,
Or else you won him with too great an ease!

And pray for all those who are in the plight
Of Troilus, as you may duly hear,
Pray that in heaven Love may their pains requite,
And pray for me, to God whom we hold dear,
That by these words of mine it may appear
Through Troilus, whose fortune turned to woe,
What suffering Love's people undergo.

And pray for those who are in hopelessness,
For whom in love no comfort there can be,
And those who suffer the invidiousness
Of slandering whispers, whether he or she;
Petition God, for his benignity,
That he will take them early from their place
Who in despair have fallen from Love's grace.

And ask also for those who are at ease
That God may grant them good continuance,
And send them strength their ladies so to please
That Love's renown and praise they may enhance.

I hope my own salvation to advance
By praying for his faithful company,
Writing their woe, living in charity,

And taking pity on them in their lot
As if I were their brother, and as dear.
Now listen with good purpose; to my plot
I'll go at once, and set my matter clear,
In loving Cressida, as you shall hear,
How Troilus with double pains was tried,
And how she played him false before she died.

   It is well known that, powerful in arms,
The Greeks went with a thousand ships to Troy,
And long besieged the city, almost ten years
Before they finished, and by various means
But with a single purpose, tasked themselves
To avenge the rape of Helen, done by Paris.
Now it happened there was living in the town
A lord of great prestige, and a great seer,
Calchas by name; such was his understanding
That he knew well Troy should be overthrown,
By the oracle of his god, called the lord Phoebus
Or the Delphian Apollo. When this Calchas,
By auguries and by Apollo's answer,
Knew that the Greeks were coming with their people
By whom Troy should be ruined, he laid his plans
To leave the city, for by divination
He knew that Troy was doomed, resist who would.
Therefore this prudent prophet thought to make
An unobserved departure; secretly
He stole to the Greek host, and they received him
With full respect and courtesy, in hope
That by his knowledge he could counsel them
In any kind of peril they might face.
   The noise rose up, when this was first perceived,

Through all the town. The word was general
That Calchas had turned traitor and joined the Greeks,
And men considered how to be avenged
On one who had so falsely broken faith,
And said that he and all his kin together
Deserved the fire, both skin and bones. Now Calchas
By this ill turn had left, all unaware
That he had done this false and wicked act,
His daughter, who in penitence and dread
Feared for her very life. She could not tell
What counsel might be best, for she was both
A widow and alone, without a friend
In whom she might confide. This lady's name
Was Cressida; in all the city of Troy
No other, for my judgment, was so fair.
Her native beauty so surpassed all flesh
That like an angel she appeared a thing
Immortal, a perfect creature out of heaven
Sent down in scorn of nature. Day and night
This lady's ear heard of her father's shame,
His falseness and his treason, until almost
Beside herself for terror, dressed as a widow
In black and flowing silk, upon her knees
She fell down before Hector. Pitiably,
And weeping helplessly, she begged his mercy,
And pleaded her excuses. Now this Hector
By nature was compassionate. He saw
How woebegone she was, how beautiful,
And in his goodness cheered her, telling her,
"A malediction on your father's treason!
Forget it, and for you yourself live here
Happily, while you like, with us in Troy.
And all the honor people ought to give you,
No less than when your father was at home,
You shall still have, with safety for your person,
As far as I can keep myself informed."

She thanked him humbly, and would have oftener
If it had been his pleasure, and took her leave.
Then she went home, and bore herself discreetly,
And in her house she lived with such a staff
As suited her position, and as long
As she was in the city, kept her estate
And lived in great affection; young and old
Spoke well of her. But whether she had children
My reading does not say; so let it pass.

Things happened, as they do in war, between
The Trojans and the Greeks, for there were days
When Troy paid dear, and then again the Greeks
Found that the people of Troy were hardly soft.
Thus Fortune, in their anger, rolled them both
After her course, now under, now on top.
But though the Greeks penned in the people of Troy
And all about their city laid tight siege,
The Trojans would not willingly give up
Their old observances and honors paid
Devoutly to their gods; and first in honor
They had a relic, called the Palladium,
Pallas Athena's image, and in this
Above all other shrines they put their faith.

And so it happened, when the time had come
For April with new green to clothe the fields
And sweetly smelling flowers, red and white,
When lusty spring was at the prime, I find
That in their various ways the Trojans held
The feast of the Palladium, and maintained
Their ancient rituals. In their best array
Went many a man and woman to the temple
To hear the service; many a lusty knight,
Many a lady and maiden fresh and fair,
And dressed becomingly in all their ranks
Both for the season and the festival.

Among these other people Cressida
Went in her widow's black; but black or not,
Even as our first letter is an A,
So stood she first in beauty, with no equal.
So gracious was her look that the whole throng
Was gladdened; nothing ever yet was seen
More dearly to be praised than Cressida,
Said all who saw her in her widow's dress,
Nor under a black cloud so bright a star.
And yet she stood quite humbly and alone
Behind the other people, quietly,
And near the door, not seeking place or room,
But dreading always to be put to shame,
Clothed simply, and of gentle disposition,
Yet self-possessed in all her look and manner.

   Now Troilus, whose habit was to give
Instruction to his young knights, led them round
The spacious temple, with a roving eye,
Now here, now there, on the ladies of the city.
He was not losing sleep for any woman,
And so he praised or found fault where he chose.
Walking about, he watched his knights and squires
To see if any in his retinue
Began to sigh, or let his vision linger
On any woman whom he could distinguish.
Then he would smile and call it foolishness
And say, "God knows, her sleep is soft enough
For love of you, no matter how you toss!
I have heard tell, by God, of how you live,
You lovers, your profane observances,
The labor people have in winning love,
And the perplexity in keeping it;
And when your prey is lost, penance and grief!
You are the fools, for certain; ignorant, blind!
None of you learns his lessons from another."
And with that word he set his brows askance

As if to say, "Is this not wisely said?"
For which the god of love maliciously
Began to scowl, and thought to be revenged.
He made it clear his bow was far from broken,
For suddenly he hit him fair and full,
And he can pluck as proud a peacock yet.
    O blind world, O blind purposes of men!
How often the vain sequel of presumption
Falls out quite opposite! Caught are the proud,
And caught the humble. So with Troilus:
Climbing the ladder, little does he think
He must come down again. But every day
Things fail the expectations of a fool.
As Bayard feels his oats, and in his pride
Begins to skip and sidle from his course
Until he feels the whiplash, then he thinks,
"Although I prance first in the tandem traces,
Plump and well groomed, still I am just a horse.
I must put up with horses' law, and pull
With other fellow creatures," even so
It fared with this fierce knight for all his pride.
For king's son though he was, who thought that nothing
Had power enough to lay hold on his heart
Against his will, yet with a look that heart
Was set afire, and he whose pride was highest
Turned suddenly most subject unto love.
    You wise, and proud, and worthy people all,
Be warned by this man from contempt of Love,
For Love can bind the freedom of your hearts
Quickly to him in service. Ever it has
And ever it shall appear that Love is he
Who can bind all things. No man has the power
To overcome the law that rules all nature.
Men do not have more wit than some of those
We read of who have been most caught by love.
The strongest have been thrown, the worthiest

And highest in the world's eye. It is well,
For love has given pleasure to the wisest,
And those in greatest woe it has relieved.
It makes the worthy worthier in repute,
And brings the greatest fear of vice and shame.
We cannot well withstand it, and by nature
It is a virtuous thing; therefore I say,
Refuse not Love. The stick that bends is better
Than that which breaks; and so my counsel is
To follow him, for he will lead you well.

Within the temple Troilus went roving,
Looking at everyone who stood about,
Now on this lady, now on that, to see
Whether she came from Troy or from elsewhere.
And then it chanced that through a knot of people
His eye pierced and went deep enough among them
To fix on Cressida, and there it stopped.
He was astonished, and in cautious fashion
He tried to see her better. "God have mercy,
Where have you kept yourself who are so fair
And goodly to the sight?" he asked himself.
With that his heart began to spread and rise,
And he sighed, softly, lest it should be noticed,
And then put on again his joking manner.

She was not of the smallest in her stature,
And yet so perfectly her figure answered
The form of womanhood that never creature
Appeared less mannish; and so gracefully
And with so pure a motion when she walked,
Men well might guess in her the womanly traits
That went with her position and her honor.
And as for Troilus, her look and motion
Began to please him wonderfully well.
She stood a little on her dignity,
Letting her eyes fall and veer off askance,

As if to say, "What, may I not stand here?"
And after that her face so cleared again
He thought he had never seen so goodly a sight.
Her look began to quicken his desire
Until the bottom of his heart received
Her fixed and deep impression, and though at first
His gaze had done its roving, he was glad
To pull his horns in now. He hardly knew
How to open his eyes or how to shut them.
Yes, he who thought himself so well prepared
To laugh at those who suffer from love's pain,
He stood where he might watch her, this in black,
This woman above all things to his liking,
Nor would he by a word or look betray
What he desired; to keep his countenance
He glanced from far away at other things
Now and again, and then at her once more,
Throughout the service. And after it was done,
Not wholly staggered yet, he left the temple
Lightly enough, but not without remorse
That he had ever poked fun at Love's people,
Lest on himself the weight of scorn might fall.
But in the fear of showing what he felt,
He hid his anguish in dissimulation.
Thus from the temple he turned and went at once
Home to his palace. The arrow of her look
Had shot him through, for all that he took care
To seem at ease. He burnished up his tongue,
Always against the followers of love,
And for his own concealment laughed at them.

"Lord, but your lives are happy ones," he said,
"You lovers! For the knowingest among you,
The one who serves most faithfully and best,
He smarts for it as often as he profits.
Your hire is paid in full, and God knows how!
Not good for good, but ill for honest service.

Your church is well run, by the eternal truth!
Your rites are all uncertainty, except
A wretched point or two; yet nothing calls
For such a strict punctilio as your creed.
You all know that. But as I hope to live,
I haven't said the worst. If I should tell
The worst point, I believe, though I spoke truth,
You'd hate me for it. But consider this:
What you avoid, or what you do, you lovers,
All with the best intentions, often the lady
Will misconstrue it and set it down as wrong
In her opinion. Or if for other reasons
She happens to be cross, you promptly hear
Complaints enough. Lord, is a man well off
Who can be one of you!"

                                But for all this,
When he could see his time he held his tongue.
It was his whole reward, for love so limed
His feathers that he hardly could pretend
Among his followers that other needs
Distracted him with business. What to do
He could not tell, for he was in hard case.
He told his knights to go wherever they liked,
And when he was alone and in his room,
Down on the bed's foot sat himself and sighed,
And thought of her unhindered, till his mind
Dreamed that he saw her in the temple again,
Her manner and her look, which he began
To study freshly. His mind became a mirror
In which he saw her figure, nothing else;
And thus he found it in his heart to think
That it might be a right good turn of fortune
To love one such as she, and if he served her
With all due care, he might yet stand in grace,
Or pass at least for one among her servants.
He told himself that neither toil nor hurt

For one so goodly as she was could be lost,
Nor his desire a fault, even if known;
It would advance his value and his name
Among all lovers, more than hitherto.
Thus at the start he argued, all unwarned
What sorrows were in store. So he resolved
To follow love's craft, and he thought at first
To work in secret, hiding his desire,
Cooping it up from every living eye
Utterly, thinking that if his love were hidden
He might recover, and remembering too
That love too widely blown yields bitter fruit
However sweet the seed when it was scattered.
And more he thought, and yet a great deal more,
On what to say and what to stifle up,
And sought what might persuade her into love,
And made a start by thinking of a song
That helped him gain a little on his sorrow;
For with good hope he gave his whole assent
To loving Cressida, with no compunction.

There is the song he wrote, both word and meaning,
Save for the difference in the tongues we speak,
As Lollius, whom I follow, has preserved it:

THE SONG OF TROILUS

If love is nothing, O God, what feel I so?
If something, what and which, I ask, is he?
If love is good, from what cause comes my woe?
If he is evil, a wonder it is to me
That all his torment and adversity
Come with so sweet a savor, as I think,
That I thirst more, the more of him I drink.

And if I burn at my own choice and will,
Whence come my bitterness and my complaint?
Why say I suffer if I thrive on ill?

I do not know, nor why untired I faint.
To welcome wounds and live in death is quaint!
Dear harm, how can I hold as much of you,
Except by my own choosing, as I do?

But if it is by choice, then wrongfully
I utter this complaint. Thus, to and fro,
Rudderless in a boat amid the sea
And buffeted between two winds I go
That ever from opposing quarters blow.
Strange malady, that such extremes can cherish!
Of heat in cold, and cold in heat, I perish.

"O Lord," said Troilus to the god of love,
"Yours is my spirit now, and should be yours.
You have my thanks for bringing me to this.
But whether she is a goddess or a woman,
She whom you make me serve, I do not know,
Only that I must live and die her man.
You have your sovereign station in her eyes,
A place fit for your power. If I, therefore,
May please you by my service, let me have
Your favor. I resign my royalty
Into her hands, humbly in every way
To be hers, as a lover to his lady."
The fire of love in him, God bless me for it,
Spared neither royal blood nor soldier's prowess,
But took and held him like the lowest slave
And burned him with so many fits and starts
He lost his color sixty times a day.
The closer to the fire, the hotter it is—
All company, I think, will grant me this!
But far or near, the heart of Troilus,
The eye within his breast, by day and night,
And whether in wisdom or in foolishness,
Was fixed on her, more lovely to behold

Than ever Helen or Polyxena.
No hour slipped from the day but he had said
A thousand times in silence to himself,
"O goodliest of good creatures, Cressida,
For whom I serve and toil as best I can,
Now would to God, dear heart, before I die
You would take pity on me! Hope and strength
And life are lost unless I have your mercy."
All other fears took flight, both of the siege
And of his soul's salvation. His desire
Bred in his heart no fawns nor other fondlings
But arguments to one sole end: that she
Should have compassion on him. The tests of war,
The onslaughts, thick as hail, that Hector made
And the other sons of Priam, did not stir him,
And yet wherever man or horse might go
He was among the best, as long to stay
Where danger was, and did such feats of arms
That men would marvel when they thought of him.
But not for any hatred of the Greeks
Nor even for the rescue of the town
He spent his fury, but only for this end,
To win her inclination by his prowess.
And for this purpose day by day he fought
Until the Greek knights feared him like the plague.
   From this time on love robbed him of his sleep
And made his food his foe, and multiplied
His sorrows till the effect showed in his color
Both night and day. To keep men from discerning
That he was scorched in the hot fire of love,
He borrowed the title of another sickness
And said he had a fever and was not well.
The woe that nearly drove him out of mind
Was this: he feared she might have loved so well
Some other man that she would never feel
The slightest care for him; this was a thought

At which he felt his heart bleed inwardly,
And yet he did not dare, for the whole world,
Speak to her of his woe. But when he felt
A moment's respite, he would chide himself,
And say, "Now you are in the snare, you fool,
Who used to laugh at lovers in their plight!
Now you are caught, now gnaw at your own chain!
The things that you condemned in other men
Are those from which you can't protect yourself.
Now what will every lover say of you
If this is known? Always behind your back
They'll laugh contemptuously, and say, 'See there,
The wise man who had small respect for us!
Praise be to God, he dances now with those
Whom Love will be in small haste to reward!'

   "But you, unhappy Troilus, O God,
Since destiny has ruled that you must love,
Why could you not have fixed on one who knew
Your anguish, though she had no pity at all!
Your lady is as cold for love of you
As the white frost beneath the winter moon,
And you conquered as quick as snow in fire.
I wish to God I had arrived already
At death's harbor, to which my sorrow leads.
Ah, Lord, that would be a comfort, and a great one!
I should be done with languishing in fear,
For if my hidden sorrow is noised abroad,
I shall be ridiculed a thousand times
Worse than the fools whose fate is sung in ballads.
But now God help me, and you, sweet, for whom
I suffer and am caught, no man so fast!
Mercy, dear heart, and save me from the plague!
As long as I have life, I will love you
More than myself. Give me some cheer at least,
A friendly look, though you never promise more."

   As he fretted in his room thus, by himself,

A friend of his, whose name was Pandarus,
Came in one day while he was unaware
And heard him groan and saw him in distress.
   "God help us, who has put you in this mood,"
Pandarus asked him, "what catastrophe
Does all this signify? Can it be the Greeks
Have thinned your ribs so soon, or is it conscience?
Are you at your devotions for some sin?
Have you been frightened into some compunction?
Blessed are they that have besieged our town,
Who cupboard up our jollity so well
And turn our lusty people to religion!"
   He used these words to anger Troilus,
Hoping that wrath would mollify his woe
And rouse his spirit; for Pandarus well knew
There was no hardier man, and none with heart
More set on valor.
                          "What unlucky business
Has brought you here to see me languishing,
An outcast among men?" said Troilus.
"For the love of God and my sake, go away,
For this disease intends to be my death.
Past question I shall die. So leave me, then;
There's nothing more to say. But if you think
I'm sick because of fear, it is not so.
Don't hold me in contempt on that account.
There's something else that troubles me far more
Than anything the Greeks have done as yet,
And which will be the death of me for sorrow.
And though I will not tell you what it is,
Don't be angry; I hide it for the best."
   Pandarus nearly melted with compassion.
Over and over he said, "What may it be?
Now friend, if there has ever been or is
Frankness or sympathy between us two,
Do not be guilty of such cruelty

As hiding from your friend so great a care!
This is I, Pandarus—can you take that in?
If it so prove I cannot bring you comfort,
I will divide your grief with you at least.
It is the privilege of a friend to share
Sorrow as well as pleasure. All my life,
In right and wrong, through false report or true,
I have loved you as a friend, and so I shall.
Don't hide your care from me, but tell me gladly."

    Then Troilus groaned unhappily, and said,
"I hope to God it's wise to let you know.
If it will give you any satisfaction
I'll tell my secret, though my heart should burst.
You cannot help me; I know that, certainly.
But rather than you thought I do not trust you,
Listen, for this is how it stands with me.

    "Love, even he against whose power the man
That most defends himself can least prevail,
Has given me a wound so desperate
My heart is on its voyage straight for death;
And my desire attacks me with such heat
That to be killed would satisfy me more
Than to be king of Greece and Troy at once.

    "Let this content you, Pandarus, my true friend.
I have said enough, for now you know my care.
And for the love of God, this fatal sorrow,
Don't let it out—I have told no one but you.
Troubles might follow, more than a handful of them,
If it were known. Be happy for yourself,
And let me keep my secret while I perish."

    "Why have you hidden this from me so long,"
Said Pandarus, "and so unnaturally?
You may be hankering after such a one,
You fool, that my advice could help us with her."

    "A likely thing!" said Troilus. "You've never
Given yourself the right advice in love.

How the devil can you turn the trick for me?"
  "Hold on a minute! Listen, Troilus.
Though I'm a poor example, it often happens
That one who suffers badly from excess
By good advice can warn his fellows from it.
What, I myself have seen a blind man walk
Where people with good eyesight lost their footing!
A fool, moreover, can often lead the wise.
A whetstone is no cutting instrument,
But it can make sharp tools. Wherever you see
That I have made missteps, you can avoid them,
For that's the way to learn. Often the wise
Are warned by fools, and if you do the same,
Your wit is well prepared. All things are known
By opposites, for how could men know sweet
If they had never tasted sour? No man
Can inwardly be happy, I feel sure,
Who's never been in sorrow or distress.
Put white by black, put merit next to shame,
Each seems the more for standing by the other,
As wise men say and everyone perceives.
And since two opposites produce one wisdom,
I, who have suffered grievances in love
So often, ought to know so much the better
How to advise you in this plight of yours.
  "One thing, you may be absolutely sure
That not for fear of torture to the death
Will I betray your secret; and by my word
It's no concern of mine to hold you back,
No, not though it were Helen, your brother's wife,
To my very knowledge. Let her be what she is,
And love her as you please. Come, as a friend,
Trust in me fully, and in so many words
Tell me what is the final cause and reason
For the distress you suffer. Have no fear;
There is nothing of reproach in my designs,

For no one can forbid a man to love
Till he elects to give it up himself.
Remember both are vices: to mistrust
All men, or to believe in all. The mean
Between these two extremes is not a vice.
That I know well. It's evidence of truth
To trust a few; therefore I would correct
Your heresy, and lead you to confide
Your woes in someone; tell me, if you like.
'A man alone is crippled,' say the wise,
'He falls, and no one helps him to get up.'
Now since you have a friend, relieve your sorrow.
The short way to success in love is not
To wallow and weep like Niobe, whose tears
Can still be seen in marble. Stop your crying,
And don't luxuriate by seeking woe
In woe, as fools do, egging on their grief
With grief, when they have fallen in bad luck,
And never hunting for the remedy.
It's consolation to a wretched man
To have a fellow in misery, as they say.
That should be our conviction, for we both
Have grievances in love. I am, in fact,
So full of misery on that head, no more
Could sit on me; there isn't room for more.
I hope to God you aren't afraid of me,
As if I might deceive you with your lady!
You know yourself the woman I have loved
This long while past, as well as I knew how.
You say you trust me more than any man;
Tell me a little, for you know my secrets."

For all this talk, still Troilus had no word,
But lay as fixed as death. Then, after a time,
He burst out sighing, and appeared to listen
To his friend's voice, and lifted up his gaze
In such a way that Pandarus was afraid

He'd fall into a frenzy, or die at once.
  "Wake up!" cried Pandarus, in a voice abrupt
And wonderfully sharp. "Are you in a trance?
Or are you as the ass is to the harp,
Who hears a noise when people pluck the strings
But in his beastly mind no harmony
Can sink for dullness?"
                              Pandarus fell silent,
But Troilus answered nothing, still resolved
That no man should be told for whom he suffered.
Men often make sticks, as the saying goes,
By which the maker is beaten; most of all
A man should keep his counsel in all points
That touch on love. He will himself betray it
Unless it is well governed, and many times
Prudence will seem to shun what it pursues.
  These were the thoughts that Troilus had in mind.
But when he heard the voice of Pandarus
Crying, "Wake up!" he gave a groan that wrenched
    him,
And said, "Friend, though I lie still, I'm not deaf.
Keep quiet now, and don't shout any more.
I've heard you and I've listened to your wisdom,
But let me vent my misery. Your proverbs
Do me no good, and there's no other cure
You can administer. And as for that,
I won't be cured; I'll die. What do I know
Of Niobe? Forget your old examples."
  "No," Pandarus declared, "that's why I said
It's fools' delight to wallow in the dumps
And never to think of looking for relief.
I see that you've begun to lose your reason.
But tell me, what would happen if I knew
For whom you suffer all this grievousness?
Would you dare let me whisper in her ear
This plight of yours, if you don't dare yourself,

And plead with her to take some pity on you?"
    "No," Troilus said, "by God and by my honour!"
    "What, even if I spoke as earnestly
As if my life depended on the mission?"
    "No, certainly," said Troilus.
                                    "Why not?"
    "You'd never succeed."
                            "You're sure of that?"
                                            "Quite sure.
It's past all doubt. Nothing that you can do
Will win her over to a wretch like me."
    Said Pandarus: "Now why have you despaired
So needlessly? For God's sake, she's alive,
Your lady. How do you know you have no hope?
Ailments of this sort are not always fatal,
For many a thing to come depends on chance.
You suffer as much, I readily admit,
As Tityus down in hell, whose bowels were torn
By birds called vultures. But let you maintain
The stupid notion that your miseries
Are past relief, that I will never do.
You will not, for pure cowardice of heart
And for your anger and headstrong foolishness,
Make a clean breast of it in your mistrust,
No, not so far as just to give a reason.
You lie there like a man who cares for nothing.
Can any woman love a wretch like that?
What would she make of it if you should die,
Except to think, not knowing why it was,
That you had given up the ghost in fear
Because the Greeks besiege us? Lord, the thanks
You'd have for that! But that is what she'd say,
And the whole town besides: 'The wretch is dead,
The devil take his bones.' All by yourself
You may get down here on your knees and blubber,
But love a woman and never let her know

And she'll requite you for it just as blankly.
Unknown, unkissed; unfound, if never sought.
What, many a man pays high enough for love
Through twenty seasons, when his lady knows it,
And never yet has kissed her on the lips!
All right! Should he despair on that account,
Or give it up to his own injury,
Or kill himself, finding her beautiful?
No, no, but still unwithered, fresh and green,
Be constant in his service, and have faith.
It is enough, and more than he deserves
A thousand times, to do what she demands
And love her as his heart's delight."

                     These words
Had their effect on Troilus. He perceived
The folly he was in, and how much truth
Pandarus uttered. If he killed himself
He would gain nothing, but he would be guilty
Both of unmanliness and of a sin.
His death would have no meaning for his lady,
For she, God knows, was ignorant of his pains.
Thus thinking, he sighed bitterly, and said,
"What is it best for me to do?"
                       "It's best,"
Said Pandarus, "if you please, to tell
All that you have to tell; and on my word,
If you don't find, before much time has passed,
That I'm your doctor, have me drawn and quartered
And hang me after that."
                    "So you keep saying,"
Said Troilus, "but that doesn't make it true.
It will be hard to help me in my case,
For I am sure that Fortune is my foe.
All men together, though they walk or ride,
Cannot withstand her cruel wheel; her whim
Plays with the free man and the slave alike."

Said Pandarus: "You put the blame on Fortune
Purely from anger. Yes, I see at last.
Fortune belongs, as you must surely know,
In some degree to every man in common.
You have this comfort, yes, by God, you have,
That as her favors do not last, so too
Her frowns are soon forgotten, every one.
For if her wheel stopped turning for a moment,
Then she would not be Fortune any more.
Now, since we know her wheel can never rest,
How if she is about to do to you
In her mutations just what you'd want done?
How if she is about to give you help?
Perhaps you should be singing! Do you know
What I implore you, therefore? Give up grief,
Stop looking downward. Those who want a cure
Must first unwrap their wounds. To Cerberus
May I be bound forever down in hell
But you should have her tomorrow, for my mind,
Although it were my sister. Cheer up, I say,
And tell me who she is immediately
So that I can go quick about your business.
Do I know her? If you love me, tell me that.
Knowing her, I'll have more hope of success."

This tapped the veins of Troilus; he was hit,
And red for shame.
                    "Aha," said Pandarus,
"The fun begins!" and shook him, crying out,
"Now, thief, who is she?"
                              Troilus began
To tremble as if he were being led to hell,
And said, "Dear God, the source of all my pain,
My sweet foe, she's called Cressida." With that
He all but died of terror.
                          When Pandarus
Had heard her name pronounced, Lord, he was glad.

"Dear friend, you're all right now, as God's in
    heaven.
Love has done well by you," he said. "Be cheerful,
For in discretion, bearing, and good name
She is well off, and in her breeding, too.
Whether she's beautiful, you know yourself.
I never saw, in her position, one
More bountiful than she, nor friendlier
In speech, more cheerful, with such graciousness
In doing well, nor one who had less need
To think what she should do, nor so disposed
To stretch all this as far as ever she can
And add to it in honor; a king's heart
By hers will seem no better than a wretch's.

    "Take comfort, then. A man should first of all
Have peace within himself, a noble heart
Kept well in order; so indeed should you.
Nothing but good can come of loving well
When love is well bestowed; don't call it chance,
But call it grace. Remember, too, that since
Your lady has all virtues, there must be
Some pity in her among other things;
And so take care you never ask of her
A thing against her honor, for true virtue
Will never stretch to shame. Now I am glad
My mother bore me, to see you so bestowed
In a good place. I would have taken an oath
That you could never have such luck in love.
Do you know why? Because you used to gird
Contemptuously at love, call him St. Idiot,
The lord of fools, and say that those who served him
Were God's baboons; for some would munch their food
All by themselves, lying in bed and groaning;
Some suffered with green sickness, pale with fever,
And even prayed God not to make them well;
And some took on about the cold, and some

Feigned wakefulness although they slept in comfort,
Thinking they might fly high by this pretense
Though always they went under in the end.
Now I can have a little fun with you
If I'm inclined; but you are not a fool,
I dare say. Beat your breast, and offer a prayer
To the god of love: 'Your grace, Lord; I repent
If I spoke wrongly, for I am in love
Myself now.' "

           Troilus answered: "I submit.
Ah, Lord, forgive my jokes, and while I live
I'll give them up forever."

                 "That's well said,"
Pandarus told him, "and I trust that now
The god has been appeased, and she from whom
Your sorrows flowed will be your comfort too.

  "For the same ground that bears the vicious weeds
Nurtures the wholesome herb; the soft rose blooms
Often beside the nettle, rough and thick.
High up beside the valley stands the hill,
And next the dark night is the cheerful morning,
And so stands gladness at the end of grief.

  "Now drive with even rein, and trust to time
To shape things for the best, or else our work
Will all be idle. He that knows how to wait
Shortens his journey. Be diligent and true,
And persevere in service; all is well
If you act so. The man who splits himself
In every quarter can be nowhere whole,
So say these learned men, and you know well
That if you plant a tree and pull it up,
No wonder it doesn't grow. And so stand fast,
For you have pulled your boat to a good port.

  "And do you know why I am less afraid
To undertake this matter with my niece?
I have heard it said by wise and learned men

There was never man or woman yet begotten
Impervious to love's heat, the love divine
Or natural. Speaking specially of her,
And thinking of her beauty and her youth,
Divine love hardly suits her at this stage,
Although she had been taught and were disposed.
But surely it would suit her at the moment
To love a worthy knight; if she refuses,
I hold it for a vice. And so I am
And will be ready always to take on
This service, for I hope to please you both
In due time. Both of you can be discreet
And keep your counsel; none will be the wiser.
We three shall all have reason to be glad.

   "I have a good opinion of you now,
As I'm a man. I'll tell you what it is.
I think, since Love in his benevolence
Converted you from sin, you will become
The pillar of his church, the greatest grief
To all his foes. Take for a good example
These learned brethren who sin most of all
Against the law, until they are converted
Through God's grace from their wicked practices
When he is pleased to draw them to himself.
They are the men who most hold God in awe
And strongest in their faith, I understand,
And quickest to oppose a heresy."

   When Troilus heard Pandarus agree
To be his aid in loving Cressida,
Then, as a man might say, he was distormented,
But all the hotter grew his love. He said,
Soberly, though his heart skipped, "Blessed Venus,
Help me before I perish! I must earn
Some thanks from you, dear friend. But Pandarus,
How shall I live till this is done? And tell me,
How will you speak of me and my distress

So that she won't be angry—this I dread
Above all else—or will not understand
Or listen how it is? I fear it greatly,
And also that because of you, her uncle,
She will not let you speak of things like this."

   "You worry admirably," said Pandarus,
"For fear the man in the moon will tumble down!
Good Lord, I hate your scruples and your fears!
Forget your part. Let me alone, I ask,
Do me that favor, for the love of God,
And all will turn out for the best."

                              "Why, friend,
Do as you like," said Troilus. "But one word,
Pandarus. Listen! I would not have you think
I am such a fool that I in any way
Wish anything that might bring down reproach
Upon my lady. I should rather die
Than have her understand a thing of me
Except for good."

                  Then Pandarus laughed, and said,
"Shall I stand bail for that? Everyone
Says the same thing. I wouldn't care, myself,
If she stood here and heard just what you say.
Good-by. I'm going. God favor both of us.
Give me the management of this affair,
And yours be all that honey of success!"

   Then Troilus fell on his knees, and took
Pandarus in his arms, gripping him fast,
And said, "Now to the devil with the Greeks!
I'm a fool if God won't help us in the end!
I tell you, if my life lasts, under God,
A few of them will smart for it! This boast
I can't keep back. Now Pandarus, that's all
That I can say. But you—you know, you teach,
You govern, you are all. My life, my death

I put entire into your hands. Help, now!"
   "I shall," said Pandarus, "on my word, I shall."
   "Good-by, friend, and above all else commend me
To her whose will I follow to the death."

   So Pandarus went, thinking of this affair
And how to make approaches to her favor
And how to find a proper time and place.
For any man who has a house to build
Knows better than to rush the work at once
With reckless hand; he bides his time a while,
And first sends out his heart's line from within.
Pandarus kept this thought in mind, and planned
Wisely and well before he set to work.

   But Troilus on his bay steed took the field,
And lying down no longer, played the lion.
Unhappy was the Greek who crossed his path
Whatever the time of day, and in the town
His manner was so irreproachable
And brought him so much favor there was no one
Who looked him in the face but loved him for it.
For he became the friendliest of men,
The kindest, noblest, and in war among
The best that were or might be in his time.
Dead were his jokes, his pride, his arrogance,
And every fault transformed into a virtue.

Book II

Out of the blackness of these waves to sail,
O wind, O wind, the sky begins to clear.
What wonder if the laboring ship should fail
In such a sea? My skill could hardly steer

Through the tempestuous matter it found here,
The black despair that Troilus was in.
But now the kalends of his hope begin.

My lady Clio, henceforth be the one
To prosper me, and help me as my Muse
To rhyme this book well till my task is done.
No other art is needed if your views
Acquit me, lovers, wherever I abuse
Your tenderness, or if I have maligned it.
I simply take the Latin as I find it.

And so I look for neither thanks nor blame
In all this work, but beg you modestly,
Exonerate me if a word is lame.
Whatever my author says, I speak as he,
And though I write of love unfeelingly
It is no wonder; the fault is hardly new.
How can a blind man judge the rose's hue?

And then you know how forms of speech will change
Within a thousand years; words long ago
Were prized that we think wonderfully strange,
And yet time was when people spoke them so,
And did as well in love as we do now.
For winning love, in various times and scenes
Various are the customs and the means.

And should it happen therefore for this reason
That someone who is listening in this place,
Some lover who shall hear, as in due season
The tale will tell, how Troilus came to grace,
May think, "That's not how I will win my race,"
Or marvel at his words, or think he blunders,
To me his luck will be the least of wonders.

The roads that lead to Rome are not the same;
Men go in different fashions year by year,
And in some countries it would spoil the game
If people dealt in love as they do here
And followed the same customs far and near
Or in the same words had to plead their cause.
But, as men say, each country has its laws.

There are not three among us here who do
Alike in love or say alike in all,
Yet all is said or shall be. What serves you
May only lead another to a fall.
Some carve a tree, some chisel at a wall,
As fancy suits them; but as I began
I shall pursue my author, as I can.

In May, the mother of the cheerful months,
When the fresh flowers, blue and white and red,
Quicken again after their winter death
And every field breathes honey, when the sun
Sheds brightness from the white sign of the Bull,
It happened, on the third day of the month,
As I shall tell, that Pandarus, for all
His knowing words, felt the sharp edge of love
Himself, with such effect that though he preached
Never so well, it turned his color green.
Often enough he tossed that night in bed
Before the daylight, and when morning came,
The swallow, Procne, with unhappy voice,
Began her lamentation for the fate
That had transfigured her; and Pandarus
Lay all the while half sleeping in his bed
Until she brought her twittering song so close,
Of Tereus and his rape upon her sister,
That he was wakened by the noise, and called,

Preparing to get up; for he remembered
His errand, still to do for Troilus,
And his great undertaking. He consulted,
And found the moon auspicious to begin
His enterprise, and to his niece's palace
Not far away he promptly took himself.
Janus, you god of entry, be his guide!

"Where is my lady?" Pandarus demanded.
Her people told him; he went in at once
And found her sitting with two other ladies
In a tiled parlor, listening to a girl
Who read the story of the siege of Thebes.

"God save you, Madame, with your pretty book
And all your pretty company," Pandarus said.

"Ah, you are welcome, uncle," she replied,
And rising, took his hand. "Three nights ago
I dreamed of you; I hope good comes of it.'

She seated him, and Pandarus said, "Niece,
God willing, you shall be the better for it
The whole year through. But I have interrupted
The reading of this book you like so much.
What's it about? Tell me, for God's sake, do.
Is it concerned with love? Ah, you can teach me
A lesson I can use."

                    With that she laughed,
And said, "Uncle, your lady is not here.
This book that we were reading deals with Thebes,
And we have just heard how King Laius died
Through Oedipus, his son, and all that story,
And we shall stop at the red letters here
Where it describes how Amphiaraus plunged
Right through the earth to hell."

                           "I know all this
Myself," said Pandarus, "the siege of Thebes
And all that grief. The tale is twelve books long.
But never mind it. Tell me how you are.

Take off your veil and let me see your face.
Forget your book. Get up, let's have a dance
And show some token of respect to May."

"I? God forbid!" she said. "Are you insane?
Is that a widow's life? You frighten me.
You talk so wild, I think you must be raving.
It would become me more to wait my time
Within a cave, and read the lives of saints.
Let girls and those who still have husbands dance."

"If ever I hope to live," said Pandarus,
"I've something I could tell to make you skip."

"Now tell us, uncle! Has the siege been lifted?
I am so frightened of the Greeks I perish."

"No, no," he said. "If I hope for my salvation,
This is a better thing than five of that."

"Now, holy God," she said, "what can it be?
Better than five of that? Heavens! I can't
For all this world imagine such a thing.
Some joke it is, I think. If you yourself
Refuse to tell us what it is, my wits
Are all too thin to puzzle it out. God help me
If I know what it is."

         "You never shall
If you depend on me!"

           "Now, uncle, why?
Why so?" she said.

         "By God, I'd tell you that
As willingly!" he answered. "Prouder woman
There isn't in all Troy, if you only knew.
I am not fooling, no, by all my hopes."

Then she began to wonder a thousand times
More than she had at first, and dropped her eyes,
For never since the day she had been born
Did she desire to know a thing so much.
At last she told him with a sigh, "Now, uncle,
I won't upset you, nor ask any more

What might disturb your comfort."
                                    So they talked
Gaily of this and that, and waded deep
In the profundities and tangled thickets
That friends discuss together, till at length
She thought to ask him how it was with Hector,
The very wall of Troy and scourge of Greeks.
    "Oh, handsomely, thank God," said Pandarus,
"But that he has a slight wound in his arm;
Also his lusty brother, Troilus,
The second Hector, worthy as he is,
In whom it pleases all the knightly virtues
To meet abundantly."
                            "In all truth, uncle,
I am glad to hear it. They are doing well,
God keep them both! It is a lovely thing
To see a king's son prove himself in battle
And be a man of character besides,
For goodness and great power in this world
Are seldom found together in one person."
    "A true word, as I live," said Pandarus.
"But, by my credit, Priam has two sons,
Hector and Troilus, as I'm mortal man,
Who are as free of vices, I dare say,
As any living soul beneath the sun.
No need to talk of Hector; in all the world
There is no better knight. He is the source
From which our prowess flows, and he has virtue
Exceeding even his prowess. Troilus
I put on the same plane. As God's my help,
I do not know another pair like them."
    "Lord knows that's true enough," she said, "of Hector,
And the same is true of Troilus, I believe.
For certainly men say, day in, day out,
He does so well in battle and bears himself
In such a friendly fashion here at home

To every one, he wins the admiration
Of all the people whose praise I value most."
　"You speak the truth, I'm sure," said Pandarus.
"Anyone who was with him yesterday
Might well have marveled, for no swarm of bees
Was ever yet as thick as were the Greeks
That flew out of his path. All through the field
The only shout that any man could hear
Was 'There goes Troilus!' He tracked them down
So fast, now here, now yonder, you could see
Nothing but Greek blood. Always where he fought
It was ordained that he should be their death
And shield and life to us. No man that day
Dared to oppose him while he had in hand
His bloody sword. And then besides all this,
He is the friendliest man of high position
That I have ever known in all my life,
And when he likes, the best in fellowship
With people that he thinks are good for something."
　With these words Pandarus got up cheerfully
To take his leave, and said, "I must be off."
　"No, uncle! Is it my fault?" she protested.
"What's wrong with you that you are tired so soon,
Especially of women? Must you go?
Sit down again. I have some business with you,
Truly, before you leave."
　　　　　　　　　　　When they heard this,
All who were standing by them drew away
To let them talk their business as they liked.
And when she brought her story to an end,
Telling him how she managed her affairs,
Pandarus said, "Now it is time I went.
But still I say, up, and we'll have a dance.
The devil with your mourning! Why go round
Disfiguring yourself in clothes like that
When you are standing in the smile of fortune?"

"Ah, you remind me! For the love of God,"
She said, "shall I not find out what you mean?"

"No," Pandarus told her. "This thing calls for leisure.
Besides, I should be grievously upset
Were I to tell and you to be offended.
It would be better not to wag my tongue
Than tell a truth you might not like to hear.
For, by Minerva, niece, by Jupiter
Who makes the thunder ring, by her I serve,
The blessed Venus, you of all alive
Are the woman I love best—leaving *amours*
Out of account—and most would hate to grieve.
You are aware of this yourself, I'm sure."

"I know it, uncle, gratefully," she said.
"I have always found that you were my true friend.
Really, I am beholden to no man
So much as you, and have repaid so little!
And with God's grace, as far as my wit goes,
I never will offend you willingly,
And if I have already, I'll make amends.
As you are the man that I most love and trust,
Give up this offish talk. Tell me, your niece,
Whatever you please."

                     With that her uncle kissed her.
"Gladly, dear niece," he said. "Take it for good,
What I am going to tell you."

                           She allowed
Her glance to fall at this, and Pandarus
Began to cough a little. "Niece, it happens,"
He said, "however some people like to wrap
Their meaning up in subtleties of art,
Right to the last, still, for all that, the tale
Is always for a purpose; it is told
For some conclusion. The strength of any story
Is in its close; and therefore, since this matter
Is full of promise, why should I dress it up

Or expatiate, to you, who are my friend?"
   He peered at her as if he meant to search
Into her mind, and dwelt upon her face,
And said, "May such a mirror find good favor!"
He was thinking: "If I talk in flourishes
Or break my news in terms the least bit hard,
She'll scarcely relish it, and she'll suspect
I'm trying to deceive her. Tender minds
Believe there is a plot in everything
They cannot plainly understand. Some way
I'll think of to cajole her wits." He looked
Intently at her, and she was aware
He studied her thus busily, and said,

   "Lord, how you look at me! Haven't you seen me
Ever before? Come, what about it—no?"

   "Yes, yes," he said, "and I shall see you better
Before I leave. I was thinking, on my word,
Whether you haven't fallen into luck,
For now's the time to learn. To every man
Some goodly chance occurs if he accepts it;
But if he does not heed it when it comes
Or willfully disowns it, then in truth
He cannot say he is deceived by fortune
But by his very indolence and meanness.
And such a man, I think, is much to blame.

   "A blessed gift of fortune, lovely niece,
Has dropped into your lap, if you will take it,
And for the love of God, and my love, too,
Snatch it at once, before the bag is empty!
Why argue out the matter any longer?
Give me your hand, for up and down the world
No one is so well circumstanced as you are!
And since my purpose is entirely good,
As I have said before, and as I love
Your honor and good name, by all the oaths
I've sworn to you, if you are angry with me

Or think I am lying, I shall never again
Look on you with these eyes. Don't be aghast,
Don't tremble, nor change color so for fear!
Why should you? For the worst of this is done,
And though my tale is new to you at present,
Yet trust that you will always find me faithful,
And if I thought it any way unfitting
I should never come to you with this affair."

   "Now, my good uncle, for God's love, I beg,"
She said, "speak out, and tell me what it is!
For I am both aghast what you will say
And yet I long to hear it. Whether for good
Or ill, go on, don't leave me in this torment!"

   "I'll do so; listen to me now, I'll tell you.
Now, niece, the king's dear son, the good, the wise,
The brave, the generous, he whose habit is
To do well always, the noble Troilus,
Loves you so that it will be his death
Unless you save him. There! That's the whole of it!
I have no more to say. Do as you like.
And let him live or die. But let him die,
And I'll die also—take my word for it,
I am not lying, niece—though with this knife
I had to cut my throat."

                With that the tears
Burst from his eyes; he said, "If you allow
Both of us, for no fault of ours, to die,
Then you'll have had good fishing! Would you gain
If we both perished? He that is my lord,
That true man and that noble, gentle knight,
Who covets nothing but your friendly favor,
I see him dying with his every step
And hurrying with all the strength he has
To meet his death, if his fate will humor him.
Ah, why did God confer such beauty on you?
If you can be so heartless as to care

No more for his death, true man as he is,
Than for some miserable fool or clown,
If such you are, your beauty will not stretch
To pay for such an act of cruelty.
It's well to be advised before the need!
The fairest jewel that has no efficacy,
What is it worth? The herb that does not heal,
What value has it? So also with the beauty
That has no tenderness, and with those people
Who trample everyone beneath their feet.
If with your loveliness you have no pity,
By all that's true, it's wrong that you should live!

    "This is no trick, remember. To my mind
I'd rather you and I and he were hanged
As high as men could see than be his pimp.
I am your uncle; the shame would fall on me
As well as you if I were his accomplice
To let your honor suffer. Understand,
I am not asking you to bind yourself
By any promise to him, only this—
Be friendlier with him than you have before,
Be gayer with him, and so save his life
If nothing further. This is our whole aim,
This, nothing else. God be my warrant for it,
I never intended otherwise. I ask
Nothing but sense; no reasonable misgiving
Can trouble you. But put the worst: you fear
That men will wonder, seeing him come and go.
I answer, everyone but natural fools
Will set it down to friendship in his mind.
What! Who imagines when he sees a man
Enter a church, he means to eat the icons?
Consider also, he behaves himself
With such discretion, overlooking nothing,
Wherever he goes he is welcomed gratefully.
And then he will be coming here so seldom,

What matter if everyone in Troy looked on?
Love between friends is the rule all over town.
Wrap yourself in that mantle constantly.
That is your course, as God is my salvation;
But, niece, at all events, to end his woe,
Sweeten a little this offishness of yours,
So that his death will not be charged to you."

    Cressida, hearing him talk in such a fashion,
Thought: "I shall smell out what he has in mind!"

    "Uncle," she said, "now what is your advice?
What do you recommend that I should do?"

    "That is well said," he answered. "Certainly
The best would be to give him love for love.
Do not forget how age wastes hour by hour
Some portion of your beauty; love, then, do,
Before you are consumed by age. Once old,
No one will heed you. Be ruled by the proverb:
'Aware too late,' said beauty as it withered.
Age tames disdain at last. The king's fool shouts
Whenever a woman puts on airs: 'Live long,
You in your pride, until the crow's feet come
Under your eyes; and then go find a glass
To see yourself in the morning.' Niece, for you
I hope there will be no more grief."

                              With that
He bent his head, and she burst out in tears,
And cried, "O misery! Why am I alive?
Faith has departed wholly from this world.
Now what will strangers do to me when he
I thought my best friend urges me to love,
The very thing he should forbid my doing?
I would have felt sure, if by some mischance
I had loved him or Hector or Achilles
Or any creature in the form of man,
You would have had no mercy, but would scold me
Beyond all measure! But this treacherous world,

Who can believe it? Is this your happy news?
Is this your counsel? Is this my great good fortune?
This the reward of all your promises?
Is all this fine veneer of argument
Said to this end? Pallas, in this dread plight,
You must provide for me! I am so struck
That I shall perish!"
                    Grievously she sighed.
  "Is it as bad as that?" said Pandarus.
"By God, I won't come here again this week,
God be my witness, I who am so distrusted!
I see you set but little store on us
Or on our death. If only he might live,
I wouldn't matter; I'm of no account.
By Mars, the lord of cruelty and spite,
By the three Furies who reside in hell,
May I not be allowed to leave this house
If I intended any low design!
But since I see my lord will have to die
And I with him, I here absolve myself
And say that you do wrong to cause our deaths.
But since it pleases you that I should perish,
By Neptune, god of ocean, from henceforth
I shall not eat bread till I have beheld
My own heart's blood; I'll die as soon as he,
You may be sure."
                    He started up to go
Until she caught him by a fold and held him.
Cressida, frightened almost to extinction,
As of all souls alive she was the most
Susceptible to fear, who heard and saw
The sorry earnestness with which he spoke,
Began to be in terror for the harm
That might still further happen, and she thought:
"Disasters every day fall thick and fast
For love, as people are wicked in their nature

Or cruel. If this man should kill himself
Here in my presence, it would be cold comfort.
What would be said of it I cannot tell.
I need to play a shrewd hand." Sighing three times,
She said, "Ah, Lord, this is a sorry turn!
My property in danger, my uncle's life
Hangs in the balance! With God's help, none the less,
I shall manage so that I can keep my honor
And his life too." With that she wept no longer.
"We must always choose the lesser of two evils,
And I should rather show some friendship to him,
Honorably, than lose my uncle's life.
You say you ask me nothing more than this?"

"No, certainly," he said, "my own dear niece."

"Well, then," she answered, "I will do my best.
I'll try to force my heart against my wishes,
Although I won't deceive him with false hopes.
I cannot love a man against my will;
But otherwise I'll try, within my honor,
To please him day by day. And as for that
I never should have said a single no
Except that I am fearful in my mind;
But vanish cause, and vanish the disease.
And now let me protest that if you spin
A deeper plot, then not for your salvation,
Though both of you should die, and the whole world
Turn hostile to me on a single day,
No other mercy shall I ever give him."

"Agreed," said Pandarus, "by all that's true.
But may I be assured that in this promise
You've given me here, you will be faithful to me?"

"Why, certainly you may," she said, "dear uncle."

"I won't have reason to complain," he asked,
"Nor preach to you more often than this once?"

"Why, no, of course not; what more can I say?"
They fell to talking pleasantries awhile

On other topics, until at last she said,
"Good uncle, by his love who made us both,
Tell me how you first learned of his distress.
Does no one know but you?"

                    He answered, "No."
  "Please tell me, can he talk well about love,"
She asked, "for I'll prepare myself the better."
  Then Pandarus began to smile a little,
And said, "I'll tell you, on my word I shall.
The other day, not very long ago,
Inside the palace garden, near a spring,
He and I spent half a day together
To talk about a scheme by which the Greeks
Might be embarrassed. Presently we began
To exercise, and throw our darts around,
Until at last he said that he would sleep
And lay down on the grass. I strolled away,
Until, as I was walking by myself,
I heard him give a miserable groan.
Then I stalked up behind him quietly,
And sure as truth, as best I can recall it,
He addressed himself to Love, and said, 'O Lord,
Take pity on my pain, though I have been
A rebel in my ways! Now, *mea culpa*,
Lord, I repent! O god whose just provision
Resolves the destiny of every man
By your foreseeing providence, accept
In good part my confession, humbly tendered,
And fix me such a penance as you please,
But lest my soul be cast out from your sight,
Be you, in your benignity, my shield
Against despair! For she that stood in black
Has with a look so sorely wounded me
It has gone down to the bottom of my heart,
For which I see that I am doomed to die.
The worst is this, I do not dare betray

My suffering; the red coals are no hotter
That people heap with ashes pale and dead.'
And then he beat his forehead on the ground
And muttered I don't know what, and I went off
Quietly, and pretended I had known
Nothing about it, and then I came again
And stood beside him, and said, 'You sleep too long!
Wake up! You hardly seem to pine for love,
Sleeping as though a man could never rouse you!
Who ever saw so dull a man before?'

   " 'Friend, give yourself a headache over love,'
He said, 'and let me live as best I can.'
But pale as he was for grief, he livened up
His face as if to lead the latest dance.
And so things went till just the other day
It chanced that I came strolling all alone
Into his room, and found him on his bed.
But never have I heard a man groan so,
For what I could not tell, for as I entered
He stopped abruptly. At that I felt suspicious,
And coming closer, found that he was weeping,
And sorely, too. As God is my salvation,
I have never seen a sight I pitied so.
I scarcely had the wisdom or the skill
To keep him from his death. Since I was born
I've never worked so, preaching to a man,
Or pledged myself to any single soul
So deep before he told me who it was
Who had the power to heal him. What he said
And all his words, don't ask me to repeat
Unless you want to see me swoon away!
Merely to save his life, for nothing else,
And for no harm toward you, I am driven to this.
Now for the love of God, be pleasant with him
So that we both may live! I pray to God
That you may profit well, you who have caught

One such as he is, and without a hook!
If you are only as wise as you are fair,
Then is the ruby well set in the ring!
Two in all time could not be better matched
When you are wholly his, as he is yours;
Almighty God, grant us to see that hour!

    "Ha, ha," she cried. "No, I said nothing of that!
So help me God, you spoil it, every bit!"

    "Spare me, dear niece," he said. "When I spoke so
I only meant well. Now, by Mars, the god
Whose helmet is of steel, do not be angry,
My own blood, my dear niece."

                        "Ah, well," she said,
"We'll let it be forgiven."

                      Hearing this,
He took his leave, and went home, Lord, how glad,
How perfectly contented!

                      Cressida rose
Immediately, and straightway sought a room
Where she could be secluded by herself.
She sat down still as any stone; each word
That Pandarus had spoken she turned over
And over again as it came into her mind.
She was no little astonished in her thoughts
At this new circumstance, but all in all,
Fully considered, she saw no danger in it
By which she need be frightened. Quite possibly
A man may love a woman so that his heart
Will break in two without her loving him
Unless it pleases her.

                    Sitting alone
And thinking thus, the tumult of a skirmish
Arose outside; men shouted in the streets,
"Look! Troilus has put the Greeks to flight!"
With that her household all began to cry,
'Come on! Let's go and see! Open the gates,

He'll have to take this street to reach his palace,
There isn't any other way to ride
From where the chain is down at the Dardanus gate."
With that he came, and all his followers,
Riding an easy pace, in double file,
As if it were in truth his fortunate hour,
Which none the less, men say, can alter nothing
That destiny will surely bring to pass.

This Troilus was mounted on his bay,
And richly armed, except for his bare head.
His horse was wounded, and the blood was running;
He rode it very gently, at a walk.
But such a knightly image as he made
Was nowhere to be seen unless in truth
A man could look on Mars, the god of battle.
So like a man of arms he was, a knight
Well proved in prowess; for he had a strength
And body for that task, as well as courage;
And then to see him put his tackle on,
So young, so lusty, and so lithe he looked
It was a heaven to watch him. Twenty ways
His helmet had been hewn, that by a thong
Hung down his back; his shield was hacked to shreds
By swords and maces; in it could be found
Many an arrow that had skewered it
Through horn and hide and sinew. As he rode
The people shouted, "Here comes our delight,
And next his brother, he that keeps up Troy."

He grew a little red, hearing the people
Shout at him; it was a noble sport to see
How soberly he dropped his glance for shame.
And Cressida, who noticed his whole bearing,
Allowed it to sink gently in her heart
Till she could only ask herself, "Whose potion
Have I been drinking?" She blushed at her own thought,
Remembering, "This is he my uncle swears

Will surely die unless I pity him."
And with that thought, she drew her head in quickly,
For very shame, while he and all the people
Were going by. And she began to turn
His valor and renown this way and that
Within her mind, his birth, his wit, his shape;
But that which most inclined her in his favor
Was that his sufferings were all for her.
She thought it would be pitiable to kill
One such as he, if he were true in purpose.

    Here might some envious listener have his joke:
"This was a sudden love! How could it be
That she should fall in love with Troilus,
By all that's true, thus lightly, at first glance?"
Whoever says so, may he never prosper!
For everything, past doubt, must have a start
Before the work is done. I do not say
That she gave Troilus her love so quickly,
Only that she inclined to like him first,
And I have told you why. And after that
His grief and manhood mined her heart with love,
Till by degrees and by his faithful service
He won her love, and in no sudden fashion.
Venus, moreover, in auspicious guise
Sat in her seventh house of heaven then,
Pleased in her aspect, favorably disposed
To help her victim in his time of need;
And truth to tell, she was not wholly hostile
To Troilus at his birth. God knows for that
He reached his goal more promptly!

                             Cressida,
Hanging her head and sitting there alone,
Began to think what measures she could take
At last, if it proved her uncle would not cease
To press with her for Troilus. And, Lord,
She argued round the matter, what was best

To do and what avoid, until she wound it
In many a wrinkle! Now her heart was warm,
Now it was cold. Remembering that she knew
The person of Troilus by sight, and knew
His breeding also, she reflected thus:
"Although it would not be the thing to do
To grant him love, still, for his worthiness,
It would be honorable to please and cheer him
And to deal virtuously with such a lord
For my position, and for his solace, too.
He is my sovereign's son; since he delights
In me so much, if I avoid his eyes
Utterly, he may take it in resentment,
And then I might be put in a worse plight.
Should I be wise to buy hate for myself,
And with no need, where I may stand in favor?
In everything, I think, there's moderation,
For though men put a ban on drunkenness
They don't mean to prohibit everyone
From drinking, I imagine, for all time.
And since I know his torment is for me,
I ought not to disdain him just for that
When the truth is, he has no wrong intention.
I've long known, too, of his good qualities.
He is no fool, nor braggart certainly,
Men say. He is too wise for such a vice,
Nor shall I comfort him in such a way
That he can ever find just cause to boast.
He'll never bind me in such terms as that!
Consider, now: the worst of it would be,
People might think he loves me. What reproach
Would that bring on me—that? Can I prevent him?
Why, no, in all truth. Every day I see
That men love women quite without their leave,
And when the whim is over, drop them flat!
I must remember, too, that he is fit

To have the woman who can serve him best
In all this noble town to be his love,
Saving her honor. For he is out and out
Our bravest except Hector, who is best.
Yet now his life lies wholly in my hands.
But such is love, and such my turn of fortune!

    "Nor is it odd to love me. I myself,
So help me God, though I want no one else
To know this thought, am well enough aware
I am among the goodliest and the fairest,
And people say so, in the whole town of Troy.
What wonder that he takes delight in me?
I'm at my own disposal, well at ease,
Thank God, in property; I am still young,
And stand untethered in the lusty pasture,
Free from all jealousy and such contention.
I'll have no husband say 'checkmate' to me
For either they are jealous to the brim
Or masterful or only love the new.
What should I do? To what end live this way?
Should I not love, supposing I should want to?
Lord, I am not a nun! If I should fix
My heart upon this knight, the best and bravest,
Keeping my honor and my fair name always,
By all that's good, it will do me no discredit."

    But just as when in March the sun shines clear,
Who often changes face, as when a cloud
Is put to flight before the wind, and spreads
Across the sun a while, a cloudy thought
Began to travel through her spirit, and spread
Across the brightness of her thoughts, until
She almost sank with fear. That thought was this:

    "Ah, heavens, free as I am, shall I now love,
Hazard my safety, turn my independence
Into a slave? How do I dare to dream
Such foolishness? Can't I observe in others

Their apprehensive joys, their miseries,
And their constraint? No woman ever loves
Who does not have her reasons for lamenting.
Love by its nature is the stormiest life
That ever was undertaken. Some mistrust
There always is in love, some petty quarrel,
Some cloud is over that sun. We wretched women,
There's nothing we can do for misery
But weep and sit and brood. Our punishment
Is this, to drink of our own grief. Besides,
These wicked tongues are evermore impatient
To slander us, and men are so unfaithful,
No sooner are they finished with desire
Than love is done with too, and off they go
To a new love. But harm once done is done,
Whoever sorrows for it; for though these men
Will tear themselves apart for love at first,
A sharp beginning makes a sudden end.
Often enough the treason has been proved
That women suffer! The purpose of such love
I cannot see, nor what becomes of it
When it is over. No one, I believe,
Has any notion where it goes; no one
Stumbles upon it. What began as nothing
Turns into nothing. How busy must I be,
If I should love, to placate those who laugh
And draw conclusions, allaying their suspicion,
Lest they malign me! Though there is no ground,
It seems to them that everything is wrong
We do to please our friends. And who can stop
All wicked tongues or silence all the bells
When they are ringing?"

                Then her spirits brightened,
And nothing undertaken, she told herself,
Is nothing gained, whether for love or loathing.
But then she trembled at another thought;

Hope fell asleep, and fear woke in its place.
Now hot, now cold; and so, between the two,
She rose, and went down to amuse herself,
Taking the stairway straight into the garden,
And there walked up and down for many a turn
With her three nieces, Antigone and Tharbe
And Flexippe, so that it was a joy
To see them in their pleasure; and other women,
A generous company of her household, followed
All through the garden. This was an ample space,
With railed walks overshadowed by green boughs
Where blossoms hung, the benches new, the paths
Covered with sand where arm in arm she walked;
Until at last the fair Antigone
Began a Trojan song, her voice so clear
It was a heaven to listen. "Love," she sang,

"O Love, to whom I ever have and shall
Be subject humbly, and with true intent,
As best I can, to you, Lord, I give all
The revenues of my heart's abandonment.
For to no other has your kindness lent
So happy a reason that her life be led
In all delight, and with no shadow of dread.

"Your servant you have taken, Lord, and set her
So in the best of love that all alive
Could not imagine how it might be better.
Free from love's jealousies and wars I thrive;
I love one whose devotion is to strive
That he may serve unwearied and unfeigning,
Truest that ever was, and least complaining,

"As one who is the fount of worthiness,
The ground of truth, mirror of excellence,
Apollo of wit, and stone of steadfastness,

The root of virtue, joy's discovering prince,
Through whom my griefs have fallen dead long since.
I love him best, indeed; so he does me.
Good grace go with him, wherever he may be!

"Whom have I, God of Love, to thank but you
For all this bath of joy whose bliss I win?
Because I love, be thanked, Lord, as is due!
This is the right life, this that I am in,
To banish every kind of fault and sin.
This makes my steps toward virtue so to bend
That in my will I day by day amend.

"Whoever says it is a vice to love,
Or slavery, no matter what distress
He feels in it, he is a fool above
All others, or he speaks in enviousness
Or cannot love for pure ill-naturedness.
Nothing of love can love's detractors know.
They talk, but they have never bent his bow!

"How is the sun the worse, in nature's rightness,
Although a man, so tender is his eye,
Cannot look on it for its very brightness,
Or love the worse for some poor wretch's 'fie'?
The joy is frail that sorrows cannot try!
The man whose skull is glass instead of bones
Should watch out in the wars for flying stones!

"But I with all my heart and all my might,
Will cherish till my very life is past
He that is wholly mine, my own dear knight,
In whom my heart has taken root so fast,
And his in me, that it shall ever last,
That love which, though I dreaded to begin it
I see now has no shadow of peril in it."

At these words, as her song came to an end,
Cressida said, "Now, niece, who made this song,
Well-meaning as it is?" Antigone
Told her. "The loveliest well-born girl in all
The town of Troy, I think, who leads her life
In greatest ease and honor."

                    "So it seems
By her song, indeed," said Cressida, and sighed,
And went on, "Lord, is there such bliss among
These lovers as they can describe so well?"

"Yes, truly," said the fair Antigone,
"For all who have ever lived or are alive
Cannot express the bliss of love too well.
But do you think each miserable fool
Can know the perfect bliss of love? Not so!
It is all love enough for one of them
If he alone is hot. Go on, go on!
They know as much of this as nothing at all.
People must ask the saints whether it's fair
In heaven—why? because the saints can say!—
And ask the fiends whether it's foul in hell."

Cressida had no answer for this point,
But said, "It will be night before we know it."
Yet every word that she had heard her speak
Began to print itself upon her mind,
And love began to frighten her the less
Than it had done at first, and so to sink
Into her heart that she became prepared
To alter somewhat.

                Day's honor, heaven's eye,
The foe of night, the sun, was westering fast,
Descending to be hidden, as if to say
He had run his day's course; white things all grew dim
For want of light, and stars began to show,
As she went in together with her people.
And when she felt inclined to take her rest,

And all had left whose place it was to leave,
Her women helped her quickly into bed.
Then in the quiet she lay still and thought
On all this matter, and a nightingale
In a green cedar by the chamber wall
Where she was lying sang to the clear moon,
Perhaps, in his bird fashion, a lay of love,
And long she listened, till at last dead sleep
Laid hold on her. And as she slept, she dreamed
How, feathered white as bone, an eagle fixed
His long claws under her breast, and all at once
Tore out her heart, and caused his heart to pass
Into her breast; and yet she did not shudder
Nor suffer pain. So off he flew with heart
Exchanged for heart.
                              But leave her to her sleep,
And we shall turn to Troilus, who had ridden
Home from the skirmish, and in his room sat down
Waiting his messengers, two or three of whom
Went after Pandarus, and sought him out
Till finally they found and brought him back.
    This Pandarus came bounding in abruptly,
And said, "Who has been soundly drubbed today
With slingstones and with swords but Troilus?
Who's got into a heat?" He joked, and said,
"Lord, how you sweat! But get up, let's have supper,
Then we can go to bed."
                              Troilus answered,
"We'll do whatever you like."
                              With all the haste
That they could manage suitably, they hurried
From supper into bed, and everyone
Went out the door and off wherever he pleased.
But Troilus, who thought his heart would bleed
For agony until he had some tidings,
Demanded, "Now, friend, shall I weep or sing?"

Said Pandarus, "Lie still and let me sleep.
Put on your hat and gird yourself for action.
Your needs are served. Choose whether to sing, dance,
    leap!
I'll tell you in a word—you can believe me:
My niece, sir, will do well by you, and love you
Best, by God, and by my honor, unless
You show your sloth by slacking the pursuit.
For I have so far entered on your work
From day to day that just this very morning
I won her friendship for you, and to that
She gave her solemn pledge. We have lamed your
    anguish
In one foot, anyway."
                Even as flowers,
Closed by the chill of night, and stooping low
On their bent stalks, recover with the sun
And open their tight files by course of nature,
Just so this Troilus lifted up his eyes
And said, "Dear Venus, praises on your power
And on your graciousness!" To Pandarus
He held out both his hands. "All that I have
Be yours," he said, "for I am healed. My chains
Are broken, one and all. A thousand Troys,
If I were to be given them one by one,
Could not so gladden me, as God's my help.
My heart, I tell you, so spreads out for joy
It will fly open! But, Lord, what shall I do?
How shall I live? When may I hope to see
My dear heart next? And how shall this long time
Be driven away until you can be at her
Again for me? Oh, you may say, 'Wait, wait,'
But anyone who is hanging by the neck
Waits, in all truth, in plenty of discomfort
Because he is in pain."
                "Now take it gently,

For the love of Mars," said Pandarus. "Everything
Requires time. Wait till the night is over.
Sure as you please, and let God be my witness,
I'll be there early. Act somewhat as I say,
Or put this burden on some other man.

    "You are, I know, wiser a thousand times
Than I, and yet if I were you, God help me,
I would in my own hand write her at once
A letter, and tell her it goes hard with me,
And ask her to take pity. Be your own help,
Don't give it up for sloth! And I myself
Will take it to her, and when you know I'm there,
Get promptly on a mount, be bold about it,
Yes, in your best gear, and ride by the place
As if by chance, and you will find us sitting,
If I can manage it, beside some window
That overlooks the street, and if you please
You can bow to us. Address yourself to me.
But as you value life, see to it well
That you don't linger—God protect our luck!
Ride on your way, and keep your self-control.
We'll say some things about you, I believe,
To make your ears burn, after you have gone!

    "Touching this letter, you are shrewd enough.
You will not write it heavily, I know,
Nor put on airs, nor fill it full of jargon,
Nor flourishes of art. Blot it a little
With tears, and if you hit on a good word,
Good as it is, don't dwell on it too often.
For though the best harper that has ever lived
Should on the jolliest harp of sweetest tone
That ever was, and though with all five fingers,
Touch but one string, or play but one same song,
Then if his nails were pointed never so sharp
It would make everyone who heard him dull
And glutted with his music. Then don't jumble

Incongruous things together, as for instance
To mingle medical terms with terms of love.
Stick to the proper form in all this matter;
Keep all your strokes alike. For if a painter
Should paint a pike with ass's feet, and head it
As if it were an ape, it would not suit,
Not even if he meant it as a joke."

    Troilus was well pleased with this advice,
But in the qualms of love he said, "Alas,
The truth is I'm afraid to write for shame,
Good brother Pandarus, lest foolishly
I put something amiss, or she for scorn
Might not accept it. Then I'd be dead for fair!"

    To this Pandarus answered, "If you please,
Do what I tell you, and let me take it with me,
For by that God who made the east and west
I hope to bring an answer in her hand
And that right soon. But if you will not do it,
Then give it up, and wretched be his life
Who tries to help you thrive in your desire."

    "In God's name, I agree," said Troilus.
"Since it will please you, I'll get up and write.
I pray the blessed Lord to prosper it,
This venture, and the letter I'll compose;
And give me wit, Minerva, to devise it."

    So down he sat, and wrote after this fashion.
He called her first his lady, his heart's life,
The healer of his sorrow, his desire,
His bliss, and added all those other terms
That lovers all resort to in such cases;
And went on humbly to commend himself
As suitor to her mercy. After this,
He begged her meekly not to be enraged
That in his foolishness he had made bold
To write to her, and said that it was love
That made him do it, or he would have died,

And piteously implored her to have mercy;
And then he said, and laughed loud as he wrote,
That he himself had little merit enough
And still less art, and hoped she would excuse
His ignorance; then too, he feared her so.
Many times over he accused himself
Of his unworthiness, and after that
Began to tell his sorrow; but that was endless,
Without a halt. He said he would be true
Forever, and read it over, and then began
To fold the letter, and with salty tears
He bathed the ruby in his signet ring
And set it hastily upon the wax.
A thousand times, before he let it go,
He kissed the letter he had sealed, and said,
"Letter, a happy destiny is yours!
My lady's eye shall see you."
                                        Pandarus
Took the letter, and early in the morning
Made for his niece's palace, where he swore
It was past prime, and joked, and said, "My heart,
Truly it is so young that though it aches
I never can sleep when these May mornings come.
I have a jolly grief, a cheerful sorrow."

   Cressida, when she heard her uncle speak,
Fearful at heart, and anxious to discover
The cause of his arrival, said, "Dear uncle,
As you hope to be believed, what kind of wind
Has blown you here? Tell us your jolly grief,
Tell us your twinges. How far have you got
In love's dance now?"
                                    "By God," said Pandarus,
"I always hop along behind,"
                                        She laughed
Until she thought her sides would burst. He said,
"See that you always laugh at my expense!

But listen, if you please. A guest just now
Has come to town, a Greek spy, bearing news,
And I have come to let you have the tidings.
Let's go into the garden; you shall hear,
In privacy, a long report about it."

    Into the garden arm in arm they went,
And when he knew that none could overhear,
He said to her, pulling the letter out:

    "He that is wholly yours commends himself
Humbly to your good favor, and through me
Sends you this letter here. Consider it,
When you have time, and with some gracious answer
Provide yourself; if not, so help me God,
He can no longer live for his distress."

    She stood still in her fear, and would not take it.
All her good humor changed, and "Writ nor bill,"
She said, "on no such matter bring to me,
For love of God! And also, my dear uncle,
Have more regard, I beg, for my position
Than his desire! And now will you consider
If this is reasonable, and don't refuse
Either for sloth or partiality
To speak the truth: now would it be becoming,
By God and by your honor, in my place,
To take this letter, or take pity on him
To my own hurt or shame? Return it to him,
By the God who gives you being!"

                                        Pandarus
Began to stare at her. "Now this," he said,
"Is the greatest marvel that I ever saw!
Forget this foolishness! May I be struck
By lightning if for the city that stands yonder
I'd bring or take you a letter to your harm!
Why see that in it? But that's the way you are,
The lot of you: the man who most desires
To serve you, you care least what happens to him

Or whether he lives or dies. But for the sum
Of all that I may ever yet deserve,
Do not refuse it," and he held her tight
And thrust the letter down into her bosom,
And said, "Now throw it away, for people to see
And stare at us."

           "I can wait till they are gone,"
She said, and then began to smile, and told him,
"Uncle, provide an answer by yourself,
Such as you like, I beg, for in all truth
I will not write a letter."

           "No?" said he.
"Then I will, if you'll copy it."

           At that
She laughed, and said, "Come, let's go in to dinner."
  Then he began to poke fun at himself,
And told her, "Niece, I am pining so for love
That every other day I have to fast."
He called on his best jokes, and made her laugh
Until she thought that she would die of laughter.
  "Now, uncle," she announced as they came in,
"We'll go and dine."

           She called some of her women
And went straight to her chamber; but among
Other concerns, she did one thing, no fear,
And that was, on the sly, to read his letter.
  She scanned it line by line and word by word,
And found no fault, thinking he well knew how
To put his best foot forward. She put it by,
And went to dine. But she found Pandarus
In a brown study, and caught him by his cape
Before he was aware, and said, "You were caught
Before you knew."

           "Granted," he said, "I'll pay
Whatever forfeit you may like."

           They washed,

And sat themselves, and ate; and after dinner
Pandarus made slyly for the window
Next to the street, and said, "Niece, who has trimmed
That house up so that stands there opposite?"

   "Which house?" said she, and looked, and knew it
      well,
And told him whose, and they fell into talk
Of this and that, both sitting in the window.

   When Pandarus saw his time, and all her people
Were well away, "Now, niece," he said, "speak up.
How is that letter you know of? Can he do
That sort of thing? I don't know, on my word,
Whether he can."

                    At that she grew all rosy,
Began to hum, and said, "I think he can."

   "Answer him kindly, for God's love," he said.
"I'll sew[1] your letter as a small reward.
He doubled his knees beneath him as he sat
And lifted his hands. "However short you make it,
Give me, good niece, the task of folding up
And sewing the letter."

                    "Yes, for if I do that,
Then I must write it, and I do not know
What I should tell him."

                    "Now, niece, do not say so.
Thank him at least for his good will, I beg,
And do not cause his death. If you love me, niece,
Do not deny my prayer just now!"

                    "In God's name,
May all be well!" she said. "The Lord so help me
But this is the first letter I ever wrote,
Yes, the first scrap of one."

                    She went alone
Into a small room to collect herself,

---

[1]Sew the parchment sheets together.

And there, if only a little, began to free
Her heart from the scornful fetters of its prison;
She sat down and began to write a letter.

She gave him thanks for all he meant toward her,
But offer him false hope she would not do,
Nor pledge herself in love; but as his sister
She would be always willing to ease his heart.

She folded it, and went to Pandarus
Where he was sitting, looking at the street,
And setting herself upon a jasper stool
That had a cushion worked in gold, she said:
"So help me God in all his greatness, never
With more reluctance have I done a thing
Than write this letter, as you forced me to."
She gave it to him, and thanking her he said,
"God knows, a good end comes of many a thing
Reluctantly begun; niece Cressida,
He should be glad, by God and yonder sunlight,
That you have been so hard for him to win,
For light impressions, people often say,
Are ready to fly lightly off again,
But you almost too long have played the tyrant;
Your heart was hard to dent. Now stop, and hang
No longer on it, though you may preserve
The appearances of being difficult,
But quickly make him glad; for trust it well,
Hard treatment for too long through pure distress
Will lead to hate."

As they discussed this question,
There, at the street's end, Troilus came riding
With a company of ten, and casually
Turned toward them where they sat, along the way
That took him homeward. Pandarus discerned him,
And said, "See, niece, look who comes riding here!
Don't hurry in (he sees us, I imagine)
Or he may think that you're avoiding him."

"No, no," she said, and her face blushed like a rose.
   At that he meekly bowed to her, his color
Coming and going, and his manner timid,
And looked up graciously and waved his hand
To Pandarus, and went on down the street.
   God knows whether he sat well on his horse
Or made a good appearance on that day!
God knows whether he looked the manly knight!
But Cressida, who noticed all these things,
Liked altogether his person, dress, and bearing
So well that never in her life before
Had she so pitied him in his distress;
And hard as she has been with him till now,
I hope to God she has a thorn at last
She will not pull out for another week.
The Lord give others, too, such thorns to pick at!
   Pandarus, who was standing close beside her,
Feeling the iron hot, began to strike,
And said, "Now, niece, I beg you heartily,
Tell me a little thing that I shall ask you.
A woman who should find that he was dead,
Not through his fault, but through her want of mercy,
Would that be well done?"
                                   "No, by my word," she said.
   "So help me God, you're telling me the truth.
You see yourself," he said, "I am not lying:
Yonder he rides!"
                              "He does, that's true," she said.
   "Well," answered Pandarus, "as I have told you
Three times, forget your shame and silliness
And talk with him to give his heart some ease."
   But toward that project much remained to do.
All things considered, it was not to be;
And why? for shame; also it was too soon
To grant him such a privilege as that.
She made plain her intention, which she said

Was to love secretly, if she could do so,
And to reward him only with her sight.

But Pandarus thought, "It shall not go that way
If I can manage; this silly resolution
Shall not be kept as much as two whole years."
But he could only bow to her decision
For the time being; and when evening came
And all was well, he rose and took his leave.

Hurrying homeward, his heart skipped for joy,
And he found Troilus, who was alone,
In bed, and lying, as these lovers do,
As in a trance, between hope and despair.
But Pandarus, on the instant he came in,
Sang out like one who calls, "I have some news,"
And said, "Who's buried himself in bed so early?"

"It is I, friend," he answered.

                           "Who? Troilus?
What, as the moon's my help, get up and see
A charm that has been sent to you just now,
One that can heal your fever, if you do
Your business quickly."

                     "Yes, through Almighty God,"
Said Troilus.

              Pandarus offered him the letter
And said, "By all that's true, the Lord has helped us.
Get a light here, and look at all this black!"

Often the heart of Troilus leaped and shook
By turns while he was reading, as the words
Moved him to hope or fear. But finally
He took all she had written him for the best,
For he saw something, as he thought, on which
His heart might rest secure, although she hid
The words beneath a shield, till what for hope
And what for all that Pandarus promised him,
He lost at least the chief part of his woe.

But as we notice every day ourselves,

The more the wood or coal, the more the flame,
Just so increasing hope, whatever its object,
Will often bring an increase of desire;
Or as an oak springs from a tiny sprout,
So through this letter she had sent to him
Grew also the desire with which he burned.
And so I say that always, day and night,
Ever the more this Troilus desired,
Through hope, than even at first. He did his best
To press on, under Pandarus' instruction,
And write to her about his bitter sorrow.
He did not let it cool from day to day,
But wrote or sent some word through Pandarus;
And all the rituals and observances
Proper to lovers he performed as well.
Then he threw dice and reckoned up his chances,
And he was glad or sorry as they fell,
And by the indications of the dice
His days were glum or cheerful. His recourse
Was constantly to Pandarus. He complained
Piteously, and often begged of him
Counsel and help, and Pandarus for his part,
Who saw the madness of his pain, almost
Grew dead for pity; busily he sought
With all his heart to slay, and that right soon,
Some portion of his anguish; and he said,

   "Lord, friend, and brother, God knows your
      discomfort
Makes me unhappy. But will you put an end
To all this hangdog bearing, and on my word,
Before two days, God be my witness for it,
I'll work it so that in a certain place
You may yourself come plead with her for favor.

   "I don't know whether you're aware of it,
But those who are expert in love declare
One of the things that most advance the cause

Is leisure for a man to make his plea
And a safe place where he may state his plight.
For in good hearts it must arouse some pity
To hear and see the innocent in pain.
Perhaps you think: Though it is true that nature
Will lead her to begin to take some pity,
After a fashion, pride will make her offish,
Will say, not so, you never shall win me!
The spirit of her heart so rules within her
That though she sways, yet she stands rooted still.

   "What bearing has this on my remedy?
Think this on the other side: when the sturdy oak
That men have often hacked receives at last
The lucky felling-stroke, with the greater swish
It comes down all at once, as boulders do
Or millstones; for the heavier a thing is,
The swifter is its course when it descends.
The reed that sways and bends with every gust
Lightly enough, the wind gone by, recovers;
But not so will an oak when overthrown.
I do not need to give you more examples.
All men rejoice at some great undertaking
Accomplished well, and standing past all quibble,
Although it took the longer to perform.

   "But Troilus, tell me if you please one thing
I mean to ask you: which of all your brothers
Do you love best, in the bottom of your heart?"

   "Truly, Deiphobus," he said.

                           "Now then,"
Said Pandarus, "before twelve hours have passed,
He'll give you ease, and never know it himself.
Let me alone, to manage as I can,"
And off he went to see Deiphobus
Who had always been his friend; save Troilus
No man meant more to him. "I beg of you,"
Said Pandarus, "befriend a cause of mine."

"Certainly," said Deiphobus, "I will,
Before God, if I can, as you well know,
If only for the sake of Troilus,
My closest brother. Tell me what it is,
For never since the day when I was born
Have I opposed you in a single matter
By which your were troubled."

            Pandarus thanked him, saying:
"I have a lady in this town, my niece,
Whose name is Cressida, and there are people
Who wrongfully would seize her property.
And so I beg your lordship this, in brief:
To be our friend."

            Deiphobus replied,
"What, she of whom you speak so formally,
Isn't she my friend Cressida?"

                "Why yes,"
He said.

      "You hardly need to tell me more,"
Deiphobus assured him, "for, trust me,
I'll be her champion with spur and shaft!
I shouldn't care if all her foes could hear me.
But tell me, since you know about this matter,
What way can I best serve her?"

              "Now let's see,"
Said Pandarus. "If you would do me honor
By asking her to come to you tomorrow
To set forth her complaints, her adversaries
Would wince at that. And if I dared to ask
More of you at this time, and give you trouble
To such extent as also to have here
Some of your brothers, that would still better help
Her situation. Then she would never lack
For aid, I think, what with your own example
And with the power of her other friends."

Deiphobus, who responded by his nature
To all the appeal of just and generous dealing,
Answered, "It shall be done; and I can find
Still more to help the purpose. What would you say
If I should send for Helen to talk this over?
I think it would be well, for she leads Paris
Just as she likes. As for my brother Hector,
There is no need to ask him to befriend us,
For I have heard him, one time or another,
Talking of Cressida in such a way
He could not speak more highly. You yourself
Must speak to Troilus on my behalf.
Ask him to dine with us."

                              Pandarus answered,
"Sir, this shall all be done," and did not wait
To finish, but took his leave, and straight as a line
Went to his niece's house. She had just risen
From eating, and so he sat with her, and said,
"By the true God, how I have run! Look, niece,
Do you see how I am sweating? I don't know
Whether you'll thank me any the more for that,
But have you heard how the scoundrel Polyphoetes
Is now about to go to law again
And bring new suits against you?"

                              "I? Why, no,"
She said, and all her color changed. "What more
Will he do now to worry me and wrong me?
What shall I do, alas? I wouldn't fear
The man himself, if he didn't have Antenor
And Aeneas as his friends in all such dealings.
But never mind it, for the love of God,
Dear uncle; let him have everything he wants.
I have enough for us without all that."

   "No," Pandarus answered, "not so in the least.
I've been just now with Deiphobus and Hector
And other of milordships, and have made

Each one his enemy, and worked so well
He'll never win, for all that he can do."
    As they considered how best to proceed,
Deiphobus, in his own person, came
To ask her to be present the next day
At dinner, which she could not well refuse,
But pleasantly accepted his request.
    When this was done, Pandarus promptly rose
And quiet as a stone betook himself
To Troilus, and told him all this business
From first to last, and how he had deceived
Deiphobus, and said, "Now is the time,
If you know how, to put your best foot forward
Tomorrow, and the whole game will be won.
Now speak, now plead, now piteously protest!
Don't let it slip for shame or fear or slackness!
A man must sometime tell his plight himself.
Believe it, and she will take pity on you.
Only your faith will save you, that's the truth!
You are afraid, I know; what troubles you
I think that I can fathom. You are asking,
'How shall I do all this? For by my manner
People must see that I am thus afflicted
For love of her.' Now spare yourself that thought,
For you commit a folly. I have just now
Hit on a trick to keep your symptoms hidden.
You must go and spend the night, and start at once,
With Deiphobus, at his house, as if for pleasure,
To drive your sickness off; for truth to tell,
You do look sick. Soon after you are there,
Lie down in bed, say that you can't stay up
A moment longer; lie right there, and wait
Your fortune. Say that the fever comes each day
At the same time, and lasts till the next morning.
Let's see how well you can do it, for in truth,
Sick is the man who is in sorrow! Now

Good-by and go, and Venus for my warrant,
I hope, if you are steadfast in this purpose,
She'll there confirm your favor to the full."

   "You advise me needlessly, and that's a fact,"
Said Troilus, "to pretend that I am sick,
For I am sick in earnest, past all question,
So much so that I nearly die for pain."

   "You'll plead your case the better," Pandarus
      answered,
"And have less need to counterfeit your part,
For people think a man hot when he sweats.
Keep close to your covert; I will drive the deer
Straight to your bow."

                           With this he took his leave,
And Troilus, happier than in all his life,
Fell in with his designs. To his brother's house
He went straightway that very night. What need
To tell you all the hospitality
Deiphobus extended to his brother,
Or his access of fever, his sick looks,
Or how when he lay down everyone piled
The covers on him and tried to entertain him?
But all to no result, for he behaved
In just the way that Pandarus recommended.

   But certainly, before he had lain down,
Deiphobus had begged him to become
A friend and help to Cressida next day.
God knows he promised readily enough
To be her friend as fully as he could;
He needed such persuasion as a madman
Might need to make him run!

                           The morning came,
And then mealtime drew near, when the fair queen,
Helen, meant to be with Deiphobus;
And as his sister, in the simplest manner,
She came to dinner. But God and Pandarus

Knew best what this was all about!
Cressida
Came also, innocent of this whole plan,
Antigone, and her sister Tharbe, too.
Deiphobus paid them much honor, truly,
And fed them well with all that they could wish.
But his refrain was constantly, "Alas,
My brother Troilus, the ailing, lies—"
Then he would sigh, and then exert himself
To entertain them all as best he could.
And Helen too lamented his condition
So genuinely it was pitiable to hear;
And promptly everyone became a doctor
To deal with fevers, and said, "This is the way
People are cured—" "I'll let you know a charm—"

But though she did not wish to teach them how,
One sat there who was thinking, "I could best
Become his doctor."
After their laments,
Then they began to praise him; as people do,
When someone has begun to praise a man,
They lift him up a thousand times beyond
The very sun: "He is, and he can do
What very few can do." And Pandarus,
In all that they maintained, did not forget
To add his confirmation to their praise.

Cressida listened to these things well enough
And carefully took note of every word.
Under her gravity, she laughed at heart;
For where is the woman who will not be flattered
If she can cause a man that she hears praised
To live or die?
Time came to rise from dinner,
And suitably they rose and talked a while
Of this and that. But Pandarus interrupted
Their small talk, saying to Deiphobus,

"Will you present the needs of Cressida,
If it is your pleasure, as I asked of you?"
    Helen, who had taken her by the hand,
Responded first, and said, "Let's do so quickly,"
And looking pleasantly at Cressida,
She said, "Jove never prosper any man
Who does you harm, but promptly take his life;
And give me grief but he'll be sorry for it,
If I have power and everyone is true!"
    "You tell your niece's case," Deiphobus
Instructed Pandarus, "for you can tell it best."
    "My lords and ladies, this is the way it stands;
Why keep you waiting longer?" Pandarus said,
And rang out charges for them like a bell
Against her adversary, Polyphoetes,
Heinous enough to make men spit. Each one
Outdid the other in answer. "Such a man
Deserves to hang, if he were my own brother!
Nothing else for it, he shall hang," they said,
And in such terms they called down maledictions
On Polyphoetes. They promised her together
To be her help in all they ever could.
    Then Helen asked, "Pandarus, does my lord,
My brother Hector know about this matter?
Or Troilus, does he know?"
                              He answered, "Yes,
But will you hear a word of mine? I think,
Since Troilus is here, it would be well
If she herself should tell him all of this,
If you agree to it, before she goes,
He'll have the greater sympathy at heart
Because, you see, she is a lady. Now,
By your leave, I'll just look in and let you know,
In just an instant, truly, whether he sleeps
Or wants to learn of this." And he dashed in

And whispered to him, "God receive your soul,
I've brought your bier!"
                    As Troilus began
To smile at this, Pandarus went at once
To Helen and Deiphobus again,
And said, "As long as people do not linger
Nor make a crowd, he wants you to bring in
My lady Cressida, and he will listen
As long as he is able. But as you know,
The room is small, and only a few people
Could make it close. Now think (for my right hand,
I wouldn't have a crowd that might upset him
Or do him harm) whether she ought to wait
Until some other time. Consider, you
Who know what should be done. For my own part,
I think it best that no one should go in
Except you two, unless it were myself,
For I can in a moment put her case
Better than she; and afterward she may
Plead with him once, briefly, to be her friend,
And so take leave. This can't disturb him much.
Also, he will exert himself the more
Because she is a stranger, while for you
He does not need to do so. One more thing—
He has a secret that concerns the town
To speak with you about."
                    And in they went,
Quite unaware of what his purpose was,
And with no further word, to Troilus.

   With all her gentle ways and pleasant manner,
Helen began to greet him and amuse him
In womanly fashion. "You must be up again,
By all means, truly! Do be well, I beg,"
She said, "good brother." And she put her arm
Across his shoulder, and tried with all her wit

To entertain him. Then at length she said,
"We ask you, brother, Deiphobus and I,
For the love of God—and so does Pandarus, too—
Be a protector and a cordial friend
To Cressida, who certainly is wronged,
As Pandarus here well knows, who can explain
Her case much better than I."
                                        Then Pandarus
Began to sharpen his tongue all over again,
Rehearsing her whole case. When it was finished,
Troilus said, "As soon as I'm about,
I'll cheerfully with all my power be one,
God hear my promise, to support her cause."

   "And may you have success," Queen Helen said.
   Pandarus asked, "Would you like her to come in
To take her leave of you before she goes?"

   "O, God forbid she shouldn't," he replied,
"If she'll consent to do so." And with that
He said, "You two, Deiphobus and my sister,
I have a matter to bring up with you,
To be advised the better by your counsel—"
And found, as if by chance, at his bed's head
The copy of a statement and a letter
That Hector had sent him, asking him to read it,
On whether a certain man deserved to die,
I know not who; but with a frightening manner
He begged them to consider it at once.

   Deiphobus began to unfold the letter,
Solemnly, and so did Helen the queen
And strolling out, they studied it intently,
Passing down a stair and into an arbor.
They read the thing between them for an hour,
Poring over it closely.
                              Pandarus,
Who saw that all was clear, went quickly out
To the main room again. "God save all present,"

He said. "Come, niece, my lady Helen, the queen,
Is waiting for you, and also both these lords.
Come, bring with you your niece, Antigone,
Or whom you will; or never mind; in truth,
The less we crowd the better. Come with me,
And take care that you give them humble thanks,
All three of them, and when you see your time,
Take leave, lest we should trouble him too long."
      Still innocent of Pandarus' design,
Cressida said, "Let us go in then, uncle,"
And arm in arm went with him, well prepared
In word and manner. Pandarus earnestly
Said, "Everyone, for the love of God, I beg,
Stop here, and quietly amuse yourselves.
Consider who are present here, inside,
Consider the plight of one of them, God heal him!"
And then he whispered, "Approach him gently, niece,
I charge you, by no means allow yourself,
For his sweet sake who gave us all our souls,
And by the double crown of virtuous love,
To slay this man who bears for you such pain.
Shame on the devil! Just think who he is,
And in what plight he lies! Come ahead, now.
Remember, all delay is but time lost.
That's what you both will say when you are one.
Secondly, no one has guessed about you two.
Come ahead, if you can! While people are blind
Then time is at your mercy. In vacillation,
Pursuit, postponement, people draw conclusions
If a straw stirs; and though you wanted later
To have your merry days, you will not dare.
Why? Because she and she spoke such a word,
And he and he looked thus! Lest I lose time
I do not dare to argue with you further.
Come ahead, then, and bring him to his health!"
      But now to you, you lovers who are here:

Was Troilus in a frenzy of suspense
Who lay and heard them whispering and thought:
"O Lord, my fate is running toward the moment
When I shall wholly die, or have my solace!"
And this was the first time he would plead with her
For love; Almighty God, what should he say?

Book III

*O happiest of lights, whose beams adorn
The whole third circle of heaven and make it fair,
Joy of the sun, Jove's daughter dearest-born,
Love's pleasure, reigning with a queenly air,
Venus, at all times ready to repair
To noble hearts, true cause of happiness,
True healer, praised be your power and graciousness!*

*In heaven and hell, in earth and the salt sea,
Your power is felt, if rightly I discern,
For man and bird, fish, herb, and the green tree
Feel your immortal influence in turn.
God loves, and will not teach a soul to spurn
Love, when all creatures in this world alive
Are worthless without love, nor can survive.*

*You first persuaded Jove to those glad ways
By which all creatures live and come to be;
You made him amorous (yours be the praise)
Toward mortal things; and as you pleased, even he
In love found comfort or adversity;
You sent him wrapped in many a form and look
To earth for love, and whom you chose, he took.*

You can appease the fierce Mars in his ire,
And any heart to whom you are inclined
You can ennoble; those you set on fire
Abhor all shame, their every vice resigned;
You make them courteous and brave and kind,
And as a man aims, whether high or low,
Your might sends him such joys as he may know.

You rule your heavenly house in unity;
You are the source from which true friendships flow;
And you know all the hidden quality
In things, about which people wonder so,
All at a loss why this with that should go,
Why he loves her, or why she should love him,
Why this, not that, fish to the weir should swim.

You set us laws throughout the universe;
And this I know by the lovers that I see,
Whoever strives with you comes off the worse.
Now, fairest lady, in your benignity,
For the honor of your service, grant to me
That as their clerk I may some part express
Of all your servants feel in happiness.

You, through the feeling of my naked heart,
Pour in, and let your sweetness fill my sight!
Calliope, let your voice have its part!
Now is the need; do you not see my plight,
How I must tell this moment the delight
That came to Troilus, for the Cyprian's praise?
Whoever needs, God bring him to like ways!

Troilus in the meanwhile lay rehearsing
His lesson thus: "Good Lord!" he thought, "I'll say
Such and such, and thus I'll plead with her.
That is a good word, this will be my comfort,

And this at all costs I must not forget."
God help him work according to his plan!
Lord, but his heart began to pound and sigh,
Hearing her come. Pandarus, leading her
By a fold in which her dress fell, drawing near,
Said, "God give health to all those who are sick!
See who has come here now to visit you.
Look, here she is for whose sake you are dying!"

   At that it almost seemed as if he wept.
"Ah, ah," said Troilus, groaning wretchedly,
"Whether I suffer, Almighty God, you know!
Who all are there? I cannot see, for truth."

   "Sir, Pandarus and I," said Cressida.

   "You, dearest heart? Alas, I cannot rise
To kneel and do you honor." He raised himself,
And she at once laid both her hands upon him,
Softly, and said, "Do not do so to me,
For the love of God! Why, what is this you say?
Sir, for two reasons I have come to you,
The first, to thank you, and also I would ask
That you continue giving me protection."

   This Troilus, who heard his lady beg
Protection of him, fell into a state
Neither alive nor dead; he could not speak
A word for shame in answer, though his neck
Were struck off for it. Lord, but he turned red,
And, sirs, his lesson that he thought he knew
For pleading with her trickled through his wits!

   Cressida took in all this well enough,
For she was wise, and loved him none the less
Because he was not brash, and did not try
To beat her down with words, like one who sings
Mass to an idiot. But when his shame
Subsided somewhat, in a voice unlike
His own for dread, a voice that quavered, too,
His face now pale, now flushed, to Cressida,

His lady, with a downcast look and air,
The first submissive word that broke from him
Twice over, was "Mercy, mercy, dearest heart,"
And stopped a moment; when he could bring it out,
The next word was, "God knows, I have been yours,
As wholly as I have had the wit to be,
Even as I hope that God will save my soul;
And so I shall, till wretched as I am,
I am in the grave. And though I do not dare
And cannot plead with you, still, in all truth,
My pain is none the less for that. This much,
Womanly as you are, I can bring out
For now; if it offends you, I will wreak
The vengeance on my life and give your heart
Some comfort if my death can comfort you.
But now, since you have heard me speak a little,
I do not care however soon I die."

To see his manly suffering as he spoke,
It might have made a heart of stone take pity.
Pandarus wept as if he would turn to water,
And nudged his niece over and over again,
Saying, "True hearts are in a sorry state!
For God's sake, bring this business to an end,
Or kill us both at once, before you go."

"Why! What?" she said. "By God and by my word,
I do not know what you would have me say."

"Why! What?" said he. "That you take pity on him,
For the love of God, and do not make him die."

"Then I will ask him this," she said, "to tell me
What is the object that he has in view.
I have not understood yet what he means."

"I mean, dear heart," said Troilus, "that with
The current of your eyes, clear, fresh, and fair,
You will look on me with a friendly glance
Sometimes, then grant that I may be the one,
Not branching into any sort of wrong,

Always to do you true and faithful service
As to my lady and my chief recourse
With all my wit and all my energy;
And I to have such comfort as you choose
Under your rod, equal to my offense—
Death, if I ever do what you forbid;
And that you condescend to honor me
By your command in all things at all times;
And I to be your true and humble servant,
Ever discreet and patient in my trials,
And ever eager that I may serve anew
And that I may be always diligent
And with good heart receive your wishes always,
No matter how I suffer. This I mean,
My own dear heart."

                    "This is a hard request,"
Said Pandarus, "a reasonable one
For a lady to refuse! Now, my good niece,
By the festival of Jove, patron of birth,
If I were a god, you'd die promptly enough
Hearing this man anxious for nothing else
Except your honor, seeing him almost die,
And you so loth to let him be your servant."

  She looked at Troilus pleasantly with this,
Choosing her course, and hurrying not too fast
At any word, and softly said to him,
"Saving my honor, I will gladly and truly,
In such a way as he has just described,
Receive him altogether in my service,
Beseeching him, for God's love, that he will
Honorably and faithfully, as I
Mean well toward him, mean also well toward me,
And keep my honor by his thought and effort
Always. If I can give him happiness,
From this time on, indeed, I won't pretend!
Now be all well. You need no longer suffer.

But none the less I warn you of one thing,"
She said. "A king's son though in fact you are,
You shall no further have the sovereignty
In love than rightfully should be the case,
Nor shall I hesitate, if you do wrong,
To make you angry; as long as you serve me,
I shall cherish you just as you may deserve.
And to be quick, dear heart, wholly my knight,
Be glad, and lift your spirits up again,
And I shall truly and with all my power
Turn bitter into sweet. If I am she
Who governs your happiness, for every woe
You shall regain a joy." She took him then
Into her arms and kissed him.
       Pandarus
Fell on his knees, lifted his eyes to heaven,
And holding high his hands, "Immortal god,"
He said, "who cannot die, Cupid I mean,
You may exult in this, and you may sing,
Venus! I think I hear each bell in town
Ring with no hand to pull it for this marvel.
But stop! No further in this matter now;
These people will be coming who have read
The letter; I hear them. But Cressida, I charge you,
And you too, Troilus, once and again,
When you can be about, come to my house
When I give notice. I will plan your coming
Carefully. There you can ease your hearts all right,
And we shall see which one will take the prize
For eloquence in love"—at that he laughed—
"For there you shall have leisure for discourse."

 "How long," demanded Troilus, "must I wait
Till this is done?"

      "When you can rise," he said,
"It shall be carried out just as I tell you."

 At this point Helen and Deiphobus

Came up and reached the stairhead. Troilus
Began to groan, Lord, how he groaned! to blind
His brother and sister.

      "It is time we went,"
Said Pandarus. "Bid the three of them good-by,
Niece. Let them talk, and come along with me."
 She took leave gracefully, as well she could,
And they paid her the greatest courtesy,
And in her absence, praised her management,
Her wit, her excellence, in the highest terms;
It was a joy to hear how they commended
Her manner and her ways.

       Dismissing lightly
The letter that Deiphobus had seen
Below in the garden, Troilus would gladly
Have been relieved of Helen and his brother.
He needed sleep, he said, rest after talk.
Helen kissed him, and took her leave at once,
Also Deiphobus; everyone went home,
And Pandarus, as fast as he could skip,
Came by the straightest line to Troilus
And on a pallet, all that happy night,
Near Troilus he lay, in a sportive mood
For talk; and they were glad to be together.
 When everyone had gone except the two,
And all the doors were shut fast, Pandarus rose
And sitting on his bedside, soberly
Spoke to Troilus, and said: "Dear brother,
God knows, and you, it sat so sorely on me
To see you languishing this year away
For love, in which your pain grew ever greater,
That I, with all my power and all my wisdom,
Have ever since been laboring to bring you
Joy out of grief; I have brought things to the point
You are aware of, so that because of me
You stand to make out well. I make no boast.

Do you know why? It is shameful to confess:
For you I have begun to play a game
I never shall play again for anyone else
Although he were a thousand times my brother.
That is to say, for you I have become,
What between sport and earnest, the kind of tool
By means of which women are brought to men.
I do not say it, but you know what I mean.
For you I have made my niece, free from all vices,
Trust so completely in your character
That all shall be exactly as you want.
But God, who is omniscient, I call to witness
I never did this out of covetousness
But only to alleviate the pain
For which you nearly died, as I believed.
Good brother, do as you ought to, for God's love,
And keep her from reproach, since you are wise,
And always guard her name. For well you know
Her reputation as yet among our people
Is, as a man might say, a hallowed one.
The man has not been born, I dare take oath,
Who knowingly can say she has done wrong.
The worse for me, that I, the cause of this,
May think she is my niece and I her uncle
And traitor in the bargain! Were it known
That I through my contrivances had put
This fancy in my niece, to do your pleasure
And wholly to be yours, why, all the world
Would cry out at it, and say that I had done
The foulest treachery in this case that ever
Had been conceived. She would be wholly lost,
And you would surely not have won. And so,
Before I take another step, again
I beg you and say plainly, secrecy
Go with us in this case; that is to say,
Do not betray us. Do not be angry with me

Though often I beseech you to conceal
So high a matter, for you know my prayer
Is to the point. Remember how much woe
Has happened before this for making boasts,
And what mischances in the world there are
From day to day, just through this wicked practice,
For which wise voices who are in the grave
Have made a proverb for us in our youth:
'The first of virtues is to hold your tongue.'

"I could recite to you a thousand tales
Of women lost through the false boasts of fools.
You know yourself proverbs enough against
The vice of blabbing, which would be a vice
Though people spoke the truth whenever they
     boasted.
Tongues, alas, have made full many a lady
Bright of cheek say, 'Oh, that I ever was born!'
Tongues have renewed the griefs of many a maiden,
And for the greater part all is untrue
Men brag about; if it were put to proof,
No braggart is to be believed by nature.
A braggart and a liar, all is one.

"Consider: suppose a woman grants to me
Her love, and says that she will have no other,
And I am sworn to keep the matter secret,
And then I make it known to two or three.
Certainly, I'm a braggart at the least,
A liar also, for I broke my promise.
Now then, consider whether they're to blame,
The kind of people—what shall I call them? what?—
Who boast by name of women who never yet
Promised them either one thing or another
And never knew them more than my old hat!
It is no wonder, as God is my salvation,
That women dread to have dealings with us men.

"I do not say this in distrust of you,

Nor any man of wisdom, but for fools,
And for the harm there is now in the world
As much because of foolishness as malice.
For I know well no woman dreads that vice
In men of wisdom; by fools' injuries
Wise people are restrained. But to the purpose:
  "Keep all that I have said in mind, good brother.
Keep close. Be in good spirits. At your day
You'll find me true; you shall be satisfied,
As God is listening. For I am sure
That you mean well, and therefore I can dare
To undertake this mission to the full.
You know now what your lady granted you;
The day is set to draw the charter up.
Good night. I can no longer keep awake,
And pray for me, since you are now in bliss,
That God will send me, quickly, death or joy!"

  Who could express one half the happiness
That Troilus in his soul felt at that moment,
Praising the outcome of his good friend's promise?
His former woe, that led his heart toward death,
Began for joy to melt and waste away;
His wealth of bitter sighs fled all at once;
He felt no more of them, but as the fields
And hedges that in winter have been dead
And dry reclothe themselves in May with green,
When every lusty spirit likes best to play,
So suddenly his heart grew full of cheer
Until there was no happier man in Troy.

  He looked up soberly at Pandarus,
And said, "Last April, friend, if you remember,
You are aware how close to death you found me
For wretchedness, and all the pains you took
To learn from me the cause of my distress.
You know how long it was that I forbore
To tell it to you, though you are the man

I trust in most, and though it was no risk
To let you know. But tell me, if you please,
When I was so unwilling to tell you,
How should I dare tell others of this matter
Who tremble now, when none can overhear us?
But none the less, by God himself I swear,
Who governs the whole world just as he will—
And if I lie, Achilles with his spear
Cleave my heart, though I had eternal life
Instead of being mortal, as I am;
If late or soon I should betray the secret,
Or dared, or should know how to, even, for all
The good that God created under the sun—
I swear I'd rather die, and make my end,
It seems to me, thrust in the stocks in prison
Among the vermin, wretchedness, and filth
As captive to the cruel Agamemnon;
And this in all the temples of the town
By all the gods I'll swear to you tomorrow
If you would like to hear it. That you have done
So much for me I never can deserve it,
That I know well, though I could die for you
A thousand times a day. I can say no more,
Except that I will serve you as your slave
Wherever you go, always, until my death.

    "But now with all my heart I beg of you
That you will never think me such a fool
As I must speak of; it seemed by what you said
That this you do for me in fellowship
I might consider as a kind of pimping.
I may be ignorant, but I am not mad!
It is not so, I know that, by my word!
Whoever goes on errands of that sort
For pay or profit, call him what you like;
What you are doing, call it courtesy,
Compassion, friendship, trust. Distinguish it

In this way; it is widely recognized,
I've gathered, that distinctions must be made
Between things that resemble one another.
And that you may be sure I do not think
Your service a disgrace or a low trick,
I have Polyxena, my lovely sister,
Cassandra, Helen, any of the pack,
Let her be never so fair or so well formed,
Tell me the one you want for yours, and then
Let me alone, and see! But since you have done
This service for me, to preserve my life
And not for hope of profit, for God's love
Push this great undertaking to the end,
For now's the time of need. In great and small,
No fear, I'll always follow your commands.
And now good night, and let's both go to sleep."

    Thus each felt well rewarded by the other,
And in the morning, after they had dressed,
Each of them went about his own concerns.
But Troilus, though he burned as in a flame
For sharp desire of hope and of enjoyment,
Did not forget how to conduct himself.
By his own manliness he held in check
Every unbridled impulse and rash act;
No one alive by any word or look
Could have detected what was in his mind.
He was as far away from those about him
As clouds, he could dissimulate so well.

    This was his life: in the service of high Mars
He spent the day, in armor as a knight;
And in the darkness, through long hours he lay
And thought how he might serve his lady best
To earn her gratitude. I will not swear,
Although his bed was soft enough, his mind
Was undisturbed, nor that he did not turn
Often upon his pillow, and would have liked

To have what he still missed; in such a case
No man is wholly pleased, by all I know,
More than he was; this is a fact I deem
Within the realm of possibility!
   But all this while he saw his lady sometimes,
And she spoke with him when she dared and wanted,
And by their common counsel they decided,
Warily, by what steps they would proceed.
But it was uttered in so brief a fashion,
So watchfully, among such witnesses,
Lest anyone should penetrate their secret,
That all the world was not so dear to them
As that the god of love should grant the favor
To bring their hurried speeches to an end.
But all the little that they spoke or did
His spirit heeded so, it seemed to her
He knew what she was thinking without words;
There was no need to tell him what to do
Or to forbid him anything. She felt
That love, though tardily, had opened to her
The gates of all delight. So well he used
His words and services, and came to stand
So fully in the graces of his lady,
That twenty thousand times before she stopped
She thanked God she had ever met with him.
She found him so obedient, so secret,
And so discreet that she could well believe
He was a wall of steel to her, a shield
From all discomfort. She no longer feared,
So wise he was, to be in his control—
So far, I mean, as it was right to be.
   And Pandarus, always blowing on the fire,
Was ever ready and diligent. His wish
Was fixed to ease his friend. He shoved things on,
He was sent back and forth. When Troilus
Was absent, he took letters. Never a man

Bore himself better than he at a friend's need.
  But for the great result: this Pandarus,
Who did all that he could for but one end,
To bring his niece and Troilus together
At his own house some night, where this high matter
Touching their love could be bound up at leisure,
Had found a time. With great deliberation
He had forecast and put in execution
Whatever might contribute to this plan,
And had not stopped for trouble nor for cost.
Come if it pleased them; nothing would be lacking,
And as for being spied on there, he knew
That was impossible. The wind was clear
Of every telltale jay and every spoilsport.
Now all is well, for all the world is blind
Toward the whole matter, tame and wild alike.
The timber is all ready, up with the frame!
We only need to fix the certain hour
When she shall come.
                Now Troilus, who knew
This preconcerted plan, and waited always,
Had made great preparations; he had his cause
And his excuse if he were missed by day
Or night about this service: he had gone
To sacrifice, and in a certain temple
Must watch alone to obtain Apollo's answer;
First he must see the sacred laurel quiver
Before Apollo spoke out from the tree
To tell him when the Greek host should take flight.
Let no man interrupt him, God forbid,
But pray Apollo to give help at need.
  Now there is little left that must be done,
But promptly with the changing of the moon,
When for a night or two the world is lightless
And when the sky was making up for rain,
Pandarus went in the morning to his niece.

There he began, as usual, to joke
And make fun of himself; and finally
He swore by this and that she should no longer
Escape nor make him lose his breath for her,
But certainly she must come sup with him
That evening at his house. She laughed at that,
Beginning to excuse herself, and said,
"How could I come? It's raining."

                          "Never mind,"
He said. "Don't stand like that and hesitate.
This must be done. You shall be there."

                                    At last
They agreed together; otherwise, he swore
Softly into her ear, he would never again
Come where she was. A little afterward
She whispered to him and asked if Troilus
Was there. He told her no, upon his oath,
For he was out of town; and added, "Niece,
What if he were? You need not fear the more,
For rather than have people see him there
I should prefer to die a thousand times."

My author does not see fit to announce
All that she thought when he said that Troilus
Had gone from town, or whether she believed
That what he told her was indeed the truth;
Only, without delay, since he had asked her,
She agreed to go with him, and as his niece
Obeyed him as she should. But none the less,
Although it was no fear to go with him,
She implored him to beware of silly tongues
Who dream up things that never did exist,
And take care whom he brought, and told him, "Uncle,
Since I put highest trust in you, be sure
That all is well, and have it as you please."

He swore his yes to her by stocks and stones,
By all the gods in heaven; or he would rather,

Body and soul, be down in hell with Pluto
As deep as Tantalus! He took his leave,
And she, when it was evening, came to supper,
With certain of the men who served her household
And with the fair Antigone, her niece,
And others among her women, nine or ten.

   Now who was glad, who, as you may suppose,
But Troilus, who stood where he could see
Through a little window in a tiny room
Where he had been cooped up since the past midnight
Unknown to everyone but Pandarus?
But to the point. When she had come, her uncle
Embraced her in the friendliest fellowship
And afterward they all went in together
To supper, when the time came, and sat down.
God knows they did not lack for delicacies!
And afterward they got up, well at ease,
And in the best of spirits. Happy was he
Who pleased this woman or that, or made her laugh.
He sang; she played; another told the tale
Of Wade. But finally, as all things end,
She said good-by, and must be going home.

   But O the executrix of destinies,
O Fortune, and the influences of these,
The lofty heavens! The truth is, under God,
You are our shepherds, though from us your flock
The causes are concealed. My meaning is
That though she started homeward, the gods' will
Determined everything without her leave,
And so she must remain. The crescent moon
With Jupiter and Saturn was conjoined
In Cancer, so that from heaven such a downpour
Began to fall that every woman there
Had of that smoking rain a very panic.

   Pandarus laughed, and said, "Now is the time
For a lady to be leaving! But, good niece,

If I ever hope in anything to please you,
Then give my heart so great a satisfaction
As to stay with me here the whole night through,
For this is your own house. Joking aside,
To go now would disgrace me, by my word!"
    Cressida, who could tell her own advantage
As well as half the world, heeded his prayer,
And since it poured and all was in a flood,
She thought, I'll do as well to stay right here
And grant it gladly in a friendly fashion
And have my thanks, as grouch and then stay on,
For going home is hardly to be thought of.
    "I will," she said, "dear uncle. Since you wish,
It should be so. I shall be very glad
To stay here with you. I was only joking
When I said that I should go."
                        "Thanks, niece, indeed,"
Pandarus answered. "Joking or not, I'm glad,
Truly, because it pleases you to stay."
    So all is well; but then the merriment
Began again. Pandarus, if he could,
Suitably, would have hurried her to bed,
And, "Lord," said he, "this is a monstrous rain!
This is the kind of weather meant for sleeping,
And I suggest that soon we all begin.
And do you know, niece, where I mean to put you,
So that we won't be sleeping far apart,
And so that you, I dare say, will not hear
Thunder nor rain? By God, in my little chamber
Yonder! I in this outer room alone
Will be the guardian of all your women,
And in this middle chamber that you see
Your women will be sleeping well and soft,
And in there you yourself, as I have said.
If you sleep well tonight, come frequently,
And never mind what weather is aloft.

But now the wine, and when you feel disposed,
We'll go to sleep; I think that will be best."

There was no more discussion, but soon after
They drank, and when the curtains had been drawn
All those who had no duties in the place
Began to leave the room; and still it rained
So violently and blew so wondrous loud
That scarcely one of them could hear another.
Then Pandarus, her uncle, just as he ought,
With women who were closest in attendance,
Conducted her with pleasure to the bedside
And took his leave, and made her a deep bow,
And said, "Here at this chamber door outside,
Just opposite, your women will be sleeping,
And you can summon any of them you want."

When she was lying in the little chamber
And all her women had gone out in order
And were abed themselves, there was no more
Tiptoeing or tramping, no course but go to bed.
A malediction on anyone who stirred
And kept those who were safe in bed from sleep!
But Pandarus, who well knew every point
And move in the game, seeing that all was well,
Thought to begin his work, and quietly
Unlatched the door where Troilus was cooped up
And silent as a stone sat down beside him.
He told him all the steps that he had taken,
And said, "Get ready at once, for you are going
Into the bliss of heaven."

                      "Now, happy Venus,
Bless me," said Troilus. "Never till this moment
Had I the need, or half such fear as now."

"Don't have a bit of fear," said Pandarus.
"For as I hope to prosper, it will go
Just as you want. I'll make it well tonight
Or else chuck all the porridge in the fire."

"Yet, blissful Venus, inspire me tonight,"
Said Troilus, "as surely as I serve you
And better and better shall until I die.
And if I had, O Venus full of joy,
Unfavorable aspects at my birth
Of Mars or Saturn, or if you were scorched
By being too near the sun, pray to your father
That he will graciously avert the harm
And make me glad again, for the love of him
You loved among the leaves, I mean Adonis,
Whom the boar killed. Jove, also, for the love
Of fair Europa, whom you carried off
Disguised as a white bull, now help! O Mars,
You with your bloody cloak, for the Cyprian's love
Do not impede me! Phoebus, remember Daphne
And how she hid herself beneath the bark
And turned into a laurel tree for dread;
Yet for her love, O help me now at need!
Mercury, for the love of Herse, too,
Which brought Athena's anger on Aglauros,
Help! And Diana, I implore you also,
Be not offended at this undertaking.
O fatal sisters, who before a garment
Was cut for me had spun me out my fate,
Help with this enterprise that has begun!"

"You wretched mouse's heart," said Pandarus,
"What are you so afraid of—that she'll bite you?
Why, put this furred cloak on over your shirt
And follow me along; I'll make you learn.
But wait, and let me go ahead a little."

At this word he unfastened a trap door
And led in Troilus by his cloak. The wind
So furiously roared that none could hear
A different noise, and those who lay outside
Beyond the door slept soundly all together.
Pandarus gravely went at once and shut it,

Quietly and unhindered. As he came
Secretly back again, his niece awoke,
And asked, "Who's there?"

               "Dear niece," he said, "it's I.
Don't be surprised, don't be afraid about it."

  He came up close, and whispered in her ear,
"No word, I beg you, for the love of God.
Let no one rise and hear what we are saying."

  "Bless me! How did you get in here," she said,
"Unknown to all of them?"

               "By this trap door,"
He answered.

          "Let me call someone," she said.

  "What! God forbid that you should be so foolish.
They might guess things they never thought before.
It's never wise to wake a sleeping dog
Or to give people reasons for supposing!
Your women are all sleeping, I can promise,
So hard that men could undermine the house
For all of them; they'll sleep on till the sun shines.
And when I've told my story to the end
I'll go out undetected, as I came.

  "Now, niece, you must fully realize," he said,
"As all you women think, to bait a man
In love, call him her darling, all the while
Pulling the wool down over his eyes—I mean
By loving another man—she shames herself
And plays a cheat on him. Now here's the reason
I tell you this: you are aware yourself
As well as anyone how your love is granted
Fully to Troilus, the best of knights,
One of the world's best, and your truth so plighted
That, saving only for some act of his,
You should not play him false for all your life.
Here is the way it stands: after I left you
This Troilus, to put the matter plainly,

Has by a secret passage, through a drain,
In all this downpour come into my room,
And not a soul knows this except myself,
Past question, as I hope to see good times
And by the faith I owe Priam of Troy.
And he has come in such pain and distress
That if he isn't wholly crazed by now
He will, unless God helps, fall suddenly mad.
The reason why is this: he says a friend
Has told him that you love one called Horaste,
At which his grief is such this night will end him."

   Cressida, listening to this marvel, chilled
Suddenly at the heart, and with a sigh
She answered bitterly, "Alas, I thought,
Whoever might tell stories, my dear heart
Would not so easily hold me untrue!
False notions, how they hurt! For now I live
Too long. Horaste! And false to Troilus?
I do not know him, God help me when I say it.
What evil spirit told him this? Now truly,
Tomorrow, uncle, if I see him then,
I will exonerate myself as fully
As ever woman did, if that will please him."
And with this word she gave a bitter sigh.
"O God," she said, "the happiness of this world,
Which the divines call false felicity,
Is mingled so with bitterness! God knows
The state of vain prosperity is anxious;
For either joys come separately, apart,
Or else no one can always have them here.
O brittle good of man's uncertain joy!
No matter with whom you are or how you play,
He knows or does not know that joy is fleeting,
One or the other; if he does not know,
How can he tell for sure that he is happy
When he is in the night of ignorance?

But if he knows that joy is transitory,
And joy in every wordly thing must die,
Then every time that he remembers this
The dread of loss puts him in such a state
He cannot be in perfect happiness;
And if he thinks that he may lose his joy
By even a mite, that joy seems little worth.
And so I say, for all that I can see,
There is no true delight here in this world.
But O you wicked serpent, jealousy,
You infidel, you envious foolishness,
Why have you led Troilus to distrust me
Who never have aggrieved him knowingly?"

   Said Pandarus, "It came about this way—"
   "Why, uncle?" she demanded. "Who told him this?
Why has my dear heart acted so?"

                      "You know,
My niece, you, what the truth is," he replied.
"I hope all will be well that has gone wrong,
For you can settle the matter if you want.
Do so at once, I'm sure that will be best."

   "And so I shall, indeed," she said, "tomorrow,
So that it shall suffice, God be my witness."

   "Tomorrow? What a bargain that would be,"
Said Pandarus. "No, no, that will not do,
Delay drags danger with it, say the wise.
No, such postponements are not worth a button.
There is a time for all things, I dare say,
For when a room or hall, niece, is on fire
There is more point in saving it at once
Than arguing and asking up and down
Just how this candle fell among the straw.
God bless us, yes, for by that kind of dealing
The harm is done—farewell and good riddance!
Moreover, niece—and do not be offended—
If you will let him stay all night in pain.

You never held him dear, so help me God—
I dare say this, with only us two present.
But I know well that you will never do so.
You are too wise for such a foolishness,
To put his life all night in jeopardy."

"Have I not held him dear? By God, I think
You never had a thing so dear," she said.

"Now as I hope to prosper," Pandarus said,
"That can be seen! For since you hold me up
As an example, if I for all the wealth
In Troy would see him sorrow the whole night,
I pray God I may never again be cheerful!
Consider then, if you who are his love
Would put his life in danger all night long
For what amounts to nothing, by God in heaven,
This dallying comes not from folly alone
But malice, if I'm not to tell a lie.
What! Flatly, if you leave him in distress,
You're doing neither a courtesy nor a bounty."

"Will you do one thing," she replied, "to end
All his discomfort? Take him this blue ring,
For there is nothing that could please him more
Save I myself, nor more appease his heart;
And tell my dear life that his pain is groundless—
That will be clear tomorrow."

                              "A ring?" he said.
"You're talking nonsense.[1] Niece, your ring would
     need
A stone with virtue to revive the dead,
And such a ring I do not think you have.
Discretion has gone quite out of your mind,

[1]Chaucer: "Hazel bushes shake," a proverbial expression,
"of which," according to Robinson, "the application is not entirely
clear." Hazel is alluded to in several situations implying nonsense
or unreality.

I see that now, and what a pity it is!
O for lost time! Sloth well deserves a curse.
Do you not know that high and noble spirits
Will neither grieve nor stop for a light cause?
If a mere fool were in a jealous rage
I wouldn't count his misery worth a jot,
But stuff him with a plausible word or two
Another day, whenever I could find him.
But this is business of a different sort.
This is a man of such a tender heart
He will revenge his sorrows with his death.
Trust me, however bitterly he feels,
He will not say a jealous word to you,
And for this reason, niece, before his heart breaks,
You must speak to him yourself about this matter,
For with one word you may control his heart.

   "Now I have told you how he is in danger,
His entrance is unknown to everyone.
My word, there can be neither harm nor sin.
I will myself be with you until morning.
Also you know this is your own dear servant,
And rightfully you owe him confidence,
And I all ready to fetch him when you want."

   So pitiable was this catastrophe
And on the face of it so like a truth,
And Troilus, her knight, so dear to her,
The place secure, and his arrival secret,
That though she granted him a privilege,
Considering how things stood, it was no wonder,
Since all she did was done with a good purpose.

   And so she said, "As surely as I hope
God will receive my soul, I grieve for him!
And, uncle, truly I would do what's best,
If I had grace to do so. But should you wait
Or should you go for him, until God gives me

A better head, I am at dulcarnon,[1]
My very wits' end."
                        "Will you listen, niece?"
Pandarus answered. "Dulcarnon is called
'The banishment of wretches.' It seems hard,
For wretches will not learn for very sloth
Or willfulness. People who talk this way
Aren't worth a pair of beans. But you are wise,
And what we have in hand is neither hard
Nor prudent to resist."
                        "Uncle," she said,
"Do as you like, then. But before he comes
I will get up, and for the love of God,
Since all my trust is in you two, and you
Are both wise men, now work this out discreetly,
That I may have my name and he his comfort,
For I am here wholly in your control."

    "That is well said," he answered, "my dear niece.
A blessing on that wise and gentle heart!
But lie still, and receive him here; no need
To go a step for him. And each of you
Comfort the other's grief, for the love of God.
I hope, praise Venus, we shall soon be merry."

    Troilus was not slow to place himself
Soberly on his knees beside her bed,
And there he greeted her in his best manner.
But Lord, she grew so crimson suddenly,
Nor could she, though her head had been struck off
For penalty, bring out a single word
To suit the moment, his coming was so sudden.
But Pandarus, whose feeling could respond
So well to everything, began to joke,
And said, "See how his lordship can kneel down!
See how polite he is, by all that's true!"

---

[1] A name by which a certain proposition in Euclid was known.

He ran to get a cushion, and said, "Now kneel
As long as you want, and may God quickly set
Your hearts at rest."
                    She did not bid him rise,
Whether her sorrow put it out of mind
I cannot say, or whether she took his kneeling
Merely as duty; but I do discover
That she conferred this grace on him: she kissed him,
Although she sighed, and bade him seat himself.

   "Now you will make a good start," Pandarus said.
"Tell him to sit down in there on your bedside
Where each of you can hear the other better."
So saying he drew over toward the fire
And getting himself a light, composed his face,
Pretending to look through an old romance.

   Cressida, with a conscience clear and safe
As Troilus' lady, though she felt her servant
Should not suspect her of the least untruth,
Yet for all that, considering his distress
And mindful that such folly springs from love,
Spoke to him thus about his jealousy:

   "Dear heart, as love willed in its excellence,
Which no man may nor rightly should resist,
And also since I felt and saw how great
Your service and your truth have been each day,
And that your heart was altogether mine,
This drove me to take pity on your pain.
And I have found you constant in your goodness,
For which, dear heart, as far as I have wit,
I give you thanks, although I cannot give
As much as would be right; and to the limit,
With all my skill and power, whatever I suffer,
I have been ever and shall be true to you
Wholly, with all my heart; and never fear,
You will find it so by trial. But, dear heart,
I must let you know what this is all about

So that you will not grieve, though my complaint
Lies against you yourself. For by this means
Once and for all I hope to slay the grief
That holds your heart and mine in heaviness
And to redress each wrong. I know not why
Nor how this wicked monster, jealousy,
Has crept without a reason into you,
Bringing this harm that I would do away with.
Alas, that whole, or even a silver of him,
He should find refuge in so noble a place!
May Jove uproot him quickly from your heart!
But Jove, author of nature, is your godhead
Honored when people who are innocent
Suffer their wrongs while he that bears the guilt
Gets off quite free? Oh, if complaint were lawful
To you who suffer jealousy to fall
Upon the undeserving, I would cry
In protest against that! I also grieve
That people in these days are used to saying,
'Well, jealousy is love,' and so excuse
A bushel of venom because a grain of love
Is laid on top. But God on high knows whether
It more resembles love or hate or rage,
And after its likeness it should have its name.
    "But certainly one sort of jealousy
Is more to be forgiven than another,
As when there is a cause; and jealous fancy
Is held so well in check sometimes by pity
It hardly goes amiss in word or deed,
And I forgive that, for its courtesy.
Then there is jealousy so full of fury
It overwhelms restraint; but you, dear heart,
Are not, thank God, in such a state as that.
And so I will not call this passion of yours
More than a fancy, born of love's abundance
And busy care that so disturbs your heart.

I am truly sorry for it, but not angry.
But for my duty, and your ease of mind,
Wherever you will, by ordeal or by oath,
By divination, or any means you like,
For the love of God, let's put it to the trial,
And if I am proved guilty, let me die!
What further can I do or say?"

                                        With that
A few fresh tears fell brightly from her eyes.
"Now, God," she said, "you know in thought nor deed
Cressida never yet has been untrue
To Troilus," and so saying turned her face
Down on the bed and hid it in the sheet,
And bitterly sighed and said not one word more.

    But now God put an end to all this grief!
And so I hope he shall, as he best can,
For I have seen, after a misty morning,
Often enough a merry summer's day,
And after winter, May with all her green.
Men have said always, and have read in story,
That after the sharp onslaught follows triumph.

    This Troilus, when he heard his lady's words,
He did not care to sleep, be sure of that!
It seemed to him no fillip of a stick
To see his lady Cressida in tears.
For every tear her eyes let fall he felt
The cramp of death constrict him at the heart,
And in his mind began to curse the hour
He had come there, and the hour when he was born.
For bad enough had now turned into worse
And all the labor he had done before
Seemed to him wasted; he felt that he was lost.
"Ah, Pandarus," he thought, "your wiles and guiles
Have served for nothing all the time, alas!"
He hung his head and fell down on his knees,
And wretchedly he sighed. What could he say?

He felt he was as good as in the grave,
For she was angry who could heal his sorrow.
Nevertheless, as soon as he could speak,
He said, "If everything were understood,
God knows I am not guilty in this game."

With that the sorrow so closed up his heart
That not a single tear fell from his eyes,
And all his spirits knitted up their vigor
As if they were suppressed. The sense of sorrow
Or fear or anything else fled out of town,
And suddenly he fell in a dead faint.

This was no small anxiety to see,
But all was quiet, and Pandarus leaped up
Quickly and muttered, "Niece, don't make a noise
Or we are lost. Now don't be terrified!"
And one way and another, in the end,
He got him into bed, and said, "What, thief,
Is this a man's heart?" He stripped off his clothes
Down to the shirt, and said, "Unless you help,
Your Troilus is lost, niece."

                                "So I would,
Gladly, if only I knew how," she answered.
"O, why did I ever live?"

                                "You can pull out
The thorn that sticks in his heart," said Pandarus.
"Say 'all's forgiven,' and stop this nonsense, niece."

  "Ah, that to me," she said, "would be more precious
Than all the goodliness the sun encircles."
She whispered in his ear, "Indeed, dear heart,
I am not angry, on my solemn word,"
And many another pledge. "Now speak to me,
It's I, Cressida." But it was all for nothing;
He could not yet recover. They began
To chafe his pulse and palms and wet his temples;
And to deliver him from the bitter chains
Often she kissed him, and did her uttermost

To call him back; and he began at last
To draw his breath again, and soon thereafter
Regained his senses and possessed himself
More firmly of his powers of mind and reason.
But in all truth, he was grievously abashed.
He said, as he became more fully conscious,
"Merciful God, what is all this?"

                              "Now why,"
Said Cressida, "do you wrong yourself this way?
Is this a man's part? Will you carry on
In such a fashion? What, Troilus, for shame!"
And saying so, she put her arm across him,
Forgave him everything, and kissed him often.
He thanked her, and began to speak with her
As fitted his heart's purpose, and she answered
Freely, and with the solace of her words
Comforted him.

                    "As far as I can see,"
Said Pandarus, "neither this light nor I
Can serve a purpose here. Light isn't good
For the eyes of sick folk. But for the love of heaven,
Since you've been brought into this happy plight,
Let no more heavy thoughts hang in your hearts,"
And carried his candle over to the chimney.

  Presently after this, when she had taken
Oaths and pledges from him of such a kind
As she was pleased to set, though they were needless,
It did not seem that she had reason to fear
Or bid him rise from where he was; yet less
Than oaths will do in many a case, for all
Who love well, as I think, mean only well.
But she desired to know of whom and where
And why he had conceived his jealousy,
Since it was baseless; and she ordered him
To tell her seriously what indications
Had put it in his mind, or else, for certain,

She accused him of having done it all in spite
To put her to a trial. This command
He must obey, and as a lesser evil,
He had to feign. He said at such a dinner
She might at least have looked at him—what more
I do not know, the sort of precious straws
A man needs who is fishing for a reason.
And she replied, "Sweet, though it had been so,
What harm was in it, since I meant no wrong?
For by the god who ransomed both of us,
I have meant only well in everything.
The reasons that you give aren't worth a pebble.
Are you going to imitate a jealous child?
Now in all fairness you deserve a spanking."

   Then Troilus, for fear she would be angry,
Said, "Oh, have pity on my sorry heart!
And if in what I said there is any wrong
I will not sin again. Do what you please,
I am wholly at your mercy."

                              And she answered,
"For sin, forgiveness. I forgive it all,
And I admonish you to keep this night
In mind forever, and to take good care
You do not err again."

                         "Ah yes, dear heart,
Truly," he said.

                  "And since I caused you pain,
Forgive me for it, my dear life," she said

   Troilus, overwhelmed by this glad stroke,
Put all in God's hand, like a man who means
Nothing but good; and suddenly resolved,
Drew her into his arms and firmly to him.
And Pandarus, with benevolent intentions,
Laid himself down to sleep. "If you are wise,
Don't faint again," he said, "lest other people
Start getting up."

What can the innocent lark
Say in the talons of the sparrowhawk?
No more can I; but though I put it off
A year, yet sooner or later I must tell
The rapture of these two, after my author,
As I have told their grief, although the tale
To one taste may be sugar, and to another
Bitter as soot.
        Feeling herself so caught,
As learned men have written in old books,
Cressida trembled like an aspen leaf;
But Troilus, healed of his long chilling cares,
Thanked all the seven planets in their bliss.
Thus various people come through various pains
To paradise.
        He strained her in his arms,
And said, "Ah, sweet, as ever I hope to live,
Now you are caught, now there are but we two!
Now yield, there is no help for you but that!"
    And Cressida replied, "Had I not yielded
Long since, dear heart, I should not be here now."
    True is the word that to be cured of fevers
Or other great afflictions men must often
Drink bitter potions, and to have delight
Must swallow many pains and great distress.
But sweetness now seems only the more sweet
For the earlier taste of bitterness; for now
They swim from woe to bliss, and such a bliss
As they had never felt since they were born.
This is a better state than two in sorrow!
Let every woman, for the love of God,
Take care to do the like in case of need!
    Cressida, free from every apprehension,
As one who trusted in him with good reason,
So pleased him that it was a joy to see;
And as the honeysuckle twines and wreathes

About a tree trunk, so they twined their arms
About each other; and as the nightingale,
At first abashed when she begins to sing,
Who stops if she should hear a shepherd's voice
Or footfall in the hedges, and afterward
Sings on full-voiced in safety, Cressida
When she had lost her fears opened her heart
And told him all her thoughts. And as a man
Who sees his death prepared, and by all signs
Must perish, who escapes by sudden rescue
And from his death is brought away secure,
In such an instant gladness Troilus was.
He has his lady; God send us no worse luck!

He stroked her slender arms, her straight soft back,
The white length of her sides with their smooth flesh,
And called down blessings on her snowy throat
And round small breasts. Thus in his paradise
He took delight. A thousand times he kissed her
Until for joy he knew not what to do.

"O god of love," he said, "O charity,
And next to you yourself, your mother too,
The lovely Cytherea, Venus I mean,
The planet of good will, praise to her name,
And the great Hymen next, for never man
Was more beholden to you gods than I,
Whom you have rescued from the chill of care.
You holy bond of things, benignant love,
Whoever hopes for grace and does not please
To honor you will find that his desire
Must fly without wings. If you did not choose
To succor in your bounty those who best
Serve and are still most constant in their toil,
All would be lost, that I dare say for truth,
Unless your grace exceeded our deserts.
And since you have to me, the least deserving
Among your files of favor, given help

When I was like to perish, and have set me
In such a lofty place that no delight
May pass the bounds of mine, I cannot say
One further word; only let praise and worship
Be to your bounty and your excellence."

    And saying so he kissed her, and she felt
No pain in that, for certain. "Would to God
I knew how I might always make you happy!
What man," he said, "was ever in such ease
As I on whom the fairest and the best
I ever saw has deigned to set her heart?
This makes it plain that mercy is more than justice.
I am the proof of that, who am not worth
So sweet a creature. But in your own bounty,
Consider that unworthy as I am
I cannot help improving in some measure
By virtue of undertaking your high service.
And for the love of God, since God has wrought me
Only to serve you—it is his will, I mean,
That you should be my guide, to make me live,
If so you please, or perish—teach me how
I may deserve your thanks, so that I may
Through ignorance do nothing to displease you.
For truly I dare say, womanly creature
And lovely as you are, that you will find
Diligence in me faithfully all my life,
Nor will I, certainly, do what you forbid.
And if I do, in presence or in absence,
For God's love let me perish with the deed
If in your womanliness you'd have me die."

    "In truth," she said, "my heart's delight, I thank you,
For in your faithfulness lies all my trust.
But let's forget this matter. What's been said
Suffices. In a word, with no regrets,
Welcome, my knight, my peace, my happiness."

    Of their delight, or the least among their pleasures,

My wits find it impossible to speak.
Judge for yourselves, you who have been at feasts
Of kindred happiness, if they were happy!
Ah, night of bliss that they had sought so long,
How welcome to them both you were at last!
Why with my soul have I never bought the like,
Yes, or the smallest pleasure that was there?
Away with hesitation and stupid fear
And let them linger in their heavenly bliss
That is so high I cannot speak of it!

    But though I cannot, as my author can
In this supremacy, express it all,
Yet I have said, and shall, as God's my witness,
Everything as he wrote it, word for word;
And if I have added here and there a phrase
In honor of love, and with the best intentions,
Do with it as you like. For all my words
I speak under correction, here and elsewhere;
You that have feeling in the art of love
Enlarge my language or diminish it;
This I beseech, and put it to your judgment.

    Left in each other's arms, these two so feared
To part or to be sundered from each other,
Or else their greatest fear was rather this,
That the whole matter was an idle dream.
Each in this fear said often, "O dear heart,
Do I really hold you thus, or am I dreaming?"
And, Lord, to see her was so goodly a thing
That never once his look turned from her face.
"Ah, sweet," he said, "can it be really true
That you are here?"
                "Yes, my dear heart," she answered,
"I thank God in his bounty," and she kissed him
So that his spirit knew not where it was
For very joy. And Troilus kissed often
Both her eyes, and said, "It was you, clear eyes,

That wrought me such a sorrow, you modest snares
Belonging to my lady! Though in your look
Mercy is written, the text is hard to find,
God knows. How is it that without a chain
You have thus fettered me?" A hundred times,
Holding her fast within his arms, he sighed,
Not bitter sighs that men in sorrow give
Or sickness, but those easy sighs and pleasant
That showed his heart's devotion. After this
They talked of various matters to their purpose,
And interchanged their rings. I cannot tell
The mottoes or inscriptions, but I know
Cressida gave him a gold and azure brooch
In which was set a ruby like a heart,
And pinned it on his shirt.

                Lord, have you met
A miser or a wretch, who scoffs at love
And holds it in contempt, who by the pence
That he could rake together, ever yet
Was given such delight as love can give?
Not so, as I hope that God will save my soul,
For perfect joy will have no parsimony.
They will say "yes," but, Lord, the scoundrels lie,
The busy wretches, miserable and fearful!
They say that love is a folly or a madness,
But it will turn out with them as I tell you:
They'll lose their silver and gold, their white and red,
And live in woe, God send them all misfortune
And prosper all true lovers! Would to God
These wretches who despise love and his service
Had ears as long as grasping Midas had
And also had drunk a potion hot and strong
As Crassus drank for his avaricious cravings,
To let them know that they are in the wrong,
Not lovers, though they hold that love is folly.
  These two of whom I speak, when in their hearts

They were confirmed in full, they talked and played,
Recalling how and when and where they first
Began to know each other, and each woe
Or fear gone by; but all that heaviness,
I thank God for it, had been turned to joy.
And always when they spoke of a past grief,
That tale was interrupted by a kiss
And turned into fresh joy. Since they were one,
They did their uttermost to be at ease
And counterbalance every outlived woe
By pleasure and recaptured happiness.

   Reason forbids that I should speak of sleep,
For it is not in keeping with my subject.
God knows they gave but little thought to that!
Rather lest this dear night escape they spent it
On joy and on the business that pertains
To courtesies of love. But when the cock,
Astronomer-in-general to the world,
Began to beat his breast and then to crow,
And Lucifer, the messenger of day,
Began to rise and spread abroad his beams,
And in the east, for such as were informed,
The stars together called Fortuna Major
Were rising, then with sore heart Cressida
Spoke thus to Troilus: "Life of my heart,
It grieves me now that I was ever born
Since day must part us. It is time to rise
And go away, or I am lost forever!
Ah, night, why will you not brood over us
As long as when Alcmena lay with Jove?
Black night, whom God, as people read in books,
Designed to hide this world at certain times
In your dark garment, that beneath it men
Might be at rest, well may the beasts complain
And people chide you that as day must come
To afflict us with its labor, you fly thus

And will not let us rest. Alas, too briefly
You do your office, hurrying night! May God,
The author of nature, for your unkind haste
Bind you so firmly to our hemisphere
That you may never again wheel underground,
For now, so fast you hie away from Troy,
I have already lost my happiness."

    Troilus, feeling with these words as though
The bloody tears were melting from his heart,
As one who had never tasted such an anguish
After so great a joy, strained in his arms
His lady Cressida. "Cruel day," he said,
"Discloser of the joy that night and love
Have stolen and concealed, may you be cursed
For coming into Troy! For every chink
Has one of your bright eyes! Why does it please you
To spy so, jealous day? What have you lost?
Why do you search this place? Bountiful God
Put out your light! What have these lovers done
To offend you, spiteful day? The pains of hell
Be yours, for you have slaughtered many a lover,
And will again. Your pouring in will leave them
Nowhere to go. Why do you offer here
To peddle your light? Go peddle it to engravers
Cutting their tiny seals; we do not want you,
We need no daylight." Tithonus the sun
He chided too, and said, "People may well
Despise you, fool, who at your side all night
Have the young Dawn, and let her rise from you
So early, to discomfort lovers. What,
Keep to your bed there, you and your fresh Morning!
God grieve you both!" Then bitterly he sighed,
And said, "My lady, of my happiness
Or pain the root and wellspring, must I rise,
Must I, indeed? I feel now that my heart
Must break in two. How can I keep my life

A single hour, since all the life I have
Is but with you? What shall I do? For truly
I do not know when I shall see the time
That I may be with you this way again,
Nor how. And God knows what my life will be.
I am so bitten by longing even now
That I shall die unless I can return.
How can I live apart from you for long?
Nevertheless, dear heart, if I could know
And utterly be sure that I your servant,
Your humble knight, were settled in your heart
As firmly as you are in mine, a thing
That would be dearer to me, in all truth,
Than both these kingdoms, I could better bear
All that I suffer."

                Cressida sighed and answered,
"Indeed, dear heart, the game has gone so far
That Phoebus shall first tumble from his sphere,
And eagles mate with doves, and every rock
Be torn from place rather than Troilus
From the heart of Cressida. You are engraved
So deeply in my heart that though I wished
To efface you from my thoughts, I could not do so,
Not for the fear of death upon the rack.
For the love of God who made us, let your brain
Allow no other fancy to creep in,
Lest it should make me die! And I beseech
That you will keep me in your mind as fast
As I keep you; if I were sure of that
God could not eke my joy out by a point.
Be true to me, or else it were a pity!
For I am yours, by God and by my faith.
And so be glad, and live in confidence.
I've never spoken so to any other,
And never shall. If it would be to you
A great delight to come back soon again

After you go, I too am just as anxious
That it should happen, as I hope that God
May bring my heart to rest."

> She kissed him often,

And since it had to be, against his will
Troilus rose and dressed. A hundred times
He took his lady in his arms, and said,
In tones as though his very heart were bleeding,
"Good-by. God keep us well, and grant us soon
To meet again."

> She answered not a word,

So bitterly his parting anguished her.
And Troilus went homeward to his palace,
As woebegone as she. With pain so sharp
He longed again to be there in delight
That he could never put it from his mind.
He thought to slink into his bed and sleep
Long, as his custom was; but all for nothing.
He found that he could lie with twitching eyes,
But sleep refused to slide into his heart,
Thinking how she for whom his longing burned
Was worth a thousand times more than he guessed.
Her every word and change of countenance
He studied in his mind, and firmly fixed
The smallest point that was to his delight.
By such remembrance longing flamed anew
And his desires bred faster than at first.
Cressida in the same way in her heart
Held Troilus, his courtesy, his prudence,
And how she had met him, and his worthiness,
Grateful to love who had dealt with her so well,
And longing often to have him with her again
Where she could comfort him.

> But with the morning,

Pandarus, who had come to greet his niece,
Said, "All night long it rained so hard, alas,

That I'm afraid, niece, you had little chance
To sleep and dream. The rain kept me awake
The whole night so, that some of us, I think,
Have headaches." He came close to her and said,
"How goes it on this merry morning, niece?
How do you do?"

                She answered, "None the better
For you, you fox! God punish you with grief!
So help me God, you're underneath these doings,
I know you are, for all your whited words.
Little he knows of you who merely sees you!"
With this she hid her face under the sheet
And grew all red for shame. Said Pandarus,
Prying beneath it, "Niece, if I must die,
Just take a sword, and whack my head right off!"
He thrust his arm suddenly under her neck
And kissed her.

              All that needs no words I skip.
What! God forgave his own death, says the proverb,
And she forgave as well, and with her uncle
Talked pleasantries; there was nothing, after all,
Against it. When the time came, she went home,
And Pandarus had accomplished his whole purpose.

   Troilus lay a long while in his bed,
Restless, and sent for Pandarus privately
To come as quickly as he could. He came
At once, and greeted Troilus, and sat down
Upon the bedside. Troilus, with all
Devotion that the love of friends can compass,
Went down upon his knees to Pandarus
And thanked him as best he could a hundred times
Before he would get up, and blessed the hour
When Pandarus had been born to rescue him
From his distress.

            "Friend, best of all friends
That ever were," he said, "and that's the truth,

You have brought my soul into its heavenly rest
From Phlegethon, the fiery flood of hell.
If I could sell my life to your advantage
A thousand times a day, that would suffice
Not even by an atom in return.

"The sun, who can survey the world entire,
Has never seen, I'll put my life on that,
So fair and goodly a creature to the inmost
As she of whom I say, 'I am wholly hers
And shall be till I die.' That I am hers,
Thanks be to the high worthiness of love
And to your generous work, I dare affirm.
Thus you have given me no little thing,
For which my life is under bond to you,
And why? Since through your help I am alive
Or else I had been dead this many a day."

So saying he lay down upon his bed,
And Pandarus listened to him soberly
Till he had finished, and then answered him:
"Dear friend, if I have helped in any way,
God knows I am pleased. I am as glad of it
As man can be. But do not take amiss
What I'm about to tell you: be on guard,
Since you have now been brought to happiness,
That you yourself don't cause your luck to fail.
For in the sharp adversity of fortune,
Misfortune of the bitterest kind is this:
Once on a time to have been in happiness
And to remember it after it is gone.

"You've sense enough, so do not misbehave.
Don't be too rash, though you are sitting warm,
For if you are, you'll surely come to grief.
You have your ease; carry your comfort well,
For just as sure as every fire is red,
It takes as great a skill to guard as gain.
Bridle your tongue and also your desire,

For worldly joy hangs only by a hair.
The proof of that is, it is always breaking,
And so it must be treated gingerly."

    "Before God, my dear friend," said Troilus,
"I hope that I shall so conduct myself
That nothing will be lost through fault of mine.
I shall not trouble her by acting rashly.
There is no need to agitate this point,
For if you knew my heart well, Pandarus,
God knows you would feel little worry about it."

    He told him then about his happy night
And what his heart had dreaded first, and how.
"I never had it half so hot," he said,
"As at this moment, by that faith I owe
To God and you, friend. And the more desire
Nags me to love her best, the more I like it.
I don't myself know what it is exactly,
But I feel now a quality that's new,
Yes, altogether different from before."

    Pandarus answered, "Once a man has been
In heaven's bliss, he feels a different way,
No doubt, from when he first heard tell of it."

    Troilus never had his fill of talking
About this matter, praising to his friend
The beauty of his lady, and thanking him,
And always he was ready to begin
The tale again, as new as a fresh chip,
Until they separated for the night.

    Soon after, Fortune willing, came the time
When Troilus was warned that he should meet
His lady, Cressida, in the selfsame place.
He felt his heart swimming in happiness
And faithfully gave praise to all the gods.
Now let us find out whether he can be merry!
The manner and arrangement of her coming
Were as before, and his in the same way,

And to come plainly to the point, in safety
Pandarus brought them happily to bed
When both of them were ready; and so they lie
In quiet and in rest. You do not need
To ask me, since they were together again,
If they were happy. If it was well at first,
Now it was better a thousand times. Each fear,
Each grief was gone; and, as they thought, they both
Possessed as much joy as heart can contain.

This is no little thing of which to speak.
To express it is beyond all mortal wit,
For each of them obeyed the other's will.
Felicity, that learned men so praise,
Will not suffice at all; this is a joy
Ink cannot write, surpassing what the heart
Can well imagine. But the cruel day,
Alas, brief time, gave signs of its approach,
At which they thought they felt the stroke of death.
Such was their woe the blood went from their faces,
And all afresh they poured contempt on day,
Calling it traitor, jealous, and worse names,
And bitterly they cursed the morning light.

"Ah, now I see that Pyrois and those three
Swift steeds that draw the chariot of the sun,"
Said Troilus, "have out of spite toward me
Taken some shortcut that has brought the day
So soon; and since the sun is in such haste
To wake, I'll never do him sacrifice."

But day must separate them; when their words
Were done, they parted, setting another time
To meet; and so they managed many a night.
Thus Fortune for a while led happily
Cressida and this royal son of Troy.
Singing in his contentment and his bliss
This Troilus passed his days. He spent his money,
Gave generously, and often changed his clothes

To make a fresh appearance; offered feasts,
Jousted, and kept about him all the time
A world of people, as well became his nature,
The choicest spirits that he could discover,
So that his reputation and acclaim
Went forward through the world until it rang
Even at the gate of heaven. As for his love,
His joy in that was such that in his heart
He thought no lover in the world so well
At ease as he. The goodliness and beauty
That nature gave to any other lady
Were helpless by a single knot to loosen
Cressida's net, that wholly bound his heart.
He was enmeshed and knit so narrowly
That to untangle it at any point
Was quite past doing, whatever might befall.
Often he took the hand of Pandarus
And led him to the garden, where he made
Such a delight and such an argument
Of Cressida, her womanhood, her beauty,
That, never fear, it was a heaven to hear him.
At every time of need, in the town's battles,
He was, and always, the first armed, and truly,
Unless books lie, most dreaded of all men
Except for Hector. This increase of courage
And prowess came from love; it was to win
His lady's thanks that thus his spirit changed
Within him so. In time of truce he rode
Hawking, or hunting the lion, bear, or boar;
He let the little animals alone.
And then when he came riding into town,
Often his lady was ready from her window,
As fresh as a falcon taken from the coop,
To give him graciously her salutation.
His talk above all ran on love and valor,
And all mean qualities he held in scorn.

He never needed urging, certainly,
To honor men of worth, or heal distress.
And he was glad if anyone fared well
Who was a lover, when he learned of it.
For he considered any man as lost
Unless he put himself in love's high service—
Such people, I mean, as ought to be by right.
And with all this he could so well contrive
His dress and manner, and so curiously,
To fit his feelings, that every lover thought
Whatever he said or did was right and well.
And though of royal blood, he never liked
To spurn a man of any sort in pride.
Gracious he was to people of all kinds,
For which he met with thanks on every side.
Thus by Love's will, whose graciousness be praised,
He turned away from Envy, Anger, Pride,
And Avarice, and every other vice.

Bright Lady, Dione's daughter, with your son,
Winged Cupid, whose keen shafts are blindly plied,
And you nine sisters who by Helicon
On Mount Parnassus from of old reside,
You who thus far my tale have deigned to guide,
Since now you will take leave, I can but say
Praise to your names, forever and a day!

Through you I have told fully in my song
What service Troilus did, and to what cheer,
Although discomforts in the tale belong
As it has pleased my author to make clear.
I end my third book in this fashion here,
And Troilus, of every joy possessed,
With Cressida, his heart's love, is at rest.

Book IV

But thanks to Fortune, all too brief a while
Such joys can last; there is no way to bind them.
Truest she seems when she is deep in guile,
And as for fools, well she knows where to find them
And tunes her song to catch them and to blind them,
The common traitor. And when her wheel throws down
Some man, she laughs and mocks him like a clown.

From Troilus averting her bright face
She turned away, and took no further heed,
But cast him clean out of his lady's grace
And on her wheel she set up Diomede,
At which even now my heart begins to bleed,
And now, alas, at what I have to write
The very pen I use quivers in fright.

How Cressida this Troilus forsook,
Or at the least how she became unkind,
Must henceforth be the matter of my book
As they through whom the tale is kept in mind
Have written it. Alas, that they should find
Reason to speak ill of her! If they lie,
They have the baseness of it, and not I!

You Furies, daughters of the Night all three,
Voicing your pains from everlasting hell,
Alecto, Megaera, and Tisiphone,
And Romulus' father, cruel Mars, as well,
So help me end this fourth book as to tell

Completely here how Troilus was crossed
And life and love together how he lost!

The Grecian host, as I have said before,
Lying in force about the town of Troy,
It came about that at the time when Phoebus
Was shining on the breast of Hercules' Lion,
Hector with many brave knights chose a day
To fight the Greeks, according to his custom,
And do them as much damage as he could.
How long or short the time between this plan
And the day they meant to fight I do not know;
But on a day, well-armed and glittering,
Hector with many valorous men went out,
Their spears in hand, their big bows bent, and promptly
Their foemen met them head on in the field.
The whole long day, with spears ground sharp, with
    arrows,
With darts and deadly maces and with swords
They fought and brought both man and horse to earth,
And dashed the brains out with their battle-axes.
But in the final onslaught, truth to tell,
The Trojans blundered, so that when night came
They fled home beaten. On that day Antenor,
For all Polydamas or Mnestheus could do,
Was captured, with Antipus, and Sarpedon,
Polites, Polymnestor, Trojan Ripheus,
And among lesser men, Phebuseo,
So that for what they suffered on that day
The Trojans feared to lose most of their comfort.

A truce was granted at the Greeks' request
By Priam, and then bargaining began
Over exchange of prisoners, great and small,
And for the balance they gave great sums of money;
A business quickly known in every street,

Everywhere, in the besiegers' camp, in town,
And with the first it reached the ears of Calchas.

    When Calchas knew this treaty would be settled,
He pushed his way in soon among the throng
In the Greek council, with the elder lords,
And took his place there as he used to do,
And with a changed expression begged their favor
That for God's love they would be kind enough
To stop their noise and let him have a hearing.
Then he addressed them thus: "I was, milords,
Trojan, as you all know beyond a doubt.
I am, if you remember me, Calchas,
Who first gave reassurance to your purpose
And told you fully how you would succeed.
Through you, in a short time, beyond all question,
Shall Troy be burned and beaten to the earth.
And by what means to devastate this town
And to accomplish all that you desire,
You've clearly heard me before now explain.
You are aware of this, milords, I'm sure,
And since I held the Greeks thus dear, I came
Myself, in my own person, to instruct you
How this might best be done, setting no store
Upon my properties or revenues
Against your comfort. All my wealth I left
And came to you, hoping by this, milords,
That I might please you. All that loss, however,
Does not disturb me. I would undertake
To lose for you all that I have in Troy,
Except for a daughter, whom I left, alas,
At home, asleep, when I fled out of Troy.
Oh hard, oh cruel father that I was!
How could I have been so hard of heart in this?
Ah, had I only brought her in her smock!
I will not be alive tomorrow morning
Unless you lords take pity on my grief.

For since I have not seen a time till now
To set her free, I have kept it to myself;
But now or never, if it pleases you,
I may obtain her quickly, past a doubt.
Give me your help and grace! In all this throng
Take pity on this old wretch in distress,
Because through you I suffer all this grief.
You have now caught and manacled in prison
Trojans enough, and if it be your will,
My child can be redeemed for one of them.
Now for the love of God and by your bounty,
One of so great a number, let me have him!
What reason have you to deny my plea
Since you will take both town and people soon?
On penalty of my life, I do not lie;
Apollo has told me faithfully, and also
I've found it by the stars, by divination,
By augury too, and dare well say the time
Is close at hand when fire and flame shall run
Through the whole town, and Troy turn to dead ashes.
Phoebus and Neptune both, who built the walls,
Are so enraged against the people of Troy
That they will surely bring it to confusion,
Such is their spite toward King Laomedon.
Because he would not pay their wages to them,
The Trojan city shall be put to flame."

   Obsequious in his voice and his look,
This gray old man kept harping on his tale,
The salt tears running down on both his cheeks.
He begged so long that to assuage his grief
They gave Antenor to him. Who was glad
But Calchas then? He quickly laid his wants
On those who were to undertake the treaty,
And pleaded with them often to bring home
Cressida and King Toas for Antenor.
And then when Priam sent out his safe-conduct

The ambassadors went immediately to Troy.
   When the reason for their coming had been given,
Priam, the old king, called his parliament
With what effect I shall describe to you:
The ambassadors received their final answer;
The exchange of prisoners and this whole affair
Well satisfied them; forthwith they marched in.
This Troilus was present in the place
When Cressida was demanded for Antenor,
At which his face changed even as though the words
Had well nigh brought his death. But none the less
He made no answer, all for fear that men
Might guess where his affection lay. He bore
His grief with a man's heart, and full of anguish
And ghastly fear, waited for what the lords
Might say about it. If they meant to grant,
Though God forbid, the exchange of Cressida,
He pondered two things, how to save her honor,
And by what way he might defeat the exchange.
He brooded hard on how all this might stand.
Love quickened him to keep her, and to die
Rather than let her go; but reason told him,
Taking the other side, "Do not do that
Except with her consent, lest for your work
She choose to hate you, seeing the love you both
Have kept unknown made public through your
    meddling."
So he began to think it for the best
That though the lords agreed to let her go,
He'd let them grant whatever they might like
And tell his lady first what they intended,
And when she had let him know her mind, thereafter
He would act quickly enough, though the whole world
Should strive against him.

                Hector, who well heard
The Greeks, how for Antenor they would have

Cressida, began to speak against it,
And soberly answered, "She is no prisoner, sirs.
I do not know who gave you this commission,
But as for me, you can go to him again
And tell him it is not our custom here
To barter women."
           The clamor of the people
Sprang up at once, as furious as a blaze
Kindled in straw. Misfortune at that time
Resolved that they should will their own confusion.
"Hector," they cried, "what spirit has possessed you
To shield this woman and let us lose Antenor?
You're taking a wrong course, bold knight and wise
Although you are. We need men, that is plain,
And he is one of the greatest in the town.
Hector, forget these notions. O King Priam,
Our vote is all to give up Cressida."
And so they begged that Antenor be released.

   Ah, Juvenal, true is your observation
That men have little knowledge what to long for
If their desires are not to bring them harm!
A cloud of error keeps them from discerning
What would be best, and here's a pat example:
These people long to see Antenor freed
Through whom they came to grief, for afterward
He proved a traitor to the town of Troy.
They paid his price too quickly. O vain world,
This is your wisdom! Cressida, who never
Had done them harm, shall swim in bliss no longer.
Instead Antenor shall come home to town,
And she be sent away; so said their clamor.
In consequence the parliament decided
That Cressida should be yielded for Antenor
And so proclaimed, though Hector many times
Pleaded his "nay." When everyone had left
Troilus hurried to his room, alone,

But for a servant or two that he dismissed,
Saying that he would sleep, and hastily
He lay down on his bed. There, as in winter
The leaves are stolen one after another
Until the tree is bare, and nothing left
But branch and bark, so Troilus lay bereaved
Of every gladness, in the black ship of sorrow
Fettered, and ready to burst out of his mind
So sore he felt the exchange of Cressida.
He rose, and shut each door and window too,
And then this wretched man on his bedside
Sat down like a dead image, bleak and pale,
And in his heart the heaped-up woe began
To burst out. In his madness he behaved
Like the wild bull that plunges here and there,
Pierced to the heart, and roars his death-complaint.
He ran about his room, and beat his fists
Upon his breast. Often he struck his head
Against the wall, his body on the floor,
As if he meant to make way with himself.
His eyes, for pity of his heart, streamed out
Like two swift springs; his bitter sobs of grief
Deprived him of his speech. Scarce could he say,
"Why, death, do you refuse to let me die?
Cursed be the day when nature ever formed me
To be a living man!" But when the rage
With which his heart swelled, through the lapse of time
Subsided somewhat, he lay down to rest.
Yet there his tears burst from him all the more.
It was a wonder his body could support
The half of all this woe of which I tell you.

At length he said, "Fortune, what have I done?
In what have I offended you? For pity
How could you so deceive me? Is there no grace,
And shall I perish thus? Must Cressida
Be thieved away because you have willed it so?

How can you find it in your heart to be
So cruel toward me? Have I not honored you
More than all other gods my whole life long?
Why will you thus deprive me of my joy?
Ah, Troilus, what can men call you now
But wretchedest of wretches, fallen from honor
And into misery, where I shall mourn
For Cressida until my breath shall fail me!
Ah, Fortune, if my life in joy displeased
Your loathsome jealousy, why did you not
Spirit away the king my father's life,
Or kill my brothers, or slay me myself
Who thus complain, I, world-encumberer
Who have no use, and constantly am dying
But never fully die? If Cressida
Were left me only, then I should not care
Where you might pilot me; and you have stolen
Her, alas! But ever it is your way
To rob a man of what he holds most dear,
And prove by that your fickle violence.
Thus I am lost. There is no help in resisting.
True lord, ah Love, who best can know my heart
And all my mind, what can my sorrowful life
Do now if I must lose what I have bought
So dearly? Since you led us into grace
And sealed our hearts, both Cressida's and mine,
How can you suffer this to be revoked?
What shall I do? I shall, while I can bear
A life of torment and of cruel pain,
Lament this evil turn of destiny
Alone, as I was born. I shall not see
Sunshine or shower, but end my wretched life
Like Oedipus in darkness. Weary spirit
That wanders to and fro, why will you not
Flee from the sorriest flesh that walks the earth?
Soul, lurking in this misery, leave your nest,

Fly from my heart and let it break, and follow
Cressida, your dear lady, to the end.
Your rightful place is now no longer here.
O my unhappy eyes, whose whole delight
Was but to see the eyes of Cressida,
What will you do but for my grief become
Of no account, and weep away your vision
Since she is quenched who used to give you light?
In vain hereafter I possess two eyes
Created in me, but their virtue gone.
Cressida, sovereign lady of the soul
That thus laments, who now shall soothe my pain?
Ah, none; but when my sorrowful heart shall perish
Accept my spirit, that hastens after you,
For it shall ever serve you; and for this
It does not matter though the body die.
You lovers now fixed high on Fortune's wheel,
God grant you find love ever as strong as iron,
And may your lives continue long in joy!
But when you pass my burial place, remember
That there your fellow lies. I also loved,
Although unworthy. You man of wickedness,
Feeble and old, Calchas, I mean, what ails you,
That you should be a Greek, though born a Trojan?
Ah, Calchas, my destruction, you were born
In a cursed time for me! Would to glad Jove
I only had you where I want, in Troy!"

   A thousand sighs, hotter than living coals,
Came from his breast, each following the other,
And anguish thwarted him and rent him so
That he was conscious neither of pain nor pleasure
But lay insensible.

                    Now Pandarus
Had heard what every lord and tradesman said
In parliament, and how by general vote
Cressida was to be yielded for Antenor.

Almost beside himself, and in his woe
Not knowing his own mind, he rushed straight off
To Troilus. A knight who kept the door
Let him into the chamber, and Pandarus,
Who wept for sympathy, crossed the dark room
And toward the bed went quiet as a stone,
So staggered that he knew not what to say.
With folded arms and face all torn with grief
He stood before this wretched Troilus,
And, Lord, his heart chilled, seeing his friend in woe.

   Troilus, feeling Pandarus his friend
Come there to see him, began to melt like snow
Beneath the sun, at which this Pandarus
Began to weep as tenderly as he,
And they were speechless; neither one could say
A word for grief. But Troilus at last
Burst out amid his sobs and bitter sighs,
"Pandarus, I am dead. There's nothing more
To say. Haven't you heard in parliament
How for Antenor my Cressida is lost?"

   Pandarus answered, dead and pale of face,
"Yes, were it only false as it is true.
I have heard it. I know how the whole thing stands.
Merciful God, who would have looked for this?
Who would have thought that in so short a time
Fortune would overturn our happiness?
No soul in all the world, I do believe,
Has ever seen a ruin stranger than this
Grow out of any chance. But who escapes
Or foresees everything? Such is this world,
And therefore I conclude: no man should think
He has a vested interest in Fortune.
Her gifts belong in common to us all.

   "But tell me this: why do you madden yourself
With sorrow so? Why lie here in this way
When you have fully had your whole desire

So that by rights it ought to be enough?
But I, who never felt a friendly look
In all my service, let me weep and wail
Until I'm done for! Then again, you know
This town is full of women on all sides,
And I'll find one or two, no question of it,
Among some company, if I can judge,
More beautiful than any twelve of her.
And so take heart, dear friend. If she is lost,
We'll get another. What! God forbid each pleasure
Should be in one thing only, and no more!
If one can sing, another dances well;
This one is gracious, that one quick and gay,
This one is fair, that one knows what to do.
Falcons that fly at herons, and those for hawking,
Both are held dear, each for his special virtue.
As Zanzis in his wisdom said, moreover,
'The new love often chases out the old.'
New cases call for new considerations.
Remember, too, you owe your life a duty.
Such fire, by nature, bit by bit will cool;
For since it is no more than casual pleasure,
Some chance will put it out of memory.
For just as sure as day comes after night,
New love, or labor, or some different care,
Or simply happening to meet less often
Makes old affections altogether fail.
You shall have one of these to shorten pain;
The lack of her will drive her from your heart."

These words he said entirely for the moment,
To help his friend, lest he should die for sorrow;
He did not care what nonsense he might utter
To make his torment sink. But Troilus
Took little notice; it went in one ear
And out the other. "Friend," he said at last,
"Your medicine would suit me very well

If I were fiend enough to play her false
Who is true to me! Pray God that such advice
May never come to pass, but let him kill me
Here on the spot at once before I do
As you would teach me. Whatever you may say,
She whom I serve, who has my heart by right
In her possession, she shall have me wholly
As hers until I die. For, Pandarus,
Since I have promised to be true to her,
I will not be untrue for any man.
As for your finding others just as fair,
Enough of that; make no comparison
With any natural creature of the earth!
Dear Pandarus, I will not take your view
About all this. You kill me with your words;
No more, I beg. You bid me love another,
A new one altogether, and Cressida
You say let go. It lies beyond my power,
And if I could, dear brother, I would not do it.
If you can play at racket, back and forth—
First one and then another, like the charm,
'Nettle in, dock out'—evil befall the woman
Who heeds your woe! You treat me, Pandarus,
Just like the man who comes in quite unruffled
When someone has been hurt, and says to him,
'Don't think about the pain, and you won't feel it.'
You must transmute me first into a stone
And rob me of my passions, one and all,
Before you overcome my grief so lightly.
Death well may tear the life out of my breast,
So deep this pain may delve; but from my soul
Cressida's dart shall never be plucked out,
But with Proserpina, when I am dead,
I will go dwell in anguish, and complain
Eternally how we two have been parted.
    "You argue that the loss of Cressida

Should grieve me less because she has been mine.
Why talk such gibberish, you who said to me,
'It's worse for him who is cast down out of bliss
Than if he had never tasted bliss at all'?
But tell me now, if it seems to you so easy
To change forever back and forth in love,
Why haven't you been at work to change the lady
Who makes you suffer? Why is your heart unwilling
To let her go? Why don't you love another
Who can set your heart at rest? If you in love
Have met with nothing but rebuffs, and still
Can't thrust it from your heart, then I, who lived
In freedom and delight with her as great
As any living soul, can I forget it,
And that so soon? Where have you been cooped up
All this long while, you who can press a point
So well and with such logic? All your counsel,
God knows, amounts to nothing. I shall die,
There is no more to say. O death, come now,
Ender of every sorrow, since I call
So often for you! Happy is that death
That often summoned comes and quiets pain!
Well do I know that while I lived in peace
I would have paid you any sort of ransom
Before I let you slay me, but your coming
Seems now so sweet there is nothing in this world
I so desire! Ah, death, since in this grief
I burn with flames, drown me at once in tears
Or with your cold stroke put my heart at rest!
You slay so many in so many ways
Against their will, unasked, by day and night,
Do me this kindness at my own request:
Deliver the world, and thus do as you should,
Of me, the unhappiest soul that ever was.
It's time for me to die, since in this world
I serve no purpose."

Troilus began,
Like liquor from an alembic, to distill
In quickly running tears; and Pandarus
Looked downward at the floor and held his tongue.
What, for God's sake! Rather than let him die,
He thought at last, I'll say a little yet.

"Friend," he began, "since you are in such grief,
And choose to find fault with my arguments,
Why don't you help yourself, and use your manhood
To stop this misery? You can't for shame
Go carry her off; then either let her go
Or keep her, and give up this foolishness.
Are you in Troy, and haven't nerve enough
To take a woman who loves you, and herself
Will be of the same mind? Now isn't this
A piece of silliness? Get up at once,
Remember you're a man, and stop this bawling,
For I'll be dead or she shall still be ours."

Troilus answered patiently, "Dear brother,
I've thought of all this often enough myself,
And more than you have mentioned; you shall hear
Why it has been abandoned. First, you know
This town has all this war because of women
Borne off by force. I never should be suffered,
The way things stand, to do so great a wrong,
And everyone would reproach me if I ran
So counter to my father's resolution
Since she has been exchanged for the town's good.

"I have been thinking, too, if she consented,
I would ask her of my father, by his favor;
But this, I see, would mean she stood accused,
And well I know I never should obtain her.
For since my father, in so high a place
As parliament, exchanged her over his seal,
He won't revoke his edict for my sake.
But my worst fear in playing such a game

Is to disturb her heart by violence.
For if I tried to hinder it openly,
She would be slandered, and I'd rather die
Than lead to her disgrace. Thus I am lost
By all that I can see. For as her knight
Certain it is that I must hold her honor
More dear at all times than I hold myself,
As lovers rightly should. Thus I am pulled
One way by reason, one way by desire:
Desire prompts me to prevent her going,
But reason, as my heart fears, will not have it."

 Weeping as if his tears would never end,
He said, "Wretch that I am, what shall I do?
For constantly I feel my love increasing
And, Pandarus, hope is ever less and less.
The causes of my care increase as well.
Why does my heart refuse to break? In love
There's little peace."

      Pandarus answered, "Friend,
Do as you like, as far as I'm concerned,
But if I had it half so hot, and had
Your rank and standing, she should go with me
Though the whole town bayed after us in chorus.
I wouldn't care a snap for all that noise!
When people have cried out loud, then they will
 whisper,
And wonders only last the town nine nights.

 "Don't delve so deep in reason and subtlety,
But help yourself. Better another wept
Than you; and since you two are one, get up,
For on my life, she shall not go! Be found
Somewhat at fault rather than as a gnat
Die here without a blow. It is no shame
To keep her whom you love in your possession,
And if you let her go to the Greek camp,
She may consider your scruples overnice.

Remember too that Fortune helps the bold
In their designs, but she deserts a wretch
For cowardice. Your lady may be vexed,
But you yourself can make your peace hereafter.

"I will myself be with you in this deed,
Though I and all my kin, if there's a scuffle,
Should lie dead in the street like dogs, pierced through
With wide and bloody wounds. At every turn
I will be found a friend. And if you please
To die here like a fool, well then, good-by.
The devil with anyone who pities you!"

With these words Troilus began to liven.
"Friend, I am with you. Many thanks," he said.
"But in all truth, you cannot egg me on
Nor torture so torment me, though I die,
To such a point that I shall carry her off,
Whatever happens, except by her own will."

"Why, so I meant," said Pandarus, "all the time.
But tell me, have you put it up to her,
You in your misery?"

                He answered, "No."

"Then what are you dismayed by," Pandarus said,
"Not knowing, since you haven't been there yet,
That if you carry her off, she will think herself
Ill used, unless Jove whispered in your ear?
Get up, at once, as if there were nothing wrong,
And wash your face, and go and see the king,
Or he may happen to wonder where you are
And send for you before you are prepared.
And once for all, dear brother, be more cheerful
And let me manage. I shall work it so
That some way, certainly, sometime tonight,
You can discuss it with her privately
And by her words and face you'll soon discover
What's in her mind and what's best at this juncture.
Good-by, for on this point I rest the case."

Rumor, reporting true and false alike,
Flew through the length of Troy with ready wings
From ear to ear, and made of this occurrence
The latest story, how the daughter of Calchas
Had been exchanged in parliament for Antenor;
Which tale, as soon as Cressida had heard it,
Caring nothing at all about her father
At this turn of events, nor when he died,
She set to work imploring Jupiter
To bring mischance on those who made the treaty.
But lest the tale be true, she did not dare
To ask the question of a single soul.
As if her heart and thought on Troilus
Were fixed and set so wonderfully fast
That all the world could not unbind her love,
She would be his while life remained in her;
And thus she burned with love and fear at once
Until she did not know what course to follow.

But as we see, in town or anywhere,
That women like to visit with their friends,
A company of women came to call
In cheerful sympathy on Cressida,
Expecting her to be well pleased. They sat,
These women who were dwellers in the city,
And chattered as I shall report. Said one,
The first to speak, "I am delighted, really,
On your account; you're going to see your father."
Another said, "Not I, and that's the truth,
For she's been all too little here with us."
Then the third said, "I hope, indeed I do,
That she will bring us peace. God guide her steps
By his almighty power when she goes."

She listened to these womanish concerns
As if she were not there. God knows her heart
Was fixed on other things! Although the body
Sat there among them, her attention dwelt

Elsewhere throughout it all; for constantly
Her soul was seeking Troilus, and she thought
Always of him.
           These women chattered on
About their nothings, thinking that they pleased her.
But vanities could give her little help,
Burning the while with quite another passion
From what they thought, so that she felt her heart
Ready to die for woe and weariness.
At last she could restrain her tears no longer,
They welled up so, signs of the bitter pain
In which her spirit was and must continue,
Remembering from what heaven to what hell
She'd fallen, losing Troilus from her sight.
   The fools who were sitting round her thought she
      wept
Because she had to take leave of their circle
And never amuse herself among them more;
And those who had known her longest, seeing her
      weep,
Mistook it for affection, and wept too
For her distress. And they bestirred themselves
To comfort her for something that God knows
She little had in mind. They thought their gossip
Amused her, and often begged her to be glad.
But the relief they gave her was just such
As a headache gets by scratching a man's heel!
   Yet after all this idle vanity
They took leave and went homeward. Cressida
Went up into her chamber sorrowfully,
And fell upon her bed as if to die,
Meaning never to rise from it again.
Her wavy hair, bright as the sun in hue,
She tore, and wrung her fingers, long and slender,
And begged God give her mercy, and by death
Cure all her care. Her once-bright color, pale

As then it was, bore witness to her woe,
And she protested, sobbing her complaint:
   "Alas, unhappy wretch, ill-fated soul,
Born under evil stars, I must go away
And leave this place, and so part from my knight!
Oh, that the day had never dawned on which
I saw him first who is the cause to me,
And I to him, of all this woe!"
                        The tears
Fell from her eyes like a sudden April shower.
She struck her white breast, and a thousand times
Cried out for death, for she must give him up
Who was her solace. At this evil turn
She held herself a lost soul.
                    "What will he do,"
She said, "and I as well? How shall I live
Parted from him? Dear heart, whom I love so,
Who shall destroy the sorrow that you feel?
Calchas, my father, yours is the fault in this!
And O my mother, Argive, would the day
You brought me into life had never been!
To what end do I live and suffer thus?
Can fishes go on living without water?
What worth am I apart from Troilus?
How should a plant or other living thing
Exist without the food that nature gives it?
I cannot say the proverb now too often:
'Green without root dies quickly.' Thus I'll do,
Because I dare not handle sword or dart:
The very day I leave you, if that itself
Won't be my end, no meat nor drink shall come
Into my body, till I unsheathe my soul
Out of my breast, and so I'll slay myself.
And Troilus, my clothes shall be all black
In token, dear heart, that I am as one
Gone from this world; and ever till my death

I shall be of the faith and company,
Deprived of you, of those whose rite and practice
Consist in sorrow, plaint, and abstinence.
   "The spirit in my woeful breast I leave
Forever with your spirit to complain,
For they shall never part: though here on earth
We be divided, in the field of pity
Known as Elysium we shall be together,
Out of all pain, like Orpheus and his love,
Eurydice. Thus for Antenor soon
I'll be exchanged; but in this woeful turn
What will you do? How will your tender heart
Bear up against it? But, dear soul, forget
The sorrow and the grief; forget me too.
If you are well, I care not if I die."
   How could the plaint she made in her distress
Be ever read or sung? I do not know;
But as for me, my little gift of speech,
If I attempted to describe her sorrow,
Would only make it seem less than it was
And childishly deface her high complaint;
And so I pass it over.
                         Pandarus,
As she lay there in the passion of her grief,
Came secretly from Troilus with his message,
And found her wet with weeping, face and breast,
And the thick tresses of her sunny hair
Hanging disheveled all about her ears,
True sign that she desired martyrdom
And longed at heart to die. When she perceived him,
She hid her face for grief between her arms,
And Pandarus at that was so distraught
That he could scarcely stay there in the house,
For if she had cried bitterly at first,
Now she complained a thousand times the more.
   "Pandarus was to me," she said, "first cause

Of more than one joy that is now transmuted
Into a cruel grief. Shall I bid welcome,
Or shall I not, to you who first of all
Persuaded me to love, whose service ends
In such a way as this? Love ends in woe?
Yes, or men lie—and all this world's delights!
Sorrow stands always at the end of joy,
And whosoever thinks it is not so,
Let him come look on me, unhappy wretch,
Who hate myself, and ever curse the day
That I was born. Who sees me sees all sorrow,
Grief, torment, woe, and anguish, all at once.
There is no suffering save in my poor body,
Whatever its name, aching or bitterness,
Vexation, frenzy, fear, sickness, and pining.
I think, indeed, that tears pour down from heaven
In pity of my sharp and cruel pain."

"Sister, full of discomfort," Pandarus said,
"What do you mean to do? Why don't you show
Respect for yourself a little? Why set about
Destroying yourself this way? Stop all this business,
Hear what I have to tell you, and be receptive
To this that comes to you from Troilus."

Cressida turned, making a lamentation
So great it was like death to witness it.
"Alas, what message can you bring?" she said.
"What does my dear heart have to say to me,
He whom I fear I shall not see again?
Will he have tears and plaints before I go?
I have enough, if he will send for them!"

To look upon her face was like beholding
The face of one bound on a bier in death;
Image of paradise, it was all changed
Into another species; and the laughter,
The gaiety that people found in her,
And every joy that she had known, were fled,

And thus she lay deserted. Rings of purple
Enclosed her eyes, true token of her pain,
A thing like death to see, and Pandarus
Could not prevent his tears from pouring down
Because of it; but still, as best he could,
He said his say to her from Troilus.
   "Well, niece, you have heard, I doubt not, how the
     king
And other lordships, with the best intentions,
Exchanged you and Antenor. What this turn
Has done to Troilus no tongue can say;
He is beside himself. We have sorrowed for it,
He and I, until we were at death's door.
But through my ministrations, finally,
He has somewhat got the better of his tears.
I have the impression he would gladly be
All night with you, to find, if possible,
Some help for this. In sum and substance, here
My message is in brief, for you can't listen,
In such a frenzy, to a long preamble,
And you can answer him immediately.
And for the love of God, dear niece, before
Troilus gets here, shed this misery!"
   "Great is my woe," she said, "and yet to me
His sorrow is much more. I think I love him
More than he loves himself. Does he so suffer
Because of me? Can he so piteously
Complain for me? This doubles all my anguish.
Grievous it is for me, God knows, to part;
Yet it is harder to behold his sorrow.
I know that it will be my death, for die
I will for certain; but bid him come," she said,
"Before the death that threatens me drives out
The spirit beating in my heart."
                           Face down,
After these words, she fell upon her arms

And pitiably wept.
            Said Pandarus,
"Why act this way, knowing the time is close
When he'll be coming? Get up immediately,
Don't let him find you draggled so with tears
Or you will have him clean out of his mind.
If he knew you were behaving in this fashion
He'd kill himself; and if I thought he'd meet
With this reception, I wouldn't have him here
For all the wealth that Priam has to spend.
For I know perfectly what course he'd take,
And so I say again, shed all this grief,
Or once for all, he'll die. Try to assuage
And not increase his misery, dear niece.
Cause him to feel the flat side of the sword,
The side that heals, and not the edge that injures.
Apply a little wisdom to his sorrow.
How will it help to weep till the streets run
Or both of you are drowned in salty tears?
Better a time of healing than complaint!

   "This is my notion: when I bring him here,
Since you are wise, and both of the same mind,
Consider how you can prevent your going,
Or after you have gone, come quickly back.
Women can show their wisdom on short notice,
And let's see what your wit is good for now.
What help I can, I will not fail to give."

   "Go then," said Cressida, "and truly, uncle,
I shall restrain myself with all my power
From weeping in his sight, and do my best,
With all my powers and pains, to comfort him.
If there is any salve to heal this sore,
It will not lack for failure on my part."

   Off Pandarus went to look for Troilus
And found him in a temple all alone,
Begging the gods to take him soon in pity

Out of this world, for he was well convinced
There was no other favor they could do him.
That day he had fallen into such despair
That he was utterly resolved to die,
For this became his constant argument—
He said he was as good as lost: "For all
That happens, happens by necessity,"
He said, "and so I am destined to be lost.
I know this much for certain: the divine
Foresight of providence has always seen
That I should have to give up Cressida,
Since God, beyond a doubt, sees everything,
Directing all things by his ordinance
To come to pass as they have been predestined.

    "Yet whom shall I believe? There are learned men,
Many and great, who set up destiny
By proof of argument; but some men say
No unavoidable destiny exists,
But that free choice is given us, every one.
Alas, the old fathers are so full of sleight
I cannot tell whose view I ought to take!
Some say, if God sees all things in advance
(And surely God can suffer no deception),
What providence foresees is bound to come
Though men had sworn it were impossible.
And so I say, if he has known beforehand
Our thoughts and acts from all eternity,
We have no free choice; for no other thought,
No other act could ever come to pass
But such as providence has known already.
If there could be uncertainty enough
To let us wriggle out of God's foreknowledge,
Prescience of things to come would not exist;
It would be only fallible opinion,
Not steadfast foresight. That, for fair, would be
A great delusion, to think that God should have

No perfect and clear knowledge more than men
Who wander amid doubtful suppositions!
To lay on God an error such as this
Would be a damnable abomination.
     "Then there are tonsured crowns both high and
          smooth
Who offer this opinion: they maintain
Not that things come about because foreknowledge
Sees in advance that they are going to happen,
But rather that because they are going to happen
Foreknowledge therefore sees them in advance.
And thus necessity slides over again
And takes the other side; for things foreseen
Need not, on this view, come about for certain,
As of necessity, but things that happen
Must all be necessarily foreseen.
     "I seem here to be struggling with the question
Which is the cause of which: is God's foreknowledge
The certain cause of that necessity
By which things happen, or is the necessity
Of things that are to come the cause instead
Of God's foreknowledge? But I will not now
Burden myself with how the order stands
Among the causes, for I well know this:
It must be that the happening of things
Assuredly foreseen is necessary,
Although it may not follow that foreknowledge
Puts into things to come, for good or ill,
Their necessary coming. Suppose a man
Sits yonder on a bench; then it must be
That your opinion, if you think he sits there,
Is true, and necessarily. Now I say
That if your thought is true because he sits there,
There, of necessity, he must be sitting;
And thus necessity is in each of you,

In him of sitting there, in you of truth.
   "But you may say, the man sits on the bench
Not for the reason that your thought is true;
Rather because he sits before your eyes,
Therefore your thought is true. My answer is,
Although the cause of truth in your opinion
Comes of his sitting there, necessity
Is meanwhile intermingled in you both.
   "By the same principle I can well pursue,
It seems to me, my reasoning on this point
Of God's foreknowledge and of things to come;
And through this reasoning men may clearly see
That whatsoever comes to pass on earth
Comes by necessity. This is enough
To make an end of free choice, every bit.
   "And yet this is a sad abuse of mind,
To say that temporal things, by their occurrence,
Can be the cause of God's eternal foresight.
For what might I suppose, if I thought that,
Except that God foresees events to come
Because they are to come, not otherwise?
Thus I might think that all occurrences,
All things that ever have happened at any time,
Are cause of that foreknowledge that is sovereign
Over all things, above all ignorance.
   "But further still, I have this yet to say,
That just as when I know there is a thing,
That thing must necessarily be so,
Thus also if I know a thing will happen,
Happen it must; and so with the occurrence
Of things foreseen before they come to pass:
They cannot be escaped on any hand.
   "Almighty Jove," he cried, "upon your throne,
Who knows what is the truth in all this matter,
Have pity on my sorrow, and take my life

Quickly, or else bring Cressida and me
Out of distress!"
                    And while he was disputing
This question with himself, who should come in
But Pandarus, and said, "Almighty God,
Who ever saw a wise man act this way?
What are you up to, Troilus? Why this rage
To be your own worst enemy? What, man,
Cressida hasn't gone yet! Is it a pleasure
To ruin yourself so that your eyes look dead
Inside your skull? Haven't you lived these years
Without her, and been happy? Were you born
For her and no one else? Did nature shape you
For nothing but her pleasure? Come out of it,
And tell yourself, in this catastrophe,
That even as the chances fall in dice,
Just so the pleasures come and go in love.

  "And yet this most of all amazes me,
Why you should grieve yourself before you know,
Concerning her departure, what will happen,
Or whether she herself can hinder it.
You haven't probed her wit by any means.
Offer your neck up when the ax is ready,
And sorrow when you have occasion for it!

  "Therefore take in what I am going to tell you.
I've spoken with her and spent a long time with her,
According to our plan, and I keep feeling
That in the secret places of her heart
She has a way to forestall what you dread.
And my suggestion is that when night comes
You go to her, and make an end of this.
And blessed Juno, through her mighty power,
Shall, as I hope, receive us in her grace.
My heart says, 'By the truth, she shall not go.
Quiet yourself a while, then, and keep firm;

That will be best.'"

                Troilus answered, sighing,
"You've spoken well, and just so will I do."
  When it was time, he came to her alone
And secretly, according to his custom.
Truth is that at the moment when they met,
Their pain so wrung their hearts that neither one
Could say a word of greeting. They took each other
Into their arms, and then they kissed. The tears
That flowed from them, beyond the nature of tears,
Were bitter as gall and aloes. I cannot find
That woeful Myrrha, turned into a tree,
Wept through the bark such bitter tears of gum.
No heart exists in all the world so hard
It would not have felt pity for their pain.
  But when their weary spirits had returned
Into their rightful dwelling place again,
And by mere length their pain had somewhat weakened,
With broken voice, all ragged from her cries,
Cressida said to him, "Ah, Jove, I am dying!
Have mercy, I implore. Help, Troilus!"
  With that she laid her head against his breast,
And lost her voice, and her unhappy spirit
Was on the very point of taking leave.
She who had been in former time so fair,
So fresh to see, above all other women,
Lay pale and green in hue. He called her name
Without an answer, and he felt her limbs
Cold, and her eyes turned upward in her head.
There was no help or counsel for him now
Except to kiss her cold lips over and over.
Whether he suffered, God knew, and he himself!
  He rose, and stretched out long and straight her body,
For not one sign of life, search as he might,
Could he discern in Cressida; he sang

Again and again the sad tune of "alas,"
And seeing her lie speechless, he declared
That she had left this world. He wrung his hands,
And said what could be said, and rained his tears
Over her breast, and then he wiped away
And dried those tears he had shed, and piteously
Prayed for her soul, and cried, "O Lord, established
Upon your throne, have mercy, for I soon
Shall follow her!"
                    Cold, and devoid of feeling
She was for all that he could tell; he felt
No breathing in her, and this was to him
A pregnant argument that she had gone
Beyond this world. There was no help for it
That he could see, and therefore he began
Disposing her as men dispose the limbs
Of those that are to be upon a bier.
And after this, resolved and stern at heart,
He drew his sword to slay himself at once,
In order that his soul might follow her
Wherever Minos, judge of all the dead,
Appointed them to go. "O cruel Jove,
And you, O hostile Fortune," he cried out,
"This I protest, that you have falsely slain
Cressida; you can do no worse to me,
And so I say, fie on you, once for all,
Your powers and your caprices. You shall never
Conquer me in so cowardly a fashion;
No death shall ever part me from my love,
For I will quit this world, since you have slain her,
And follow her spirit, high or low. No lover
Shall say that Troilus did not dare for fear
To keep his lady company in death.
But since you will not suffer us to live
Here on the earth, suffer our souls at least
To be together. O city that I leave

In your distress, and Priam and my brothers,
Farewell, and you, my mother, for I go;
And Atropos, make ready now my bier,
And Cressida, my sweet, receive my spirit!"
These were the words he said, with sword at heart,
Ready to die. But as God willed, she woke
That moment from her swoon with sighing breath,
And cried out, "Troilus!"

                      "Cressida, my lady,
Do you still live?" he answered.

                          "Yes, dear heart,
Thanks to the Cyprian."

                      She sighed grievously,
And Troilus did his best to comfort her,
Took her into his arms and kissed her often,
Until her hovering spirit had come back
Into her woeful heart again. At last
She looked and saw his sword, lying unsheathed,
And cried aloud, and asked him why he had drawn it.
Troilus told her the reason. "Merciful God,
Think what a deed!" she said. "Alas, how near
We both have come to dying! If by good grace
I had not spoken, you would have killed yourself?"
  "Unquestionably."

                    "By the very Lord who made me,
I should have gone few steps alive," she said,
"After your death, no, not to be crowned the queen
Of all the land on which the sun shines bright.
With this same sword I should have killed myself.
But let's cry halt; we've had enough of this.
Let's get up now and go at once to bed
And there speak of our woe, for by the wick
That I see burning, I know well that day
Is not far off."

                  When they were in their bed,
Fast in each other's arms, it was not like

The nights they had spent before; in wretchedness
They looked upon each other, as two might look
Who had lost their every joy. But finally
Cressida said: "Dear heart, you know this well,
That if a man does nothing but complain
And seeks no help, that is mere foolishness,
And makes his woe the greater. And since we are here
To find some cure for what we are suffering,
It's high time to begin. I am a woman,
As well you are aware, and what I think
On the spur of this disaster I will tell you
While it is hot. The truth is this, our woe
Is for no other reason, if I am right,
Except that we must part. What help for this
Except to plan how we may quickly meet?
That I shall manage to come back again
Soon after I go, I do not doubt at all.
No fear of it, within a week or two
I shall be here. I'll tell you heaps of ways,
As briefly as I can; for time once lost
Can never be recovered. The fact is
Our parting will distress us cruelly,
But he that serves love and will have his pleasure
Must sometime suffer pain. Since I shall go
No farther away from Troy than I can ride
In half a morning, that should ease our sorrow;
For I shall not be cooped so close, dear heart,
But day by day, during this time of truce,
You shall be kept informed of how I am.
Before the truce is finished, I'll be here;
Then you'll have gained Antenor and me too.
So take heart if you can, and think this way:
'True, Cressida has gone, but she will come
Speedily home again.' How soon? By God,
Before ten days, I dare say that for certain!
And when that moment comes, we'll be so glad,

Since we shall be together all our lives,
That the whole world could not express our joy.

"Often as we are now, to hide our minds,
You do not speak with me nor I with you,
Nor watch you ride, a fortnight at a time.
And can't you wait ten days, then, for my honor,
In this turn of events? If not, there's little
You can endure! You know that all my kin
Are here as well, except my father only,
And all my other things, and more than that,
My dear heart, you, whom I would rather see
Than all this world even to the farthest shore.

"Why do you think my father so desires
To see me but for fear that in this town
I'm hated for his sake? How does he know
The life I lead? For if he could imagine
How well I fare in Troy, we'd have no cause
To worry about my going! And moreover,
Peace talk is gaining all the time, you know.
Queen Helen, so they say, will be restored.
The Greeks will give us back whatever is right.
And if peace comes, the very nature of peace
Will force men to communicate together;
They'll have to travel back and forth all day,
Walking and riding, thick as a swarm of bees,
Everyone free to stay where he best likes.

"Or if peace doesn't come, still I must come.
Wherever should I go, how should I live
Among those warlike men, in constant fear?
If all this leaves you still unsatisfied,
Here's yet another way: my father is old,
And age is covetous. I've thought just now
Of how to catch him, and without a net.
You cannot have a full wolf, people say,
And also a sound lamb. Men have to spend
Something of what they own to save the rest.

Gold always makes its mark on covetous hearts.
Now let me tell you what I mean to do:
Whatever I have in Troy that I can take
I'll carry to my father, and I'll tell him
A friend or two have sent it to him in trust,
And these friends beg him fervently to send
For more, and in a hurry, while the town
Lies in such peril. The amount is huge,
That's what I'll say; but lest it be detected,
It can be sent by no one except me.
And if peace comes, I'll let him know besides
What friends I have at court to stay the wrath
Of Priam, and to bring him back to favor.
So, what for one thing and another, sweet,
I'll cast him under such a spell of words
That he will dream his soul has gone to heaven.
Apollo won't be worth a fig to him,
Nor all his learned tricks and auguries.
And if he tries to prove by divination
Whether I'm lying, I shall find the way
To interrupt him. I'll twitch him by the sleeve
While he's about it, and tell him out and out
That he has failed to understand the gods,
Because the gods talk ambiguities—
For every truth they utter twenty falsehoods.
I'll tell him also, 'Fear, as I suppose,
First found the gods,' and that his coward's heart
Led him to put a false gloss on the words
The god spoke, when he fled in fear from Delphi,
And if I do not make him change his mind
And do my will within a day or two,
My life be forfeit."

         It is down in writing,
Truly, as I have found, that all these things
Were spoken with good purpose, and that her heart
Was kind and faithful to him, and she spoke

Just what she thought; and when she went, she died
For grief, always intending to be true
Forever. They who knew her life and acts
Have so recorded.
             With open ear and heart
Troilus heard this matter through and through.
It seemed to him that he was of like mind;
To let her go, however, was a thought
At which his heart misgave him constantly.
But in the end he reconciled himself
To trust in her, and take it for the best.

The frenzy of his grief was quenched with hope,
And so for joy the amorous dance began
Between them. As the birds delight in song
Among the green leaves when the sun is shining,
So they delighted in their speech together.
But none the less, for the wealth of all this world,
Cressida's going would not leave his mind.
He begged her many times and piteously
That he might find her faithful to her pledge.

"If you are cruel," he said, "unless you come
To Troy on the promised day, I'll never again
Have honor, health, or joy. Sure as the sun
Will rise tomorrow morning, sure as God,
I hope, will bring me from this cruel sorrow
And give me rest, I will destroy myself
If you delay. And though my death is nothing,
Rather than let me suffer so, dear heart,
Stay here. The shifts that I have heard you scheme
Are likely altogether to collapse.
The saying is, 'The bear has one idea,
His master has another.' Your father's wise,
And it is said, 'Men may outrun the wise,
But not outwit them.' It's no easy thing
To limp before a cripple undetected;
He knows the art. Your father is in sleight

As Argus with his eyes. He may have lost
His coin, but his old craft so stays with him
You won't deceive him by your womanhood
Nor fool him by your acting; that's my fear.

"If peace will ever come again, I know not.
But peace or no peace, whether in sport or earnest,
Since Calchas has once taken the Greek side
And foully lost his honor, I am sure
He will never dare come here again for shame.
And so that plan, for all I can perceive,
Is no more to be trusted than mere fancy.

"You'll see, too, that your father will cajole you
To marry someone. He knows how to talk,
And he'll so praise and represent some Greek
He'll ravish you with words, or make you do
By force what he demands. Then Troilus
Will die unpitied in his faithfulness,
And for no cause. Your father will despise us,
Moreover, and say this city is but lost,
And that the siege, because the Greeks have sworn it,
Will never be lifted till we have been slain
And our walls leveled. He will frighten you
So that my fear is you will stay with him.
Also you'll see so many a lusty knight
Among the Greeks, each with his heart and wit
Busy to please you, that you'll soon grow tired
Of simple Trojans, unless your truth or pity
Have power to trouble you. This is to me
A thought so grievous it will wrench my soul
Out of my breast. I cannot make myself
Think well about your going. A thousand times,
With humble and true heart, I beg you mercy.
Take pity on my sharp and bitter pain,
And do as I shall ask. Let's steal away,
We two, and think of what a folly it is,
When choice is given us, to lose the essential

In the accidental. This is what I mean:
Since we can steal away before the daybreak,
And be together so, then where would be
The wit in putting our safety to the test,
And finding out, by going to your father,
Whether you can come back again or not?
This is my point: it would be foolishness
To put that certainty of ours in danger.
And speaking vulgarly of wealth, we both
Can take sufficient with us for a life
Of honor and of pleasure till we die.
And in this way we can avoid all risk,
But every other way that you propose
My heart cannot subscribe to. Have no fear
Of any poverty, for I have friends
Elsewhere, who if we came in our bare shirts
Would never let us lack, but honor us
As long as we were with them. And let's go off
At once; for that, to my mind, will be best,
If you agree."

           Cressida, with a sigh,
Answered, "Dear heart, we can indeed steal off,
Just as you said, and take up with such new
Unprofitable ways; but afterwards
We shall be sorry. And as I hope that God
Will help me in my bitterest hour of need,
You suffer all this fear without a cause!
That day when I for love or fear of father
Or any other man, or for my pleasure,
Or for the sake of wealth or state or marriage,
Am false to you, my Troilus, my knight,
May Juno make me dwell like Athamas
Mad forever in Styx, the pit of hell!
And this I swear to you by every god
And every goddess in the span of heaven,
Each nymph and each infernal deity,

And by the fauns and satyrs, great and small,
Who are the half-gods of the wilderness.
May Atropos break off my thread of life
If I am false! Now trust me if you want!
And Simois, you, that like a shining arrow
Run evermore through Troy down to the sea,
Bear witness to the word that I say here,
That on the very day when I prove false
To Troilus, my own, my noble heart,
You shall return and flow back to your source
And I with body and soul sink down in hell.

   "As for the talk you made of going away
And leaving all your friends, may God forbid
That you for any woman should do so!
And all the more now Troy so much needs help.
Remember, too, if this were known, my life
Would hang in the balance, and your honor too.
And if a peace were brought about hereafter,
As always, after a quarrel, things come round
To pleasantness, why, Lord, the howl you'd make
Because for shame you couldn't come back again!
Before you risk your honor so, don't press
This rashness; haste is never in want of grief!
What do you think the people all around
Would say about it? That's easy enough to guess.
They'd say you were not driven to this deed
By love, but by the luxury of lust
And cowardice. Your honor, now so clear,
Would all be lost. And think of my good name,
Still in the flower; how foully I should stain it
If I went off with you. If I should live
To the world's end I'd never restore my name.
So quench this heat with reason. Patience triumphs,
Men say; he that will have his want must lose it.
So make a virtue of necessity
By patience. Remember that the lord of Fortune

Is he who does not waste his care upon her,
And she can frighten no one but a wretch.
And trust me, dear heart, when I say that truly
Before Apollo's sister, bright Diana,
Shall pass from Aries and beyond the Lion,
I will be here. So may the queen of heaven,
Juno, give me her help, on the tenth day
I'll see you without fail."

                   "If it be so,"
Said Troilus, "I will suffer out the time
Till the tenth day. But for the love of God
Let's privately steal off to live in quiet
Ever and ever. My heart says that is best."

   "Merciful God," she said, "what's this life worth?
Alas, you are killing me for very grief!
I see now that you have no faith in me.
For bright Diana's sake, do not distrust me
Without a cause. Remember it is wise
To spend a while sometimes to gain a while.
If only you knew how sore it makes me smart
You would put an end to this. The very spirit
Weeps is my heart, God knows, to see you weep
Whom I love best, and that I have to go
To the Greek camp. If I had not to my knowledge
A cure to help me come again, I'd die
Here where I am. But I am not so stupid,
Honestly, as not to contrive the means
Of coming back on the day that I have promised.
For who can hold a thing that will not stay?
Not my father, in spite of all his cunning!
And so with all my heart, and by the love
With which I love you, I beg, before I go,
That I may see you comforted and cheered
Enough to put my heart at rest, that now
Is on the point of breaking. And this too
I beg, since I am altogether yours:

Let no delight in any other woman,
While I am absent, drive me from your mind.
There is no lady in the world alive,
If you were faithless (as may God forbid!)
Who would be so betrayed and woebegone
As I; and so for God's love be not cruel!"

   Troilus answered, "God, from whom no cause
Is hidden, comfort me as in truth I never,
Since the first day I saw her with my eyes,
Was false to Cressida, and until I die
Shall never be so. I can say no more.
It will prove true on trial."

                    "Now blissful Venus
Keep me from dying," she said, "until I stand
At the point of pleasure where I can reward him
Who well deserves reward. For trust my word,
Neither your royal birth, nor vain delight,
Nor the prowess that you showed in war alone,
Nor pomp, nor wealth, nor worldly circumstances,
Made me take pity on you in distress,
But strength of virtue, founded upon truth—
That was the reason I first showed you mercy!
Your gentleness of heart and manhood, too,
And your contempt of all things, as I thought,
That savored of the vulgar, low desires,
And all discourtesy; and that your reason
Bridled your pleasure, this it was that made me,
Above all souls, your own. No length of years
Can undo this, nor Fortune in her changes
Deface it. But Jove, who has it in his power
To cheer the sorrowful, so favor us
That we may meet in ten nights at this place,
And your heart and my own be satisfied!
And now farewell, it is time for you to rise."

   After they had complained, and often kissed,
Clasped tight within each other's arms, the day

Began to dawn, and Troilus dressed himself
As one who felt the stroke of death fall cold.
Whether he suffered I hold is not a question,
For mortal head cannot conceive, nor thought
Consider nor tongue describe the cruel pains
Of this unhappy man, exceeding all
The torments down in hell. For when he saw
She could not stay, with soul torn from his breast
And with no further word, he left the chamber.

᪣᪣ ᪣᪣ ᪣᪣ ᪣᪣ ᪣᪣ ᪣᪣ ᪣᪣ ᪣᪣ ᪣᪣ ᪣᪣

Book V

On came the destiny that Jove commits
To you, the Parcae, you three fatal sisters,
To execute according to his will,
And by which Cressida must quit the town
While Troilus shall linger on in pain
Till Lachesis no longer spins his thread.
The golden-haired Apollo, high aloft,
Has three times by the brightness of his rays
Melted the snows, and Zephyr no less often
Brought back again the green and tender leaves
Since first the son of Hecuba the queen
Began to love her for whose sake came all
His grief; and in the morning she must go.

Diomede at the hour of prime was ready
To go with Cressida to the Greek encampment,
At which for sorrow she felt that her heart bled,
And in all truth, as may be found in books,
No woman ever known had half the care
Or left a city so reluctantly.

Troilus, who could see no scrap of counsel,
Still waited on his lady, as the root

And bud of all his joys and his desires.
But Troilus, good-by to all joy now,
For you shall never see her again in Troy!

    Truth is that while he waited in this fashion
He hid his anguish manfully, so well
It hardly could be noticed in his manner.
But at the gate through which she would ride out
He hovered, with a few souls, waiting for her,
So woebegone, although he would not show it,
That he could scarcely sit his horse for grief.
He shook with rage, his heart gnawed at him so,
When Diomede mounted, and asked himself, "Alas,
Why do I let myself endure so foul
A wretchedness? Why will I not redress it?
Were it not better to die all at once
Than to endure this constant languishing?
Why will I not give rich and poor alike
Enough to do before I let her go?
Why will I not throw all Troy in a turmoil?
And why not slay this Diomede as well?
Or why not rather with a man or two
Steal her away? Why do I bear with this?
Why can't I take my cure in my own hands?"

    But why he would not do so cruel a deed
Was for this reason; he always had at heart
A kind of terror that in such a brawl,
With all its rumors, Cressida would be slain.
Certainly, but for this, he would have done it.

    Cressida, when she was prepared to go,
Sighed sorrowfully, and said, "Alas!" But go
She must, whatever happened; and she rode
Slowly upon her way; there was no help.

    Troilus, in the guise of courtesy,
With hawk on hand, and a throng of knights about him,
Keeping her company, rode far beyond
The outlying valley, and would have gladly ridden

Farther, no doubt, and heavy it was for him
To turn so soon; but turn he had to do.
And just then from the Greek camp came Antenor,
And everyone was glad, and welcomed him.
Troilus, though his heart was far from light,
Exerted all his strength to keep at least
From weeping, and he made much of Antenor
And kissed him; then he had to take his leave.
Pitiably he looked at her, and rode
Close by to plead his case, and soberly
To take her hand. But Lord, how she began
To weep for tenderness! He spoke to her
Slyly and softly. "Now keep your day," he said,
"And do not kill me." Then he turned his horse,
His face pale; not a word to Diomede
He spoke, nor any of his company.

The son of Tydeus took due note of this,
As one who had done more than learn the creed
In such affairs. He took hold of her reins,
And Troilus went the homeward way to Troy.

This Diomede, who led her by the bridle,
When he perceived the Trojans gone, he thought:
"My work shall not be wasted if I can help it.
I'll try a word or two, for at the worst
It still can shorten our way. I have heard it said
A score of times and more, 'The man's a fool
Who will forget himself.' " But none the less
He reflected also, "It will go for nothing
To speak of love; for if she has in mind
The man I think, no doubt he won't be ousted
As soon as this. But I will find a way
So that she won't know what I mean as yet."

As one who knew well how to further himself,
Diomede talked of this and that, and asked
Why she appeared unhappy, and pleaded with her
That if he could contribute to her ease

In any way, she would give him her command
And he would do it. He swore that as a knight
Whatever he could do to ease her heart
He would attempt to do with all his power.

   "It will give pleasure to us Greeks," he said,
"To honor you, no less than to the Trojans.
I know you think it hard—no wonder so,
New to you as it is—to change acquaintance,
The Trojans for the Greeks you have never known.
But God forbid you should not find a Greek
Among us all as true as any Trojan
And no less kind. And since I took an oath
Just now to be your friend, and I'll have more
Acquaintance with you than another stranger,
I beg you, from now on, both day and night,
Command my service. Treat me as your brother,
Don't take offense at the friendship I have offered,
And if your grief, although I don't know why,
Is for great things, yet when more time has passed
My heart will take great joy in healing it.
And if your wrongs are past my power to right,
I am truly sorry for your heavy lot.

   "For though you Trojans have been many a day
Enraged against us Greeks, yet, truth to tell,
We both have served one god of love alike.
So, for the love of God, whomever you hate
Spare me your anger. Were we not so near
The tent of Calchas, who can see us both,
I'd let you know my whole mind about this;
But let it be sealed up for another day.
Give me your hand. I am, and ever shall be,
So help me God, yours while my life shall last.
I never said this before to woman born,
For I never loved a woman until now,
And never shall again. So for God's love,
Be not my foe, although I cannot plead

My case in the right terms, being yet to learn.
And do not wonder though I speak of love
So soon; for I have heard that many a man
Has loved a thing that he has never seen
In all his days. I have no power to strive
Against the god of love. I will obey him,
Always, begging your mercy. In this place
Are such deserving knights, and you so fair,
That every one of them will do his best
To win your grace. But could so fair a favor
Be mine as to have you take me for your servant,
None of them would so humbly and so truly
Serve you as I shall till the day I die."

    Cressida answered little to the purpose,
Oppressed with sorrow so that in effect
She did not hear his tale. She thought her heart
Would break in two for grief, for when far off
She spied her father, she began almost
To sink down from her horse. But none the less
She gave her thanks to Diomede for his trouble
And his good cheer, and for his proffered friendship,
And she accepted it, and would do gladly
What he found welcome, and would trust in him,
As well she might, she said. So she dismounted.

    Her father kissed his daughter twenty times
And took her in his arms, and said, "Dear daughter,
Welcome!" She said that she was glad to see him,
And meekly stood there with him, mute and mild.

    To Troy had come the unhappy Troilus
With sullen look and desperate face. Abruptly
He leaped down from his horse, and through his palace
Went to his room with swollen heart. He paid
No heed to anything, and no one dared
To speak a word to him. There to the griefs
He had repressed he gave a generous issue.

"Death!" he cried out, and in his frenzied throes
Cursed Jove, Apollo, Cupid, Ceres, Bacchus,
The Cyprian, and his birth, himself, his fate,
And nature, and excepting for his lady,
All creatures. To his bed he went, and there
Wallowed and rolled in fury as Ixion
Wallows in hell, continuing in this fashion
Almost till day. But then through tears his heart
Subsided somewhat, and he piteously
Complained for Cressida, and asked himself:
"Where is my lady? Where is her white breast?
Where is it? Where her arms and her clear eyes
That yesterday this very hour of night
Were with me? I can now weep many a tear
Alone, and grope about, but save a pillow
Find nothing here to clasp. What shall I do?
When will she come again? And why, alas,
I let her go is past my understanding!
Ah, would to God I had been slain right then!
My lady whom I love, and none besides,
Cressida, my sweet foe, to whom I leave
My heart forevermore, see how I die!
You will not rescue me! Who sees you now,
My star, my true north? Who sits in your presence
Or stands there now? And who can comfort now
The tumult of your heart? Now I am gone,
Who is received into your company?
Who speaks for me now, absent as I am?
No one, alas, and that is all my care!
For well I know you suffer no less than I.
How can I bear to wait for ten whole days
When on the first night I have all this pain?
And what will she do in her tenderness,
How will she bear such misery for me?
Ah, pitiful, pale, and green shall be your fresh
And womanly face before you come again!"

If he fell into a doze, he would begin
To mutter, and to dream of horrible things,
Finding himself alone in ghastly places,
Or in the midst of all his enemies
And helpless in their hands. His flesh would jump
And with a start he would suddenly awake,
Such tremors at his heart that for pure fear
His body quivered. With that he would cry out,
And feel as if he were falling from great heights,
And sorrow for himself so pitiably
His fantasies were wonderful to hear.
Again he would take comfort mightily,
And call it foolish to endure such dread
Without a reason, and then all over again
Begin his lamentations. Who could tell
Or properly describe his woe, his anguish?
Not all who are or ever were alive!
You, reader, can yourself well understand
That my poor wit cannot describe such pain.
Idle would be the toil I spent to write it
When thinking of it makes my wits grow weary.

In heaven as yet the stars could still be seen,
Although the moon had paled, and in the east
The clear horizon whitened, and soon after
Phoebus prepared to drive his rosy chariot
When Troilus sent out after Pandarus.
The whole preceding day this Pandarus
Could not have come, although he had sworn an oath
On penalty of his head; he had been with Priam,
The king. But in the morning he went off
To Troilus, when his friend had sent for him,
For in his heart he could guess well enough
That Troilus had not slept all night for sorrow
And would tell of his pain. As much as this
He knew without a book. He came at once
Into the chamber, and greeted Troilus

And soberly sat down with him on the bed.
  "My Pandarus, the sorrow I have borne
I can endure no longer," Troilus said.
"I know I shall not see another day.
And so I will describe to you the form
To follow at my burial; and my goods
You must dispose of just as you see fit.
Take care, dear brother, of the fire and flame
In which my body shall burn down to coals,
The feasting and the contests at my wake,
That they are suitable; and offer Mars
My horse, my sword, my helmet; give to Pallas
My shield that shines unstained; and of my heart
Take the burned powder, I beg you, and preserve it
In a vessel such as people call an urn,
A golden one, and give it to my lady
For love of whom I die. Do me the pleasure
Of asking her to keep it for remembrance.
For I know by my sickness and my dreams
Now and long since that I shall surely die.
The owl, that people call Ascalaphus,
These two nights has been hooting at me also.
Ah, Mercury, of my unhappy soul
Be now the guide, and fetch it when you will!"
  Pandarus answered, "Troilus, my dear friend,
I have told you long ago what folly it is
To grieve yourself this way, and for no reason.
I can say no more about it. But the man
Who heeds no counsel, I can see in him
No help except to leave him to his fancies.
But tell me now, I ask you, Troilus,
Whether you think that any man before
Has loved as much as you do? Yes, by God!
From many a knight his lady has been gone
A week or two, and no such fuss been made,
Not by the half. What need of all this frenzy,

Since you yourself can see, day in, day out,
A man must unavoidably be parted
From his love, or else his wife. Although he loves her
As he loves his own breath, he will not fight
Such battles with himself. For well you know
Friends cannot be together all the time.
What do these people do who see their loves
Married at the insistence of their friends,
As often happens, and bedded with their husbands?
God knows they take it wisely, fair and soft.
It is because good hope keeps up their spirits,
And since they can endure a time of sorrow,
As a time hurts them, so a time will heal.
That's how you should bear up. Let time slip by,
Try to be cheerful. Ten days are not so long
To wait, and since she promised you to come,
She will not break her word for any man.
She'll find a way to come again, don't fear.
I'll put my life on that. As for your dreams
And all such stuff and nonsense, drive them out;
They are the product of your melancholy
That gives you all this misery in your sleep.
A fig for all significance in dreams!
So help me God, I count them worth a straw!
What dreams may mean no man can truly say.
For in the temple the priests will tell you this,
That dreams are revelations of the gods,
And just as readily they'll say that dreams
Are devilish illusions. Doctors hold
They come from states and humors of the body,
From gluttony or fasting. Who in fact
Knows what they signify? Others will say
That through impressions, when men have a thing
Much in their minds, these visions will result;
And others, as they find in books, maintain
That men dream by the seasons of the year

Or the influence of the moon. But trust no dream,
There's nothing in it. Leave dreams to old women,
And also all these auguries of birds,
The boding raven and the hooting owl
For fear of which men think that they will die.
It's false and wicked, both, to give them credit.
Alas, that such a noble creature as man
Should fear such rubbish! Get up, we'll talk about
The gay life we have led in Troy, we'll drive
The time away, and we'll delight ourselves
Over the coming time that quickly now
Shall bring our comfort. This town is full of people,
The truce is lasting all the while. Let's go
And visit Sarpedon and join the crowd
That frolics there, only a mile away.
Get up now, Troilus. Trust me in one thing,
If you lie here this way a day or two,
People will think that you are feigning sickness
Because you are a coward, and don't dare rise!"

Troilus answered, "Those who have suffered pain
Know this: it is no wonder if a man
Who smarts in every nerve is far from cheerful.
And if I am lamenting all the time,
It's not my fault, for I have lost the cause
Of all my joy. But since get up I must,
Get up I will as soon as ever I can.
And God, to whom I consecrate my heart,
Send us the tenth day quickly! Never a bird
Has been so glad for May as I shall be
When she returns to Troy! But where do you think
We can best amuse ourselves?"

                                    "I say, by God,"
Said Pandarus, "we should visit Sarpedon."

They talked this matter over at great length,
Till Troilus at last agreed to rise
And off they set.

           Now Sarpedon, as a man
Both honorable and generous all his life,
Set such a table day by day, supplied
With every delicacy, though at great cost,
That such magnificence, as all agreed,
Had never graced a banquet till that time.
Nor is there in the world an instrument
Lovely of breath or touch of string, as far
As foot has gone or tongue can tell or heart
Record, but it was heard in harmony
Accompanying that feast; nor ever had eyes
Looked on so fair a group of ladies dancing.

  But what was this to Troilus, who for sorrow
Cared nothing for it all? His busy heart
Sought always and alike for one thing only,
His lady, Cressida. On her was ever
The thought of his whole heart, now this, now that
Imagining so eagerly that no feast
Could give him pleasure. The ladies who were there,
In the absence of his lady, it was his grief
To see them or to hear their instruments.
When she who held his heart's key was away
His feeling was that no one had the right
To make a sound of music. Day or dark,
No hour went by when none could overhear him
But he would say, "Ah, in your loveliness,
Lady, how have you fared since you were here?
Welcome, dear heart, in truth!" But it was all
A maze he wandered in. Fortune intended
To fit him with a better fool's cap still!

  From noon to morning he would read alone
A hundred times her letters of old days,
Within his heart repicturing her shape,
Her womanhood, her every word and act.
And so he drove the fourth day to an end,
And said that he would go. "Dear Pandarus,

Do you mean that we should stay till Sarpedon
Dismisses us? We ought to take our leave.
For God's sake, let's go home when evening comes!
For on my word, I will not stay here so."

"Have we come hither only to fetch fire,"
Pandarus answered, "and run home again
Before it cools? God help me, I don't know
Where any man will be more glad to see us
Than Sarpedon. And if we go away
So suddenly, I hold it will be rude,
Seeing we told him that we'd stay a week;
And if we took our leave on the fourth day,
He'd wonder at it, certainly! Let's keep
Our purpose firm, and since you promised him
To spend a while, hold on, and then we'll go."

Thus in his misery Pandarus made him stay,
And when the week was up they said good-by
To Sarpedon, and hurried to return.

"Now," Troilus said, "may the Lord give me grace
At my homecoming to find that Cressida
Is here again," and he began to sing.

"Yes, yes, still chasing bubbles," Pandarus thought,
And said to himself, "The heat of all this frenzy
Will have time to cool down before this Calchas
Lets Cressida come back to Troilus!"
But still he joked, and swore his heart confirmed
That she would come as soon as ever she could.

When they had reached the palace, they dismounted
And took their way to the chamber, where they talked
Until the darkness came of Cressida.
And afterward from supper went to rest.

Next morning, when the day began to brighten,
Troilus woke, and said to Pandarus,
"For the love of God, why don't we go and see
Cressida's house? We have nothing else to do,
We can see her house at least."

To blind suspicion,
He found some cause for going into town,
And they set out. But Lord, what wretchedness
This innocent Troilus felt! He thought his heart
Would break in two, for when he saw her doors
All barred, he nearly tumbled down for grief!
Beholding every window shut, his heart
Grew cold as frost. With deathly countenance
He passed by speechless, and began to ride
At such a clip that no one saw his face.
"O palace empty and disconsolate,"
He said, "O house once worthiest of the name
Among all houses, lamp of which the beam
Has been extinguished, house that once was day
And now is night, surely you ought to fall
And I to perish, for she who governed us
Has gone away! O palace once the crown
Among all dwellings, lit by the sun of bliss,
O ring from which the ruby has been lost,
O cause of grief that once brought happiness,
I should be glad, since I can do no better,
To kiss your cold doors, but for all these people.
Ah, farewell, shrine from which the saint is absent!"
   With this he turned his eyes on Pandarus,
And when he saw his time, riding about,
Made known his new grief and his former joys
With such a deathly face that any man
Might well have pitied him. So up and down
He rode, and as he passed familiar places
Where once he had had his pleasure to the full,
Each joy came back to him in memory.
"There last I saw my lady dance; there first
With her clear eyes she caught me, in that temple.
There I have heard her laugh out heartily,
And there I saw her once when she was playful,
And yonder once she said to me, 'Now sweet,

Love me well,' and yonder she looked at me
With such a goodly look that to the death
My heart is grateful. In that corner house
I heard her sing with such a womanly voice,
So clear and true, that in my soul it seems
I can still hear the sound. In yonder place
My lady took me first into her favor."

   And then he thought, "O Cupid, blessed lord,
When I recall how you have warred on me
At all turns, men could make a book about it
As if it were a story. Why do you need
To triumph over me, since I am yours
And wholly at your will? What joy do you take
In slaughtering your own people? Well have you wreaked
Your anger upon me, you mighty god
And dreadful to provoke! Have mercy on me!
You know well that of all delights I crave
Your favor most, and I will live and die
A member of your faith, for which I ask
But one reward, that you will quickly send
Cressida home to me! Constrain her heart
As eagerly to come as you do mine
To long for her, for well I know that then
She will not linger. Deal not with Trojan blood
As cruelly, I beg, as Juno did
With the blood of Thebes, for which the Theban people
Fell under her destruction."

                After this
He went out to the gates where Cressida
Had ridden away, and there walked back and forth
Many a turn, and said, "Alas, from here
My joy, my comfort rode! Now would to God
That I might see her come again to Troy!
I took her yonder over to that hill,
And there I said good-by. From there I watched her
Ride to her father, for which my heart will break,

And hither I came home when it was evening,
And here I live, cast out from all delight,
And shall, until I see her again in Troy."

Often he fancied that he was disfigured,
And pale and shrunken, and that people whispered,
"What can the trouble be? Has anyone guessed
Why Troilus is in the dumps this way?"
But it was only from his melancholy
That he conceived such notions of himself.

At other times he took it into his head
That every one who passed was pitying him
And saying, "I am sorry, indeed I am,
That Troilus is going to die." And thus
He wore out still another day or two
Between his hopes and fears. In songs it pleased him
To trace the reason for his miseries,
As best he could, and so he made a song,
No more than a few words, to lighten somewhat
His heavy heart. With no one near to see him,
He sang with soft voice of his absent lady:

*"O star, of whom I have wholly lost the light,
With bitter heart well may I now bewail,
Since ever in dark torment, night by night,
Running before the wind, toward death I sail;
For which if on the tenth night I should fail
To find your guiding beam by even an hour,
My ship and me Charybdis will devour."*

When he had sung this song, he fell again
To sighing as of old, and every night
He stood where he could watch the shining moon
And told her all his sorrows. "When your horns
Are new," he said, "then I'll be glad in truth,
If the world is faithfull. I noticed your old horns
In the morning when my lady rode away.

Ah, bright Diana, run fast around your circle,
For when your horns are waxing new again,
Then she shall come who can bring back my bliss!"

It seemed to him there was more of every day
And every night was longer than its wont.
The sun went round its course improperly
And took a longer path. "I fear," he said,
"That Phaëton, the sun's son, is alive,
And drives his father's chariot amiss."

He walked the walls, and saw the Greek encampment,
And said to himself, "There yonder is my lady,
Or yonder, where the tents are. And from there
This breeze is coming, so soft that in my soul
I feel it gives me help. Surely this wind
That by the moment on my face increases
More and more is the breath of her deep sighs.
This is my proof, that in no other place
In the whole town except this very spot
Do I feel a wind that sounds so much like sorrow.
It says, 'Alas, why must we two be parted?' "

And thus he drove the weary time away
Until at last the ninth night had gone by.
Pandarus was beside him all the while,
Doing his best in every way he knew
To comfort him, giving him constant hope
That with the tenth day she would end his sorrow.

Among the turbulent Greeks was Cressida,
Where women were but few. Often enough
She cried, "Alas, that ever I was born!
My heart may well desire my death, for now
I have outlived my time. I cannot help it,
Alas, for this is worse than ever I thought!
My father will not let me go again
For anything. I cannot gain his favor.
And should it be that I outstay my time,

My Troilus in his heart will think me false,
And so it may well seem. Thus I shall meet
With nothing but reproach wherever I turn.
And if I take the risk of stealing away
By night, and should I happen to be caught,
I should be taken for a spy; or else—
And this is my worst fear—if I should fall
Into some villain's hands, then I'd be lost
No matter how I may be true at heart.
Almighty God, have pity on my sorrow!"

 Her bright face had grown pale, and her limbs thin,
For all the livelong day, whenever she dared,
She stood and watched the place where she was born
And where she had always lived; and all the night
She lay and wept, and so she led her life
Despairing of all help, this wretched woman.
Often she sighed, and always went about
Picturing to herself the worthiness
Of Troilus, and remembering all his words
Since that first day her love began to spring;
And so she set her woeful heart on fire
By keeping what she longed for in remembrance.
In all the world there is no heart so hard
That hearing her lament would not have wept!
She did not need to borrow tears! And this
In all her sorrow was the sharpest point:
Her pain had none in whom she dared confide.

 Sadly she looked on the high towers of Troy.
"Alas," she said, "the pleasures and delights,
All turned now into gall, that I have had
Often within those gates! O Troilus,
What are you doing now? Lord, do you think,"
She cried, "of Cressida still? Had I but taken
The counsel that you gave, and gone with you,
I should not now be sighing half so sorely!
Who could have said that I had done amiss

To steal away with such a one as he?
But all too late the medicine reaches him
Whose corpse is being carried to the grave.
Too late to talk about the matter now!
Ah, prudence, I had always lacked, alas,
Before I came here, one of your three eyes!
For well I could remember time gone by,
And also present time I could see clearly,
But future time, before the trap had caught me,
I could not see; that is my sorrow now,
But none the less, let happen what will happen,
I shall tomorrow night, by east or west,
At one point or another, steal away
Out of this army, and go with Troilus
Wherever he likes. This purpose I will hold.
No matter for the gossip of lewd tongues,
For love was ever the envy of the mean.
The man who scruples over every word
Or rules himself by everyone's advice
Will never prosper, for the very thing
That some consider wrong, others uphold.
In these diversities, I say for one
That happiness is my sufficiency.
So, wasting no more words, I'll go to Troy,
For that is my decision."

                    But God knows,
Before two months were out, she was far away
From that intention. Troilus and Troy
Shall slip alike unknotted through her heart;
She will resolve to stay.

                    This Diomede
Now spends his time debating in himself
With all his cunning how with least delay
To catch the heart of Cressida in his net.
With this ambition he was never done;
Fishing for her, he laid out hook and line.

But in his heart he none the less believed
That she was not without a love in Troy,
For he had never since he brought her thence
Seen her once laugh or make a moment's cheer.
He did not know how best to soothe her heart.
"But still," he said, "to try will cost me nothing.
The man who never tries will never succeed."
And yet he thought, "Mustn't I be the fool,
Knowing she sorrows for another's love,
To try her now? I ought to understand
It will not help; wise heads have said in books,
'Never make love to anyone in sorrow.'
But if he won a flower such as she
From him for whom she mourns both day and night,
A man might call himself a conqueror."
And bold as always, he thought within himself,
"Whatever happens, I shall probe her heart
For life or death. I can only lose my trouble."

This Diomede, as we are told in books,
Was prompt in his undertakings, full of mettle,
Square-limbed and gruff-voiced, headstrong and
        powerful,
And valorous, like Tydeus, his father.
Some also say that he was loose of tongue;
And he was heir of Calydon and Argos.

Cressida was but moderately tall,
And in her face and figure and all her ways
No fairer creature could have lived than she.
Often she went about with her bright hair
Braided down by her collar behind her back
And bound by a thread of gold. She had no blemish,
By all I know, save that her eyebrows met.
As for her clear eyes, truly, those who saw her
Have written that paradise in her eyes took form.
And ever with the riches of her beauty
Love strove within her always to decide

Which of them should be greater. She was prudent,
Demure, and simple in manner, and well spoken,
Perfect in education, dignified,
Affectionate, gay, and generous; never wanting
In pity; tender-hearted and inconstant.
But what her age was, truly, I cannot tell!

    And Troilus in stature was well grown,
His figure so completely in proportion
That nature could not have improved upon it;
Young, strong, and lusty, hardy as a lion,
As true as steel in every quality,
One of the best endowed among all men
Who live or ever shall live, while the world lasts.
And certainly it is found in all the records
That Troilus was never in his time
Second to any in daring to do all
The duty of a knight. Although a giant
Might have surpassed him in brute strength, his heart
Stood equal with the first and with the best
In daring to accomplish his desires.

    On the tenth day since Cressida left Troy,
This Diomede, fresh as a branch in May,
Came to the tent where Calchas had his quarters
And feigned some business with him. Cressida
Gave him her welcome and sat down beside him,
And it was easy enough to make him stay!
Spices and wine were put before them soon,
And they began to talk of this and that
As friends do. First he spoke about the war
Between them and the people of Troy town,
And asked her what she thought about the siege;
And from that question he went on to ask
Whether she thought Greek ways and customs odd,
And why her father waited for so long
To marry her to some deserving man.
Cressida, in the pains of her strong love

For Troilus, answered as best she could;
It seemed she did not know what he intended.
Diomede none the less plucked up his courage,
And said, "If I have understood you rightly,
It seems to me, my lady, Cressida,
That since I first laid hands upon your bridle
When in the morning you came out from Troy,
I have never seen you yet except in sorrow.
Now what the cause may be I cannot say,
Unless it might be for some Trojan's love,
Which would for my part be a grievous thought,
That you should shed a quarter of a tear
For any soul there, or deceive yourself
In such a wretched way; for past all question
It isn't worth your while. The people of Troy,
As everyone says, and you yourself observe,
Are shut in prison, nor shall a single one
Come out alive, for all the gold there is
Between the sun and sea. Take my word for it,
And understand me: not a one shall go
Alive in mercy, although he were the lord
Over ten worlds, for we shall so avenge
Their theft of Helen before we leave this place
The very Manes, who are gods of pain,
Shall live in terror lest the Greeks destroy them;
And men will dread from now till the world's end
Ever again to carry off a queen,
So cruel our vengeance on them shall appear.
Unless it proves that Calchas leads us on
With ambiguities and sly double meanings,
The kind of talk that men call two-faced words,
You shall discover that I do not lie,
And see all this with your own eyes at once,
You will not know how soon. Consider well;
That is the thing to do. What! Do you fancy
That your wise father would have given Antenor

For you immediately unless he had known
The city would be razed? No, as I live!
He knew full well no Trojan should escape,
And for his very terror did not dare
To let you live there longer. What will you have
Beyond this, lovely lady? Troy and Trojans
Dismiss out of your heart! That bitter hope
Renounce! Be happy, and resume again
The beauty of that face you so disfigure
With salty tears. For Troy is in such danger
That nothing now can save it. And be sure
That you shall find before long with the Greeks
A love that is more perfect and more kind
Than any Trojan, one who will spend his strength
To serve you better; and if you will vouchsafe,
Dear lady, I myself will be your servant,
Yes, rather than be lord of Greece twelve times!"
    With this he reddened, and faltered in his voice
A little, and turned his head aside a little,
And stopped a moment, and afterward recovered
And soberly regarded her, and said,
"I am, although it may give you no pleasure,
As nobly born as any man in Troy;
For if my father, Tydeus, had lived,
I should have been a king already," he said,
"Of Calydon and Argos, Cressida.
And so I hope in fact I shall be still.
But he was killed too soon, alas, at Thebes,
Polynices and many a man as well,
More's the pity. But since I am yours, dear heart,
And you the first whose grace I ever sought
To serve you ever as truly as I can
While I have room to live, grant me at least
Before I go that I may come tomorrow
To speak at greater leisure of my pain."
    Why should I set down every word he uttered?

The tale he told was plenty for one day.
He spoke to such effect that Cressida
Consented on the morrow, at his desire,
To talk with him at least, if he would say
No more about such matter. Distantly
She said to him, as one whose heart was fixed
So fast on Troilus that none could move it:
"O Diomede, I love that selfsame place
Where I was born. Jupiter in his kindness
Deliver it soon from all that gives it care!
Almighty God, protect it! I know well
The Greeks, if so they can, will vent their wrath
On Troy; but it shall not happen as you say,
No, before God! I know my father's wisdom,
And since he bought me at so dear a price,
As you have said, I am bound to him the more.
And that the Greeks are noble in descent
I well know too; but certainly in Troy
As worthy people may be found, as perfect,
Clever, and kind as any there may be
From India to the Orkneys. I know too
That you could serve your lady well enough
To win her thanks, indeed. But as for love,
The lord who was my husband had my heart
Entirely, till he died; and other love,
So help me Pallas, is not and never was
Within my heart. I have often heard it said
That you come of a high and noble lineage,
And that is just what makes me wonder so
Why you should have such scorn for any woman.
God knows that love and I are far apart!
I am more disposed to grieve until my death.
What I may later do, I cannot tell;
As yet it does not please me to be gay.
My heart at present is in tribulation,
And you are busy fighting day by day.

Later, perhaps, when you have won the town,
When I see what I never yet have seen,
I may do what I never yet have done!
This word should satisfy you for the moment.
Tomorrow I shall gladly talk with you,
As long as you don't bring this matter up;
And when you like, you may come here again.
I'll say this much to you, before you go:
So help me Pallas with her shining hair,
If ever I should take pity on a Greek,
It would be on yourself. I do not say
That I will love you, nor do I say I won't;
Only that I mean well, by God above!"

   She cast her eyes down, and began to sigh,
And said, "O town of Troy, I still pray God
That I may see you happy and at peace,
Or else that he will cause my heart to break!"

   But in effect, to put the matter briefly,
This Diomede began all over again
To urge his case, and plead with her for mercy.
And truth to tell, he later took her glove,
At which he was much pleased; and finally,
When evening came, and all was favorable,
He said good-by.

                         Venus in all her brightness
Followed and showed the broad path where Apollo
Made his descent, and Cynthia urged on
Her chariot steeds to whirl out of the Lion
While all the zodiac showed its glittering candles
When in her father's fair tent Cressida
Went to her bed, always within her mind
Turning over and over again the words
This sudden Diomede had said to her,
His great position, the peril of the town,
And how she was alone and needed friends.
Thus, truth to tell, began to breed the reason

Why she made up her mind that she would stay.
   Day came (to tell my tale religiously)
And Diomede came to Cressida. In brief,
And lest you turn your backs upon my story,
He spoke to such advantage for himself
That all those bitter sighs of hers he solaced,
And stole away the chief part of her pain.
She later gave him back the fair bay steed,
The story tells us, that he had taken once
From Troilus; and she gave him, too, a brooch
That had belonged to Troilus—of that
There was little need!—and for his comfort also
She made him wear, as a token from his lady,
Part of her sleeve. And elsewhere in the records
I find, too, that when Diomede was wounded
By Troilus through the body, then she wept
Many a tear, seeing his wide wounds bleed,
And that she took good care of him. They say
That for the healing of his pain, she gave
Her heart to him—I do not know; but truly,
There never was woman, as the story tells us,
More grieved when she played false to Troilus.

   "Alas, clean gone now is my name," she said,
"For constancy in love, forever more!
I have been false to one among the noblest
That ever lived! No good word will be said
Or sung, alas, of me, to the world's end.
Books will revile me. Oh, I shall be rolled
On many a tongue! The bells of the whole world
Will ring my infamy, and most of all
Women will hate me! Ah me, for such misfortune!
They'll say that I have done the very best
I could, alas, to bring them in dishonor.
And though I am not the first who has done amiss,
How will that help to take away my blame?
But since I see there is no better way,

And that it is too late now to be sorry,
To Diomede at least I will be true.
But Troilus, since I can do no better,
And we have thus been parted, you and I,
Still I pray God, may all be well with you
As one who was the noblest, in all truth,
I ever saw, and faithfulest to keep
His lady's honor."

          And with that word she wept.
"I'll never think of you with hate, be sure;
And friendly love, that you shall have from me,
And my good word, though I should live forever.
And I shall grieve to see you in misfortune,
Truly; and not through any fault of yours
I leave you, well I know. But all things pass,
And so I say good-by."

          How long it was
Before she gave him up for Diomede
No writer, to my knowledge, has informed us.
Go, study the books. Take notice what they say—
You will not find the term there, never fear;
For though he lost no time in wooing her,
Yet there was more to do before he won.
Nor do I care to chide this hapless woman
Further than the story itself demands.
Her name, alas, has been so widely punished
That it should be sufficient for her guilt.
And if I could excuse her in any way,
She was so sorry for her faithlessness
Indeed I would excuse her still for pity.

  This Troilus, as I have said already,
Wore out the time as best he could. His heart
Was often hot and cold, especially
On that ninth night when she had promised him
To come back on the morrow. Little rest

He had that night, God knows; the thought of sleep
Gave him no pleasure.
                         Phoebus, laurel-crowned,
Began, as he went upward in his path,
To warm the wet waves of the sea to eastward,
And the lark, Nisus' daughter, freshly sang
When Troilus sent after Pandarus.
They whiled away their time on the town walls
Looking for any sign of Cressida
That they might see. Till it was noon they stood there,
Watching whoever came; and everyone,
No matter of what sort, who came in sight
From far away, they said that it was she
Until they knew for certain who it was.
First he was heavy at heart, then light again,
And thus this Troilus and Pandarus
Stood there hoodwinked, and staring after nothing.

   Troilus said to Pandarus at length,
"For all I know, before noon, certainly,
Cressida won't be coming back to town.
She has enough to do just slipping away
From her old father, that's what I believe.
No doubt he'll make her eat before she goes,
God wring his heart!"
                         "True enough," Pandarus answered.
"It may be as you say. Therefore, I beg,
Let's go and have a bite to eat ourselves.
This afternoon you can come back again."

   And home they go, and back they come; but long
May they stand gaping there before they find
What they are seeking. Fortune is resolved
To make fools of them both!
                         Said Troilus,
"I see now she has tarried for so long
With her old father that before she comes
It will be almost evening. Come along,

I'm going to the gate. These gatekeepers
Are always lunkheads, and on some excuse
I'm going to make them hold up the portcullis,
However late she is."

> The day goes fast
And after that the evening comes, but still
Cressida does not come to Troilus.
He peered at hedges, peered at trees and thickets,
Craning his neck far outward over the wall,
And finally he turned and said, "By God,
I know now, Pandarus, what she means to do!
My griefs almost began again, for certain!
But never doubt this lady knows what's best.
I think she plans to ride home secretly,
And I commend her wisdom, on my word.
She will not have the people gawking at her
Foolishly when she comes, but on the quiet
She means to ride into the town, by night.
And please don't think it tedious to wait.
We've nothing else to do, you know, dear brother.
And Pandarus, will you believe me now?
Take my word for it, I see her! There she is!
Lift up your eyes and look, man! Can't you see?"

Pandarus answered, "No, as I hope to live!
All wrong, by God! What are you saying, man?
Where are you, anyway? All I see there
Is just some traveler's wagon."

> "You are right,"
Said Troilus. "But still, it's not for nothing
That I feel such a joy now in my heart.
I can't help thinking it must be for good.
I don't know why, but never since I was born
Have I felt such assurance. Come she will,
Tonight—I'll dare to stake my life on that!"

Pandarus answered, "It may be, true enough,"
Agreeing with him in everything he said,

But in his heart he softly laughed, and thought
Soberly to himself, "What! Out of nowhere,
The hazelwood where jolly Robin played,
Shall come all that you stand here waiting for.
Yes, farewell all the snows of yesteryear!"
  The warden of the gates began to call
Those left outside to drive their cattle in
Or stay there for the night. And Troilus,
Deep in the night, rode home and wept the while,
For well he saw it would not help to wait.
But none the less he cheered himself by thinking
That he had wrongly reckoned up his day.
"I have misunderstood, that's all," he said.
"For on the last night Cressida was with me,
She said, 'I shall be here, if I can do it,
Before the moon has passed beyond the Lion
From Aries,' and she still can keep her promise."
He went in the morning to the gate, and walked
Up and down on the walls for many a turn,
Both east and west, but it was all for nothing;
His hope still blinded him. And so at night,
In sorrow and in sighing, he went home.
His hope took flight, clean gone out of his heart.
He had nothing now to hang on any longer.
But in his pain he thought his heart was bleeding,
So mighty were his throes. For when he saw
How long she stayed away, he did not know
What he should make of it, since she had broken
Her promise to him. The third day and the fourth,
The fifth day and the sixth, after those ten
Of which I have told, his heart turned first to hope
And then to fear, for still he trusted somewhat
In her first promises. But when he found
She would not keep her term, he saw no help
Except to plan how he might quickly die.
With this the wicked spirit, God defend us,

That men have called mad jealousy began
To worm its way inside him; for which reason,
Because his heart was set on dying soon,
He neither ate nor drank for melancholy,
And he refused all company as well.
This was the life that all the while he led.
He was so changed that people were hard put
To know him in the places where he went;
So lean and pale and feeble that he used
A staff to walk with. In his anger thus
He brought himself to ruin, and if questioned,
He said his trouble lay about his heart.
Priam many a time, his mother too,
His brothers and his sisters also asked him
What caused his pain and why he was unhappy,
But all for nothing; he would not let them know,
But said he felt a grievous malady
About his heart, and would be glad to die.

So one day, lying down to sleep, it happened
That as he slept, he dreamed that he was walking
Deep in a forest, weeping for love of her
Who gave him this distress. And in his dream,
As he searched up and down amid the forest,
He came upon a boar who with great tusks
Lay sleeping in the warmth of the bright sun.
And by this boar, fast folded in his arms,
Lay, kissing him, his lady Cressida.
In grief, when he beheld it, he awoke,
And cried out loud to Pandarus, and said,
"O Pandarus, now I know it, root and branch!
I am no better than dead; there's no help now.
My lady has betrayed me, Cressida,
In whom I put my trust above all souls.
Now she has given her heart away elsewhere.
The blessed gods, in their almighty power,
Have showed me what the truth is in my dream.

As I was dreaming, I saw Cressida—"
And he described it all to Pandarus.

   "Ah, Cressida, what plot, what change of heart,
What beauty, what dark science—what just cause
Have you against me? What dread experience,
What fault of mine has stolen your thoughts away?
Who is it that has robbed me of Cressida,
My sun of joy? Why did I not prevent
Your going off, at which I was almost
Beside myself? Who now will ever believe
In any oath again? But who, if he likes,
Can better deceive than he that is most trusted?
What shall I do, Pandarus? I feel now
So new and sharp a pain that it were better
To slay myself at once with my own hands
Than grieve forever. Through my death my woe
Would have an end, while I disgrace myself
With every day of life."

                  Pandarus answered,
"Alas that I was born! Haven't I told you
Already that dreams make fools of many a man?
Why? Because people interpret them all wrong!
How do you dare to say your lady is false
Because of any dream? Forget this notion;
You haven't the art of understanding dreams.
As for the dream you had about this boar,
It may mean that her father, who is old
And grizzled too, is lying in the sun
On the point of death, and she for grief is crying
And kissing him as he lies there on the ground.
That is the way you ought to read your dream!"

   "What could I do, then," Troilus demanded,
"No matter how little, to be sure of this?"

   "Now you are talking sense," Pandarus answered.
"My counsel, since you write so well, is this—
Write her a letter quickly; by this means

You'll learn the truth where now you are in doubt.
Consider why: I dare say this for certain,
That if she is untrue, I can't believe
She will write back again, and if she writes,
You'll soon learn whether she has any chance
To come again; or if she's being prevented,
She will, by some phrase, let you know the reason.
You haven't written her since she went away,
Nor has she written you. I'll hazard this:
There may be such a reason in her mind
That you yourself will say her tarrying there
Is best for both of you. Write, then, and learn
The whole truth soon. There's nothing else to do."

The two agreed at once in this conclusion.
Troilus quickly sat down, and at heart
Considered how he might express his woe
To best effect, and said as you shall hear:

"Fresh flower, to whom I have been and shall be
Forever your own in body, life, and thought,
I, woeful man, humbly as tongue can speak,
As many times as there are motes in space
Commend myself to you and your high favor.
May it please you, sweet, to think how long ago
You left me, when you went, in bitter pain,
For which with fearful and with faithful heart
I write, as one whom sorrow drives to write,
Complaining as I dare and as I can
With blotted words, that you may know what tears
Rain from my eyes, and if they could, would speak.
First I beseech you that you will not hold
Your clear eyes blemished if they look on this,
And for my cares' sake, that destroy my wits,
If anything that is amiss escapes me,
Forgive it! If any servant dared or ought
Rightly against his lady to complain,
Then I believe that I should be the man,

Seeing that you have tarried for two months
When in all truth you said that you would stay
No more than ten days there amid the army—
And yet in two months you have not returned!
But inasmuch as all that pleases you
Must needs please me, I dare complain no more,
Only desiring day by day to know,
If it should be your will, how you have been
And done while you were there; whose happiness
May God increase, and grant what you desire
As truly as in all things I am true
To you, my lady. And if it pleases you
To know how I have fared, I say no more
Except that at the writing of this letter
I was alive, the cabinet of all cares,
Ready to drive my woeful spirit out.
But I delay, and put him off awhile
To see what matter you may have to send us.
My eyes, with which I see in vain, are springs
Of sorrowful salt tears; my song, a plaint
Against adversity; my good is harm,
My comfort turned to hell, my joy is woe;
I can tell nothing else but that all joys
Have been transformed into their opposites,
Which by your coming home again to Troy
You can redress, and by a thousand times
Increase my joy more than I ever knew.
For never was heart so glad to beat with life
As I when I shall see you. And if pity
Leaves you unmoved, remember still your truth.
Or if I have through fault deserved my death,
Or if you never wish to see me more,
Yet in reward for the service I have tendered
Write me, I beg, for the love of God, that death
May end my struggle. If some other cause
Compels you to remain, then with your letter

Give me some comfort. Your absence is to me
A hell, but I will bear my woe with patience
And draw hope from your letter. Write me, sweet;
By hope or death deliver me from pain.
When next you see me, my dear heart, in truth
I have so lost my health that Cressida
Will not know how to tell me from another.
For I so thirst to see your beauty again
That I can scarcely keep myself alive.
I say no more, though I have more to tell you
Than I can say. But though you save or slay me,
I pray God still, may all go well with you.
In you, when it shall please you, lies the day
My grave shall clothe me, in you my life, in you
The power to rescue me from every pain.
And now farewell, dear heart.

> Your Troilus."

This letter was dispatched to Cressida,
To which her answer in effect was this:
Compassionately she wrote to him, and said
That she would come as soon as ever she could
To mend all that was wrong; and finally
She wrote that she would come, but knew not when.
But in her letter she swore she loved him best
And made so much of him it was a marvel.
He found in all of it but promises
That had no bottom. Now, Troilus, you may go
And whistle through your fingers, if you like!
So runs the world! God shield us from misfortune
And prosper all whose hearts are set on truth!

By day and night increased the wretchedness
This Troilus felt at Cressida's delay.
His hope and strength diminished; he lay down
In bed, and neither ate nor drank nor slept,
Nor spoke a single word, imagining
Incessantly that she had proved unfaithful;

And with this thought he nearly lost his senses.

The dream of which I have already spoken
Would never leave his mind. He was convinced
That he had lost his lady, and that Jove
Had showed him by his providence in sleep
The evidence of her inconstancy
And his misfortune, and he thought the boar
Had been revealed to serve him as a symbol.
On this account he called his sister to him,
Cassandra, and to her told all his dream,
Begging her to solve the enigma for him
Presented by this boar with the stout tusks.

The prophetess, Cassandra, after a moment,
Interpreted his dream. But first she smiled,
And said, "Dear brother, if you want to know
The truth about all this, you'll have to hear
A few old stories of how ancient lords
Were overthrown by Fortune; by this means
Quickly enough you'll recognize this boar
And of what line he comes.

                                   "Enraged against
The Greeks, who would not do her sacrifice,
Diana took a marvelous cruel vengeance,
For by a boar as great as a stalled ox
She caused their corn and vines to be devoured.
To slay this boar the country rose as one,
Among whom came, to see the boar, a maid
Praised as hardly another was on earth.
And Meleager, the lord of all that land,
So loved this maid that summoning his manhood
He slew this boar and sent the head to her.
And from this lord descended Tydeus."

She told how on behalf of Polynices
Tydeus laid claim to Thebes; how seven kings
Besieged the city all about; and down
From struggles and feats of arms long past she came

To Diomede. "This boar of which you dreamed
Signifies Diomede, son of Tydeus,
Who comes down by descent from Meleager.
Your lady, wheresoever she may be,
Diomede has her heart, and she has his.
Weep if you will, or stop. There is no question
This Diomede is in, and you are out."

    "You are not telling the truth, you sorceress,"
He cried, "with your false spirit of prophecy!
You are a great diviner, so you think—
Now isn't it plain that this incredible fool
Is trying her best to spread lies about women?
Get out! Jove wring your heart! You will be false
Yourself, most likely, by tomorrow morning!
You might as well tell lies about Alcestis,
The kindest and the best among all souls
That ever were, unless men have deceived us,
For when her husband was in danger of death,
She chose to die for him, as the books tell us,
And die she did at once!"

                     Cassandra left,
And he forgot his sorrows in his rage
At what she said. He sprang up suddenly,
As if some doctor had made him whole and sound,
And day by day he sought with all his care
To find out what the truth of it might be.

    Fortune, to whom the providence of Jove
Commits the permutations of events
When power from one people to another
Must be transferred, or realms must be struck down,
Began to pluck the bright plumes of the Trojans
From day to day till they were bare of joy.
Amid all this, the end of Hector's term
Drew quickly near. The fates willed that his soul
Should be disbodied, and contrived the means
To drive it out, against which destiny

Availed him not at all, but on a day
He went to fight, and caught, alas, his death.
It seems to me that every sort of man
Who follows arms ought to lament his death
Who was so noble a knight; for as he dragged
A king by the mouthpiece, unaware of this
Achilles thrust him through his coat of mail
And through his body, and so this worthy knight
Was brought to death. For him, as old books tell us,
A woe was made past power of tongue to tell,
And most of all the grief of Troilus,
Who after Hector was the fount of prowess.

   In this woe Troilus lived till what for sorrow
And what for love and for his troubled mind,
Often enough he told his heart to break.
But none the less, beginning to despair,
And dreading that his lady had played him false,
It was to her his heart still had recourse,
And as these lovers do, he was always seeking
To win again his bright-hued Cressida,
And went about excusing her at heart
On the ground that Calchas caused all her delay.
Often he purposed to disguise himself
As if he were a pilgrim, and visit her,
But knew he could not pass unrecognized
By people who were shrewd, nor plead excuse
If he should be detected by the Greeks.
Over and over again he wrote to her,
Piteously, and begged, since he was true,
That she would come again and keep her faith.
And for this reason Cressida one day
For pity—so I take it—wrote back to him
About this matter, and said as you shall hear:

   "O son of Cupid, sword of knighthood, type
Of every gentle and high quality,
How should a soul in torment and in dread

Send you at this time any joyful word?
I comfortless, I sick, I in distress—
You cannot deal with me, nor I with you,
And hence I cannot send you heart nor help.

"Your letters, full, and covered with complaint,
Bring pity to my heart. I have seen, too,
How every letter has been stained with tears,
And how you bid me to come home again,
Which may not be as yet. But why, for fear
This letter may be found, I do not now
So much as mention. Grievous to me, God knows,
Is your impatience; what the gods ordain
It doesn't seem that you accept as best.
Nothing at all is in your memory
Save only, as it seems to me, your pleasure.
But don't be angry—that I beg of you;
I only wait because of wicked tongues.
For I have heard much more than I expected
Touching us two, how things have stood between us,
Which I shall set right by dissimulation.
And—don't be angry—I have understood
That all your pleas are mere cajolery.
No matter, now; I can imagine nothing
But all truth and all honorableness in you.

"Come I will; but in such an evil juncture
As I stand now, I cannot set the year
Nor day when it shall be. But I beseech
Your good word and your friendship; for as long
As life shall last me, you may count on me,
Faithfully, as a friend. And think no ill,
I beg of you, if this I write is brief.
I hardly dare write letters, where I am,
Nor have I ever learned yet to write well.
Men write to great effect in little space;
The meaning is the letter, not the length.

Farewell, God keep you now!
                    Your Cressida."
   Troilus thought this letter, when he saw it,
Distant enough, and grievously he sighed.
It seemed like an inaugural of change.
He could not fully take it in at last
That she would never keep her promise to him.
For he that loves well is but ill inclined
To stop, in such a case, although he suffers.
   But people say that truth will out at last,
In spite of all; and such an incident
Occurred, and very soon, that Troilus
Well understood that she was not so kind
As she should be; and in the end he knew
That all he had gone about was lost, past question.
For one day as he stood in melancholy,
Suspecting her for whom he thought to die,
It happened that throughout the town was carried,
As custom was, a sort of coat of arms
Before Deiphobus in sign of triumph;
Which coat, as Lollius tells us, he had torn
From Diomede that very day. Troilus
Began to study it closely, length and breadth
And all the workmanship; but as he looked,
He felt a sudden stroke of cold at heart,
For underneath the collar he discovered
A brooch that he had given Cressida
In memory of him and of his sorrow
That morning when she had to part from Troy.
And she had pledged her faith to keep it always!
But now he knew full well he could no longer
Trust in his lady. Home he went, and sent
Quickly for Pandarus, and of this brooch
And this new turn he told him chapter and verse,
Complaining of her heart's inconstancy,

His truth, his long love, and his grievous pain.
  "Ah, lady Cressida, where is your faith,"
He said, "and where your promise, where your love?
Now you are reveling in this Diomede!
Alas, if you would not stand true to me,
I should have thought that at the very least
You would not have deceived me so! Who now
Shall ever put his faith in oaths again?
I never would have thought till now that you,
Cressida, could so change! No, in all truth,
Unless I had been at fault and done amiss,
I could not have believed your heart so cruel
As thus to kill me. Your name for constancy
Is now undone, alas—that is my grief!
Was there no other brooch that you were willing
To part with as a present for your love
Except the very brooch that I with tears
Gave you as a remembrance of myself?
You had no reason save for spite! You meant
To show your meaning, too, past all mistake.
Through this I see that you have cast me clean
Out of your mind; and I, for all this world,
I cannot for a quarter of a day
Find it within my heart to unlove you,
I, born beneath a curse since I still love
Above all creatures you who cause my woe!
  "God in his grace grant me that I may meet
This Diomede," he cried, "and by the truth,
If I have strength and opportunity,
I'll make his sides, I hope, run blood even yet.
O God, who should take care to further truth
And punish wrongs, why will you not take vengeance
On this betrayal? O Pandarus, you who have blamed me
And often upbraid me for putting faith in dreams,
Now, if you care to, you may see yourself
How true your niece is, glorious Cressida!

In sundry forms, God knows," he said, "the gods
Reveal in sleep tidings both glad and sorry,
And by my dream this is now obvious.
From this time on, with all the strength I can,
I shall go seek for my own death in battle.
I do not care how soon the day may be.
But Cressida, my sweet, to whom I have given
My service always and with all my might,
This that you do, in truth I have not deserved!"

    Pandarus, as he listened to these things
And knew well that he spoke the truth about them,
Said not a word in answer, sorry enough
For the sorrow of his friend, and shamed because
His niece had erred. Beneath this double reason
He stood confounded, silent as a stone,
And could not utter a syllable. At last
He spoke and said, "Dear brother, I can do
No more for you. What can I say? I hate
Cressida, and God knows that I shall hate her
Forever! What you begged me long ago
To do, regardless of my ease and honor
I did it all according to your wish.
If I did anything that may have pleased you,
I am glad of that; as for this treason now,
God knows it grieves me! For your ease of heart
I'd gladly set it right, if I knew how.
And from this world I pray Almighty God
Deliver her quickly! I can say no more."

    Great was the grief of Troilus; but Fortune
Kept always on her path. Cressida loves
The son of Tydeus, and Troilus
Must weep in his cold care. Such is this world
To those who can perceive it; God help us take it
All for the best!
                In many a cruel battle,
As men may find by reading these old books,

Appeared the prowess and the knightliness
Of Troilus. By day and night the Greeks
Paid cruelly for his rage, and always most
He sought for Diomede. And many times
They met, I find, with words and bloody swords,
And put to trial how their spears were whetted.
God knows that Troilus hammered on his helmet
In many a bitter passion! None the less
The will of Fortune was that neither one
Should die by the other's hand. Had I set out
To tell the exploits of this worthy man,
I would have made a record of his battles;
But since I undertook at first to write
About his love, I have spoken as I could—
Whoever wants to hear his feats of arms,
Read Dares, he can tell them first and last—
Beseeching every lady fair in hue,
Although it be that Cressida was false,
Not to be angry, for that sin, with me.
I will more gladly write of good Alcestis,
Or Penelope the faithful, if you please.
Nor do I speak for men alone, but most
For women whom false men betray. God grieve,
Amen to that, those that by subtlety
Betray you, and by wit! And I am moved
By this to speak, and to implore you all
Beware of men! Remember what I say!

Go, little book! If only God would send
Your author still, my little tragedy,
Some comedy to write before his end!
Go, and on no man's work look enviously,
But be a servant of all poetry,
And kiss the steps their passing has made gracious—
Vergil, Ovid, Homer, Lucan, and Statius.

And since there is so great diversity
In English and the writing of our speech,
For lack of language may you never be
Miswritten nor mismetered, I beseech,
And read or sung, wherever your words may reach
May you be understood, to God I pray!
But now for what I first set out to say:

The Greeks bought dear the wrath of Troilus;
His hands made thousands die. From all I hear,
He was without a rival in his time
Save Hector. But alas (under God's will)
Contemptuously the fierce Achilles slew him.
And when he had been killed his happy spirit
Rose to the hollow of the seventh sphere,
Leaving below all earthly elements.
There in full view he saw the erratic stars
And heard the sounds of heavenly harmony.
And down from that high station he began
To look upon this little spot of earth
Enfolded by the sea, with full contempt
For this unhappy world; he held it all
A vanity compared with that clear joy
That is in heaven above; and at the last
He looked down on the place where he was slain,
And laughed within himself at all the woe
Of those who wept and sorrowed for his death,
Condemning all our work that so pursues
Blind lusts that cannot last, when our whole hearts
Ought to be fixed on heaven. And so he went
Where Mercury ordained that he should dwell.

Such end has, lo, this Troilus for love!
Such end has all his knightly worthiness,
The royal state that set him high above,

Such end his lust, such end his nobleness!
Such end has all this false world's fickleness!
And thus his love of Cressida began,
And thus he died. I have told it as I can.

O young and lusty people, he or she,
Whose loves come with your season to invade you,
Bring home your hearts from worldly vanity
And lift them up, before love has betrayed you,
To that same God who in his likeness made you,
And think of it as but a fair, yes, all
This world, as quick to fade as flowers fall.

Love him that on a cross for very love
The bitter ransom of our souls to pay
First died, and rose, and sits in heaven above.
He will be false to no one, I dare say,
Who will his whole heart frankly on him lay.
Since he is best to love, since he is meek,
What need for some pretended love to seek?

Here you have heard of cursed old pagan rites,
Here, what their gods are worth, both low and high,
Here, of these wretched worldly appetites,
Here, of what end, what payment toil can buy
From Jove, Apollo, Mars, and such canaille!
Here, forms of speech old scholars and divines
Have left in verse, if you will read their lines.

O moral Gower, I dedicate this book
To you, who will not be at any loss,
And you too, philosophical Strode, to look
Benignly on it and correct its dross;
And to that faithful Christ who on the cross
Perished, with all my heart I ever pray
Mercy, and to the Lord I speak and say:

Eternal One in Three on whom we call,
Who, Three in One, reign ever and transcend,
Uncircumscribed, and circumscribing all,
From visible and invisible foes defend
Each one of us, and take us in the end
Into your mercy, Jesus, for her love,
The maid and mother who is yours above.

SELECTIONS
AND
SHORT POEMS

From *The Book of the Duchess*

This work is an elegy on the first wife of John of Gaunt, Blanche, Duchess of Lancaster, who died during an outbreak of plague in September 1369. (Katherine Swynford, sister of Chaucer's wife Philippa, became first John of Gaunt's mistress and later his third wife). The *Prologue* to *The Legend of Good Women* mentions the "Deth of Blaunche the Duchesse" as one of Chaucer's writings, and in the poem itself the name of the lady whom the knight in black laments is "White" (Blanche). At the end the knight rides homeward toward a "long" castle (Lancaster, also known as Longcastel) which has white walls and is set ("by St. John !") on a "rich hill" (Richmond, in Yorkshire, a seat belonging to John of Gaunt).

The Book of the Duchess has been patronized as an apprentice work. A product of Chaucer's French period, written in the tumbling four-stress couplets he later outgrew when he came under Italian influences, it draws heavily on the fashionable dream visions of Chaucer's French contemporaries. Nonetheless the reader should be prepared to find it a far more delicate, original, and sophisticated work than its conventional affiliations would suggest.

The dream in the conventional love visions was a pretext for allegory, more like a fantasy consciously elaborated according to well-established expectations that like an actual dream. In *The Book of the Duchess* much is far more truly dreamlike, the strayed hound puppy, for example, who melts from the scene and is forgotten after leading the dreamer to the knight in black, or the castle that mysteriously appears close by at the end as the knight, suddenly mounted without any explanation, rides homeward.

The poem may appear diffuse in construction, but its episodes are more tightly related than they may seem on a casual reading. We are introduced to an insomniac who has been suffering from an unrequited love affair. The only physician who could heal him is obviously a lady who declines the role. To while away the small hours he reads the story of Ceyx and Alcyone (Chaucer knew it in Ovid's Latin but makes much use of French treatments). He falls asleep and in a dream encounters the knight in black, who mourns a lost mistress. Thus the grief of a bereaved wife, the grief of a bereaved lover, and the disappointment of an unsuccessful suitor come together in the theme of the transience of happiness: "To[o] lytel while oure blysse lasteth!" All this is fiction. The first-person narrator, as G. L. Kittredge insisted long ago, is a character in the poem, not Chaucer writing autobiography. It is much more likely that Chaucer slept normally while writing *The Book of the Duchess* than that he was in the state he ascribes to the lovelorn insomniac who becomes the dreamer. The only connection of the poem with fact lies in the identification of the knight with John of Gaunt and of the lady "White" with the Duchess Blanche.

The apparent obtuseness of the dreamer has caused critical to-do. The knight does not know that his initial lament has been overheard, but the dreamer has overheard it and thereby possesses explicit knowledge of the knight's loss from the start. Nonetheless the dreamer maintains an air of studied ignorance which can lead the unwary reader to wonder whether Chaucer himself wasn't napping as he wrote. But the dreamer is playing a game of deferential courtesy, trying to alleviate the knight's grief by inducing him to make a clean breast of his story, to come out plainly with the fact that each knows. As B. H. Bronson puts it, "Never presuming on his private knowledge, the Dreamer leads the knight from point to

point to disclose everything, and at the knight's own
pace and pleasure." The dreamer's feigned obtuseness
throws into sharp relief the knight's final forced admis-
sion, after which the scene dissolves rapidly and dreamily
into the sound of the huntsman's horn, the ride home-
ward, and the dreamer's awakening with the tale of Ceyx
and Alcyone still in hand.

The extreme simplicity of the diction in the poem may
give an impression of naïveté, but it is calculated naïveté,
delicately suited to the dream state in which the action
takes place, and part of the charm of the work. My
version renders the opening episode of Ceyx and Alcyone
closely and completely. The more than eleven hundred
lines that follow have had to be drastically reduced and
more freely treated.

I wonder greatly, by this light,
How I live, for day or night
I scarcely sleep the merest whit.
Such idle fancies fill my wit
Purely for lack of the sleep I need
That on my word I do not heed
What comes or goes, what stays or leaves.
Nothing pleases me, nothing grieves;
All is equally good to me,
Joy or grief, whichever it be,
For nothing is able to make me feel,
A creature bewildered, ready to reel
And tumble down in desolation,
For sorrowful imagination
Is always wholly in my mind.
    You know that Nature has not designed
A soul on earth to live this way.
None who draws breath under her sway
Can, no matter what she may give,
For any length of time still live
Both lacking sleep and being in sorrow,
And I cannot, by night or morrow,

Sleep; thus wearily I lie
In melancholy, dreading to die,
For lack of sleep and dull distress
Have robbed my spirit of lustiness
Until I am no better than dead.
Such fantasies are in my head
I doubt what course is best to try.

But if someone should ask me why
I cannot sleep, and what it is
That ails me, he would ask me this
Only to forfeit his own question,
For I myself have no suggestion
As to the truth; but at a guess
I think it is a sore sickness
That I have suffered these eight years,
And still no remedy appears,
For no physician except one
Can heal me; but all that is done.
Put by for now that bygone cup.
What cannot be men must give up,
And to our main theme we should keep.

So when I knew I could not sleep
Till early hours the other night,
Upon my bed I sat upright
And asked someone to fetch a book,
A romance, which I straightway took
To read and drive the night away,
For that seemed better than to play
Either at backgammon or chess.
This book I read for sleeplessness
Told fables of a former time
That scholars and poets put in rhyme,
Tales to be remembered and read
As long as men are born and bred.
This book spoke only of such things,
Of queens' lives and of lives of kings

And much else on a lesser scale.
Among all this I found a tale
That struck me as a wondrous thing.
   This was the story: Once a king
Named Ceyx took himself a wife,
The best that ever drew breath of life,
And she was called Alcyone.
Soon afterward across the sea
This king set sail, and to be brief
His ship and company came to grief.
The sea put on a dreadful guise
And such a storm began to rise
It broke her mast and made it fall
And split their ship and drowned them all.
Never was found, as the book tells,
Plank nor man nor anything else.
   But now to turn back to his wife:
At home alone, she felt concern
Grow as the king did not return,
And as the time passed more and more
She wondered, and her heart grew sore.
It seemed not well for him to go
Over the sea and linger so.
She pined so for her lord the king
That it would be a piteous thing
To dwell upon the sorrowful life
That she endured, this peerless wife,
Longing for him that she loved best.
She sent for word of him east and west,
But nothing was found. By sorrow torn,
"Alas," she cried, "that I was born!
And may it be my lord is dead?
Truly, I shall eat no bread,
I vow it to my goddess here,
Till word of my lord shall reach my ear."
Such was the grief her spirit took

That verily I who made this book
Felt such compassion for her sorrow
I fared the worse for it all the morrow.

When nothing was found in any place
Touching her lord, nor word nor trace,
She often swooned and cried "Alas!"
Almost mad in her sorrowful pass,
Nor could she think of help at all
Except down on her knees to fall
And weep so it was pity to hear.

"Ah, Juno, lady whom I hold dear,"
She cried to her goddess in her grief,
"Let my distress have some relief,
And grant me grace my lord to see
Soon, or learn where he may be
And how he fares or in what plight.
With sacrifice I will requite
Your mercy, and be wholly yours,
Heart, body, and all while life endures.
But if this cannot be the case,
Then, sweet lady, grant me grace
To sleep, and meet with a true dream
Which will enable me to deem
My lord for certain alive or dead."

With that word she hung down her head
And swooned stone-cold; she could not stir.
Quickly her women lifted her
And laid her in her bed all bare.
She slept before she was aware,
Worn with her weeping and her waking.
Sleep had her merely for the taking,
Through Juno, who had heard her plea
And made her sleep immediately.
For as she prayed, so it was done.
The goddess, Juno, summoned one
To do her bidding, and told him thus:

"Go straight," she said, "to Morpheus,
The god of sleep whom you well know.
Now understand before you go
And take good heed. Bid him for me
Go straightway into the salt sea.
Tell him by every sacred thing
To take the body of the king,
Ceyx, where it lies drowned and pale.
Creep into the body without fail
And bear it to Alcyone
Who lies alone in her misery.
Show her what no one can gainsay,
How it was drowned upon a day,
And make the body speak just so
As it was always used to do
During the time it was alive.
Go quickly, as you hope to thrive."
    This messenger went on his way.
He made neither stop nor stay
Until he came to the valley, dark
Between two rocks that stand up stark,
Where grass nor grain can never spring,
Nor nothing worth the reckoning,
No tree, nor man, nor animal,
Only runnels of waterfall
That sliding from the cliffs around
Murmur a deathly sleeping sound.
Right past a cave in a rocky hollow
Their path these watercourses follow
Within this valley wondrous deep.
There these gods lie fast asleep,
Morpheus and Eclympasteyr
Who was the god of slumber's heir.
They slept and did no other work.
This cave as black was in its murk
As is Hell's pit from rim to floor.

There they had ample time to snore,
Rivals in who could sleep the best.
Some of them sat with chin on chest,
Some slept upright with covered heads
And some lay naked in their beds
Sleeping while the days went past.

    This messenger came flying fast
And cried, "Wake up!" but nothing stirred.
His breath was wasted; no one heard.
"Come to!" he cried. "Who's sleeping here?"
And blew his horn in the god's ear
And shouted "Wake up!" ever so high.
The god of sleep opened one eye
And asked, "Who is it calling there?"
"I am," answered the messenger.
"Juno has set a task for you,"
And told him what he was to do
As I have told it all before—
There is no need for saying more—
And went his way when he had spoken.
The god of sleep, his slumber broken,
Roused from his trance, prepared to go.
As he was bidden, even so
He took the body from the sea
And bore it to Alcyone,
The wife of Ceyx, where she lay
In bed three hours before the day,
And at the bed's foot took his place
And called to her through his drowned face
By name, and said, "My sweet, my wife,
Awake! Forget your sorrowing life,
For to no cure your grief can lead.
Truly, my sweet, I am dead indeed.
You shall see me alive no more.
But good, true heart, this I implore:
Bury my body, for some day's tide

Will cast it up by the sea side.
And farewell, sweet, my world's delight.
All your grief may God requite.
Too little while delight may last."
  Upward with that her eyes she cast,
But they saw nothing. "Alas!" she cried
For grief. Within three days she died.

[The narrator reports that if he had not read the story
of Ceyx and Alcyone and the gods of sleep, he would
have died of insomnia. Instead he fell sound asleep him-
self on the book he had been reading and dreamt "so
inly sweet a dream" that not even "Joseph of Egypt," who
interpreted Pharaoh's vision, would know what to make
of it. He dreamt that he was awakened at dawn in May
by the singing of innumerable small birds. The windows
of the room in which he found himself were "well glazed,"
and the glass was etched with the story of Troy and *The
Romance of the Rose*, "both text and gloss."]

In this chamber as I was lying
I dreamt I heard a huntsman trying
Whether his horn was clear or hoarse.
Hunters were crowding in great force
With mounts and hounds on every side
And all was talk of how they would ride
To hunt the hart that very day.
Exulting, I rose up straightway
And took my horse and led it out
To where in a field had gathered a rout
Of hunters with their coupled hounds
And remounts thronging all the grounds.
Off toward the forest fast they hied
And I rode with them. To the woodside
Hot-foot the master huntsman drew.
On a great horn three notes he blew
At the uncoupling of his hounds.

Within a short while after these sounds
The hart, discovered, was hallooed
And long by horse and hound pursued,
But circled at last and stole away
Secretly, leaving the hounds astray.
They lost his scent, checked once for all.
The master-huntsman blew a recall.

As I was quitting my post by a tree,
A lost hound-whelp crept up to me
As if I were someone he might know.
He fawned on my hand with head hung low,
His ears lapped under it, and his coat
Sleek, unruffled from tail to throat.
This whelp had followed the chase from the start
But was too young to carry his part.
I would have caught him, but off he fled
Along a path so thickly spread
With flowers it seemed the earth would vie
To outdo all the stars in the sky
And show itself more gay than heaven
Multiplying the stars by seven.
I followed among huge trees that stood
Ten feet or twelve apart in the wood,
Their clean trunks climbing toward the sky
Forty or fifty fathoms high.
Their tops were not an inch asunder
And all was in deep shade thereunder.
The forest swarmed with bucks and does
And squirrels sitting as they chose
High up in trees to hold their feasts.
I saw so many kinds of beasts
That Algus with his reckoning-board
Could never count so great a horde.
But they fled from me ever so fast
Into the wood; and so at last
I grew aware of a man in black

Seated alone, who leaned his back
Against an oak, a mighty tree.
"Lord," I thought, "who may that be?
What ails him to be sitting here?"
Promptly I went on and drew near,
And saw, as he sat there upright,
A wondrously well-favored knight,
In age some four and twenty years.
His beard still boasted but few hairs.
His clothing was entirely black.
I stalked up to his very back
And stood as still as still can be.
But he was unaware of me
Because his head drooped toward the ground,
And with a deathly sorrowing sound
He made himself some lines of rhyme
Which I remember to this time:

 "I am by sorrow so undone
 To no joy can I now be won
 Since my lady, my heart's delight,
 Whom I loved with all my might,
 To death away from me has gone.

 "Alas, death, could you blinded be
 Taking her instead of me,
 My lady, whom I held so dear,
 Who was so fair, so fresh, so free,
 So kind no man could fail to see
 In kindness she could have no peer."

When he had finished his complaint
His heart for wretchedness grew faint,
His spirits faltered as if dead
And from his face the warm blood fled.
Seeing his state, I thought to greet
This knight, and stood right at his feet
And spoke to him; he said no word.
Heavy with thought, he had not heard.

At last he saw me where I stood
Before him, taking off my hood.
"Sir, do not hold it for a slight.
I neither saw you," said this knight,
"Nor heard." "That does not signify.
But, good sir, I am grieved," said I,
"If I have put your thoughts astray."
"Amends for that are light to pay,
For none are due," he said at this.
"No act nor word has been amiss."

 He spoke as fair as a knight can,
As if he were another man,
Composedly and courteously
However sore his grief might be.
I sought some way by which to find
A closer entrance to his mind.
"Sir," I said, "this hunt is done.
Clean away the hart has gone.
They will not find him anywhere."
"Little enough for that I care,"
Said he. "I give it never a thought."
"Lord knows you seem indeed distraught,"
I answered, "for it does appear
You are in grief. But will you hear
One thing? If you would tell your woe,
I would, and may God help me so,
Assuage it, if I may, perchance."
With that he looked at me askance
As who should say, "That cannot be."
"Good friend, I thank you," answered he,
"But no man may assuage the pain
By which my happiness was slain
Leaving me with a mind so torn
I grieve that I was ever born.

 "Death is itself so much my foe
That I would die, but death says no,

For when I follow, death will flee.
I would have death, but not death me.
Pain without hope I have instead,
Always dying, never dead.
Sisyphus, who lives in hell,
Could of no greater sorrow tell.
Truly, if one who knew the whole
Could stifle pity in his soul,
Feel no compassion for my smart,
That man would have a fiendish heart.
Who meets me first on any morrow
May say that he has met with sorrow,
For I am sorrow, sorrow I.

　　"Alas, and I will tell you why.
Fortune, that traitress, full of guile,
Played chess with me in an evil while,
And with her sly moves and false mien
She stole on me and took my queen,
And when I saw my queen away
I knew no longer how to play,
But 'Farewell, sweet,' I said at this,
And 'Farewell everything that is.'
Yet Fortune is the less to blame.
I should myself have done the same
If she were I and I were she.
From fault she should be counted free,
For in this matter I say still
Had I God's power to do my will
I should have made the selfsame play
As she did, taking my queen away.
So may God's wisdom give me rest
But I will swear she took the best.
My bliss from me that move has torn.
Alas, that ever I was born!"

　　"Good sir," I told him, "say not so.
Let Fortune's favors come or go.

Have mercy on the gift of nature
That made of you a living creature.
Remind yourself of Socrates.
He never would have bent his knees
To Fortune, not for any cause.
He counted her not worth three straws.
Though you had lost a dozen queens,
To slay yourself would be the means
Of being damned, like Medea, she
Who slew her children cruelly.
No man who draws a living breath
Would for a chess queen court his death
Or yield himself to so great woe."

   "Why not?" he answered me. "You know
But little what you mean. I grieve
A greater loss than you perceive."

   "Yet how can that be, Sir?" said I.
"Tell me wholly how and why
Your joy has so been overthrown."

   "Gladly," he answered. "Come, sit down.
But I will make one stipulation:
Promise me, on your salvation,
To hear me closely, with all your wit."
   "Yes."

       "On your honor, swear to it."
   "By heaven, I'll listen as well as I can."
He said, "In God's name!" and began:
"Sir, from my youth when first I could
In any manner have understood
What love is, my course was set.
From that time forth I have ever yet,
His tributary, paid my rent
To Love, with only good intent.
I served with pleasure as his thrall,
Both will and body, heart and all.
That was my state for many a year

Before my heart fixed anywhere.
   "I came to a place one day by chance
Where ladies gathered in a dance,
Truly the fairest company
Men's eyes were ever given to see
Together in a single place.
Was I led there by chance or grace?
No, Fortune brought me, that perverse
Traitress—God help me call her worse,
For now she works me bitter woe
And I will straightway tell why so.
   "Among these ladies I saw one
That truly as the summer sun
Outshines the planets in the heaven,
Or the Great Bear with all its seven
Stars, so she excelled no less
All others in her comeliness,
Her look, her eyes, her womanly way.
To put it shortly, what shall I say?
By Christ and by the twelve that he
Chose for apostles, it was she,
Her very self, my love, my sweet,
That I thus happened there to meet,
Who suddenly in my heart and thought
So fast forevermore was caught
I rather would serve her in vain
Than with another stand to gain.
   "I saw her dance with comely pace
And heard her sing with such good grace,
Sport and laugh and speak so fairly,
So womanly, so debonairly,
So friendly that in all time's measure
Never was seen so rich a treasure.
Her life with such a zest she led
That dullness skulked from her in dread.
Of nature's work, done with such care

To make her every feature fair,
She was in all truth no mere sample
But pattern rather, and chief example.

    "Her love of justice, too, was strong.
No living creature would she wrong,
And none could do her any shame
So well she cherished her good name.
No man was sent by her commands
Hoodless to the Goby sands
To come back after faring far
By the Black Lake, the Carrenar,
With 'Sir, before you dare return,
Word of your prowess let me learn.'

    "Her name was hers as by due right,
The good, the fair, the peerless White."

    "By God," I said, "from what you tell
You have bestowed your service well.
But tell me further, I beseech,
How you approached her first in speech
And how she first your thought divined
And what the loss that haunts your mind."

    "You scarce know what you mean. I grieve
A greater loss than you perceive."

    "What is it that I do not know?
Will she not love you? Is it so?
Or have you done something amiss
And has she left you? Is it this?
For God's love, tell me the whole tale."

    "By God, I shall tell without fail.
As I have said before, good Sir,
My whole love settled fast on her,
Yet for a long time never a whit
Was she herself aware of it.
For all this world I did not dare
Confess to her my secret care
For dread to meet with her displeasure.

But then, as it were some sort of measure
Against pure idleness, I made
Songs that I sang, with little aid
From art, for I knew not at all
The lore of Lamech's son, Jubal,
Who first found out the craft of singing.
He heard his brother's hammer ringing
As on his anvil he would pound
And from that captured song's first sound,
Though some the fount of song would seek
In Pythagoras, the Greek.
But I, for all my want of art,
Made songs, and sang to cheer my heart.
This one was the very first.
For all I know, it's not the worst:
   'Lord, it makes my heart grow light
  To think on her, that blissful sight,
  Who is so comely to behold;
  And would to God I might be told
  That in her eyes, so fair, so bright,
  I stood accepted as her knight.'
This was the first song that I made.
Then one day in my thoughts I weighed
The woe I bore for her, while she
Knew nothing of it utterly,
Nor dared I speak of my distress
Fearing her wrath should I confess.
'Alas, what can I do?' thought I.
'Unless I tell her, I shall die.'
I saw no help. It seemed my heart
In conflict would be torn apart.
At last it came into my thought
That Nature never yet had wrought
So fair a creature, so benign,
Who would not in her heart incline
To mercy. In that hope I broke

My silence, but in fear I spoke,
Mumbling and quaking out my tale.
I felt my wits, my manners fail,
My color veer from pale to red.
Bowing to her, I hung my head.
I dared not once look at her plainly
And all I said came out inanely.
'Mercy!' I cried at last resort.
I was hard hit. It was no sport.

    "And when my tale was done, I saw
She did not count it worth a straw.
The gist of her reply was 'No,'
Utterly. But at that the woe
Cassandra felt, who so bewailed
Troy's fall, could never have prevailed
Against my woe. I dared not say
Another word, but stole away.
I had no need to seek for sorrow
Thereafter, for with every morrow
I found it at my bedside near.

    "But as it chanced, another year
I found a time to make her know
And fully take to mind my woe,
And well my lady understood
That all I meant was but for good,
To guard her worship and her name
And to protect her from all shame,
And I had served so faithfully
It seemed a pity I should die.
So when she was aware of this
She raised me up from death to bliss.
Her noblest gift she wholly gave me,
Her mercy, which alone could save me.
With that she gave another thing,
The first pledge of her grace: a ring.
But if my heart was set afire

With joy, there's no need to inquire!
Sweet as she was, so far from spite,
When I was wrong and she was right
She would forgive me out of hand.
She took my youth under command.
Always she was herself so true
Our joys were ever the same as new.
Many a year together thus
We lived in bliss, all one to us,
Sorrow or joy as it befell.
Beyond a doubt we lived so well
It would surpass me to say how."
   "Sir," said I, "where is she now?"
   "Now?" he stopped and grew stone-dead.
   "Alas that I was born," he said.
   "That was the very loss I bore.
Remember how I said before:
'You scarce know what you mean. I grieve
A greater loss than you perceive.'
God knows, alas, that loss was she."
   "Alas, good Sir, how may that be?"
   "She's dead."
              "No!"
                      "Yes, by all that's true!"
   "Is that your loss? God pity you!"
Even as he spoke the huntsman's horn
Called hounds and hunters to return.
Finished for good was that day's course.
With that I dreamt the knight took horse
And homeward he began to ride
Toward a place that was close beside,
A little before us, well in sight,
A long castle with walls of white
Set, by St. John! on a rich hill.
So it seemed to me, sleeping still,
And in my dream it seemed as well

That in the castle hung a bell
Which just had finished its twelfth stroke.
But with that I myself awoke
Finding myself propped up in bed
Holding the book that I had read
Of Queen Alcyone doomed to weep
For Ceyx, and of the gods of sleep.
It lay there in my hand held fast.
"For strangeness this is unsurpassed,
This dream," I thought. "In course of time
I'll try to put this dream in rhyme
As best I can, and that right soon."
Such was my dream; now it is done.

అము అము అము అము అము అము అము అము అము అము

From *The House of Fame, Book II*

TRANSLATOR'S NOTE

The House of Fame is another early work in which
Chaucer again follows widespread medieval fashion by
presenting his matter in the guise of a dream. Like *The
Book of the Duchess*, the poem plunges along in loose
four-stress couplets; Chaucer had not yet adopted for
consistent use the pentameter line that forms the basis
of his mature work. The poem is unfinished.

On the night of December 10, Chaucer relates, he
dreamed that he found himself in a temple of glass, sacred
to Venus. On a tablet were inscribed the first lines of
Vergil's *Aeneid*. Chaucer translates them, and then in
pictures or designs he "sees" the story of the poem. The
episode of Dido leads him to list other betrayals or
desertions of women by men. Chaucer decides to go
outside and try to learn in what place or country this
wonderful temple is situated. He finds himself in a field

of sand "as fine as men may still see lying in the desert of Libya," and looking up, he notices a golden eagle, shining so brilliantly that it could only have been equaled if the sky had gained another sun.

> This eagle of which I have told
> With feathers glittering as of gold
> And which so high began to soar,
> I watched and studied more and more
> To see the beauty and the wonder.
> But there was never bolt of thunder,
> That stroke which by its sudden power
> One time smote into dust a tower
> And came so rapidly it burned,
> That swiftly as this eagle turned,
> Descending, when its eye beheld
> That I was strolling in the field,
> And with his grim legs rough and strong,
> Using his talons sharp and long,
> Me, as I fled, seized in a swoop,
> Then rising on his upward loop
> Carried me in his talons stark
> As light as if I were a lark,
> I cannot tell you just how high;
> I don't know how, but up came I,
> For so astonished, dazed, and blind
> Were all my faculties of mind,
> What with his upswing and my dread,
> That all my feelings were as dead.
> I was too frightened, that's the cause!
>   I hung a long time in his claws
> Until at last he spoke to me
> In a man's voice. "Wake up!" said he,
> "And don't be so aghast, for shame!"
> And then he called me by my name,
> And to make certain that I woke

I dreamed the next "Wake up!" he spoke
Was in an accent just the same
As the voice of someone I could name.
And hearing that voice, truth to tell,
My mind came back again, for well
The words were said, and pleasantly,
In a way they never used to be!

My limbs began to stir once more,
And my body in his claws he bore
Until he felt in me some heat
And felt my heart begin to beat,
And then as if to entertain
And to relieve me of my pain
By speaking, twice he said, "St. Mary,
You're a vexatious piece to carry,
And there's no need of it, on my word!
The Lord so help me," said this bird,
"No harm will come to you through this!
All that is happening to you is
For instruction you may profit by.
Let's see! Do you dare yet open an eye?
I am your friend, play a man's part."

I began to wonder in my heart.
"O God," I thought, "Lord of creation,
Will Jove make me a constellation,
Or what does this business signify?
Have I no other way to die?
Enoch, Elijah, Ganymede
Who was carried up, as men may read,
To heaven by Don Jupiter
To serve the gods as cup-bearer,
Nor Romulus, I am none of these."
Of such sort were my fantasies.

My bearer, seeing my thought was this,
Told me, "You judge yourself amiss.
Jove's mind—don't worry—is not set

On turning you into a star just yet.
But now, before I carry you
Much farther, I will let you know
Just who I am, and why I'm found
Upon this errand, and where you're bound,
Always provided that you take
Courage in hand, and do not quake."
  "Gladly," I said.

                "First, then, for me,
Who carry you in my feet," said he,
"Which fills you with such fear and wonder.
My home is with the god of thunder,
He that is known as Jupiter,
Who sends me as his messenger
Flying often and far to do
All his commandments; and to you
For this cause he is moved to send me.
Now listen closely, and attend me!
He has taken pity, it's plain to see,
On you that so long and faithfully
Have served his nephew, Cupid the blind,
And the fair Venus, heart and mind;
And though without reward as yet,
The small wit in your head have set
To making books and songs and lays
In rhyme or cadence in love's praise,
And in honor of his servants, too,
Both those who have and seek to do
His service; and with all your care,
Though you have never had your share,
As best you can have praised his art.
Wherefore, so may God bless my heart,
Jove counts it great humility
And virtue in you, certainly,
That in your study you should make
Your head at night so often ache

Writing away at such a pace
Ever of Love and of his grace,
In honor of him and in his praise
And furtherance of his people's ways,
Their rites exhaustively explaining,
Love nor his people never disdaining
Although you foot it in the dance
With those he is not pleased to advance.
    "And hence, as I've already said,
Jove, my good sir, has been led
To consider this, and other things;
That is, you hear no whisperings
Or news how Love's glad game is played,
Or of anything else that God has made.
Not only from far lands, I fear,
No tidings ever reach your ear;
Your very neighbors, those who dwell
Beside your doors, you miss as well
Their ins and outs and goings on,
For when your work has all been done
And your accounts are all set true,
Instead of rest or something new
Home to your house you go alone
And just as dumb as any stone
You sit down to another book
Until you wear a glassy look,
And thus you live like an eremite—
Although your abstinence is slight!
    "Jupiter, therefore, through his grace
Wills that I carry you to a place
Known as the House of Fame, to give
Diversion to the life you live
And recompense with a little pleasure
The zeal you pour out in such measure
Without a reason or reward
To Cupid, that indifferent lord!

Thus Jove in his merit will accord you
A glimpse of some sort to reward you,
Provided that you show good cheer.
For you can rest assured, you'll hear,
In the place we'll presently be at,
More marvelous things, I'll wager that;
More of the news that always flies
About Love's folk, both truth and lies;
More loves that newly have begun
And loves long served and lately won;
More loves that casually arose
By chance, it seems, why no one knows,
As a blind man happens to start a hare;
More merrymaking and welfare
With those who find love true as steel
And all for the best, or so they feel;
More discords and more jealousies,
More murmurs and more novelties,
More lies and more dissimulations
And more feigned reconciliations;
More beards made[1] in two hours by far,
And without razors, than there are
Grains in the sand; more ways to cheat
And more cajoling for deceit;
More patchings-up by which love mends
Ties between old, forgotten friends;
More quarrels healed on arbiters' day
Than the strings on all the harps men play;
More shifts in love and more exchanges
Than all the kernels in barns or granges."

[1]To "make a man's beard" meant to deceive him.

࿔࿓ ࿔࿓ ࿔࿓ ࿔࿓ ࿔࿓ ࿔࿓ ࿔࿓ ࿔࿓ ࿔࿓ ࿔࿓

From *The Birds' Parliament*

TRANSLATOR'S NOTE

Still another dream vision, *The Birds' Parliament* begins with Chaucer's familiar humorous deprecation of his inexperience or lack of success in love, which he claims to know only through books. He takes a roundabout path to the story of the birds and their gathering on St. Valentine's Day to receive their mates. This story, when Chaucer reaches it, resolves into a courtly-love contest among three eagles for the favor of a formel (female) eagle perched on the hand of the goddess Nature. The royal eagle, or tercel (male), speaks first, only to have his claim disputed by two other tercels. All three are impatiently mocked by lower feathered orders in this stratified bird society, in which birds of prey are the aristocrats while "worm-fowl," waterfowl, and "seed-fowl" represent lower classes.

For the *Parliament*, Chaucer used the rhyme-royal stanza he employed in his mature work in a number of the *Canterbury Tales* and in the *Troilus*. The poem thus represents a stage in his assimilation of Italian rather than French influences.

Some of his medieval bird lore would require footnoting at inconvenient length for full, perhaps even then doubtful, explanation. The stork, for example, is called the avenger of adultery, perhaps because of the belief that the male stork would kill his mate if he found her unfaithful. The pheasant is "the scorner of the cock by night," perhaps because it will mate with a barnyard hen.

In the next to the last line of the poem, Chaucer may be hinting that he would appreciate greater rewards for his work from one or another patron.

The life so short, the craft so long to learn,
The attempt so hard, the victory so keen,
The fearful joy, so arduous to earn,
So quick to fade—by all these things I mean
Love, for his wonders in this worldly scene
Confound me so that when I think of him
I scarcely know whether I sink or swim.

For in love's practice though I lag behind
And know not how he pays his troops their wage,
Yet often it happens that in books I find
Tales of his miracles and cruel rage.
There he is shown as lord on every page!
I dare not say his lashes are so sore,
But "God save such a despot!" Why say more?

For pleasure, or to learn a thing or so,
I often, as I said, turn to a book.
But why all this? A little while ago
I happened, as my habit is, to look
In an old-lettered treatise that so took
My fancy with its theme that to pursue it
I read on all the livelong day right through it.

For out of old fields, as the saying goes,
Comes all the new grain garnered year by year,
And speaking truly, out of old books flows
All the new knowledge men learn to revere.
But now to the purpose of my subject here:
To read on through this book proved such delight
The whole day's time I gave it seemed but slight.

[The book that Chaucer pores on all day is Cicero's Latin *Somnium Scipionis*, the Dream of Scipio, to which Chaucer refers elsewhere, notably in the Nun's Priest's Tale. Chaucer summarizes the dream, in which Scipio Africanus, the Roman conqueror of the Carthaginian general Hannibal, appears to his descendant, the younger Scipio, and tells him of the life after death in a "blessed place" enjoyed by those devoted to the public good. Eventually Chaucer is driven from his reading by nightfall, and in turn dreams that Africanus stands by his bed, telling him that he has conducted himself so well in reading "my torn old book" that he will reward Chaucer's labor. Africanus leads Chaucer to a park full of the standard properties of the dream-vision—singing birds, harmonious instruments, trees, blossoms, and a whole catalogue of mythological and allegorical figures, all described at length. At last, still in his dream, Chaucer sees, on a hill of flowers, the "noble goddess, Nature," and in attendance on her all birds of every sort that "come by procreation."]

For this was on St. Valentine's, the day
When every bird comes there to choose his mate,
All kinds that have a name that men can say,
And such a noise they made, a din so great,
And earth, air, tree, and shore were such a spate
Of clamoring birds that I could scarce command
In all that crowd a place on which to stand.

As in his *Plaint of Nature*, Alain de Lille
Describes the goddess' raiment and her face,
So she was robed to hear the birds' appeal.
Nature, this queen endowed with every grace,
Bade every bird to go to his own place
As they did yearly, following her design,
On the day sacred to St. Valentine.

The highest perches went to birds of prey
As rightfully they should, without dissension;
Then smaller birds, who under Nature's sway

Eat worms or things that I don't care to mention.
The lowest in the ranks at this convention
Were waterfowl; but seed-birds on the green
Sat in such numbers as were never seen.

The royal eagle there a man might see
Who with his sharp look pierces even the sun,
And other eagles, lesser in degree—
The learned could describe them every one.
There, too, the tyrant with his feathers dun
And gray, I mean the goshawk, a sore spite
To other birds with his fierce appetite.

The noble falcon who with foot and claw
Clutches the king's hand, and the small quail's foe,
The hardy sparrowhawk, I also saw;
The merlin, eager to bring larks to woe,
The ring-dove whose mild eyes her meekness show,
The jealous swan that sings before his death,
The owl whose shriek foretells a man's last breath.

The crane, the giant with his trumpet's bray,
The treacherous lapwing and the chough who steals,
The chattering magpie and the scornful jay,
The starling who mysteriously reveals
Men's secrets, and the heron, foe to eels,
The friendly robin and the coward kite,
The cock, timekeeper of the village night.

The sparrow, Venus' son, the nightingale
Who calls forth the green leaves when spring is new,
The swallow, slayer of bees who ply the dale
To make clear honey of flowers fresh in hue,
The wedded turtle-dove, forever true,
The peacock with his feathers angel-bright,
The pheasant, cuckolding the cock by night.

The ungrateful cuckoo and the watchful goose,
The parrot, sensual in his luxury,
The drake who kills his mate by his abuse,
The stork, avenger of adultery,
The cormorant, hot in his gluttony,
The wise raven, the crow that croaks his care,
The long-lived throstle and the shy fieldfare.

What should I say? All birds of every kind
That in this world have feathers, men could see
Assembled there as Nature had designed.
Before the Goddess each in his degree
Was going about his business eagerly,
Seeking to choose, according to his state,
With her consent, his partner and his mate.

But to the point: Nature held on her hand
A formel eagle, peerless among the rest
Of all the works that sprang from her command.
For shape and grace she was the goodliest.
In her was every virtue at its best,
So much the very Goddess took delight
Kissing her beak and keeping her in sight.

Nature, the vicar of the almighty Lord
That hot, cold, heavy, light, moist, dry has bound
By harmony of numbers in accord,
Began to speak to all the birds around
And said, "Now hear, I ask, what I propound,
And for your comfort, mindful of your need,
As fast as ever I can I shall proceed.

"You well know, every year, how on this day,
St. Valentine's, you come as I ordain
To choose, before you fly off on your way,
The mates I spur you with desire to gain.

But none the less my statute must remain
In force, although I had the world to win,
That he who is the worthiest shall begin.

"The tercel eagle, you are well aware,
The regal bird, above you in degree,
Worthy and true as steel, wise in his care
To keep love's secrets, and as you may see,
Formed every whit as it delighted me—
But why describe him to you? His own voice
Shall speak for him, and he shall have first choice.

"And after him in order you shall choose,
Each in his kind, wherever his fancy flies,
And as your luck is you shall win or lose.
But he who in love's snare the deepest lies,
God send him her who sorest for him sighs!"
Then to the tercel she began to call,
Saying, "My son, to you the choice must fall.

"But still your choice is subject to condition,
And this for everyone who is gathered here,
That she herself consent to his petition
Whoever it be she is to hold for dear.
This is our custom always year by year,
And anyone who at this time wins grace,
A happy hour has brought him to this place."

With head inclined and royal modesty
This tercel spoke: "With heart and will and thought,
My sovereign lady, I choose faithfully
The formel on your hand, for she has caught
My heart in hers, so comely is she wrought.
To her my service wholly shall I give
Do what she likes to make me die or live,

"Beseeching her for mercy and for grace,
My sovereign lady whom I hope to gain,
Else let me perish straightway in this place,
For not long, truly, may I live in pain
Since she has pierced my heart through every vein.
For my distress have pity on your part
If only for my faithfulness, dear heart.

"And if I ever should be found untrue,
Boastful, heedless, or disobedient,
Or should I change a sworn love for a new,
I pray that this should be my punishment,
That by these birds I be to tatters rent
The very day that I am found so hateful
As to be false in loving or ungrateful.

"And since none other loves her as I do,
Although she has not pledged to me the same,
Then ought she to be mine if only through
Her mercy, the one bond that I can claim.
But never, for no torment men can name,
Shall I stop serving her wherever she goes.
Say what you will, for with these words I close."

Even as a red rose blooming fresh and new
Takes on her color from the summer sun,
So crimson red became this formel's hue
For very shame when the tercel's speech was done.
She spoke no word for good or ill, not one,
So sore abashed she was, till Nature said:
"Daughter, trust me, you have no cause for dread."

At this another tercel took the floor,
Of lesser rank, and said, "'This shall not be,
For by St. John, I say I love her more,
At least your love has no edge over me!

And I have served her longer in my degree.
She should have long been mine, by all that's vital,
If length of loving brought love in requital.

"I say, too, if she finds me a turncoat,
Ungrateful, boastful, any whit astray,
A rebel or jealous, hang me by the throat!
And if I fail her service day by day
As well as my poor wit can show the way
To guard her honor as my queen and wife,
Let her take all my goods and end my life!"

Then a third tercel spoke up in reply:
"Now, Sirs, you see we have small time to lose,
For every bird among us longs to fly
Off with his lady, the mate he means to choose.
Nature herself, to speed us, will refuse
To listen to the half that I would plead.
Yet if I do not speak, I die indeed.

"No boast of lengthy service can I bring,
But I may just as likely die today
For woe as he who has been languishing
These twenty winters, and a man well may
Serve better and work harder for his pay
In half a year, to ask him for no more,
Than he who has been serving for a score.

"I speak not of myself. I know I can
By my own service never hope to please
My lady, but I am her truest man,
I dare say, and most eager for her ease.
To make short work of it, till death shall seize
My body and soul, I am hers awake or sleeping,
And true in all that heart has in its keeping."

I never heard, from the day my mother bore me,
Such pleas, delivered in so noble a guise,
In love or anything. No man before me
Has ever heard the like who could devise
A record of their speeches and replies.
From morning they continued till at last
The sun sank downward wonderfully fast.

The clamor of the birds to be delivered
So loudly rang—"Have done, and let us go!"—
I thought the very tree trunks had been shivered.
"Lay off!" they cried. "You ruin us, spouting so!
Curse on your pleadings! How should a judge know
In favor of which party to decide
When proof is just what neither can provide?"

The goose, the cuckoo, and the duck, all three,
Cried out, "Honk, honk, cuckoo, quack quack," so high
I thought my ears would be the death of me.
The goose said, "All this isn't worth a fly!
But I know of a remedy to try.
I'll give a verdict, one both quick and fair,
For waterfowl, no matter who may care."

"And I for worm-fowl," said the base cuckoo.
"For right now, by my own authority,
I'll take this challenge, for our joint good, too,
That we may all be set at liberty."
"Contain yourself a while, for decency,"
Answered the turtle-dove, "for by your will,
Sometimes a man speaks who would best keep still.

"I am a seed-fowl, one of the humblest birds.
And I have little learning, I admit,
But better it is a man should swallow his words
Than meddle in things for which he is not fit.

Where he can neither read nor sing, his wit
Will strain itself in mere impertinence,
For proffered services may give offense."

Nature, who always had a ready ear
For such unlettered protests from below,
Said in compelling tones, "Keep silent here,
And soon, I hope, a counsel I can show
To free you from this noise and let you go.
In every rank, I judge, men ought to call
On one to represent and speak for all."

To this conclusion all the birds agreed,
And first of all to choose, the birds of prey
Elected as the spokesman for their breed
The tercel falcon, bidding him convey
Their verdict, his to give in his own way.
They led him to the Goddess for consent,
Who gave him her approval, well content.

The falcon spoke thus, while the birds gave ear:
"It would be thankless effort to decide
By reason who best loves this formel here.
Each suitor has so spoken or replied
That no man's wit can set his claim aside.
Arguments in this case are useless prattle.
It seems the issue must come down to battle."

"All ready!" the three tercels cried as one.
"No, Sirs," the falcon said, "for let me say
You do me wrong. My tale is not yet done.
For, Sirs, and take it not amiss, I pray,
It will not do to flout us in this way.
Ours is the voice, we have the charge in hand,
And by the judge's verdict you must stand.

"And therefore, quiet! According to my wit,
I should consider the most eminent
In knighthood, who has longest followed it,
Highest in rank and noblest in descent
Fittest for her, if she will be content,
And she herself must know which of the three
He is, for that is easy enough to see."

The waterfowl then put their heads together
And after holding a brief confabulation,
When each had gabbled according to his feather,
They said as one united congregation
The goose, whose eloquence had such reputation,
"Who is so anxious to present our need,
Shall speak for us," and prayed for her, "Godspeed!"

Thus for the waterfowl the goose began
To gobble out her view of this debate.
"Quiet," she said. "Now listen, every man,
And hear what a reason I am going to state!
My wit is keen. I do not love to wait.
I'd tell a man, although he were my brother,
If one won't love him, let him love another!"

"Now here's a perfect reason from a goose!"
Answered the sparrowhawk. "Plague on her soul!
But so it is when a fool's tongue gets loose.
Better than play so ignorant a role
You might have kept your tongue under control.
It lies not in his wit nor in his will,
But true's the word, 'A fool cannot keep still'!"

From all the nobler birds laughter arose,
And then the seed-fowl gathered to decide
Who should present their view. They promptly chose
The bird whose true heart never strays aside,

The turtle-dove, and begged that she would guide
Their minds to the solid truth of this affair,
And her plain view she promised to declare.

"Now God forbid that love should ever waver,"
Proclaimed the turtle. For shame she grew all red.
"Although his lady never grant him favor
Still should a lover serve till he is dead.
I cannot praise the words the goose has said,
For though she died none other would I woo.
I will be hers until death takes me, too."

"A good joke," the duck answered, "by my hat!
That men should love forever for no gain,
Who can discover sense or wit in that?
Does a man dance for joy who is in pain?
What's unexplainable, who can explain?
Quack!" said the duck. He spoke out full and fair.
"We see more stars in the sky than just a pair!"

"What, low-class oaf!" the noble tercel said.
"You speak as from the dunghill by good right.
You can't perceive what's proper or well bred.
You deal with love as owls behave toward light.
Day blinds them; they can only see by night.
Your nature is so low in wretchedness
That what love is you cannot see or guess."

The cuckoo then pitched into this affray
For birds whose appetite on worm-fare thrives.
"If I may have my mate in peace today
I don't care how long any suitor strives,"
He said. "Let them go single all their lives.
That's my advice, since they can't reach consent.
This lesson is short. It needs no document."

"What, is the glutton stuffed full to the marrow?
Then we're well off!" the merlin answered him.
"You murderer of the innocent hedgesparrow
Who nurtured you, you glutton to the brim,
Live single yourself! Worm-rot in every limb,
What does it matter if you lack all caste?
Go, and be churlish while the world shall last!"

"Hush!" Nature told them. "I am in control!
All your opinions I have fully heard
And still we are no nearer to our goal.
To make an end, this is my final word:
She shall decide who is to be preferred.
No matter who may suffer or rejoice,
She shall be his at once by her own voice.

"Who loves her best, as we can plainly see,
We cannot solve here, as the tercel said.
I grant her then this privilege, that she
Shall have the one to whom her heart is wed
And he have her for whom his heart has bled.
I, Nature, rule it thus, who cannot lie.
Toward no class do I turn a biased eye.

"But for advice on how to choose a mate,
If I were Reason, truly I'd advise
The royal eagle as best matched to your state.
To heed the tercel's counsel would be wise,
Then you should have the noblest for your prize,
The worthiest, whom I formed so for my pleasure
That he should satisfy you in full measure."

The formel eagle answered timidly,
"Nature, my lady Goddess, truth to tell
I only live beneath your sovereignty
As every other creature does as well,

And must be yours while on the earth I dwell.
Then grant me the first favor that I ask.
To make it quickly known will be no task."

"Granted," said Nature. Promptly, with eyes downcast,
The formel answered in such terms as these:
"Almighty Queen, until this year is past,
I ask a time to weigh my thoughts at ease,
And then to have my free choice as I please.
This is the sum of all I have to say.
No more, though you decree my death today.

"Venus nor Cupid, in no sort of guise
Will I serve yet, nor come within their reach."
"Now, since it cannot fall out otherwise,"
Nature announced, "I have no further speech.
My will is that these birds fly, all and each,
Off with their mates. No tarrying further here!"
And thus she spoke, if you will lend an ear:

"To you I appeal, you tercels," Nature said.
"Keep up your spirits and serve faithfully.
A year of waiting will be quickly sped,
And strive to do well, each in his degree.
From all your claims for this year she is free.
Whatever happens on another day,
Your table is furnished with this entremets."

And when this work was done, by joint consent
Nature bestowed a mate on every bird,
And on their way at last they freely went.
But Lord, the bliss by which their hearts were stirred!
With wings entwined they showed the joy conferred
By Nature on them, and with necks enlaced
Thanked her by whom their longings had been graced.

But certain birds were chosen first to sing,
According to their custom year by year,
A roundelay before they all took wing,
To honor Nature and to please her ear.
As for the tune, it's one that you may hear
In France; the words are such as you will find
In the next lines—I have them now in mind:

> Now welcome, summer, who with your soft sky
> Have routed winter's weather, dour and gray,
> And the long nights of blackness driven away.
>
> St. Valentine, set over us so high,
> Thus sing the little birds who own your sway:
> Now welcome, summer, who with your soft sky
> Have routed winter's weather, dour and gray.
>
> They have good cause in lusty song to vie.
> Each has a mate for comfort and for stay.
> Waking, they sing in bliss to greet the day:
> Now welcome, summer, who with your soft sky
> Have routed winter's weather, dour and gray,
> And the long nights of blackness driven away.

And when the song was done the birds all took
To wing by rank, and at their parting flight
I woke and went to find another book
To read in, as I still read day and night.
My reading, as I hope, may sometime light
On something that will profit me at need,
And so, year in, year out, I still shall read.

෴෨ ෴෨ ෴෨ ෴෨ ෴෨ ෴෨ ෴෨ ෴෨ ෴෨

From *Prologue to*
The Legend of Good Women

TRANSLATOR'S NOTE

Chaucer relates that almost at the end of May, after he had spent a whole summer's day "beholding the daisy," he came home and ordered his bed made up in a small arbor. He dreams that he is in the meadows again, among the daisies. The god of love appears, leading a queen by the hand. The god demands why Chaucer has dared to appear in his presence; a worm, he says, would be worthier. "Why, sir?" Chaucer asks. The god indicts him for translating *The Romance of the Rose*, with its diatribes against women, and for writing in English the story of Cressida's unfaithfulness. The queen intercedes for Chaucer, pleading that he "kept love's estate" while young, and has led many people into love's service. She instances many of his writings in his favor. As a penance for writing *Troilus and Cressida*, she commands him to compose "a glorious legend" of good women, both wives and maidens—good, of course, because they were faithful in love—and of false men who betrayed them. (These women, the "xix Ladies" referred to in the retractation at the end of *The Canterbury Tales*, belong to the company of Cupid's saints, paralleling the Christian saints, and their "legend" parallels the Christian "golden legend" of the saints' lives.) The god asks Chaucer whether he knows who it is who has pleaded for him. He answers no, and the god tells him he ought to remember that he has a book lying in his cupboard that records the virtues of Alcestis, who chose to die for her husband, was rescued by Hercules, and was transformed (this touch is Chaucer's addition to the classical story) into a daisy.

The Prologue to *The Legend of Good Women* was revised at some time by Chaucer, and now exists in two versions. In rendering the opening lines, I have drawn on both.

A thousand times have I heard people tell
That there is joy in heaven and pain in hell,
And readily I grant that this is so.
Yet true as it may be, I also know
That not a soul who is living in this land
Has been in either, nor can understand
Or know of hell or heaven in any way
Save through the written word or through hearsay.
Proof by experience no one can achieve.
Yet God forbid but that men should believe
Many a thing unseen by human eye!
A man shall not think everything a lie
Because it hasn't come within his view.
What everyone can't see is no less true,
God knows! Of all that might be seen or heard
Bernard the Monk missed some things, mark my word!
    Then surely we must go to books we find,
By means of which old things are kept in mind,
And grant in every reasonable way
Belief to what these wise old authors say,
Accepting all the old established stories
Of saints and realms and conquerors in their glories,
And other sundry things, of love, of hate,
Which here I may not recapitulate.
And if the old books were no more to be,
Lost then of all remembrance were the key.
Where proof is lacking by some other test,
Believing in old books becomes us best.
And as for me, I grant my wit is slight,
And yet in reading books I find delight.
I reverence old books in such a measure,

My heart believes them so, and takes such pleasure
In reading them that hardly a game I know
Can ever tempt me from my books to go,
Unless it is either on some holiday
Or else within the jolly month of May.
Such time as when I hear the small birds sing
And when the flowers begin again to spring,
Farewell my book until that season's past!
  My nature also is of such a cast
That of all flowers with which the fields are spread
My best love is those flowers white and red
Known in our town as daisies. For this flower
Has over my affection such a power,
As I have said already, that come May
There never dawns upon my bed a day
But I am up, and in the fields I walk
To see this flower open on its stalk
Awakened by the sun with its first light.
My grief is softened by this blissful sight,
So glad I am, finding myself with her,
To do all reverence as a worshiper
To her of all the flowers the very flower,
All honor and all virtue hers by dower,
Ever the same, still fair, still fresh of hue.
I love it ever the same and ever new
And ever shall until my heart shall die.
I need no oath for this, I do not lie.
A hotter love than mine I yield to none!
And when the evening comes I quickly run
As soon as ever the sun sinks toward the west
To see this flower, how it goes to rest
For fear of night, she hates the darkness so.
Her face will open fully to the glow
The sun gives, for to that she will unclose.
Alas, if I had English, rhyme or prose,
Sufficiently to praise this flower aright!

But woe is me, it lies beyond my might,
For well I know that men have reaped before
In poetry, and taken the full store
Of corn, I follow, gleaning here and there,
Happy enough if I can find an ear,
A good word overlooked by other men.
And if it happens that I tell again
Matter on which in their fresh songs they seized,
I hope that none of them will be displeased.

Nobility

TRANSLATOR'S NOTE

A passage in the Wife of Bath's Tale (p. 237f.) treats
more fully the theme of this "Moral Balade of Chaucier"
and acknowledges Dante as one of its sources. The "first
stock" is ultimately Christ or God, but seems to be fused,
in stanza two, with a notion of uncorrupted human proto-
types from the mythical Golden Age.

The first stock, father of all nobleness—
That man who lays claim to gentility
Must follow his steps, and his whole mind address
To seek out virtue, and from vice to flee.
To virtue alone belongs all dignity,
Not to the opposite, I dare lay it down,
Though he wear mitre, coronet, or crown.

The first stock stood complete in righteousness,
Of pure heart and true word kept steadfastly,
Gracious, merciful, and shunned idleness,
Spurning the deadly vice of lethargy.
Unless his heir loves virtue, as did he,

He is not noble, however rich his gown,
Though he wear mitre, coronet, or crown.

Vice may inherit riches, and possess
Old wealth, but no man, as men plainly see,
Can hand on to his heir his worthiness,
The property of no rank or degree
But of the first father in his majesty
Whose heir must win his pleasure, not his frown,
Though he wear mitre, coronet, or crown.

Truth: Ballade of Good Advice

TRANSLATOR'S NOTE

The French word *vache* (cow or beast) in the Envoy has
suggested to scholars the possibility that this poem was
addressed to Sir Philip de la Vache and perhaps sent to
him as an expression of sympathy for a reverse at court.

Flee from the crowd, and live in steadfastness.
Let what you have suffice, though it be small,
For wealth brings hate, luck blinds, and enviousness
Makes ticklish climbing of ambition's wall.
Tastes that exceed your means will turn to gall.
You who can give advice self-ruled must be,
And have no fear, the truth shall set you free.

Do not waste strength by storming to redress
All that is crooked; trust the turning ball!
The less to do, the greater restfulness,
And there's no profit kicking at an awl.
Don't fight like pot and kettle. You who appall

Others, regard your own soul fearfully,
And make no doubt, the truth shall set you free.

What you receive, take in submissiveness.
Who wrestles for this world asks for a fall.
Here is no home, here is but wilderness.
On, pilgrim, on! Come, beast, out of your stall!
Know your own country. Look up, thank God for all.
Keep the plain path, be guided spiritually,
And have no fear, the truth shall set you free.

ENVOY

Leave to the world your former wretchedness
Therefore, you Vache, and give up being a thrall.
Beg mercy of him that in his righteousness
Made you from nothing; draw toward him, and call
In prayer, for you and men in general,
On him, for his rewards are heavenly,
And have no fear, the truth shall set you free.

Lack of Steadfastness

TRANSLATOR'S NOTE

The Envoy is addressed to King Richard II, Chaucer's
patron, whose weaknesses and fall were dramatized by
Shakespeare.

This world so steadfast and dependable
That once a man's word was his obligation
Is now so lying, false, and changeable
That word and deed are out of all relation.
So upside down, by all my observation,

This world has turned for gain and selfishness
That all is lost for lack of steadfastness.

What makes this world of ours so variable
Except that men delight in altercation?
We hardly think a man respectable
Who cannot manage, by some machination,
To work his neighbor harm or depredation.
What is the cause but willful wickedness
That all is lost for lack of steadfastness?

Truth is put down, reason is held a fable,
And virtue now has lost all domination.
Pity is exiled, wisdom only able
To follow blindly at greed's invitation.
The world has suffered such a transformation
From right to wrong, from truth to fickleness,
That all is lost for lack of steadfastness.

ENVOY TO KING RICHARD

O prince, crave always to be honorable,
Abhor extortion, cherish this your nation!
Let nothing that is reprehensible
Be done to bring reproof upon your station.
Show forth the just sword of your castigation,
Fear God and law, love truth and worthiness,
And wed your people again to steadfastness.

෴ ෴ ෴ ෴ ෴ ෴ ෴ ෴ ෴ ෴

Chaucer's Envoy to Bukton

When Christ our king was asked, as you have heard,
My master Bukton, "What is truth?" he chose
To answer not so much as by a word.
He meant, "No man is all true," I suppose.
And therefore, though I promised to disclose
The griefs and miseries that are in marriage,
I do not dare speak evil of its woes
Lest I fall in the folly I disparage!

I will not tell you how it is the chain
Of Satan, on whose links he is gnawing ever,
But I dare say, take him out of his pain
And he would willfully be fettered never!
As for the doting fool who could deliver
His limbs, but who prefers his dungeon-keep,
Him from his woes may God refuse to sever
And no man mourn for him, although he weep!

But still, lest you do worse, marry a wife.
Better to wed than burn in a worse way.
And yet your flesh will suffer all your life
And you will be her slave, as the wise say.
If Holy Writ won't do, you'll learn some day
Through hard experience that the dread mishap
Of capture by the Frieslanders is play
Compared to falling into Hymen's trap.

To you I send, proverbially expressed
In figurative speech, this little screed.
Respect it, I advise! Who cannot rest

Content with welfare is a fool indeed,
And when you are in safety, there's no need
For courting risks. I beg of you, go read
The Wife of Bath—she covers all this ground.
In freedom may God help you freely lead
Your life; it is a hard lot to be bound.

Chaucer's Words to Adam, His Own Copyist

Adam, my copyist, should you try for me
To write out *Troilus* or *Boëthius* newly,
I hope your scalp will peel with leprosy
Unless you follow what I write more truly!
I have to rub and scrape it so unduly
And often write it over to correct
Your work, all through your haste and your neglect.

Chaucer's Complaint to His Purse

TRANSLATOR'S NOTE

The Envoy is addressed to Henry IV, who was confirmed
by Parliament as king on September 30, 1399. The course
of action by which he gained the throne from Richard
was dramatized by Shakespeare, who represents Henry
as viewing with royal and parental disapproval the re-
lations of his son Prince Hal with Falstaff. On October 3,
"Chaucer received the royal grant of an additional stipend
of forty marks" (Robinson).

To you, my purse, you whom I will not slight
For any other, you my lady dear,
Bitterly I complain. You are so light
That certainly you give me heavy cheer.
I had as lief be laid upon my bier,
And hoping for your mercy, thus I cry:
Be heavy again, for if not I shall die.

Grant me this very day, before the night,
Your blissful jingle once again to hear,
Or like the sun to see your hue flash bright
That for its golden brilliance has no peer.
Rudder by which I teach my heart to steer,
Queen of good company, to whom I fly,
Be heavy again, for if not I shall die.

Now purse, you are my solace, life, and light,
My savior, down here in this earthly scene!
If you won't be my treasurer, ease my plight
By helping me away at least, my queen,
Out of this town, for I am shaved as clean
As any friar! Yet still your grace I'll try:
Be heavy again, for if not I shall die.

ENVOY

O conqueror of Albion, realm of old
That Brutus founded, you who truly hold
Kingship by lineage and free suffrage, too,
With power to heal all wrongs, I send to you
This song, and do not let my prayer grow cold!

Chaucer's Envoy to Scogan

TRANSLATOR'S NOTE

A "pestilential deluge," probably the floods of September and October, 1393, occurred when the position of the planets ought to have meant good weather. The poem explains why, in a vein that Americans would call kidding, and adds a practical reminder that Chaucer's young friend Henry Scogan could put in a word for him at court.

Although this poem is not Chaucer's last recorded utterance, I have placed it last, because in stanza six Chaucer expresses in his happiest and most graceful way his humorously unassuming attitude toward himself and his poems. The stanza can be taken as his personal farewell to his work, and also as a motto for all writing founded on simplicity and worldly good sense.

Confounded are the high designs of heaven
That were ordained forever to stand sure,
Since I perceive the planets, the bright seven,
May weep and wail, and do not shine secure
From passion such as we on earth endure.
Alas, whence comes this thing? In deathly terror
I quake for dread of this celestial error.

The eternal word that gave the heavens their shape
Forbade that the fifth circle shed a tear
Or ever let a downward drop escape.
But Venus now is weeping in her sphere
So hard she promises to drown us here.
Alas, Scogan! This comes of your offense.
You cause this downpour and this pestilence.

Blaspheming that bright goddess throned above,
Did you not say, through pride or recklessness,
A thing forbidden in the laws of love,
That since your lady laughed at your distress
Therefore you gave her up at Michaelmas?
Alas, Scogan! By neither old nor young
Was Scogan ever yet scolded for his tongue!

Cupid in scorn has seen fit to record
That same, that rebel word that you have spoken,
For which he will no longer be your lord.
And, Scogan, though his bow is not yet broken,
He will not with his arrows make a token
Of you nor me. On figures such as ours
For hurt nor heal he will not try his powers!

I dread, friend, truly, this ill-starred affair.
Love, for your guilt, in vengeance may proceed
On all those with round figures and white hair,
Who are such likely folk in love to speed!
Then we shall have no solace for our need.
But well I know what answer I'll provoke:
"Old graybeard wants to rhyme and have his joke!"

No, Scogan, say not so! For I refuse
In any rhyme—so help me God, I pray!—
Ever again to wake my sleeping muse
That in her sheath rusts peacefully away.
While I was young I put her in the fray,
But what men write shall all pass, prose or rhyme.
Take every man his turn in his own time.

ENVOY

You, Scogan, you who kneel at the stream's head
Where honors are conferred and fortunes rise,

While at the stream's end I am dull as dead,
Forgotten under waste and lonely skies,
Put in for me the word that fructifies!
Farewell! Remember Tully on friendship's duty,
And never again defy the queen of beauty!

FOR THE BEST IN PAPERBACKS, LOOK FOR THE

In every corner of the world, on every subject under the sun, Penguin represents quality and variety—the very best in publishing today.

For complete information about books available from Penguin—including Pelicans, Puffins, Peregrines, and Penguin Classics—and how to order them, write to us at the appropriate address below. Please note that for copyright reasons the selection of books varies from country to country.

In the United Kingdom: For a complete list of books available from Penguin in the U.K., please write to *Dept E.P., Penguin Books Ltd, Harmondsworth, Middlesex, UB7 0DA.*

In the United States: For a complete list of books available from Penguin in the U.S., please write to *Dept BA, Penguin*, Box 120, Bergenfield, New Jersey 07621-0120.

In Canada: For a complete list of books available from Penguin in Canada, please write to *Penguin Books Ltd, 2801 John Street, Markham, Ontario L3R 1B4.*

In Australia: For a complete list of books available from Penguin in Australia, please write to the *Marketing Department, Penguin Books Ltd, P.O. Box 257, Ringwood, Victoria 3134.*

In New Zealand: For a complete list of books available from Penguin in New Zealand, please write to the *Marketing Department, Penguin Books (NZ) Ltd, Private Bag, Takapuna, Auckland 9.*

In India: For a complete list of books available from Penguin, please write to *Penguin Overseas Ltd, 706 Eros Apartments, 56 Nehru Place, New Delhi, 110019.*

In Holland: For a complete list of books available from Penguin in Holland, please write to *Penguin Books Nederland B.V., Postbus 195, NL-1380AD Weesp, Netherlands.*

In Germany: For a complete list of books available from Penguin, please write to *Penguin Books Ltd, Friedrichstrasse 10-12, D-6000 Frankfurt Main 1, Federal Republic of Germany.*

In Spain: For a complete list of books available from Penguin in Spain, please write to *Longman, Penguin España, Calle San Nicolas 15, E-28013 Madrid, Spain.*

In Japan: For a complete list of books available from Penguin in Japan, please write to *Longman Penguin Japan Co Ltd, Yamaguchi Building, 2-12-9 Kanda Jimbocho, Chiyoda-Ku, Tokyo 101, Japan.*

Some volumes in
THE VIKING PORTABLE LIBRARY